21.00

Dionysus Since 69

Greek Tragedy at the Dawn of the Third Millennium

Edited by

Edith Hall, Fiona Macintosh,
and Amanda Wrigley

OXFORD
UNIVERSITY PRESS

OXFORD

UNIVERSITY PRESS

Great Clarendon Street, Oxford OX2 6DP

Oxford University Press is a department of the University of Oxford.
It furthers the University's objective of excellence in research, scholarship,
and education by publishing worldwide in

Oxford New York

Auckland Cape Town Dar es Salaam Hong Kong Karachi Kuala Lumpur
Madrid Melbourne Mexico City Nairobi New Delhi Shanghai Taipei Toronto

With offices in

Argentina Austria Brazil Chile Czech Republic France Greece
Guatemala Hungary Italy Japan Poland Portugal
Singapore South Korea Switzerland Thailand Turkey Ukraine Vietnam

Oxford is a registered trade mark of Oxford University Press
in the UK and in certain other countries

Published in the United States
by Oxford University Press Inc., New York

© Oxford University Press 2004

The moral rights of the author have been asserted
Database right Oxford University Press (maker)

First published 2004

First published in paperback 2005

British Library Cataloguing in Publication Data

Data available

Library of Congress Cataloging in Publication Data

Data available

ISBN 0-19-925914-3 (hbk.)
ISBN 0-19-928131-9 (pbk.)

1 3 5 7 9 10 8 6 4 2

Typeset by Kolam Information Services Pvt. Ltd, Pondicherry, India
Printed in Great Britain
on acid-free paper by
Biddles Ltd,
King's Lynn, Norfolk.

Acknowledgements

We would like to thank the Leverhulme Trust, the Passmore Edwards Trust, and above all the Arts and Humanities Research Board, whose generous grants made possible the research and guest lectures underlying this volume. We are grateful to all the contributors to the volume for their cheerfulness and cooperation; the support of Helene Foley in particular, on several aspects of the project, has been indispensable. Isobel Hurst, Chris Weaver and Avery Willis at the Archive of Performances of Greek and Roman Drama in Oxford have provided help of various kinds. We would like to thank the numerous individuals who have helped by supplying important documentation or information relating to productions; especially significant contributions have been made by Robert Auletta, Paul Cartledge, Johannes Haubold, Tony Harrison, Philip Hooker, Brian Jackson, Richard Poynder, Francesca Schironi, Betine Van Zyl Smit and Amy Wygant. In Durham, remarkable patience was shown by Esther McGilvray with the typescripts and by Margaret Parry with the administration of finances relating to the reproduction of photographs. Carol Greunke, Marianne McDonald, Carey Perloff, and Nora Polley helped generously with the provision of images. At Oxford University Press, Hilary O'Shea has been a staunch supporter of the project from its inception; we would also like to .thank Jenny Wagstaffe, our copy-editor David Sanders, and our indexer Barbara Hird. Support of other, equally important, kinds has come from Julia Sleeper and from the Hilton family.

Contents

Illustrations

For further information relating to the productions featured in the illustrations, see their captions and also the table of production details in Wrigley, below, Chapter 15, which lists all performances of Greek tragedy discussed in this book in the chronological order of their first productions.

Contributors

PETER BROWN is a Lecturer in Classics at Oxford University and a Fellow of Trinity College. He is a Director of the Archive of Performances of Greek and Roman Drama at the University of Oxford, with particular responsibility for Roman Comedy and for operatic versions of ancient drama. He has published extensively on both Greek and Roman Comedy.

ERIKA FISCHER-LICHTE is Professor of Theatre Research at the University of Berlin. Between 1995 and 1999 she was President of the International Federation of Theatre Research. She has written more than a hundred articles and twenty books, several of which have been translated into English, including *The Semiotics of Theatre* (1992), *The Show and the Gaze of Theatre* (1997), and *History of European Drama and Theatre* (2002).

HELENE FOLEY is a Professor of Classics at Barnard College, Columbia University. She is the author of *Ritual Irony: Poetry and Sacrifice in Euripides, The Homeric Hymn to Demeter,* and *Female Acts in Greek Tragedy*; co-author of *Women in the Classical World: Image and Text*; editor of *Reflections of Women in Antiquity*; and author of many articles and reviews on Greek epic, drama, women and gender in antiquity, and modern performance and adaptation of classical drama. She has been the recipient of Guggenheim, NEH, National Humanities Center, and ACLS fellowships.

EDITH HALL is Leverhulme Professor of Greek Cultural History at the University of Durham, and Co-Founder and a Director of the Archive of Performance of Greek and Roman Drama. Her books include *Inventing the Barbarian* (1989), an edition of Aeschylus' *Persians* (1996) and (with Pat Easterling) *Greek and Roman Actors* (2002). She is working, with Fiona Macintosh, on a history of Greek tragedy in Britain since 1660 (forthcoming with Oxford University Press).

LORNA HARDWICK teaches in the Department of Classical Studies at the Open University, where she is Professor of Classical Studies and Director of the Research Project on the reception of the texts and images of ancient Greece in modern drama and poetry in English (www2.open.ac.uk/classicalstudies/greekplays). Her initial academic training was in Ancient History. She also studied European Literature and the History of Ideas and these fields came together to generate her interest in Reception Studies. She is currently working on the relationships between classical texts and their receptions in post-colonial drama and poetry. Her publications include *Translating Words, Translating Cultures*, published by Duckworth (2000).

FIONA MACINTOSH is Senior Research Fellow at the Archive of Performances of Greek and Roman Drama and a member of St Cross College, Oxford. Her publications include *Dying Acts: Death in Ancient Greek and Modern Irish Tragic Drama* (Cork 1994) and Sophocles' *Oedipus Tyrannus: A Production History* (forthcoming with Cambridge University Press). She has also published numerous articles on the performance history of Greek drama internationally and is working, with Edith Hall, on a history of Greek tragedy in Britain since 1660 (forthcoming with Oxford University Press).

PANTELIS MICHELAKIS is Fixed-Term Lecturer in Classics at the University of Bristol and Honorary Research Fellow at the Archive of Performances of Greek and Roman Drama. He is the author of *Achilles in Greek Tragedy* (2002), and co-editor of *Homer, Tragedy and Beyond: Essays in Honour of Pat Easterling* (2001). He is currently working on a Duckworth companion to Euripides' *Iphigenia in Aulis*.

KATHLEEN RILEY is writing the authorized biography of Sir Nigel Hawthorne, which will be published in 2004 by the University of Hertfordshire Press under the title *Nigel Hawthorne On Stage*. She is also a doctoral candidate at Corpus Christi College, Oxford, writing a diachronic study of the reception of Euripides' *Heracles*, and a Graduate Associate at the Archive of Performances of Greek and Roman Drama. Other publications include a study of

Robert Browning's translations of Greek tragedy, forthcoming in the Australian journal *Literature and Aesthetics*.

OLIVER TAPLIN has been a Tutorial Fellow of Magdalen College at Oxford since 1973, with the title Professor since 1996. He was Co-Founder with Edith Hall of the Archive of Performances of Greek and Roman Drama and is currently one of the Directors. His books include *The Stagecraft of Aeschylus* (1977), *Greek Tragedy in Action* (1978), *Greek Fire* (1989), and *Comic Angels* (1993). He has always been concerned to disseminate interest in the ancient Greek world and in its reception; and this has extended to working with productions in the theatre, including *The Thebans* at the Royal Shakespeare Company (1991–2), and *The Oresteia* at the National Theatre (both 1981 and 1999). He is developing research on the reflections of Greek tragedy in the vase-paintings of the fourth century BC.

TIMBERLAKE WERTENBAKER is a playwright, translator, and author. Amongst her plays are *New Anatomies, Abel's Sister, The Grace of Mary Traverse, Our Country's Good, The Love of the Nightingale, Three Birds Alighting on a Field, The Break of Day, After Darwin, Dianeira, The Ash Girl*, and *Credible Witness*. Her translations include *False Admissions, Successful Strategies, La Dispute, Mephisto, Pelleas and Melisande*, Sophocles' *The Theban Plays*, Euripides' *Hecuba, Filumena*, and Jean Anouilh's *Wild Orchids*. Her publications include *Plays One* (1996) and *Plays Two* (2002), both with Faber & Faber.

DAVID WILES is Professor of Theatre at Royal Holloway, University of London. His publications in the classical field include *The Masks of Menander* (1991), *Tragedy in Athens* (1997), and *Greek Theatre Performance: An Introduction* (2000). He is currently completing a short history of western performance space.

KATHARINE WORTH is Emeritus Professor of Drama and Theatre Studies and Honorary Fellow of Royal Holloway, University of London. She was given permission by Samuel Beckett in the Seventies to produce new versions of the television play *Eh Joe* and the radio plays *Embers, Words and Music* and *Cascando*, the latter two with new music by Humphrey Searle. Her many books and articles on theatre include: *Beckett the Shape Changer*, an edited symposium (Routledge & Kegan Paul, 1975); *The Irish Drama of Europe from Yeats to Beckett* (Athlone Press, 1978); *Waiting for Godot and Happy Days: Text and Performance* (Macmillan Press, 1990); *Samuel Beckett's Theatre: Life Journeys* (Oxford University Press, 1999; paperback edition 2001).

AMANDA WRIGLEY is full-time Researcher at the Archive of Performances of Greek and Roman Drama and an Associate Member of Magdalen College, Oxford. She is a Classics graduate, a qualified librarian, and specializes in archival investigation of theatre history. Her forthcoming publications include an historical study of the performance of ancient drama in the University of Oxford. She is currently working on the performance reception of Sophocles' *Ajax*.

FROMA I ZEITLIN is Charles Ewing Professor of Greek Language and Literature and Professor of Comparative Literature at Princeton University. She has published extensively in the field of Greek literature (epic, tragedy and comedy, novel) and in gender studies. Author of *Under the Sign of the Shield: Semiotics and Aeschylus' Seven against Thebes* and *Playing the Other: Gender and Society in Classical Greek Literature*, she also edited *Mortals and Immortals: Selected Essays of Jean-Pierre Vernant* and coedited two collective volumes, *Nothing to Do with Dionysos? Athenian Drama in its Social Context* and *Before Sexuality: Structures of Erotic Experience in the Ancient Greek World*. She is currently at work on a project entitled 'Vision, Figuration, and Image from Theater to Romance'.

Lectures at the Archive of Performances of Greek and Roman Drama 1997–2002

18 Nov. 1997	Erika Fischer-Lichte	The *Antiquity Project* at the Berlin Schaubühne
5 May 1998	Helene Foley	Some Modern Productions and Adaptations of Greek Tragedy
10 June 1998	Hellmut Flashar	Sophocles and Mendelssohn: The *Antigone* of 1841
30 April 1999	Mae Smethurst	The Japanese Presence in Ninagawa's *Medea*
2 Feb. 2000	Fiona Macintosh	Oedipus in France
4 May 2000	Pantelis Michelakis	Lecture to accompany 'Performances of Greek and Roman Drama: An Exhibition of Posters', Wolfson College
14 June 2000	Froma I. Zeitlin	'Dionysus in 69'
15 Nov. 2000	Don Chapman	*Agamemnon* and After: How Classical Greek Drama Helped Rekindle Oxford's Interest in Modern Theatre
31 Jan. 2001	Katharine Worth	Greek and Roman Notes in Samuel Beckett's Scenography
28 Feb. 2001	Timberlake Wertenbaker	The Voices We Hear

9 May 2001	David Wiles	The Use of Masks in Modern Performances of Greek Drama
17 Oct. 2001	Jane Glover	The Opera House of Atreus
21 Nov. 2001	Marina Warner	How Do We Believe in the Gods?
30 Jan. 2002	Abd' Elkader Farrah	An Algerian's Ventures Into Ancient Greek Territory
27 Feb. 2002	Lorna Hardwick	Decolonizing Classics: Greek Drama as a Catalyst for Change
8 May 2002	David Raeburn	Modern Revival of Greek Tragedy: Letter, Spirit, or Something Else?
29 May 2002	Colin Teevan	Inventing the Greek
23 Oct. 2002	William K. Zewadski	Greek Theatre in the Cinema and on Television
20 Nov. 2002	Freddy Decreus	Postmodernism and the Staging of Classical Tragedy

Note on Nomenclature, Spelling, and Texts

The spelling of proper names varies enormously between different modern translations and adaptations of ancient Greek tragedy, even between those in the English language alone (Clytemnestra, Clytaemnestra, Klutaimestra, etc.) Our policy has been to use the forms of the names as they appear in each modern author, adaptor or translator during the discussion of that individual writer's work. But elsewhere, when discussing the plays in more general terms, we have adopted traditional spellings, largely in line with those used in the third edition of the *Oxford Classical Dictionary*.

When referring to ancient Greek works in the original language we have used the most recent edition published in the Oxford Classical Texts series.

Unless otherwise indicated, all websites and email addresses were valid at the time this volume went to press at the beginning of 2003.

I

Introduction

Why Greek Tragedy in the Late Twentieth Century?

Edith Hall

By May 1968 the President and the administration of the most powerful state in the world found themselves in an unprecedented crisis. US involvement in an armed conflict—the war in Vietnam—was opposed not only by large portions of the world but by the mainstream consensus of domestic American opinion. On 5 June the last hope was shattered that a president with an anti-war ticket could be elected the following November. Bobby Kennedy was assassinated. The very day after, 6 June, a play opened in New York. Richard Schechner's *Dionysus in 69* was a socially, politically, and above all theatrically radical interpretation of Euripides' tragedy *Bacchae*. The crisis in American society which was dividing doves from hawks, young from old, long-haired from short-haired, and prophets of sexual and psychic liberation from moral conservatives, found thrilling and lucid theatrical expression in the nightly Dionysiac explosion taking place in a vast space called the Performing Garage in downtown New York City.

This book is about the reawakening of interest in Greek tragedy heralded by Schechner's remarkable production. This reawakening was just one result of the seismic political and cultural shifts marking the end of the 1960s. Greek tragedy began to be performed on a quantitatively far greater scale, from more radical political perspectives, and in more adventurous performance styles than it had been before. This demands an attempt at explanation. All revolutions, including cultural and aesthetic ones, of course have their harbingers. There had been sporadic productions of Greek tragedy before the 1968–9 watershed. They rarely challenged mainstream political ideology, or indeed the performance traditions of western naturalism, but there were exceptions. In 1965 it was the *cancellation* of a planned *Antigone* in South Africa which eventually inspired Athol Fugard's *The Island* of 1973 (see Hardwick's chapter in this volume). *Persians* was important in 1965–6; Karolos Koun's version revolutionized attitudes to the potential of the chorus as 'protagonist' (see Wiles), while Mattias Braun's East German production, which had premiered in 1960, was revived in order to protest against US policy in Vietnam (see Hall). The 1960s also saw one or two interesting experiments with operas on Greek tragic themes (see Brown). Yet the tidal wave of productions of Greek tragic theatre which was about to flow was of a different nature and order.

More Greek tragedy has been performed in the last thirty years than at any point in history since Greco-Roman antiquity. Translated, adapted, staged, sung, danced, parodied, filmed, *enacted*, Greek tragedy has proved magnetic to writers and directors searching for new ways in which to pose questions to contemporary society and to push back the boundaries of theatre. The mythical, dysfunctional, conflicted world portrayed in the archetypal plays of Aeschylus, Sophocles, and Euripides has become one of the most important cultural and aesthetic prisms through which the real, dysfunctional, conflicted world of the late twentieth- and early twenty-first centuries has refracted its own image.

In Euripides' *Bacchae* Dionysus challenges many of the social, chronological, spatial, and other boundaries with which the ancient Greeks tried to demarcate and control the world around them: he is an effeminate male, an ancient god of youthful appearance, a *Greek* god who leads hordes of oriental barbarians, a god worshipped both in the untamed wild and within the walls of the civilized city, the tutelary deity of both tragic and comic theatre, instigator of total ecstasy but also absolute terror. Recently Dionysus, the theatre-god of the ancient Greeks, has transcended nearly *all* boundaries created by time, space, and cultural tradition, for staging Greek tragedy is now emphatically an international, even worldwide phenomenon. This seminal art-form, born two and a half thousand years ago in democratic Athens, rediscovered in the Renaissance as prestigious pan-European cultural property, has evolved in recent decades into a global medium. Since 1969 Greek tragedies have been performed in every continent of the world and in many languages: Dionysus has now crazed his Bacchants in Cameroon (Figure 1) and at the

FIGURE 1. Agaue taunted by the Rastafarian-influenced Dionysos of *Les Bacchantes inspirées par Euripide* at the Goethe-Institut, Yaoundé, Cameroon (1992).

Beijing Opera.[1] He has entranced directors, authors, actors, and audiences in Hawaii, Malaysia, and Mexico as well as in Britain, France, and Germany.[2] Over the last three decades the Australian Ajax, the Georgian Medea, the Taiwanese Antigone, the Japanese Electra, the African and Egyptian Oedipus, the Colombian Clytemnestra and the Muscovite, Philippine, and Brazilian Trojan Women have enthralled audiences quite as much as their West European and North American counterparts.[3]

Greek tragedy has always been special, but it is particularly special to our specific moment in human history. It is true that a few of the Greek comedies by Aristophanes are sometimes staged outside Greece, for example Stephen Sondheim's *Frogs*, performed in Yale University Swimming Pool in 1974 by a cast including Meryl Streep and Sigourney Weaver.[4] Much more recently, Luca Ronconi's satirical realization of the same play, and Sean O'Brien's circus adaptation for the National Theatre in London of *Birds*, both premiered in 2002. It is also true that the best of the Roman tragedies by Seneca have enjoyed important revivals: in 1968, at the beginning of the era traced in this book's narrative, Peter Brook (one of an increasingly small group of prominent directors never to have attempted a Greek tragedy)

---

[1] The Cameroon production of a modernized French version of Euripides (not Soyinka) was performed by the Francophone La Troupe d'Ébène, directed by Lukas Hemleb. It dramatized the rejection of a new voodoo-influenced Rastafarian cult by a modern African businessman: see Breitinger (1996), 253. The Chinese production of *Bacchae* was directed by Chen Shizheng (1996), a former Beijing Opera singer who became interested in the Greek classical repertoire after moving to work in the United States in 1987.

[2] *Dionysus 96: The Bacchae of Euripides* (a reworking of Schechner's *Dionysus in 69*) was performed by an all-female cast at the University of Hawaii in Manoa (directed by Ramon Arjona IV). In 2001 the controversial Malaysian movie director U-Wei Saari was invited by his Ministry of Culture to stage a Malay adaptation of *Bacchae* (www.asiaweek.com/asiaweek/97/0404/feat7, accessed 25 June 2002).

[3] On the African Oedipus see Macintosh (2002). Arabic adaptations of *Oedipus Tyrannus* by Ali Salem and Fawzi Fahmi were performed in Cairo in 1970 and 1977 respectively. Pieces from *Trojan Women* were performed in ancient Greek by students at the Russian Academy of Theatre Arts in March 2002; on other Greek tragedies at the Taganka Theatre, Moscow, in the 1990s see Smeliansky (1999), 392. *Muslim Babae*, an adaptation of *Trojan Women*, written by Sedfrey Ordonez while he was the Philippine Chairman of the Commission of Human Rights, was produced in Manila in 1998. The Brazilian *Trojan Women*, performed by the Macunaima theatre company, was directed by Antunes Filho at the 11th International Istanbul Theatre Festival in June 1999.

[4] The production was directed by Burt Shevelove and opened on 20 May.

directed Ted Hughes's translation of Seneca's *Oedipus*.[5] But the ancient European texts which have offered the public imagination of the last three decades overwhelmingly the most important theatrical material have been Greek tragedies. In Britain the sheer number of productions has occasionally made these ancient plays rival the English-language classics of the repertoire. In the first half of 1995 more Euripides was performed in London than any other playwright, including Shakespeare.

This volume seeks above all to ask *why* this should be so. *Why* has Greek tragedy proved so consistently popular during these specific decades? At the book's core lie some of the lectures which have been given at the Archive of Performances of Greek and Roman Drama (henceforward APGRD), an organization dedicated to researching the history of the reception of ancient drama in performance, founded by Oliver Taplin and myself at the University of Oxford in 1996 (a list of all the APGRD lectures delivered before the end of 2002 is included at the beginning of this volume). The lectures published in the volume were delivered by invited guest speakers from the worlds of the professional theatre (Wertenbaker), Theatre Studies (Fischer-Lichte, Wiles, Worth), and Classics (Foley, Hardwick, Zeitlin). These papers have been supplemented by chapters specially conceived, written, and edited by the staff and researchers at the Archive (Brown, Hall, Macintosh, Michelakis, Riley, Taplin, Wrigley).

All the chapters document recent performances of ancient dramas and works inspired by them (for the production details of the première of the performances mentioned in the book see Wrigley, below, Chapter 15). But the more significant part of the enterprise is the drawing of connections with the social, aesthetic, and intellectual agendas of the directors and the societies within which they were operating. This project is not always easy at such a short chronological distance as a few years or a couple of decades. Yet the remarkable recent and continuing appeal of the Greek tragic repertoire demands that we at least try to make sense of it, while

---

[5] Richard Schechner also directed Ted Hughes's version of Seneca's *Oedipus* in New York in 1977, in an 'environment' partly suggested by ancient theatres and designed by Jim Clayburgh (Schechner (1985), 133 and 147 fig. 32). More recently, an innovative multimedia production of Caryl Churchill's translation of Seneca's *Thyestes* at London's Royal Court Theatre (1994) met with some critical acclaim. See also George W. M. Harrison (2000).

acknowledging that the eye of history in fifty or a hundred years from now will see causes, consequences, contexts, and patterns as yet invisible to us.

It already looks as though a revival of the epic film set in ancient Greece or Rome is imminent in the early third millennium. Following the success of Ridley Scott's *Gladiator* (2000), we await the release of blockbuster films based on Steven Pressfield's *Gates of Fire: An Epic Novel of the Battle of Thermopylae* (1998), Valerio Manfredi's trilogy of novels about Alexander the Great (1998), and even on the *Iliad*.[6] Yet we can also already see that in the middle of the 1960s, theatrical interest in ancient Greek drama *replaced* cinematic interests in spectacular myth and in imperial Rome. For the two important strands in the performance reception of classical Greece and Rome from the mid-1950s to the early 1960s were both cinematic. There were numerous popular Italian 'peplum' movies, which used ancient myths about Hercules or Aphrodite as opportunities for the display of special effects and gorgeous bodies of both sexes (a light-hearted genre which reached its widest audience through an American example, *Jason and the Argonauts*, in 1963, and lies behind the mildly sexualized use of classical imagery which has continued to appear in advertising and the fashion industry[7]). But there was a rash of extremely significant and serious American films set against the background of ancient Rome. They almost all used triangular and even rectangular relationships involving pagan Romans, Christians, Jews, and Arabs to work through issues relating not only to the Middle East but also to the anti-communist persecutions led by Senator Joseph McCarthy, blacklisting, censorship, imperial responsibilities, the role of the military, and the possibility of a just war. These issues were related to the USA's self-definition as world leader in the face of what was perceived to be an increasingly threatening Soviet Union. The films included William Wyler's *Ben Hur* (1959), Stanley Kubrick's *Spartacus* (1960), and Richard Fleischer's *Barabbas* (1962).

---

[6] David Benioff is currently adapting the *Iliad* for Warner Bros.

[7] On the eroticization of ancient Greece in popular culture see Taplin (1989), 112–41. Hartigan (2002) discusses classical imagery in advertisements, especially for cosmetics, toiletries, perfume, and clothes. On the most recent wave of 'Greek goddess' designs in haute couture, see Polychronaki (2001), Finn (2001) and McDowell (2002).

The Roman epic movie as a genre reached its zenith in 1959–62, just as the Berlin Wall was initiated. Yet the genre's basic motifs of armies, miracles, mad emperors, and slave uprisings began, with Joseph Manciewicz's *Cleopatra* and Antony Mann's *Fall of the Roman Empire* (1963 and 1964 respectively), to give way to more ironic approaches. By the middle of the 1960s both the 'peplum' and the 'epic' history film were dead, a cultural shift related to the social and psychic changes involved in the questioning of middle American 'suburban' values, and above all the worldwide challenges to long prevalent notions of empire and the rights of First World states to intervene abroad. The mirror of the Roman empire no longer worked in the increasingly complicated imagination of the First World; attempts to make popular cinema out of Greek history, with the exception of Rudolph Maté's *The Three Hundred Spartans* of 1962 (a transparent legitimation of NATO at the time of the erection of the Berlin Wall), never took off at all. By 1969 films interested in classical antiquity were profoundly non-epic and heralded the turn towards Greek theatre as the most important avenue to Mediterranean antiquity in modern entertainment. Pasolini's *Edipo Re* (1967) and Fellini's *Satyricon* (1969), both pessimistic films by Italian directors, reveal new artistic responses, from anti-authoritarian and subversive angles, to the challenge posed by the legacy of antiquity.[8]

The 1960s were a remarkable decade. But 1968, the year in which our main story begins, stands out as a year in which seismic global shifts in political consciousness took place. The year 1968, quite simply, brought an end to the ideological settlement of the early post-war period. Greece itself, the ancestral home of both democracy and tragedy, had just fallen victim to a brutal military dictatorship which, until its collapse in 1974, banned many of the ancient plays (see further Hall, Chapter 6 below). International sympathy with the oppressed people of Greece certainly helped awaken interest in their theatre. But this is only one small part of a much larger story; 1968 was fundamentally to challenge both international alignments and power relations between different ethnic groups, sexes (and up to a point socioeconomic classes) within individual countries. Struggles framed in the media as

[8] See Elley (1984), J.P. Sullivan (2001), Wyke (1997), Christie (2000), J. Solomon (2001).

clashes between authoritarian and radical forces were fought all over the world; young people were openly challenging the establishment run by their parents and grandparents. It was a sign of the times that the play Jan Kott chose to direct at the University Theater in Berkeley that year was the Greek tragedy most marked by overt inter-generational conflict, Euripides' *Orestes*.[9] Protest movements, led in many cases by students and other young people, and urging pacifist, civil rights, anti-racist, and women's liberationist causes, were perceived as achieving unprecedented successes: the fatal showdown between police and anti-war demonstrators at the Democratic Convention in Chicago in August was felt to have forced the US government to announce a halt to the bombing in Vietnam. Violent riots and suppression of them, footage of which circulated on the television screens of the world, featured in North America, Mexico, Paris, London, Northern Ireland, Prague, South Africa, and elsewhere.

In April Martin Luther King was assassinated, sparking riots across America. In May millions of French students and workers put up their famous barricades, held the country to ransom, and forced changes in the hierarchical French education system. In August the Soviet Union invaded an increasingly dissident Czechoslovakia. In September women's liberation groups staged a widely publicized protest at the Miss America Contest in Atlantic City, an occasion which prompted the first attested use of the term 'bra-burning' to derogate feminists.[10] By the end of this momentous year it began to seem that practically nothing was impossible; with the launching in December of Apollo 8, the first US mission to orbit the moon, the human race seemed to have entered an entirely new—exciting but disturbing—era.[11] Young people added to their excitement at the political developments in the outside world by transforming their inner worlds through unprecedented experimentation with psychedelic drugs. They also

[9] Barker and Trussler (1994), photograph on p. 381.
[10] Although no bras were actually burnt, an article in the *New York Times* of 8 September quoted one angry contest organizer as using the term.
[11] The space programmes were more relevant to the global reception of Greek tragedy than might be imagined. In a pathbreaking paper on the performance reception of Greek tragedy, Helene Foley pointed out that a recent Chinese translator of *Oedipus Tyrannus* referred to all the gods generically as Apollo, since he could count on his audience's ability to recognize this name from the US space programme (Foley (1999), 1–2).

revelled in their own new cultural forms and media, especially dedicated radio stations and rock music, which had pronounced Dionysiac elements and imagery—psychotropic substances, long hair, patterned garments, exaggerated priapism, ecstatic crowds and loud percussion. Jim Morrison, the lead singer of the Doors (whose albums were all released between 1967 and 1971), the self-styled omnipotent 'lizard king', encouraged his fans to see him as a shaman dedicated to Dionysus, god of drama and ecstasy.[12]

SEX

The social forces unleashed in this period, with their focuses on race, authority, imperialism, and sexual politics, are suggestive of the reasons why Greek tragedy has proven so attractive subsequently. This volume divides these reasons into four broad (although always interrelated) categories: social, political, theatrical, and cerebral. The order in which the categories are presented does not indicate a hierarchy of perceived importance. Yet the section 'Dionysus and the Sex War' comes first partly because the most *obvious* reason for the recent renaissance of Greek tragedy in performance has been the rise and continuing impact of the feminist movement. From the 1857 Divorce Act in Britain to the early twentieth-century Northern European campaigns for women's suffrage, as in the late twentieth century, Greek tragedy has invariably been rediscovered when women's rights have climbed to the top of society's agenda.[13] Indeed, it had already been observed (rarely with approval) in antiquity, by Aristophanes, Plato, Plutarch, and Origen (among others) that Greek tragedy gave a surprisingly loud voice to the women it portrayed, and was fascinated by the social problems created by conflict between the sexes.[14]

---

[12] 'I like to think of the history of rock & roll like the origin of Greek drama. That started out on the threshing floors during the crucial seasons, and was originally a band of acolytes dancing and singing. Then, one day, a possessed person jumped out of the crowd and started imitating a god . . . ' (www.expage.com/jimsquotes4). This line of thought owes much to Nietzsche, popular campus reading in the late 1960s. Thanks are owed to Richard Poynder for help on rock & roll. On one scholar's 'hippie'-influenced reading of Dionysus and his entourage see Edith Hall (1998), 35. Padel (2000), a study of the masculinities at stake in rock & roll, rightly emphasizes their Dionysiac affinities.

[13] See Edith Hall (1999a) and (2000); Macintosh (2000b).

[14] See especially the pioneering studies by Zeitlin (1978) and Foley (1981).

'The personal is political' was the slogan which will always epitomize the feminism of the 1970s. The women's movement first seems to have used it in an essay written in 1969 by the revolutionary feminist Carol Hanisch, although the phrase had been developed rather earlier in relation to the specific plight of black American women. 'The personal is political', in a slightly different sense, could equally well serve as a description of Greek tragedy, where individual, private, intimate, domestic stories of sex, parenthood, and power struggles within the family, are told from the collective, communal, political perspective of the society within which the tragic family resides.[15] In Greek tragedy the dialectical relationship between an individual's personal conduct and her or his public conduct is a central dynamic. Creon's neglect of his responsibilities as a father, uncle, husband, civic leader, and legislator are scrutinized both personally and politically by the other characters and the chorus of Sophocles' *Antigone*. One reason why Greek tragedy has proved so appealing is, quite simply, that its personal stories are political.

Yet the story of feminism's rediscovery of Greek tragedy does not make full sense unless it is set in the context of the slightly earlier 'hippie' movement, and in particular the so-called sexual revolution. The feminism of the 1970s could not have happened without the (hetero)sexual liberation of the 1960s, itself predicated on the availability of oral contraception, which (after cynically being tested in the 1950s on women in the colonial territories of Puerto Rico and Haiti) first began to become available in the USA in 1960 and in Northern Europe between 1961 and 1968. By 1969 millions of women were able to control their fertility in a manner unprecedented in history. The sexual revolution had been further facilitated by the decriminalization of both abortion and homosexual activity in many countries (in Britain these landmark legislative changes were both made in 1967): such social developments created a need for theatre which talked freely about sexual drives and relationships. In Britain the theatrical censorship which had been in place for over two centuries was abolished in 1968, resulting in the immediate production of several plays, including

---

[15] See Hanisch (1969), but also Claudia Jones (1995), which was originally published in the periodical *Political Affairs* in 1949. On the applicability of the phrase to ancient Greek society see Cartledge (2000), 12–14.

the innovative rock musical *Hair!* (banned on the grounds of nudity and obscenity), and John Osborne's *A Patriot for Me* (banned for its male homosexual scenes). *Hair!* was also first performed on Broadway in 1968, followed by the explicit sexual acts in *Che!* and extensive nudity of *Oh, Calcutta* in 1969. There was, however, a particular need for plays which were frank about *female* sexuality. Aristophanes and Plato had long ago established a precedent for criticizing the tragedians, specifically Euripides, for writing plays with a sexually motivated woman or one who 'reviled her husband' at their centre (see *Frogs* 1041–4 and *Republic* 3. 395d5–e3). But their derogatory discussions were responses to certain rhetorical passages in tragedy which still make a remarkably uninhibited impact. In the tragedies of the Greeks, where erotic passion is much discussed, deeply respected, but also portrayed as one of the most dangerous forces in the family and society, late twentieth-century directors quickly discovered ways of exploring the repercussions of the sexual revolution.

By the late 1990s Greek tragedy could be used to create public sympathy for a totally new community of victims, sufferers from HIV, seen in some quarters as the first and most graphic of all casualties of the increasing social endorsement of sexual promiscuity. In the Kaaitheater in Brussels in early 1994 Jan Ritsema directed a powerful performance entitled *Philoktetes-Variations*, consisting of three plays deriving from Sophocles' *Philoctetes*, by John Jesurun, Heiner Müller, and André Gide respectively, each in their original language. In all three parts the diseased Greek hero was played by a gay actor and gay rights campaigner, Ron Vawter (Figure 2), who was publicly dying of Aids (his death came in April that year). His naked body, covered with purple Kaposi rash, 'clearly spoke a more forceful language than his and his fellow actors' words'.[16] But the aetiology of Greek tragedy's complex relationship with the sexual revolution can clearly be traced to *Dionysus in 69*, which not only explored the homosexual reverberations of the relationship between Dionysus and Pentheus, but featured what was then perceived to be a scandalous amount of nudity. Even the title, which used no apostrophe before the

---

[16] Laermans (1994), 68. At the Edinburgh Festival in 2002, the Canadian Opera Company's highly praised performance of Stravinsky's *Oedipus Rex* explicitly equated the plague ravaging Thebes with Aids.

Edith Hall

FIGURE 2.   The gay rights activist Ron Vawter, shortly before his death, as Philoctetes in *Philoktetes-Variations* at the Kaaitheater, Brussels (1994). Photograph by Maarten Vanden Abeele.

numeral, did not refer to the date of the production's première, which was actually in 1968. Its predominant signification was certainly intended to be sexual.[17] Our own volume's title (the suggestion of Oliver Taplin) is of course intended to mark our approximate chronological coverage. But, more importantly, it pays tribute to the vision and courage of Schechner's production. Although not without its problems, *Dionysus in 69* was a significant landmark in the history of theatrical experimentation, and also, as Froma Zeitlin (an eyewitness to it) writes in the next chapter, a landmark in the history of the reception of Greek drama in the twentieth century.[18]

[17] Knox (1979), 6.
[18] For a more negative assessment of *Dionysus in 69*, arguing that the nudity was voyeuristic and the company 'self-deluded, imprisoned by the dogma of '60s psychobabble', and doomed to disintegration, see Eyre and Wright (2000), 363.

The sexual liberation of the 1960s was of course a crucial factor in the creation of the women's movement of the 1970s. One corollary has been not only the liberation of women from entirely double standards in the judging of their sexual behaviour, but young women's questioning of the myth of romantic love. Social historians have been able to document this group's increasing cynicism, since 1970, about the possibility or even desirability of finding an exclusive lifelong male partner.[19] Divorces, especially those initiated by women, have increased exponentially. The single most important reason why Greek tragedy was rediscovered by women in the 1970s and 1980s was because it gave an appearance of honesty concerning the opportunities life afforded their ancient counterparts, and especially concerning the relatively greater importance of affective ties with children, siblings and parents compared to those with lovers and husbands. Greek tragic narratives are strong on marital breakdown and stepfamilies, but weak on what we call 'romantic' liaisons.

The two most important intellectual missiles in the artillery of this new popular feminism were both published in 1970: Kate Millett's *Sexual Politics* and Germaine Greer's *The Female Eunuch*. The intellectual leaders of the tidal wave of social change (now retrospectively described by social historians as 'early second-wave feminism') found in Greek tragedy, especially the *Oresteia* and Euripides' *Medea*, prefigurative articulation of the unfairness of women's lot. *Medea*, a play in which an abandoned wife and mother kills her own children in order to hurt her treacherous husband, touches on a wide range of issues still fundamental to the 'sex war' in the twenty-first century: economic inequality, limits on women's freedom outside the domestic sphere, social condemnation of female sexual appetite, the question of whether rape is technically possible within marriage, divorce law, and rival male and female claims to parental power over children. These issues were faced head-on in the influential early feminist production of Gloria Albee's adaptation, performed at the Westbeth Playwrights' Feminist Collective in New York City in 1975.[20] The importance of adaptations of Euripides' *Medea* to our era has previously been explored in the first book published by the

---

[19] McRobbie (1978); White (1977), 27. See especially Brown (2001), 176–7.
[20] See Van Zyl Smit (2001), 270–1

APGRD.[21] But Helene Foley's paper in *Dionysus since 69* offers an important complement by exploring how, over the last three decades of debate about gender roles in society, *Medea* and other Greek tragedies have been rewritten and adapted to alter the emphasis, upgrade the importance of female experience, and challenge the gender roles and sexualities canonized in the history of western theatre. Greek heroines such as Jocasta and Clytemnestra have exerted a magnetic force over actors of both sexes, including transvestite entertainers, and especially female writers seeking to re-envision and reconfigure the gender relations of the plays altogether. For a crucial factor has been the growing frustration of women theatre professionals with the standard repertoire. Female actors in search of interesting roles have discovered in the texts of ancient Greek drama far more challenging parts, especially for mature women, than in almost any period of later theatre. There is, for example, a distinguished gallery of outstanding women actors very recently drawn to play Medea (long a favourite with opera divas): Diana Rigg, Fiona Shaw, Isabelle Huppert, to name but three.[22] Greek tragedies make extensive use of female subjectivity and interiority, which are explored in virtuoso speeches. They also move from the periphery of the plot to the centre such issues as female experience of parenthood, marriage, sexual relations, and even (in the case of Aeschylus' Clytemnestra) of political power.[23]

One of the corollaries of the feminist movement has been the emergence of 'gender studies'. Along with recent theatre's challenge to traditional gender roles has come the desire to explore the nature of the individual's gendered self-presentation (what anthropologists since Erving Goffman have also called 'display' or 'performance' of gender), and in particular of her or his sexuality. Gay men and lesbians have been interested in Plato and Sappho for very much longer than the last three decades, but Michel Foucault's *The History of Sexuality* (1976, the first volume of which was published in English translation in 1978), with its heavy emphasis on ancient Mediterranean behaviours, made the

---

[21] Hall, Macintosh, and Taplin (2000).   [22] Macintosh (2000*a*).

[23] The appeal of the Greek tragic heroines to a serious actress was emphasized in a discussion by Diana Quick after her muscular performance of scenes from Aeschylus' *Agamemnon* in Oxford's Holywell Music Room, on Thursday 20 September 2001; the discussion formed part of a conference on the *Oresteia* organized by the APGRD, the proceedings of which are to form the subject of our next published volume.

ancient Greeks honoured participants in all public discussions of the constitution of sexuality. One factor in the revival of Greek theatre has therefore been gay liberation and the new acceptance of open expression of homosexuality. A fascinating fringe gay art-work drawing on Greek tragedy is a comic film noir by Peter Demas, which has links to the plots of several Euripidean plays. *Soldier Boy* (1995) features a Greek mother going mad and decid-ing to sacrifice one child while failing to digest the other's increas-ingly camp and obvious homosexuality. Another, more widely familiar example, is John Fisher's coruscatingly funny Californian *Medea the Musical* (1994, but much revived), which through its metatheatrical action and gay realization of the role of Jason ex-plored the relationship between the sexual orientation of actors and those of the characters they portray (see further Foley, Chapter 3).

Greek tragedy, so attractive to gay and lesbian actors, has also been hospitable to experiments with cross-dressed performances, sometimes (but not always) facilitated by the use of masks, for example in Tony Harrison's *Oresteia*, directed by Peter Hall (see Wiles). Cross-dressing has often been scrutinized in performances by directors working in quite different, eastern traditions of theatre, as in Yukio Ninagawa's *Medea*. Men have played women many times, women have played men occasionally (for example in a 1991 all-female Finnish *Oresteia*),[24] and some choruses osten-sibly of one sex (and indeed ostensibly of identical sexualities) have been played by men and women, straight and gay, together. The transvestite roots of western theatre, in the male impersonation of female figures by the original actors of Greek tragedy, are un-doubtedly interconnected with the gay interest in Greek tragedy. Alisa Solomon recently argued in *Re-Dressing the Canon* that west-ern drama's promise of the mutability of human identity, revealed above all in its aboriginal figure of female impersonation, is pre-cisely what makes theatre 'the queerest art'.[25]

The critique of conventional gender roles has led to an increasing conviction that women's position cannot be understood without analysing the role of men, and indeed without confronting the unpalatable truth that society's view of ideal masculinity—indom-

itable, physically powerful, decisive, autarkic—is complicit in the
oppression of both women and children. Kathleen Riley's paper
uses a perspective informed by depictions of violence in other forms
of theatre and cinema, by research into the psychological damage
suffered by war veterans, and by gender studies, in order to explain
why Euripides' famous *male* infanticide, Heracles, long avoided as
too problematic in mainstream theatre, has in very recent years
suddenly become a popular choice. Directors have seen that he
offers an opportunity to question culturally legitimized models of
male heroism, to explore the social evils of wife and child abuse, and
in particular to examine the relation they bear to militarism and to
organized violence. The idea of Heracles as military hero was
brought home in the Euripidean section of Theodoros Terzopoulos' *Heracles Trilogy*, which premiered in Istanbul in 1999, and was
performed by both Greek and Turkish actors. Heracles' story has
become painfully relevant in an era which has seen an alarming rise
in wife and child murder committed by members of the police and
armed forces: in the summer of 2002 three US Special Forces
soldiers killed their wives shortly after serving in Afghanistan.

Two Greek tragedies are foundling tales. The Sophoclean Oedipus' quest to discover his true parentage, and the reunion of
Creusa and Ion in Euripides' *Ion*, have always had resonances for
adopted children and their parents. In the west the last great wave
of adoption was rather suddenly ended in the late 1960s by the
availability of oral contraception and safe, legal abortions. But a
large number of reunions are still taking place between mothers
and the adult children from whom they were separated at birth in
the mid-1960s and before, including the moving high-profile 1996
reunion of the popular British politician Clare Short with the son
she had given away thirty-one years previously. Reunions of this
kind—currently staples of daytime talk shows—have lent a particular charge to the outbreak of performances of Euripides' *Ion*
since the mid-1990s. In late 1994 there were two quite different
Ions in London: Jude Law, before his transubstantiation into the
darling of Hollywood, shone as the idealistic young hero at the
RSC's Barbican version in September, while the Actors Touring
Company brought nearly every woman in the audience to tears at
the Lyric, Hammersmith, a few weeks later.[26]

[26] See Padel (1996).

Greek tragedy's exploration of parenthood and its discontents prompted Euripides and Sophocles to experiment with the impact that little children can make on an audience. In *Alcestis* a young boy weeps while his mother dies; in *Medea* small boys scream for help from backstage while their mother assaults them. Children torn from the arms of a parent feature in Sophocles' *Oedipus Tyrannus* and Euripides' *Trojan Women*; and the most distressing moment in western theatre is arguably Hecuba's entrance bearing the corpse of her murdered baby grandson Astyanax (also in *Trojan Women*). The pronounced presence of children in these and other Greek tragedies has certainly been a factor in the texts' theatrical rediscovery during a period when the sensitivity of children to conflict between adults and to emotional trauma has been far more widely recognized. This is a result in particular of the popularization of the views of the liberal pacifist Dr Benjamin Spock, whose *Baby and Child Care*, the earliest version of which was published in 1946, became ever more influential in the 1960s and beyond as it sold more than 50 million copies and became the 'bible' of the post-war baby boom. It was attacked by social conservatives who regarded Spock as the 'father of permissiveness' and the mentor of a 'Spock-marked' generation of hippies, but it certainly helped to put the child's rights and needs much higher up the social agenda than they had been hitherto.

The perceived contemporary relevance of the children in Greek tragedy is also connected with the acknowledgement that children are terribly vulnerable to parental *violence* (Medea, Heracles). During the later end of the period under discussion, it has also been increasingly acknowledged that children are the last subgroup of the species *homo sapiens* whose human rights to have their views heard and to a life free even from physical assault have, in almost all parts of the world, not yet been legally recognized. Over the next few years it is likely that the emphasis laid on children through European productions of Greek tragedy will intensify as children's legal rights are scrutinized in Brussels. Moreover, until now the children of Greek tragedy have been used to highlight domestic and familial issues rather than political ones. But in Peter Sellars's adaptation of *The Children of Herakles*, which opened in Germany just as this book was going to press, groups of 'real-life' children—Kurdish refugee asylum-seekers—sat silently

throughout the entire performance, making a more 'macro-polit-
ical' appeal to their audience.[27]

POLITICS

Greek tragedy was itself born in a moment of political change,
coinciding with the first signs of democratic revolution in late
sixth-century Athens. Certainly since the time of Aristophanes in
the later fifth century it has been seen as a medium which could
fan political fervour in its audiences. The late twentieth century
has reawakened its political potential. The difficulties associated
with direct critique of the government of East Germany in the
1960s pushed Heiner Müller towards Greek tragedy, notably in
his *Philoktet* (premiered Munich 1968), which was not performed
in the GDR until 1977.[28] Subsequently many of the texts have
been appropriated to serve diverse political causes, including, recently, even environmental issues (in Tony Harrison's *Prometheus*
of 1998, see Hall below, Chapter 6, with Figure 15). The heroine
of Sophocles' *Antigone* is a hardy perennial who has protested
against South African apartheid (1973), Polish martial law (1984,
see Figure 3), and Yugoslavian civil war in the no man's land
between Greece and the former Republic of Yugoslavia (1994).[29]
In early 2003 an Irish production identified her as a contemporary
Arab, arguing her case in a prophetically war-torn Middle East.
Brecht's adaptation of *Antigone*, first performed at Chur in Switzerland in 1948, was revived by the New York Living Theater
company in 1967, a production performed over the course of two

---

[27] *The Children of Herakles* opened at the Ruhr Triennial Festival in Bottrop at
the Bottroper Lichthof on 19 September 2002. It was previewed in *Kultur* magazine
(1 Sept. 2002) and reviewed in the Culture section of *Der Tagesspiegel* (24 Sept.
2002). It was subsequently taken to Paris, Rome, and Boston, Massachusetts. All
performances were in English, with subtitles where necessary. The production used
Ralph Gladstone's 1955 translation from the University of Chicago Press, *Complete
Greek Tragedies*, vol. i.

[28] Kalb (1998), xvi, 10.

[29] See Hardwick (this volume), Macintosh (1997), 321, and, on Andrzej Wajda's
Kraków *Antygona*, in which the chorus members were dressed as either Gdansk
dockyard workers or military commandos, Karpinski (1989), 102–6. Antigone is
said to have returned recently to Southern Africa, to protest, in the artistically coded
form of a samizdat adaptation circulating underground, against the government-
endorsed brutalities afflicting Zimbabwe.

FIGURE 3. The chorus members dressed as military commandos (others were dressed as dockyard workers) in *Antygona*, directed by Andrzej Wajda, at the Stary Teatr, Kraków (1984). Photograph by Stanisław Markowski.

decades in no fewer than sixteen countries, including Franco's Spain.[30]

In Euripides' war plays, in particular, there has been discovered painful resonance. *Trojan Women* has been used to reveal the terrible consequences of war for people all over the world, in productions in the former Eastern bloc (for example, in Schwerin, East Germany in 1982), in Japan, and in the west; the implied victims have most often been those targeted by US bombs, whether in Hiroshima, Vietnam, or Libya in the late 1980s, although in the Romanian director Andrei Serban's famous version, which was first produced in 1974, Romania's experience of the

---

[30] See Judith Malina's Preface to her translation of Brecht's play (Bertolt Brecht (1990), vii): '... whenever we played it, it seemed to become the symbol of the struggle of that time and place—in bleeding Ireland, in Franco's Spain, in Poland a month before martial law was declared, clandestinely in Prague—the play is uncannily appropriate to every struggle for freedom'. On Brecht's version see also Michelakis, below, Chapter 7.

Ceauşescu family was a more obvious point of reference.[31] *Hecuba*
has been revived as a regular performance text largely since the fall
of the Berlin Wall (see Wertenbaker, this volume). It portrays war
atrocities committed by no fewer than three neighbouring ethnic
groups, and their nauseating attempts at self-justification. It is set
in the southern Balkans; in the early 1990s the parallels with the
genocidal violence in the war which broke out in agonizing stages
during 1991–2, in what had so recently been Yugoslavia, seemed
almost unbearable. This was particularly apparent in a searing
1992 production by Laurence Boswell at the tiny Gate Theatre in
London, starring Ann Mitchell and Don Warrington as Hecuba
and Polymestor.[32] *Phoenician Women*, the archetypal 'civil war'
tragedy, has also been discovered to offer incomparably powerful
theatre in the period of the violent dissolution of communist
Yugoslavia and the former Soviet republics, especially Georgia
(notably Katie Mitchell's RSC version (1995), informed by Georgian performance traditions). As Helene Foley has said, the stories
dramatized in Greek tragedy ceased, during the twentieth century,
to belong in any exclusive sense to the west.[33] The deaths caused
by a suicide bomber in Tel Aviv in early 2003 lent dark immediacy
to a production in the same city of Rina Yerushalmi's *Mythos*, an
adaptation of the *Oresteia*, in which the conflicted Orestes was
played by an Arab-Israeli actor. With the deepening of the third-
millennium war between the USA and Islam it is certain that
Greek tragedy will once again become a medium for the exploration of east–west tension.

The 'politics' section of the book consists of studies of individual
but we hope exemplary topics within a huge field. The first two
chapters look at particular sites of political conflict in the English-
speaking world. Civil war and military occupation are the subject
of the first. The year 1968–9 was a watershed in Ireland as in so
many other parts of the globe, since it is to civil rights marches by
Catholics in Derry in August 1968 that the original outbreak of the
late twentieth-century wave of violence in Northern Ireland, eu-
phemistically known as 'The Troubles', is now conventionally

---

[31] On *Trojan Women* and war see Taplin (1989), 261–3; on Serban, Macintosh
(1997), 319–20. In January 2003 an Australian production located the action of
Trojan Women in the Contemporary Persian Gulf, in order to protest against the
imminent war in Iraq.

[32] Edith Hall (1992*b*).   [33] Foley (2001*b*), 424.

dated. For much of the period covered by this book Northern Ireland was under military occupation by British troops, and Greek tragedy has proved to be a resonant medium for exploring issues related to the Irish 'problem'. The intense examination of the psychopathology of revenge enacted in Sophocles' *Electra*, for example, which was performed in Deborah Warner's uncompromising production in Derry shortly after a particularly shocking outbreak of reciprocal violence in 1992, was perceived by its audiences to be almost unbearably topical.[34] A recent adaptation of Euripides' *Iphigenia in Aulis* by Colin Teevan, developed at the time of the worst post-war loss of Irish civilian life in the Omagh bombing of August 1998, unmistakably transplanted the barbarous story of the politically expedient killing of an innocent young woman to contemporary Ireland. It was performed at the Lyric Theatre, Belfast, in March 1999. But, perhaps, the most prominent productions in this category have been Sophoclean and have emerged from the Field Day Theatre Company, founded in 1980 by Stephen Rea and Brian Friel; they included Tom Paulin's *The Riot Act*, which is an adaptation of Sophocles' *Antigone* (1984), and Seamus Heaney's *The Cure at Troy* (1990). The place of Heaney's poetic tragedy within the performance reception of Sophocles' *Philoctetes* and in the cultural politics of contemporary Ireland is explored in this volume in an essay by Oliver Taplin.

Sometimes the political energies within Greek tragedies are unleashed unexpectedly, when unanticipated events coincide with particular productions. An example was the London performances of the driven *Ajax* directed by Stephane Braunschweig in May 1992.[35] The second half of this play consists of military leaders refusing to hand over the corpse of one of their own men for burial by his family. Braunschweig had no way of knowing the headlines were to be dominated that very week by the furious Anglo-American dispute, reflected in almost daily British parliamentary showdowns, over the unreturned corpses of nine British soldiers killed by American pilots in one of the many 'friendly fire' incidents which had so blighted the Gulf War. The audience cared about the treatment of Ajax's corpse to a degree rarely experienced. The USA's role in the 1991 war with Iraq is also the starting-point of my own discussion of two Greek tragedies

---

[34] Edith Hall (1999*b*), 261–2.   [35] See Edith Hall (1992*a*).

attributed to Aeschylus (*Persians* and *Prometheus Bound*), plays with a long history of involvement in revolutionary politics. In the 1990s they provided arenas where the most radical of directors, such as Peter Sellars and Tony Harrison, could urge political causes which took them into dangerous territory on the very edges of the ideologically acceptable—the plight of the bombed people of Iraq in 1993, and of the unemployed British working-class male in the wake of Thatcher's assault on the British trade union movement in the 1980s. Greek tragedy, as Sellars has recently urged, can offer a venue for saying the otherwise unsayable, to represent the unrepresentable. In Harrison's use of Io's journey to the abattoir in *Prometheus*, Greek tragedy has also offered a profound and moving mythical language in which to address the most sensitive of all subjects, especially for a non-Jewish writer—the Holocaust.

Harrison's film reveals its director's fascination with the way that his inner world has been informed by images of the Nazi death camps he has seen in newsreel and documentaries. Harrison is one of several recent directors of Greek tragedy for whom the possibilities of plural media, a variety of historically divergent source materials, and generic inter-referentiality have combined to stimulate the creation of postmodern experiments. In 1970 Robert Wilson was already using an eclectic collage of media and images in his *Medea*-inspired *Deafman Glance*, creating a nearly surrealistic effect; by 1986, in his *Alcestis* at the Loeb Drama Theater, he was mixing Euripides with parodic themes from a Japanese Kyogen drama, Heiner Müller's *Description of a Picture*, and also laser projections, thereby 'spilling a cool, architectonic-technological brilliance' over the stage.[36] One of the reasons why Greek tragedy has attracted directors in the electronic age is that some of ancient theatre's formal devices find unexpected modern analogies in the machines we have designed for the electrical recording and retrieval of experience, such as the audiotape recorder, whose theatrical potential was revealed in Samuel Beckett's influential *Krapp's Last Tape* in 1958. Peter Sellars, for example, has talked about how the ancient Greek mask offered both 'an amazing sense of public address, but also this private interior monologue', a combination which is profoundly suggestive to him of cameras, shooting from

---

[36] Birringer (1991), 62–3 and fig. 10.

multiple angles, and the different levels of address that can be created with a microphone.[37] Michelakis's chapter in this volume looks at a group of aesthetically diverse but politically committed European film versions of Greek tragedy, made since the mid-1980s; they include Tony Harrison's *Prometheus* and a film version of Sophocles' *Antigone* by Jean-Marie Straub and Danièle Huillet (1992). The discussion shows the vitality of the relationship between these films and the current popularity of Greek tragedy on the stage, and how important a role that relationship has played in the self-definition of avant-garde cinema in opposition to mainstream Hollywood movies. Michelakis also reflects on the interaction between cinema and other screened media in contemporary society, the socioeconomic basis of that interaction, the role of vision and memory in contemporary art and culture, and the potential of Greek tragedy to allow sensitive revisiting of critical moments of the west's experience.

Greek tragedy has been discovered as a fertile place in which to explore cultural difference. The prominence of this theme in the texts themselves is so remarkable that some classical scholars have even argued that confrontation with the ethnically 'other' is what constitutes the Dionysiac about the genre, an argument which can be supported by pointing to the importance of the pattern of arrival and resistance that characterizes several myths about this god.[38] Be that as it may—and there are several alternative (and/or complementary) explanations for the relationship between Dionysus and tragedy—almost all the plays do indeed stage encounters between characters from different Greek states—Theban, Athenian, Argive, Thessalian, Cretan—and an astounding half of them portray Greeks interacting with individuals or groups (often the chorus) of an entirely different ethnic background and first language (Egyptian, Asiatic, Levantine, Black Sea).[39] The plot-types involve many heroes and heroines displaced from their own lands

---

[37] Delgado and Heritage (1996), 228.

[38] Bibliography in Zeitlin (1993), 152.

[39] Burkert (1966), 115, argued that the popularity of female and foreign choruses in tragedy stems from its origins in goat sacrifice, a violent ritual action at which the male citizens performing it may have assumed anonymity through ritual disguise. On exoticism and the tragic chorus see also Edith Hall (1989), especially 115–16; on the connection between marginal choral identities and tragic music, see Peter Wilson (2002), 56–9.

by war, abduction, banishment, death sentences, or pollution
taboo; rhetoric, dialogue and choral song tend, consequently, to
return ineluctably to themes of nostalgia for homeland, exile,
asylum, immigration, statelessness, vagrancy, cultural hybridity,
and alienation.[40]

Some Greek tragedies, especially *Medea*, have as a result had a
long relationship with European colonialism and imperialism.[41] It
has even recently been argued that this relationship goes all the
way back to fifth-century Greece, in that tragedy's representation
of foreign cultures, such as Persia and Egypt, originally represented an identifiably 'pre-colonial' discourse adumbrating the
Greek mindset which would by the end of the following century
bring these countries, through Macedonian rule, under Greek
dominion.[42] Greek tragedy was rediscovered on the stages of
Europe at exactly the moment of the discovery of the New
World, and by the eighteenth century the connection between
some of the myths enacted in Greek tragedy and the European
experience of far-flung colonies became explicit: the popularity in
the eighteenth century of Euripides' *Iphigenia among the Taurians*,
for example, was a result of that play's portrayal of the experience
of Greek adventurers on the wild northern shore of the Black Sea.
Such uses of Greek tragedy are part of the larger conceptual
programme by which Early Modern Europe invented in classical
Greece a 'pure', 'western' cultural ancestor, while systematically
playing down the significance of Africa and Asia in the cultural
melting-pot of the ancient Mediterranean.[43] What is much more
surprising is that in the period which has seen the final stages in the
slow, painful process of decolonization, especially in Africa,

---

[40] See further Edith Hall (1997*a*), 97–8.

[41] On Medea see Macintosh (2000*a*), especially 19–29 and Macintosh (forthcoming *a*); on *Iphigenia in Tauris* in the seventeenth and eighteenth centuries see Hall
and Macintosh (2004), ch. 2.

[42] Vasunia (2001).

[43] For details of the white, Northern European invention of Greece see the first
volume (1987) of Martin Bernal's controversial *Black Athena: The Afroasiatic Roots
of Classical Civilization*, whose analysis of the ideological agenda behind the
accepted eighteenth- and nineteenth-century picture of ancient Greece (an analysis
inspired by laudable anti-racist motives) was marred by his insistence on substitut-
ing an equally misleading alternative model. For a variety of responses see Lefkowitz and Rogers (1996). It must also be stressed that staged adaptations of Greek
tragedy have been used by radical playwrights to protest *against* racism and indeed
slavery since at least as early as the 1830s (see e.g. Edith Hall (1997*c*)).

writers searching for new forms of identity and cultural expression of it have found promising material in the texts which could be said to epitomize imperial Europe: the dramas of classical antiquity. Yet the fact that the ancient Greek language is so 'incontrovertibly dead' (in Louis MacNeice's phrase) has itself proved liberating; its deadness has actually *helped* writers from brutally colonized countries explore the part of their own heritage that is undeniably European. Greek drama has often felt like a root which it can be pleasurable and legitimate to dig towards, bypassing some of the pain connected with literature in the actual language of the colonial power—English, French, or Afrikaans. This is not dissimilar to the pleasure expressed by the Aboriginal Australian poet Jack Davis in reading the English dictionary to feed his fascination with the 'hidden roots of English, in particular Latin and Greek'.[44]

Lorna Hardwick's study of the relationship between performances of Greek texts and the creation of post-colonial identities, especially in Cuba, the Caribbean, and western Africa, offers a new theoretical framework for understanding this tension, and provides concepts with which to analyse the reconfiguration of ethnicities in new versions of canonical ancient plays. Her discussion also illuminates the ways Greek tragedy has been used in relation to the experience of immigrant communities, coerced or voluntary, in First World countries. *Medea* was a crucial text in the war against South African apartheid,[45] but there have been many versions of Greek tragedy which have explored 'domestic racism' elsewhere: 1998, for example, saw both Phylicia Rashad's African-American *Medea* in the USA, and in Canada a CBC radio play called *The Trojan Women*, a two-part exploration of slavery based on Euripides featuring black Canadian actors, with music based on traditional black blues.[46] The complex ethnic identity of Asians

---

[44] The phrase 'incontrovertibly dead' comes from the opening of the thirteenth canto of MacNeice's autobiographical poem 'Autumn Journey' (1938), where the narrator has been musing on how learning Latin and ancient Greek has qualified him to escape blue-collar wages and earn a professional salary. See MacNeice (1979), 101–53, at p. 125. MacNeice was a classicist and a poet, whose works also included a translation of Aeschylus' *Agamemnon* for stage performance. For the Davis quotation see Davis and Chesson (1988), 55.

[45] See Van Zyl Smit (1992).

[46] Rashad starred as Medea in Atlanta with the Alliance Theatre Company, directed by Kenny Leon. The composer of the CBC *Trojan Women* was the guitarist Colin Linden.

driven out of Kenya to Britain in the 1960s informed Jatinder
Verma's Tara Arts production *Oedipus the King* (London 1991),
while Ruksana Ahmed's recent play *River of Fire* is an *Antigone* set
in Mogul India; through it this dissident feminist, a British
Muslim whose family originated in Pakistan, uses Greek tragedy
as an alternative 'third way' when navigating a route through both
Muslim and British traditions.[47]

PERFORMANCE AESTHETICS

Interculturalism has been intimately connected with artistic experimentation in the theatre. Richard Schechner was an anthropologist by training, and has maintained extensive collaboration
with key figures in the anthropology of performance, especially
Victor Turner.[48] Interculturalism therefore forms a natural link
into the third section of the book, 'Dionysus and the Aesthetics of
Performance'. Stage versions and adaptations of Greek tragedy
have reflected every trend in contemporary western theatre and
every important focus of postmodernism—the body, artifice, the
arbitrariness of narrative; indeed, the *Oresteia* has been one of
the most important charter texts of the theatrical avant-garde, as
we hope to show in our next volume.[49] Euripides and Seneca
underlie even one important example of the confrontational 'In-
yer-face Theatre' of the 1990s (itself so derivative of the Artaudian
Theatre of Cruelty), Sarah Kane's *Phaedra's Love* (1996). This
play offered the alienated 'yoof' of Britain the most 'in-yer-face'
assault on the Greek tragic canon since Schechner, and the most

---

[47] Verma founded the Asian community theatre company Tara Arts in response
to the murder of a Sikh boy in South London during the Southall riots in June 1976;
see Delgado and Heritage (1996), 278, 280. At first the company produced plays
with Kenyan settings, exploring the Asian experience of the British empire in
Africa, but by the late 1980s began 'a more overt dialogue with England through
texts'; more specifically, the 'tradaption', 'through Asian eyes and ears' of the
authors who seemed to epitomize European culture—Gogol, Shakespeare, Sophocles, Chekhov, Brecht (Verma (1998), 129). On Ahmed's *River of Fire*, as yet
unperformed, see www.guardian.co.uk/Archive/Article/ 0,4273,3950810,00.
[48] See especially Schechner (1993).
[49] *Agamemnon in Performance 458* BC–*2002* AD (Macintosh, Michelakis, Hall,
and Taplin (forthcoming)). See also the fundamental article by Chioles (1993). For
the relationship between postmodernism and performances of Greek tragedy, especially as reflected in framing devices and the deconstruction of the mechanics of
illusion, see Decreus (forthcoming).

rebarbative Hippolytus of all time, a malodorous, foul-mouthed couch potato much given to onanism.[50]

The prominence of Greek tragedy since 1969 begins at the same moment as theatre historians now conventionally place a chronological boundary dividing recognizable periods in world theatre generally: Brockett's standard *History of Theatre* traces the history of contemporary western theatre until the present in a chapter entitled 'Theatre and Drama after 1968'.[51] But it has most to do with the so-called Performative Turn in theatre, the moment when 'physical' theatre, especially in Central Europe, began to supersede the theatre of 'the spoken word', a process discussed by Wiles and Fischer-Lichte in this volume. The (counter-) cultural watershed of the late 1960s saw vast experimentalism in theatre; one well publicized example was the anarchist San Francisco street theatre group The Diggers, whose activities combined art happenings, direct action and above all street theatre. For many groups, radical politics and unconventional dramatic performances were inseparable (in 1968 the already anti-authoritarian Théâtre du Soleil decided that every one of its members should receive an identical salary).[52] Others were calling the very nature of theatre, of autonomous performance art, into question. The classics of the repertoire were useful sites for confronting such issues: in Frankfurt Joseph Beuys notoriously allegorized the relationship between organic life and dead, inert master texts of cultural tradition in his 'action/ event' *Iphigenia / Titus*; Beuys sat in an enclosure alongside a real, live horse that was munching hay, while a tape recorder monotonously played readings from Goethe's *Iphigenie auf Tauris* and Shakespeare's *Titus Andronicus*.[53]

Above all this process continued with renewed vigour the assault on the proscenium arch, with its constraining separation of the worlds of the audience and of the stage. This assault can be dated from at least the 1880s onwards. The rediscovery, then as now, of ancient Greek drama had been fuelled by encounters with other, non-western theatrical traditions. Indeed, the western avant-garde

[50] Sierz (2001) 107–12. *Phaedra's Love* is, however, particularly popular in Germany and is often performed there.
[51] Brockett (1999), ch. 17; see also the chronological dividing line in Bradby and Sparks (1997).
[52] See Bradby and Sparks (1997), 21.
[53] See Birringer (1991), 12–14 and fig. 1.

theatre practice of the first part of the twentieth century developed
in large measure from its encounter with alternative theatrical
traditions.[54] What was different, however, in the second part of
the century was that now the (often former) colonial subject began
to take centre stage in the cultural interchange. One of the reasons
why the Algerian stage designer Abd' Elkader Farrah was so highly
regarded in avant-garde (and later mainstream theatrical) circles in
France and Britain from the mid-1950s onwards was that he was
able to bring to the plays of Brecht, Genet, and the ancient Greeks,
'theatrical' elements from his own culture that Michel Saint-
Denis, Jan Kott, Peter Brook, and now their audiences increasingly yearned to know more about.[55] The proscenium arch stage
had in many colonized countries been the most concrete symbol
of the aesthetic culture of the imperial oppressors.[56] With its
abandonment came a powerful desire to explore new types of
performance space, both roofed and (like ancient Greek theatres)
out-of-doors, the capacity to explore different configurations between audience and performance group, for which the Greek
chorus proved extremely useful (see above all Fischer-Lichte's
section on Einar Schleef, below, pp. 355–9), and the potential to
watch performances from different angles and levels in a constantly shifting perception of the action.

Out with the proscenium arch stage went the taste for the type of
dramatic action it had been developed to contain: western naturalism. There was a marked new interest in exploring other, more
interactive and vital forms of indigenous theatre, new respect for
the traditional, ritual, pantomime or mime-related, processional
and choreographical conventions of theatre in India, Africa, Japan,
and China, and above all new emphasis on performative styles,
conventions, and self-consciousness. It has become a directorial
commonplace to fuse the 'western' classics of Greek theatre with
'eastern' Kathakali or Noh conventions; but the most important
example of all was the combination of electrifying Indian- and

---

[54] In general see Innes (1993), and for Yeats's complicated relationships with
both Noh and Greek drama, Macintosh (1994), especially 60–3.

[55] Farrah gave a talk, 'An Algerian's Ventures into Ancient Greek Territory', at
the APGRD on 30 January 2002, to accompany an exhibition of some of his designs
for ancient Greek plays and also plays with Greek or Roman settings. A transcript of
the talk is held at the APGRD.

[56] Crow and Banfield (1996), 11–13, 112–13.

Cambodian-derived chorus work in Ariane Mnouchkine's *Les Atrides*, in which the design of the performance space, with its partially buried statues, like the buried army of Qin Shuang, also had Chinese resonances.[57] The Performative Turn began to penetrate even the Classics academy, which was not then conspicuous for its radicalism. By 1977 Oliver Taplin's landmark reappraisal of Greek tragedy from a performative perspective, *The Stagecraft of Aeschylus*, could be received seriously in the bastions of conservatism throughout the world of classical scholarship.

The Return to the Greeks was thus (in hindsight) a virtually inevitable consequence of this potent cultural coincidence of the hippie challenge to the traditional notion of theatre, the Performative Turn, and the exploration of non-western theatre conventions. It was also related to the emergence of television (which became instantly more popular after the introduction of colour transmission in 1968). Television has not proved particularly successful as a medium for Greek tragedy. A notorious example is provided by *The Serpent Son* (1979), a televised adaptation of the *Oresteia* which failed precisely because of the means by which its creators tried to convert a theatrical text into visual entertainment for the small screen.[58] What television does brilliantly, however, is contemporary social realist drama. Some have even argued that television's preeminence in this genre has severely compromised its potential in live theatre, which has, as a result, been left much more open to non-naturalistic stage styles

---

[57] See Gauthier and Ertel (1992), 31; Kiernander (1993), 135–8. Mnouchkine's actors included the Kathakali-trained Catherine Schaub, Nirupama Nityanandan (who had studied Bharata Natyam dancing in India), Simon Abkarian (an expert in Caucasuian folk-dance), and Juliana Carneiro da Cunha (who had studied dance in Brazil, Germany and Belgium). See Bradby (2002), 124 and Figure 21 in Wiles's chapter, below. On intercultural theatre see Balme (1999), 13–14, and Fischer-Lichte, Gissenwehrer, and Riley (1990); for the perception of Asian theatre in the eyes of European directors and dramatists see the fine bibliographical survey in Savarese (1992).

[58] The adaptation unfortunately conveyed the impression of a camp burlesque of science fiction, its design and visual effects drawing on those developed for the popular genre of television serial constituted by *Dr Who* and *Star Trek*. It was written by Kenneth McLeish and Frederic Raphael, and broadcast on BBC2 in March 1979. It boasted a stellar cast including Diana Rigg, Denis Quilley, Helen Mirren, Billie Whitelaw, Siân Phillips, and Claire Bloom. For further details see Raphael and McLeish (1979), and the major feature in *The Radio Times* for 3–9 March. On a problematic German attempt to broadcast a theatrical adaptation of a Greek play see Schanze (1979), 123.

and forms.[59] All these trends came together in Richard Schechner's participatory 'Dionysus Group' in *Dionysus in 69*. Here a very particular target was conventional theatre architecture and design, to which the ritual dancing floor of the ancient Greeks provided a conceptual counterweight. Even more important to Schechner were the barriers between audience and actor, and between individual actors and the performance group. In the subversion of both these boundaries, the convention of the Greek tragic chorus proved as inspirational to Schechner as to many directors subsequently.

Masks are ubiquitous to almost all non-western cultures. Perhaps more relevantly, they appear repeatedly in the metaphorical discourse surrounding the colonial experience of double ethnicity, especially since the Antillean-born psychiatrist Frantz Fanon's influential *Peau noire, masques blancs* (*Black Skin, White Masks*), was translated into English in 1967. Hardwick's discussion of the use of Greek tragedy in the theatrical exploration of colonialism in the Third World therefore leads naturally into the third section of the book, and especially into David Wiles's consideration of the dramatic mask. Directors and adaptors, especially Tony Harrison, have evolved special relationships with the Greek tragic mask, indeed with particular designers: Harrison's collaboration with Jocelyn Herbert, for example, extended over two decades (see Figure 4). Wiles, however, begins not with the director, adaptor, designer, or even the audience, but with the masked *performer*. Masks (re)entered the western theatre through the radical innovations of the modernists, and in the first half of the twentieth century were intimately tied up with the way in which our culture came to terms with pagan antiquity. In the last three decades, however, some of the most important theatrical innovations have occurred within the realm of physical theatre; the Greek tragic mask has allowed actors to attempt to combine a 'Grotowskian' notion of performance rooted in the body of the actor, with the text-based, cerebral, metaphysical dimension of Greek tragedy, rooted linguistically in the power of its ancient words.

[59] This plausible point was maintained vehemently by Colin Teevan (who translated Euripides' *Bacchae* for the 2002 Royal National Theatre production, directed by Sir Peter Hall) in a public discussion at the APGRD on 29 May 2002. For an incisive account of television's special relationship with naturalism and realism see Caughie (2000), 88–124.

FIGURE 4. The chorus of Oceanids, women workers from a fish canning factory, transformed by Jocelyn Herbert's masks, float on an industrial barge in Tony Harrison's film *Prometheus* (1998).

Greek tragedy was not only a masked performance but a profoundly musical one. It inspired influential choreographers much earlier in the twentieth century, above all Martha Graham, the continuing influence of whose important *Night Journey* (1947), based on Sophocles' *Oedipus Tyrannus*, is discussed below by Helene Foley (Chapter 3). Graham maintained her interest in Greek themes until as late in her life as *Phaedra's Dream* (1983). Recently her mantle has been assumed by Pina Bausch, the creator of the Wuppertal Dance Theater. Her danced version of Euripides' *Iphigenia in Tauris* (1974), to Gluck's music, is regarded as a landmark in modern ballet, especially for the manner in which it replaces narrative storytelling with exploration of the emotional implications of the myth. But Greek tragedy has played an arguably much more important role in late twentieth-century opera, discussed in Chapter 11 by Peter Brown. His wide-ranging survey yields fascinating results. Although the repertoire which has attracted opera composers (above all *Bacchae*, *Medea*, and the *Oresteia*) closely mirrors that which has been dominant in the theatre and cinema (and for similar reasons), the sheer number of recent operatic productions based on Greek tragedy is intriguing. So are the ways in which composers have used Greek tragedy to explore the dramatic and mythic potential of a variety of non-elite vocal traditions, of much more recent invention than opera, such as jazz and gospel music.

The flexible potential of the human voice supplies another important reason why Greek tragedy has been so attractive. Its Greek originals, composed in a variety of poetic metres, offer an outstanding opportunity for writing new poetry for dramatic delivery. In the English-speaking world alone, the list of poets who have created versions of Greek tragedies over the last few decades is remarkably distinguished—it includes Tony Harrison, Ted Hughes, Simon Armitage, and Seamus Heaney.[60] The poetry of Aeschylus, Euripides, and Sophocles thus runs in strong currents beneath the waters of contemporary poetry. Yet the aesthetic impact of Greek tragedy, of course, goes far beyond even performances in translation or adaptations. It would be impossible for a single volume even to begin to map this enormous cultural terrain. A great deal of work remains to be done on the sizeable number of important novels drawing, in one way or another, on Greek tragedies: Christa Wolf's recuperation of Euripides' heroine in her anti-racist *Medea–Stimmen* (1996), Donna Tartt's murderous antics, centred on an enactment of *Bacchae* in *The Secret History* (1992), William Golding's allusions to *Ion* in his unfinished posthumous *The Double Tongue* (1995), or Barry Unsworth's *The Songs of the Kings* (2002), in which *Iphigenia in Aulis* becomes a tragedy created by Public Relations.[61] In the case of dramatic works rather than fiction, the recent 'influence' of Greek tragedy

[60] On Tony Harrison's *Oresteia* see Taplin (forthcoming). On Ted Hughes's *Alcestis* see Macintosh (2001), and on his *Oresteia*, Gervais (2002). On Armitage see Riley, below, Chapter 4; on Heaney's *The Cure at Troy* see Taplin, this volume, Chapter 5. For remarks on all three poets see Taplin (2002). One outstanding new poetic *Oedipus*, composed in Yorkshire dialect by Blake Morrison and directed by Barrie Rutter, was performed by Northern Broadsides in Halifax in 2001 (see Figure 5). This company also produced the première of Ted Hughes's *Alcestis* in 2000, and is planning a production of *Antigone* for Autumn 2003.

[61] For a discussion of novels using *Medea* see Van Zyl Smit (2001). On a lighter note, A. A. Gill's *Starcrossed* (1999) concludes with a performance of *Antigone*.

becomes impossible to chart and raises huge theoretical problems. Sometimes it can be proven that a pronounced similarity between a modern work of art and one of the ancient plays results from conscious borrowing on the part of the author or director, but more often it can not. To anyone acquainted with Euripides' *Bacchae*, for example, it is impossible not to hear resonances of that ancient play in Jane Campion's *Holy Smoke*, a psycho-sexual film drama about the nature of true spiritual enlightenment (1999). The film's climax provides a powerful parallel with the famous 'transvestism' scene in Euripides' *Bacchae*, where Dionysus attends to Pentheus' cross-dressing. At the climax of Campion's film Harvey Keitel, as the 'cult exiter' P. J. Waters, is forced into dressing up as a woman and dancing in the wild Australian outback because of his sexual obsession with the young cult member he is supposed to be deprogramming (Kate Winslet as Ruth). Yet it is not clear in this case whether the similarity between modern drama and ancient Greek tragedy is the result of the author making direct allusion, revealing unconscious absorption, or tapping into familiar and currently valent patterns of narrative.

A salutary reminder of the pitfalls in this area was provided by the Coen Brothers, who have both claimed little knowledge of the *Odyssey*, yet whose movie *O Brother Where Art Thou?* (2000) contained several seemingly detailed allusions to that epic. Sometimes the relationship may simply be a matter of negotiation with the handful of 'archetypal' emotional and familial relationships which have been instantiated in most human mythological and narrative complexes. Those explored in many Greek tragedies— brothers in conflict, insult avenged, parents rediscovered, children expiring—are also, of course, staples of that most successful of all late twentieth-century dramatic genres, the television soap opera.[62]

---

[62] Dupont (1991) discusses *Dallas* in the light of Homeric epic, but nobody, to my knowledge, has yet written about the relationship between Greek tragedy and soap opera. This is surprising, since the best theoretical discussion of soap opera as a genre argues that what distinguishes it from other genres of TV dramatic fiction (police, detective, and hospital series, adventure narratives, romance) is that its central topic and source of narrative energy is the threatened integrity of the *family*. Most conflictual relationships set parent against child, husband against wife, or sibling against sibling, rather than a hero or romantic couple against an external or foreign opponent (Ang (1985), 68–72, a section entitled 'Dallas and Family Tragedy'). This is of course, very precisely, what distinguishes Greek tragedy from other forms of ancient narrative fiction, such as epic or the novel.

Yet sometimes the resemblance between situations in Greek tragedies and scenes in specific soap episodes may not be quite as
accidental as it seems; one scriptwriter for a famous British soap
opera (who sadly wishes to remain anonymous) confided to me that
he has found stimulus in the conscious rewriting of famous scenes
from theatrical classics, including Greek tragedies. And one emi-
nent theatre critic has drawn convincing parallels between Greek
tragedy and the television advertisement.[63]

Brecht's *Antigone* (like Anouilh's) has been one of the more
important avenues by which audiences have approached Greek
tragedy since the late 1960s. Yet it is not only in this actual
adaptation of an ancient play that Brecht's dialogue with the ancient Greeks is apparent. Indeed, the creative aesthetics of both
Brecht and the other most influential playwright of the twentieth
century, Samuel Beckett, were clearly shaped in direct response to
the drama of the ancient Greeks.[64] Brecht's greatest aesthetic
impact was felt in the 1950s, but Beckett was central to the public
agenda in 1969, when he won the Nobel Prize for literature. The
presence of Greek theatre in his plays is so unique, all-pervasive,
and identifiable that no book on Dionysus' impact on the theatre-
going public of the last few decades would be adequate without a
discussion of his work. Popular ideas about theatre see Beckett as
the inheritor of a tradition of pared-down, relationship-centred,
philosophical drama which originated in ancient Greece: Bennett
Simon's popular *Tragic Drama and the Family* (1988) is subtitled
Psychoanalytic Studies from Aeschylus to Beckett. In the current
volume Katharine Worth examines the subterranean influence of

[63] Esslin (1974). As long ago as 1962 Sophocles was praised in a book addressed to aspiring writers of TV drama (Barnouw (1962), 10). The nature of the
representation of the family on television changed greatly in the 1970s, coinciding
with the rediscovery of Greek tragedy. Ella Taylor's discussion of families across
genres on prime-time north American television (1989) shows how the post-war
depiction of the family as a haven from external problems was replaced in the 1970s
by the family as 'a repository for conflict, anxiety, and fear' (p. 2; see especially
the chapter 'Trouble at Home: Television's Changing Families 1970–1980',
pp. 65–109).

[64] See Eyre and Wright (2000), 214: 'There is a polarity between which most of
the modern theatre finds its place. Brecht at one pole: Samuel Beckett at the
other...Brecht revived the 'epic': the theatrical string of beads, leaping from
place to place and time to time. Beckett took the one-place, time-unbroken drama
of Sophocles or Racine and distilled it to the point where its off-stage life is reduced
to nothing.'

Greek dramatic form, convention, and of specific texts on what have emerged as some of the most seminal plays of our *own* time—*Waiting for Godot*, *Happy Days* and *Endgame*. But what makes Beckett different from all the hundreds of modern authors demonstrably influenced by Greek tragedy is that admiration for his work has been a crucial factor in the turn back to the Greeks themselves.

This is partly because of the impact made in the early 1960s by existentialism, the philosophical school with which Beckett was associated, on two directors who have been crucial to the revival of Greek tragedy, Mnouchkine and Suzuki. The ideas of existentialism, especially of Jean-Paul Sartre and Maurice Merleau-Ponty, prepared the intellectual ground for the revolution that was to be marked both by the rediscovery of Greek tragedy and by post-structuralism (Sartre's own intellectual version of *Trojan Women*, *Les Troyennes*, was first performed at the Théâtre National Populaire, Paris, in 1965). But the formal aspects of Beckett's theatrical aesthetic have been just as significant. One reason why Dionysus has been on the world stage since 1969 is that Beckett's plays, which were by that time themselves standards of the repertoire, fostered an appetite for him. The impact of Beckett on Heiner Müller's adaptations is enormous; the wheelchair motif from Beckett's *Endgame* has become a standard feature of Greek tragic productions, via the Believers' wheelchairs in Suzuki's *Bacchae*. Several other famous directors, including JoAnne Akalaitis, decided to attempt Greek tragedy after Beckett's dramas led them there.[65] The experiments of the Theatre of the Absurd (and of Beckett above all) made audiences more receptive to Greek tragedy, and the productions of Greek tragedies which they saw, in response, became more stylized and minimalist.

[65] For Beckett's influence on Müller's use of Medea see Kalb (1998), 165–6; on Suzuki and Beckett see Allain (2002), 17–19, 163–4, 186. See also Riley, this volume, p. 118. Akalaitis's reputation was established with a fully staged version of Beckett's *Cascando* with Mabou Mines in New York (1975), and confirmed by *Endgame* (1984). Recently, however, she has become identified, rather, with Euripides, following *The Iphigenia Cycle* (Euripides' two Iphigenia plays) at Chicago's Court Theatre (1997), and *Trojan Women* at the Shakespeare Theatre in Washington, DC (1999). The features she has said attract her to Euripides are also elements of Beckettian drama: irony, interest in psychology, female protagonists, and, in *Trojan Women*, pronounced 'repetition . . . that becomes more intense . . . as the evening goes on' (www.shakespearedc.org/troplay).

MIND

When Aristotle listed the elements of tragedy in his *Poetics*, he placed 'the representation of intellect' high in his list of the dramatist's priorities (6. 1449b–1450a). Recent theatrical fashions have tended to neglect the cerebral dimension of Greek tragedy in favour of its social, political, and theatrical potential. But Greek tragic heroes and heroines talk about psychology, cognition, the power of oratory, moral relativism, the relation between emotion and reason, and especially about religion and metaphysics—the relation between humans and whatever unseen forces are really in charge of the universe. Ariane Mnouchkine said in 1995 that the dominant interest the Greeks hold for her is 'metaphysical and psychoanalytical'; she wanted to actualize *Les Atrides* because she 'wanted to show how strange we are, deep inside. Our unconscious is hidden and the Greeks knew that, and they did theatre with that very far away part of ourselves'.[66] Greek tragedy has partly proved so popular in recent decades not because of the specific directions taken by late twentieth-century society, politics or theatre, but because of the 'far away parts of ourselves', the psychological, intellectual, and emotional directions taken by the late twentieth-century consciousness, and so our last section is entitled 'Dionysus and the Life of the Mind'.

The increasingly widespread use of psychotherapy since the 1960s, but more especially in the 1980s and 1990s, has also certainly helped to keep Greek tragedy on the public mind. Several currently influential psychoanalysts have used Greek tragedy, especially its fascination with children (see above), to develop 'transhistorical' models of the human psyche going far beyond Freud's interest in Oedipus or Jung's in Electra. C. F. Alford's *The Psychoanalytic Theory of Greek Tragedy* (1992) and Bennett Simon's *Tragic Drama and the Family* (1988) are cases in point. Fiona Macintosh takes a fresh new angle, informed by the history of psychoanalysis, on the most famous of all Greek tragedies, Sophocles' *Oedipus Tyrannus*, and Steven Berkoff's shocking adaptation and repudiation of it, *Greek*, first performed in 1980. She relates the performance history of *Oedipus* (and plays based upon it) to the other cultural site where this tragedy has had such an epochal

---

[66] Quoted in Delgado and Heritage (1996), 180.

influence—Freudian and post-Freudian psychoanalysis. Berkoff's *Greek*, an extremely important play (which has in turn inspired a significant opera, discussed by Brown), is the clearest example of the contemporary process by which Freudian views of the subconscious have been dethroned, at the same time as Sophocles' own play has been losing its central position within the mainstream performance repertoire in favour of plays more transparently susceptible to interpretations of perceived contemporary relevance, or, more particularly, plays which replaced the question of fatherhood with the child's relation to its mother. The *Oresteia* and *Medea*, probably the two most important Greek tragedies in the last thirty years, both stage massive contests between the importance and the claims of fatherhood and motherhood. Clytemnestra loses eventually, but Medea wins.

Various elements in *Greek* reveal that Eddy is no more impervious than the rest of society to the gradual impact of the feminist revisioning of Freudian analysis. With the motif of birth trauma, and Eddy's explicit 'splitting' of the mother-figure into Good and Bad typologies (both discussed by Macintosh), Berkoff demonstrates, however unwittingly, that Melanie Klein's assault on her mentor Freud's theories has truly acquired popular currency. Klein, who was forced to reassess her training in the light of her own experience of siblings, and especially of motherhood, began publishing even before World War II, but it was with her books *Envy and Gratitude* (1957) and *Narrative of a Child Analysis* (1961) that heterosexual eros, rivalry, and the penis began to be challenged, in popular understanding of psychology, by ambivalence from and towards the mother, envy, and the breast. The priority of the infant's relationship with the mother, and the centrality to the human psyche of birth, breast, and physical severance/individuation, became, in the last third of the twentieth century, part of popular discourse. The Kleinian revolution has toppled the Father in favour of the Mother, just as Medea and Clytemnestra have threatened, at least, to oust Oedipus from the contemporary stage.

The post-Freudian revision of psychoanalytical theory in the works of Lacan as well as Klein was one important factor in the intellectual developments which, together with the 1968–9 tremors affecting politics and society, were to shake the foundations of western scholarship. The Performative Turn in the theatre existed in tandem with what has been called the Linguistic Turn in the Academy. When cultural historians look back on the late twentieth century, one phenomenon they will undoubtedly bring into connection with the theatrical trends of the period will be the revolutionary intellectual currents, most of which have been dedicated to scrutinizing the way that we are creatures constructed out of language, and most (although by no means all) of them emanating from Paris. An astonishing proportion of the seminal work in literary and cultural theory still dominating the syllabuses today was published between the late 1960s and the very early 1970s, whether deconstructionist, post-structuralist, semiotic, or Marxist (the last usually now known as 'cultural materialist'): Jacques Derrida's manifestoes *De la grammatologie* and *L'Écriture et la différence* (both 1967), Michel Foucault's *L'archéologie du savoir* (1969), Roland Barthes' *S/Z* and *L'empire des signes* (both 1970), Jean-François Lyotard's collection on aesthetics *Discours, figure* (1971), Frederic Jameson's epoch-making *Marxism and Form* (1971) and *The Prison-House of Language* (1972). This intellectual phenomenon, generally seen as part of 'postmodernism' and often labelled collectively (if misleadingly) as 'post-structuralism', exactly coincided with the publication of the great works of feminist theory by Kate Millett and Germaine Greer. There are also vital links (as Richard Schechner has himself argued) between postmodern analytical tools and interculturalism,[67] but the emergence of a cultural theory adequate to the dissection of colonialism's fictional ethnicities, although adumbrated by Frantz Fanon's *Wretched of the Earth* (the 1967 English translation of his 1961 *Les damnés de la terre* (1961)), did not penetrate mainstream academia until a little later, with Wole Soyinka's *Myth, Literature, and the African World* (1976), and Edward Saïd's *Orientalism* (1978), discussed in this volume by Hardwick and Hall respectively.

These authors, and others like them, have provided the intellectual vertebrae for the culture of the last thirty years. Many of them are influenced by Greek theatre, and the relationship of their work to the epidemic of Greek tragedy is manifested in at least four ways. They often cite examples from the tragedians or use them as evidence in their own very widely read texts, thus bringing

---

[67] Schechner (1982).

Greek tragedies to the notice of wide audiences: Lyotard on Oedipus as Jew, Millett on the vote of Athena in *Sexual Politics*, and Saïd on the role of Aeschylus' *Persians* in the aetiology of the west's denigration of the 'Orient'.[68] Secondly, the analytical vocabulary of 'post-structuralism' is often informed by experience of Greek dialectic in both drama and Plato: deconstruction's *aporia* and *choreography*, French feminism's *chora*. Thirdly, some leading intellectuals, especially women, have been directly involved in productions and adaptations of ancient Greek dramatic texts; Germaine Greer performed *Lysistrata* as a solo act in New York (1971), and staged it in London nearly thirty years later (1999). In France the Théâtre du Soleil performed the feminist thinker Hélène Cixous's Aeschylean *The Perjured City, or the Awakening of the Furies* in 1994 (see further Michelakis, Chapter 7). Most importantly, avant-garde Classicists have tended to go to Greek tragedy (rather than, for example, Ciceronian prose) when exploring the potential of literary theory.[69] The earliest theoretically sophisticated uses of feminist theory in Classics, by our first two contributors Froma Zeitlin and Helene Foley above all, were addressed to Greek tragedy; but equally distinctive examples have been Zeitlin's use of semiotics in her revolutionary study of Aeschylus' *Seven against Thebes*, Vernant and Vidal-Naquet's synthesis of post-Marxism, post-structuralism, and ritual anthropology in their groundbreaking works on myth and tragedy, Charles Segal's psychoanalytical structuralism, and Simon Goldhill's deconstruction of the *Oresteia*.[70]

---

[68] Lyotard (1970); Millett (1970), 114–16; Saïd (1978), 56. See also Roland Barthes's less serious remarks, in his autobiography (Barthes (1975), 37), about his own experience of the role of Darius in a production of Aeschylus' *Persians* at the Sorbonne in 1936. I am grateful to Ruth Bardel for drawing my attention to this: see further Bardel (2001), 247 with n. 8, and fig. 8.2, with further bibliography.

[69] See Hexter and Selden (1992), xiv.

[70] See Zeitlin (1982) and the influential articles, some of which originally date back to the 1970s, in Zeitlin (1996); see Foley (1975) and her classic article (1981) on women in Greek drama, a revised version of which appears, along with many of her subsequent articles on gender and tragedy, in Foley (2001*a*). Much of Vernant and Vidal-Naquet's work from the 1960s to the 1980s has been translated into English and collected in Vernant (1979) and (1983), Vidal-Naquet (1986), and Vernant and Vidal-Naquet (1988). For Segal see the essays, some of which date from the 1960s, in Segal (1986), and especially the new afterword in the 1997 edition of his book *Dionysiac Poetics and Euripides' Bacchae* (349–94), which discusses the issues in that play which have most interested classical scholars since the book was first published in 1982; Goldhill's revolutionary study of the *Oresteia* was published in 1984.

Huge differences exist between the ideas of the 'post-structuralist' intellectuals. Yet they do share two certain commitments which are relevant to the contemporaneous turn to Greek tragedy. One commitment is to epistemology, or rather to the systematic problematization of the grounds of human reason, truth, and knowledge, especially within our 'prison-house' of language. Can words and other sign systems ever have universal, essential, or immanent meanings that do not change with the reader, audience, or spectator? And, if language is unstable, how can we truly know what we know?

Peter Brook's *Orghast* of 1970–1 was the dramatic experiment that most notoriously addressed this question, and if its venue at the ancient Persepolis royal tombs partly functioned as a compliment to the earliest surviving Greek tragedy, Aeschylus' *Persians*, in which the ghost of Darius arises from his tomb, Brook has not actually said so. *Orghast* was Brook's first production as director for the Paris-based International Centre for Theatre Research, which used actors from all over the world in an idealistic attempt to discover theatrical means for transcending the barriers created by different languages; the group aimed to create a hieratic theatre work made up of esoteric vocal and gestural abstractions.[71] *Orghast* used Avestan, a pre-Iranian sacred language, but in order to create a new phonetic dialect where sound took priority over meaning (aural signifier over signified), Brook also confronted the actors with transliterated passages of Aeschylean Greek. These were not translated, explained, or even divided into separate words; one was the almost unvoiceable ELELEUELELEUUPOMAUSFAKELOSK AIFRENOPLEGEIS. Ted Hughes, who collaborated on *Orghast*, had been working on the Aeschylean *Prometheus Bound*, and this string of sound is actually taken from a strong expression of pain, Io's last, agonized cries as she is chased from the stage by the gadfly that torments her (877–9).[72] But for Brook and his actors the meaning of the words was constituted solely by the affective power of their aural shape. The very deadness of the language in which Greek drama was written has appealed to other directors. It was central to the German *Antiquity Projects*

[71] Williams (2002), 41–2, 45. For a photograph of the ancient Persian tomb setting of *Orghast* see Brook (1987), 214.
[72] Brook briefly discusses the role of Aeschylus' Greek in *Orghast* in Brook (1987), 108–10.

of the 1970s (see below), to Peter Sellars when he used deaf actors and deaf signing (see Hall), and to numerous productions which have combined vernacular translation with fragments of poetry in the original Greek, especially at moments of musical intervention or extreme emotion.

The other recognizable joint project of post-structuralism is the investigation of the instability of human subjectivity; the argument flows interminably back and forth between advocates of absolute relativism (which argues that every era and culture remakes its artefacts in its own image, and denies any permanent, essential or lasting commonality of human experience), and the more humanist, psychoanalytically inflected construction of an at least partially transcultural subject.[73] Producing Greek tragedy entails unceasing oscillation between these two interpretative poles, these two contrasting ways of relating to the past. Any audience of a Greek tragedy shifts and drifts between awareness of the dimension of the performance that is determined by the attitudes, tastes and views of their own era, and a (usually) pleasurable sense that certain dimensions of human experience are truly transhistorical. Since the work of Vernant and Vidal-Naquet above all, it is now a commonplace of Greek tragic criticism that the Greeks are both supremely Other and also surprisingly Similar. But at an *emotional* level of apprehension there is nothing like hearing live theatrical delivery of speeches first formulated thousands of years ago, even in a quite different language, to bring this tension home.

In the 1970s several of the strands in the intellectual revolution came together in the work of the experimental German directors Klaus Michael Grüber and Peter Stein, in their *Antiquity Projects* at the Berlin Schaubühne. Erika Fischer-Lichte's chapter, 'Thinking about the origins of theatre in the 1970s', explores the way that academic interest in ancient Greece informed German theatre in this period, and how German directors invited their audiences to think self-consciously about challenging intellectual questions. Grüber's *Bakchen* drew on the ritual anthropology, informed by structuralism, of both René Girard and Walter

---

[73] The definitive philosophical work on relativism, belief and knowledge in the late twentieth century was Richard Rorty's *Philosophy and the Mirror of Nature* (1979). The relationship between post-structuralist literary theory and theatrical productions of Greek tragedy has been little investigated, but for some suggestive pointers see Decreus (2000).

Burkert;[74] Stein's *Die Orestie* wrestled with the tough post-structuralist issues of semantic instability and the impossibility of accurate translation, as well as the relative priority in theatre of visual or auditory space. Later, in the 1980s, Einar Schleef's experiments with the chorus in *The Mothers* (*Die Mütter*, a combination of Euripides' *Suppliant Women* and Aeschylus' *Seven against Thebes*) took to new levels of sophistication the examination of the relationships connecting spectator to actor and individual to collective. Fischer-Lichte concludes that all three directors used Greek tragedy not only to reflect on the actual, historical origins of theatre, but also in the creation of aetiologies for their own practice, their own new theatre, whether ritual, textual, or choric.

Greek tragedy has had an inherent appeal, therefore, to our psychological and intellectual subjectivity over the last three decades. The life of the mind, however, also covers our apprehension of the moral and the legal. What have Greek tragic ethics been able to do for us in the late twentieth century? They have certainly offered opportunities for exploring our modern problems of crime and punishment. Many of the plays, especially the conclusion of *Children of Heracles*, ask whether the emotional need for revenge on the part of victims of serious crime and their families should be a factor in the way that decisions about punishment are made and implemented. *Hecuba* asks to what sort of trial, in front of what sort of tribunal, should political and military figures accused of war crimes be subject. Medea, who does plan her murders but only under enormous pressure of time, challenges the distinction between premeditated murder and suddenly provoked manslaughter (an issue in which gender plays a role, as several women who have attacked their husbands, but only after years of abuse, have recently argued). She and other tragic criminals certainly allow exploration of the topical relationship between crime and physiological factors—hormones, genes, or neurological breakdown. Euripides' own Medea famously says that although she knows that what she is about to do is wrong, her internal organ of aggression (*thumos*) has subordinated her capacity to deliberate (1078–9). In court today, she could argue that her dysfunctional limbic amygdala made her do it.

---

[74] Girard's *La Violence et le sacré* and Burkert's *Homo Necans* were both published in 1972; see also Burkert's earlier article 'Greek tragedy and sacrificial ritual' (1966).

FIGURE 5. The chorus use stones as percussion instruments to accompany their hymn summoning the gods to Thebes in Northern Broadsides' *Oedipus* at the Viaduct Theatre, Halifax, Yorkshire (2001).

Yet it is the gods who are blamed by many Greek tragic characters, and it is the gods who provide a final possible answer to the question of Greek tragedy's relevance today. The opportunity to create charged, spiritual atmospheres through the performance of religious ritual, especially the collective rituals of the chorus, has certainly proved an attractive dimension of Greek tragedy (see Figure 5 and Zeitlin, Chapter 2). Yet Peter Stein has given a (rather unsympathetic) description of the difficulties experienced by some of his Russian actors, unrivalled in expressing emotional conviction, during the 1994 Moscow revival of his *Oresteia*. They were uncomfortable when performing the choral hymn to Zeus in *Agamemnon* which begins by doubting whether the supreme god's name is Zeus at all (*Agamemnon* 160–1). Stein felt that the problems arose because these actors' spirituality had been conditioned by orthodox models, whether Christian or atheist.[75] Although Stein's diagnosis of the situation may well not have told the full

[75] Stein, quoted in Delgado and Heritage (1996), 258. This production of the *Oresteia* was with the Moscow Army Theatre in 1994.

story, his premise—that the questing, sceptical tone of Greek tragedy does not fit minds moulded in monotheistic or monolithic certainty—is surely correct. On the other hand, in portraying a universe run by a multitude of pagan gods in whom nobody now believes, Greek tragedy can offer an important site, free from contemporary cultural specificity, for reflecting on metaphysical and (in the broadest sense) theological issues—the crucial 'tragic' questions of right and wrong, humankind's place in the universe and relation to the unknowable forces that shape it—especially in the fragmented, multicultural (and, in north-western Europe at least), post-Christian world of the late twentieth and twenty-first centuries.

This new role for Greek tragedy is related to the drastic recent secularization of western society, a phenomenon now traced by religious historians to exactly the same watershed as the others discussed in this chapter—the ethical and spiritual crisis of the late 1960s.[76] Albert Camus said that the necessary condition for the production of tragedy is the moment of historical transition 'between a sacred society and a society built by man'.[77] Although there have been occasional fusions of Christian energy with Greek tragedy, most importantly in Lee Breuer's *Gospel at Colonus* (1983, discussed by Brown), it is more likely that the necessary condition for the recent *re*-production of Greek tragedy has been the moment of transition into a far more secular world. Greek tragedy happens to offer modern agnostics exactly the disturbing combination of open-ended metaphysics, aesthetic beauty, and hard-core suffering which Terry Eagleton's new theory of tragedy suggests is the only way forward for serious dramatic art in the third millennium.[78]

Timberlake Wertenbaker has herself recently translated and adapted several Greek tragedies for the professional stage, and thought at length about Sophoclean and Euripidean presentation of human emotion and human apprehension of the divine. She offers a new answer to our central question, *Why* has Greek tragedy been so prominent recently? She suggests that the answer lies

---

[76] See the title of B. R. Wilson's *Religion in a Secular Society* (1969), and especially the excellent account in C. G. Brown (2001), 170–80.

[77] Camus (1970), 199.

[78] Eagleton (2002). Eagleton's book is rich in insights into Greek tragedy.

in one important and little noticed difference between Greek tragic men and Greek tragic women—the men claim to arrive at self-knowledge, to understand why they have done what they have done, to have learned from it, and to be capable of action grounded in reason derived from experience. The women, such as Hecuba, *feel* rather than know themselves, and act without making claim to self-knowledge at the time or subsequently. Wertenbaker urges that it is the voices of these Greek tragic women which must have such resonance in an age which has seen how 'enlightened' thinking, science and reason, humanity's claim to understand itself and the universe, actually produced the worst catastrophes, wars, barbarisms, even systematic genocides, that the human race has ever seen. The voices of Greek tragic women teach us not to Know Ourselves, but to be properly humble in the face of the Unknowable.

The term 'survivor' is one of the hallmarks of our age. It was originally just a legal term denoting relatives of a deceased person who were to be beneficiaries of a will; by the early twentieth century its use was extended to include those who had escaped alive from physical catastrophes. But the term now covers those who have suffered from disease, addiction, and especially damage knowingly inflicted by and on people. Incest survivors, rape survivors, child abuse survivors, concentration camp survivors, genocide survivors, Holocaust survivors, Hiroshima survivors—our new tragic heroes are those who have learned somehow to accommodate unbearable memories of acute trauma, including trauma for which they are themselves responsible, and live with their psychological pain.[79] In the judgemental Christian moral universes of Renaissance, Jacobean, and neoclassical tragedy, large numbers of the principal *dramatis personae* die. Outliving their plots when they have suffered or committed incest, rape, adultery, sexual betrayal, or murder was unusual. Not so in Greek tragedy, most of whose heroes are true survivors in the most modern sense of the term. The incestuous Oedipus, the infanticidal Heracles, Medea, and Agave, the mother-murdering Orestes, the bereaved women of Troy—they all survive their terrible experiences and

---

[79] Some of the ways in which Greek tragedy has proved helpful in the late twentieth-century attempt to come to terms with the Second World War are explored below in the chapters by Hall, Michelakis, and Brown.

stagger from the stage leaving the audience wondering how they
can possibly cope with their psychological burdens. It is perhaps in
this respect more than any other that Greek tragedy has chimed
with the obsessions of an age which has itself only just survived the
man-made horrors of the twentieth century.[80]

---

[80] This chapter has benefited greatly from comments by several of the other
contributors to the volume. I would particularly like to thank Peter Brown, Oliver
Taplin, Froma Zeitlin, and Helene Foley for their suggestions. Paul Cartledge's
help was, as always, invaluable. Several sections, especially the two discussing the
proscenium arch and Samuel Beckett, could simply not have been written without
Fiona Macintosh; Amanda Wrigley's commitment to the pursuit of accuracy has
been unshakeable.

Section I

DIONYSUS AND THE SEX WAR

2

Dionysus in 69

Froma I. Zeitlin

Here I am once again. Now for those of you who believe what
I just told you, that I am a god, you are going to have a terrific
evening. The rest of you are in trouble. It's going to be an hour
and a half of being up against the wall. Those of you who do
believe can join us in what we do next. It's a celebration, a ritual,
an ordeal, an ecstasy. An ordeal is something you go through. An
ecstasy is what happens to you when you get there.

William Finley as Dionysus

Although I saw Richard Schechner's production of *Dionysus in 69*
over thirty years ago, memories of the performance remain vivid in
my mind. I recall my astonishment at the novelty and power of the
experience, from start to finish. It began with the ritualized 'initiation' of the audience, one by one, into the unusual theatre space,
where we found seats above and below scaffoldings of towers and
platforms, and ended with the triumphant, if sinister, exit of
Dionysus out of the theatre itself, while the chorus came with
mops and buckets to clean up the 'blood' spilled in the 'death
ritual' of Pentheus. I realized even then that I was a witness to an
event whose impact reached far beyond the spare and vast space of
the Performing Garage, the site of the production, which was
located in downtown New York in a seedy area that was not yet
called Soho. Hence, as I revisited this long distant event that has
become part of theatre history, I have also had to revisit its context,
that convulsive moment in American social history towards the
end of the 1960s, which so altered all our lives, even for those too
young to have lived through that era. For *Dionysus in 69*, a
reworking of Euripides' *Bacchae*, was nothing if not a child of its
time. In fact, until the 1960s, *Bacchae* had never been performed in
any version on a commercial stage in the United States during the
earlier twentieth century.[1]

---

[1] Interestingly, there were a few productions of Euripides' drama performed
by students on American college campuses, especially in élite women's colleges,

It is perhaps ironic that a production which, for the year and a half of its run, thrived on spontaneity and improvisation and continued to evolve as it went on, has left such a substantial record. At the time, of course, there was the cacophony of professional reviews by all the best New York theatre critics, some of them writing more than once. But far more remarkable for such an ephemeral event is the fact that a number of aspects of the production were captured for posterity. First, there was a volume produced by the Performance Group itself, published shortly thereafter in 1970.[2] It consisted of over 350 photographs, information on the origins of the group, comments by the participants, and the text with its many variants, which were contributed by the actors when they played those roles. Second was the film of the same name directed by a precocious Brian De Palma at an early stage of his career.[3] Next, Richard Schechner himself has written extensively on the production in connection with the principles of his Environmental Theater and those theories of ritual and drama on which the play was based.[4] Above all, there is a later, extended account of the history and experience of the play from its very first inception written by the actor, William (Bill) Shephard, who had

---

including Smith in 1934 and Bryn Mawr in 1935. See Hartigan (1995), 97 n. 20. She refers to Pluggé (1938) for this information. At Smith and Bryn Mawr, the play was directed by an alumna, Eva Palmer-Sikelianos, who, together with her husband, the noted Greek poet Angelos Sikelianos, is credited with the revival of the dramatic festivals at Delphi (see further Wiles, below, Chapter 9). Eva also composed the music and created the choreography. The costumes were copied from ancient Greek vase paintings of dancing maenads and the actors were masked. The outdoor production at Bryn Mawr was one of the very few pre-war performances of Greek tragedy at the college, which, with the exception of a *Medea* in 1909, had previously maintained a tradition of producing Elizabethan plays.

[2] Entitled *Dionysus in 69*, the book, unfortunately, is unpaginated. I refer to it throughout as Schechner (1970). The epigraph by William Finley is from this same volume.

[3] *Dionysus in 69* was a split-screen documentary, the first film directed by Brian De Palma (see further Michelakis, below, Chapter 7). It was made from two actual performances of the play, directed by Richard Schechner, adapted by Schechner and The Performance Group, and staged at The Performing Garage in 1968–9. It was nominated for a Golden Bear Award at the Berlin Film Festival in 1970. (Information from http://www.colba.net/~jecr/dionysus.htm.) The film is very difficult to obtain, although videos of it can be found in several American university libraries, and a copy can be purchased from Richard Schechner himself.

[4] See especially, Schechner (1968*b*) and (1971); McNamara *et al.* (1975), ch. 10, 80–99.

played the original Pentheus.[5] In this detailed study, submitted as a doctoral dissertation, Shephard gives us unparalleled access to all the proceedings from both inside and outside perspectives in his dual capacity as 'ethnographer (observer/recorder) and subject (actor/participant)'.[6]

Considering this unprecedented wealth of material, and thinking too of the intense scholarly interest that has focused on the *Bacchae* (and the cult of Dionysus) in recent years,[7] I am reminded that with all its faults, all its lapses in tastes, its experimental risks (and there were many), *Dionysus in 69* remains a landmark in the history of the reception of Greek theatre in the twentieth century. If anything, it demonstrates the degree not only to which each era chooses the interpretations that correspond to its own preoccupations, but to which those preoccupations regulate even the choice of a particular drama itself.

Even so, perhaps the match between the *Bacchae* and the age that embraced it is stronger than almost any other. The run of the play extended from June 1968 to July 1969 (for a total of 163 performances). Its opening night took place the day after Robert Kennedy was assassinated in Los Angeles, preceding by only a few months the election of Richard Nixon to his first term as president of the United States. One month after its closing, the renowned Woodstock rock concert took place, an event that has assumed legendary status in the annals of hippie utopia. The title *Dionysus in 69* was chosen, not only for its more naughty associations, but also to propose a revolution that 'would elect Dionysus president' in the coming year. This was a time of radical social transition, 'reflected in diverging social values between old and young, rich and poor, whites and blacks, male and female sexual roles, and above all, between advocates and opponents of war in Vietnam'.[8] As Karelisa Hartigan puts it, 'protests against this conflict escalated to protests by the young against all authority figures; freedom of expression carried over to the realm of sex as well as speech'. It

---

[5] Shephard (1991).

[6] Shephard (1991), xviii.

[7] For the most recent survey and discussion of the critical literature, see Segal (1997), 349–93, with bibliographies, 405–11. In addition, there has been a remarkable number of translations of the play in the last decade alone. There are ten of them, some by distinguished poets. No other Greek tragedy has fared this well.

[8] Shephard (1991), 238–9.

was a time too when drugs in the search for ecstasy and relaxation
of inhibitions took over. 'Free love blended with a subconscious
narcissism.' The insistence on self-expression was often combined,
paradoxically, with a quest for community outside the ordinary
social rules and institutional conventions.[9] The themes of *Bacchae*—violence, madness, ecstasy, release of libidinal energy, relations between extremes of group and individual, challenges to
authority, transgressions of taboos, and freedom of moral
choice—are precisely those which found quite uncanny analogues
in the cultural conflicts of the day. It seemed in truth like a
Dionysiac age in more ways than one: the long hair, androgynous
dress, rock concerts, communes, and 'dropping out' of the bourgeois rat race. It was a time of an exaltation of life on the margins.
Schechner himself went so far as to say: 'Dionysus' presence can be
beautiful or ugly or both. It seems quite clear that he is present in
today's America—showing himself in the hippies, in the "carnival
spirit" of black insurrectionists, on campuses; and even, in disguise, on the patios and in the living-rooms of suburbia.'[10]

At the same time, experiments with different lifestyles and attitudes went hand in hand with artistic experimentation in theatre,
which challenged both actors and audience in new and unsettling
ways. Important precedents were set by Julian Beck and Judith
Malina's Living Theater (1947) and Joseph Chaikin's Open
Theater (1963), but the greatest inspiration was provided by the
Polish director Jerzy Grotowski, and his so-called Poor Theater
(1959).[11] Richard Schechner contributed concepts from anthropological theory and studies of primitive ritual to develop the idea of
an Environmental Theater, which was to be realized through his
Performance Group. *Dionysus in 69*, its one major success, was to

---

[9] Hartigan (1995), 67 (quotation and paraphrase). Also in 1968, the famed rock
musical, *Hair!*, which opened in 1967, moved to Broadway. In its celebration of 'the
dawning of the Age of Aquarius', this tribal love rock musical is described in terms
similar to *Dionysus in 69*. It touched on the 'drug culture, hippies, the new sexual
morality, the generation gap, and most enduringly, peace demonstrations and a
strong anti-war message' (Clasz (1991), 13, 15).

[10] Schechner (1968*a*) in Schechner (1969), 217–18.

[11] The dates given allude to the dates of foundation. For convenient discussions
of these theatrical groups, see Innes (1993), 125–92 and Aronson (2000), 42–107.
Grotowski came to the United States for the first time in 1968 and even attended a
performance of *Dionysus in 69*. His famed book (1968) was also published that year
and is back in print once more.

prove the perfect vehicle for testing the principles of his theatrical vision as a communal experience.[12]

All these avant-garde companies were idealistic and iconoclastic in outlook and technique, designed to challenge and overthrow time-honoured theatrical conventions. This alternative theatre movement aimed to break both commercial and psychological restraints by bonding spectator and actor and by reducing the theatrical illusion of an imagined space and time to one of immediacy and presence. There was a new emphasis on the actors, trained now in psycho-physical exercises, who could collaborate creatively in the production, even to the extent of improvisation, and who were urged to find ways to reveal, rather than conceal, themselves on stage in the roles they played. It was held, especially by Grotowski and Schechner, that 'theater... regarded as merely one phenomenon in an entire spectrum of human events... and life experience were part of the same continuum and could at given moments intersect or even interpenetrate.... Virtual reality could be experienced by an actor in performance, a reality which originated with ordinary life experience but somehow transcended it.'[13] The idea, in other words, was to break down the barriers between person and performer. Likewise, the intention was also to break down the barriers between spectators and performers. In this way, the audience could be placed in a confrontational, or even better, a participatory, relationship to the actors in the context of a theatrical event. 'The Dionysus Group hoped to create a more dynamic, spontaneous atmosphere in which the play could function as medium for a dialogue between actors and spectators on an artistic level.'[14] To this end, any thought of an illusionist stage production was banished in favour of 'found spaces'. Rather than the rigid structure of the proscenium theatre, these spaces constituted environments which determined how a play was to be staged, rather than vice versa. These spaces might even be created and constructed by the actors themselves as an essential ingredient of the entire collaborative experience. In the case of *Dionysus in 69*, there was no stage as such (see Figure 6). Instead, there were constructions consisting of platforms and towers, with spaces underneath and everywhere,

---

[12] Two other plays, *Commune* and *Makbeth*, were performed by the group. Subsequently, the group disbanded and the Performing Garage was taken over by the Wooster Group, which is still in existence today.
[13] Shephard (1991), 3.   [14] Shephard (1991), xiii.

FIGURE 6. A partial view of the seating area on and below the scaffolding for Richard Schechner's *Dionysus in 69*, New York (1968). William Finley as Dionysus, gesturing, is just right of centre. The author of this chapter is seated on the bottom, second from the right.

where the audience could perch on high at different levels or sit low on the carpeted floor, and thereby themselves become part of the environment, which they shared with the actors.[15]

The actors themselves could mingle with the spectators, as they often did, to appear here, there, and everywhere. But there was also a central space for a number of the main actions as well as a 'pit', which functioned as a behind- or off-stage for scenes in Euripides' drama that took place inside the palace. The bacchants hunted Pentheus over and under the towers and platforms in preparation for his sacrificial death. Earlier, after the Teiresias-Cadmus scene, the king had tried to silence them through a game of tag, running after one, now another, throughout these same spaces, as they chanted lines from Euripides' first stasimon (*Bacchae* 370–432). Since the object of the play is to win recognition of Dionysus' divinity, which means accepting his rites and the ecstasy they bring, the spectators too could be included, it was thought, in the same process of recognition and revelation. In practice, the group eventually had to discard most of their inclusionary efforts, except for the ecstasy dance towards the beginning of the play, which followed the 'birth' of Dionysus.

A good case in point was what happened to the experiment of the Total Caress. This activity took place towards the end of the play when Pentheus and Dionysus had briefly retired from the scene for a homoerotic encounter. (In Euripides' play, this would have been the 'dressing scene' inside the palace, when Dionysus dresses Pentheus as a woman[16]). The chorus now begins to sing, 'When shall I dance once more with bare feet the all night dances, tossing my head for joy in the damp air, in the dew?' (*Bacchae* 862–5), and they circulate among the spectators throughout the theatrical space. After the choral song, 'the performers were supposed to engage various members of the audience in sensory-exploration dialogues, in order to lead members of the audience toward greater freedom of interpersonal expression'.[17] In its quiet intimacy, the Total Caress was meant to be a substitute for the peacefully sensual behaviour of the bacchants in Euripides, as the messenger reports it, before they are disturbed by the intrusion of men.

---

[15] For detailed discussion of the space and its transformation into a theatre, see McNamara *et al.* (1975), 80–99.

[16] This major change in Euripides' play will be discussed further below.

[17] Shephard (1991), 85.

But, as Schechner ruefully put it, 'As audiences became accustomed to moments where they could freely interact with performers, the theatrical event became less and less controlled by the Group. With increasing frequency, audiences gawked, talked, or wanted to make out with performers. As an experiment, the caress was fine. As part of a well-known play that attracted culture tourists and not a few skin freaks, to say nothing of repeat spectators, who came again and again, it became dangerous and self defeating.'[18] Instead, a highly stylized dance, called the 'moiety' dance (modelled on a reduced version of the 'ecstasy dance'), was devised in which the group divided in half. One section engaged with the spectators in a more formal way, while the other did not.

The substitution of a formal ritual-like activity for a spontaneous, improvised, and ultimately risky encounter with the spectators brings me to the most significant point of intersection between Richard Schechner's ideas about the theatre and Euripides' *Bacchae*. Dubbed 'Professor of the Dionysiac Theater' in a newspaper profile of the time, Schechner is perhaps the most intellectually oriented of producer-directors.[19] Since 1967 a professor in the Performance Studies Department at the Tisch School of the Arts, New York University, he has been an editor, first of the *Tulane Drama Review*, then of its successor, *The Drama Review* (*TDR*), a journal which rapidly became the premier forum 'for much of the theoretical foundation on the avant-garde and a premier source of information on new performance for most American and even world theatre practitioners'.[20] Although he was influenced by such disparate figures in the counterculture as Antonin Artaud, John Cage, Marshall McLuhan, Norman O. Brown, and R. D. Laing, along with the avant-garde theatre companies mentioned earlier, what concerns us here in particular is his abiding interest in ritual. This engagement with ritual in an anthropological context has lasted throughout Schechner's distinguished career and is constantly rehearsed and refined in his numerous publications, with such titles as *Ritual, Play, and Performance* (1976), *Between Theater and Anthropology* (1985), *By Means of Performance: Intercultural Studies of Theatre and Ritual* (1990), *The Future of Ritual: Writings on Culture and Performance* (1993),

---

[18] Quoted in Shephard (1991), 178.
[19] Lester (1969).   [20] Aronson (2000), 97.

and *Performance Theory* (1988). His mentors in this field include such scholars of myth and ritual as anthropologists Mircea Eliade, Clifford Geertz, Claude Lévi-Strauss, and above all, Victor Turner, who throughout his influential career championed the interrelationships between ritual, performance, and theatre. At the heart of Schechner's anthropological investigations, along with his study of rituals in many other societies (he even conducted fieldwork of his own) is the conviction that theatre needs to 'attempt to rediscover the efficacy of performance as a ritual experience'.[21] Therefore, it needs to include 'formally patterned behaviors with ceremonial significance',[22] such as dances, ritual combats, and similar forms of activity.

While ancient Greek tragedy is itself a ritualized event, it is not, of course, a ritual as such, even if it incorporates actual rituals into its scenario, such as prayer, supplication, or sacrifice. Schechner's bias towards ritual is a way of 'sacralizing' the theatrical event, especially in the notion of creating a kind of group or tribal identity, and for this reason he was especially attracted to the use of a broad cross-cultural repertory from which to draw his inspirations. His fascination with Greek tragedy is reflected in many of his writings. Nietzsche's ideas about the Dionysiac are clearly an influence, and he makes frequent references to Aristotle, whom he both admires and reproaches. But what strikes him most about the ancient theatre is the civic nature of performance in Athens:

I suppose the Athenian community that saw *Oedipus* and *Lysistrata* in their original productions (a community) . . . sensed the affirmation—even in terror and satire—which these public events offered. Here in a single circular arena the whole community came to see its reality enacted. Although we have always known about the topicality and obscenity of Aristophanic comedy, we are just beginning to discover an equivalent topicality and sexuality in the great tragedies. Aeschylus, Sophocles, and Euripides did not conceive abstract art works. These plays related directly to the social life of Athens.[23]

It is not only Greek dramas in and of themselves which attract his attention, but the conditions of their performance. For Schechner, 'the failure of theater in America is more than a question of poverty. We are simply not brought up to believe in groups; we are trained

---

[21] Shephard (1991), xv.   [22] Shephard (1991), xii.
[23] Schechner (1968c), 20.

towards an individualistic ethic that makes us want to achieve things on our own, by ourselves. These values are inimical to theater.'[24]

While Schechner can also praise the communality of medieval Christian morality plays, he wants to make other, more distant, connections, then and now: 'There is a qualitative link between the Orokolo Fire Fight, the Greek chorus, and our own folk-rock discothèques. LSD is contemporary chemistry, but freaking out is ancient. I take this special ecstatic quality to be essentially theatrical.'[25]

Schechner's manifesto is romantic in its idealization of the Greeks in their purported links with other quite different cultural manifestations. 'We can even hear in Euripides' chorus from the *Bacchae* echoes of rhythms and customs hundreds, perhaps thousands, of years more ancient than the Athens of the fifth century BC.' The lines, 'When shall I dance once more with bare feet the all-night dances' can be compared to the 'molimo dances of the Bambuti, who roam the African forest at will, in small isolated bands or hunting groups'.[26]

Theatre, in Schechner's view, should also be highly political in its espousal of contemporary alternatives to the mainstream culture. This is the trait that all these avant-garde theatres of the time shared. At the time of writing the essay, 'The politics of ecstasy', from which I have quoted several times, the Performance Group was still working up plans for a production of Euripides' *Bacchae*. It will 'treat the text as if it were part of an oral tradition', Schechner advertises in advance. 'Only parts of Euripides' text will be used, and these parts will be joined to and set against fragments of other texts. The event will be a dance, an ecstasy, and the audience will perform along with members of the Group. Our Bacchanale will not be completely celebratory: that would not be true to our social context. We hope to explore the "politics of ecstasy." ' Yet what exactly are 'the politics of ecstasy'? He acknowledges the danger in this joyous vision—the other side of the Dionysiac frenzy—when he admits at the end that he harbours a 'hidden fear' about the new expression in that its forms come perilously close to 'ecstatic fascism'.[27]

[24] Schechner (1968*b*), 218.   [25] Schechner (1968*b*), 218.
[26] Schechner (1965–6,1968) in Schechner (1969), 59–60.
[27] Schechner (1968*a*) in Schechner (1969), 228. More specifically, he acknowledges that 'this same ecstasy, we know, can be unleashed in the Red Guards or horrifically channeled toward the Nuremberg rallies and Auschwitz. There too, at the vast extermination camps, an ecstasy was acted out.'

Euripides' *Bacchae* was always among Schechner's favourites. He wrote two essays on the play before undertaking the production of *Dionysus in 69*, although he later acknowledged that they no longer 'reflected what I learned about Euripides by directing him'.[28] His fascination with producing the play is not difficult to grasp. It has all the necessary ingredients for Schechner's ideas about theatre. As Shephard recalls:

When we first read *The Bacchae* together out loud, we were amazed how well it suited the Group.... [T]he basic themes of the play—violence, madness, ecstasy, challenge of authority, moral choice—were all issues of great concern in American society at the time, and they seemed particularly suited to the Group's extremely physical, impulse-oriented way of working. Moreover, the basic conflict in the play ... seemed remarkably similar to the Group dynamic which fluctuated between precision and order on one hand and impulsive abandon on the other. In both the play and the structure of the Group the dramatic tension between social order and anarchy, discipline and impulse, created a highly charged atmosphere of social instability poised between change into a new society and self-destruction.[29]

Additionally, in a later essay, entitled 'Actuals: primitive ritual and performance theory', Schechner advanced a series of five basic qualities that he saw as common to life, ritual, and theatre: '1) *Process*, something happens *here and now*; 2) *consequential, irremediable*, and *irrevocable* acts, exchanges or situations; 3) *contest*; something is *at stake* for the performers and often for the spectators; 4) *initiation: a change in status* for participants; and 5) space used *concretely* and *organically*.'[30] The two categories 'contest' and 'initiation' immediately command our attention as essential to the structure and interpretation of *Bacchae*, along with Schechner's other favourite terms such as ritual, celebration, ecstasy, communality, and group participation.

One of the most striking effects in Schechner's reworking of *Bacchae* was the introduction of the so-called 'birth ritual' just after the formal opening of the play (see the cover of this book and Figure 7). This ritual followed the entrance of Dionysus, when he introduced himself to the audience and announced he was about to be born. Modelled after an Asmat rite of passage in New Guinea, the ritual passed Dionysus through a 'birth canal'

---

[28] Schechner (1967) in Schechner (1969) and Prefatory Note.
[29] Shephard (1991), 52.   [30] Schechner (1971), 58.

FIGURE 7.   Studio photograph by Max Waldman of The Birth Ritual
scene in Richard Schechner's *Dionysus in 69* (1968).

composed of four women in alternating formation with five men.[31] The very same ritual, but in reverse, was matched at the end of the play as a 'death ritual' for Pentheus. 'Now, instead of facing away from Pentheus, the women faced toward him; instead of helping him through, they raised their bloody hands over their heads. Front and back were reversed in this formation in a perfect symmetrical counterpoint with its opposite, and taken together, these two rituals served as unifying elements of the entire play.'[32]

The 'birth ritual', however, was given an even greater valence of meaning on the symbolic level. The performance of the play—and even the script, with its different improvisations—issued eventually from the collaborative efforts of the entire group. The dynamics of this group were established through the workshops and group exercises, many of which were subsequently translated to the stage performance. Inevitably, along with group solidarity, there were also rivalries and conflicts, especially with respect to the libidinal energies that were essential to the group but were also compromised in part when some of the actors paired off into couples in real life. The 'birth ritual', as Shephard observed, was essential 'not only in our work but also in our collective existence', because it 'gave us the opportunity of experiencing and expressing our common bonds in a non-rational and symbolic form . . . It became an expression of both our sexual dynamic and its realization in creative form.'[33] Even more, its placement at the beginning of the play transformed the ritual into a kind of 'symbolic procreation'. As performing artists, 'the child of our labors' was supposed to be 'the performance itself', renewed and recreated each time.[34]

Earlier I remarked that the ruling idea of the actor in this kind of theatre, common both to Grotowski's Poor Theater and to

---

[31] The Asmat are a primitive tribe on the south-west coast of New Guinea, formerly headhunters and cannibals. They are noted for their highly developed spiritual beliefs, especially concerning the relations between life and death, manifested in prized wood carvings and elaborate rituals. The ritual adopted by Schechner in group exercises and later in performance was used by the Asmat to mark the occasion of intermarriage among different tribes as a way of integrating the two.

[32] Schechner in Schechner (1970), n.p. The 'death ritual' took the place of the reported *sparagmos* in Euripides.

[33] Shephard (1991), 88.   [34] Shephard (1991), 113.

Schechner's group, was participation in a performance which offered the challenge of coming to know oneself—even to surpass oneself—in the process of impersonating a character in the play. 'Schechner gradually formulated a concept of the "personal" actor, who used the role to reveal the conflicts of his or her own life. In addition, he felt that the actor's confession or revelation of self should be articulated into the structure of the performance, not merely through the character but also through the person of the actor.'[35] This merging of identity was expressed, above all, in the simultaneous use of two names—one's own and that of the mythic character. This technique was used especially in the case of the figure of Dionysus, whereby the performer would speak in his own name and in the name of the god. But elsewhere too, as in the 'mortification scene', designed to destroy Pentheus' self-esteem (a substitute for the destruction of the king's palace in Euripides), the actors spoke colloquially about their own concerns, as if in a psychodrama or group therapy session, while still maintaining their identity as a chorus of worshippers. These interjections and disruptions of Euripides' text were startling innovations, but the personal information, the free associations, the game playing among the actors and with the audience, were also sometimes a distraction or worse. The inconcinnity between tragic diction and colloquial modernisms sometimes produced witty results. At other times, it seemed like a high price to pay for the creative benefits of the interfusion between the ancient drama and contemporary goings-on. Moreover, while the group constituted itself as a democratic entity, with all sharing in its decisions, it was also inevitable that their creative work would reflect their off-stage dynamics, 'its antagonisms as well as its affinities'. As a result, the entire

---

[35] Shephard (1991), 89. Cf. Schechner (1971), 61:'The actor does not "play" Dionysus, nor Shephard Pentheus. Neither "are" they the characters. During rehearsal the performer searches his personal experiences and associations, selects those elements which reveal him and also make an autonomous narrative and/or action structure, strips away irrelevancies and cop-outs, hones what remains until everything is necessary and sufficient. What results is a double structure... The first is the narrative and/or action structure of the play. The second is the vulnerability and openness of the performer. Each performance he risks freshly not only his dignity and craft, but his life-in-process. Decisions made and actions done during performance may change the performer's life. The performance is a set of exchanges between the performer and the action. And of course among the performers and between them and the audience.'

'performance became the vehicle for projecting the interplay of personal forces within the Group onto a mythological plane'.[36]

It was therefore inevitable that internal conflicts would arise, whether between members of the group or in an individual. The problem could be one of under- or over-identification, in which the dangers of crossing the boundary between art and life became evident. This was what happened in particular to Bill Shephard, the poor fellow who played Pentheus for a large part of the play's run. Taunted by Dionysus, mortified by the bacchants, and rejected by the community, he began to feel anxious and depressed: 'My symptoms of dissociation both inside and outside the production, feelings of increased isolation from everyone around me, and the conflicts between incompatible elements of my own personality were increasing. Instead of being overjoyed at the Group's apparent success, I was withdrawing more and more into myself.'[37] He even went so far one time as to sabotage the performance by refusing to capitulate to Dionysus on cue, thereby confusing cast and audience alike and arousing their fury. Shephard internalized the role of Pentheus but also resisted it.[38] When the decision was ultimately taken to rotate the actors in different roles (including a woman to play Dionysus at times), far more was at stake than in a typical repertory theatre. Under these circumstances, others too expressed the anxieties they experienced between role and person, whether in playing Agave or in presuming to impersonate a god.

These tensions and conflicts within the individual as well as between members of the group were not, of course, obvious to the audience. But their existence contributed in no small part to the intensity of the performances and the degrees of improvisations within the highly structured sequence of actions and basic elements of the original script. Given the dangerous situation created by the premises of the plot in the antagonism between Pentheus and Dionysus, between the forces of liberation and those of repression, the actor as well as the character was often at risk.

---

[36] Shephard (1991), xvi.   [37] Shephard (1991), 143.

[38] Despite the obvious differences, Michael Frayn's hilarious farce, *Noises Off*, comes to mind in its outrageous interplay between the characters on stage and the actors off stage. The game becomes ever more complex and more chaotic as the production deteriorates over its long run. For Shephard, of course, this conflict (but also confusion) between role and character produced real effects.

Let me turn now to some of the more formal aspects of *Dionysus in 69*, its various techniques and choices, and their implications, before concluding with some further thoughts on the *Bacchae* in the light of this re-presentation.

The plot of *Bacchae* and a good deal of its text were maintained in the performance. According to Schechner, 'Of the more than 1300 lines in Arrowsmith translation of the *Bacchae*,[39] the group used nearly 600, some more than once. There were also 16 lines from Sophocles' *Antigone* [the speech in which Creon speaks of need for order in the state, 659–80] and 6 lines from Euripides' *Hippolytus* [215–21].'[40] The rest of the text was composed by the group, some on their own at home and some in the workshops. The textual montage, arrangements and variations, as well as repetitions, particularly in the use of the chorus, were worked out during rehearsals and throughout the run. The performers wrote their own dialogue in a spirit that respected Euripides' text, even if it was altered, paraphrased, or otherwise personalized. Schechner wanted as much individual expression as possible in a play that deals so effectively with the liberation of personal energy. Although techniques of displacement, montage, and split emphasis of Arrowsmith's translation were used, 'there was a formal pattern to the text's construction' that excluded pure improvisation. One important device was to insist that Pentheus had to keep to the original text as much as possible—except at the time when he becomes so deeply threatened by Dionysus that his performance mask falls away and the person playing the role is revealed. By contrast, 'Dionysus, from the very start of the play, says his own text', with a number of asides and ad libs, as if to exemplify his own freedom. 'But as the play goes on, he moves closer and closer to Euripides' text. It is as though Pentheus starts out as a character in

---

[39] Arrowsmith (1959).

[40] Schechner in Schechner (1970), n.p. Shephard (1991), 141–2, mentions the lines from the *Antigone*, which he insisted on inserting near the beginning, so as to make himself a more sympathetic character and because he personally approved of Creon's 'sense of discipline and order', so as to maintain some vestige of dignity as a ruler in the face of the humiliation inflicted on him by the Performance Group. The lines from *Hippolytus* are drawn from Phaedra's maddened fantasies in the opening of that play. These are the lines that express her desire to go to the mountain and hunt with the hounds and the javelin. In *Dionysus in 69*, Pentheus seems to speak these lines instead of expressing his voyeuristic desire to see the women at their rites. I will return to this substitution below.

a play and learns about the person underneath.' Or put somewhat differently, his restriction to Euripides' words functions to empha-size his rigid character and also spells his alienation from the spontaneous processes of self-realization. 'Dionysus, however, starts out as one of the group and elevates himself to the rigidity of godhood.'[41] Yet it is equally possible to understand both the liberties Dionysus takes with the text and his subsequent return to it as signs of the freedom he promotes as well as his formal exercise of divine authority. Gods can do what they want, after all. One of the lines that brought down the house, as I recall, was when the actor playing Dionysus (William Finley) said to Pentheus (Bill Shephard): 'Bill, you don't understand. You're a man. I'm a god. This is a tragedy. The odds are against you.'[42]

Euripides' text functions as the foundation but also as the ground of conflict or compromise between the old and the new, the then and the now. Schechner judged the final script (or scripts, since no actor taking on a given role exactly replicated the words of his/her predecessor) as being both conceptual and affective, and as reflecting the complicated internal dynamics of the Group while also, as he claimed, doing justice to Euripides' genius, despite the serious dislocations of the text.[43]

From this point of view, the intersection between Schechner's use of *Bacchae* and the very aims of his theatre gains additional significance, albeit on a more metatheatrical level. The heart of Schechner's enterprise for his actors was not just to blur the boundaries between performer and role, but to question that rela-tionship in a radical way. At the heart of *Bacchae* is the very question of identity. Who am I? For Dionysus, it is the fact that he is a god and demands to be accepted as such, even though he appears within the play and pretends to be the Stranger. For Pentheus, who knows he is the son of Echion and Agave, but not much more, the play punishes his stubborn resistance in his own mother's failure to recognize him, when he goes to the mountain disguised as a woman. The injunction to 'know thyself', so prom-inent in Theban narratives—whether Oedipus or Pentheus, and later in the case of Narcissus—addresses a Greek preoccupation about questions of social and personal identity. Schechner's

[41] Schechner in Schechner (1970), n.p.
[42] McDermott in Schechner (1970), n.p.
[43] Schechner in Schechner (1970), n.p.

production addressed these questions in a theatrical, rather than ontological way. At the same time, the fact that the performers could change roles, in the fluidity of casting, means that any identification between role and person, any influence of personality on role and role on personality, was not necessarily stable within the continuity of performances. But, like so much else that was improvised each time during the play's run, this factor too that involved changes of roles contributed not just to the group's creative freedom. It also in a way substantiated the mobility associated with Dionysus himself, as the god who comes from without but who lodges within—the god who through theatrical means (costume, role playing, illusionistic devices) can compel the recognition of himself as a divinity.

As for the structure of the drama itself, it generally followed the plot of *Bacchae* quite faithfully, with some important exceptions. It included all the initial elements: the introduction of Dionysus and his followers, the appearance of Teiresias and Cadmus, and Pentheus' modes of resistance—his crude threats and brutal attempts to exercise authority, especially in the imprisoning of Dionysus. For all its alterations and improvisations, the play also dramatized the essential phases of the later actions in the Euripidean version: Pentheus' subsequent capitulation to the god's seductive wiles and the ensuing journey to see the bacchants on the mountain; his exposure and ultimate dismemberment at the hands of his mother, Agave, and the other Theban women; the scene between Agave and Cadmus in which he brings her back to sanity and she realizes what she has done; and finally, the appearance of Dionysus on the equivalent of the *theologeion* to deliver his last messages and predict the unhappy future of Agave and her father.[44]

The miracle of the palace earthquake was, of course, eliminated. In keeping with the principles of the Environmental Theater, there was no single structure in the performance space that could function as a house or stable structure. Likewise, stage devices for creating special effects would have been utterly out of the question. Its substitute was a kind of 'circle of transformation'. Its purpose was to isolate Pentheus at first from the group and then treat him to

---

[44] The *theologeion* was the roof of the ancient stage building, a high platform, generally used for appearances of the gods on-stage.

humiliating exposure by his interlocutors, who both taunted and ignored him, while talking to one another in the 'group therapy' style I described earlier. The idea of this 'mortification scene', as earlier observed, was to replace the 'destruction of the palace' with the 'destruction of Pentheus' pride or self esteem' through 'encounter-group strategy'.[45]

Other major changes, however, were even more striking; and they worked both with and against the spirit of Euripides' vision. Here is where the all-important question of sexuality and libidinal display enters into discussion. In the first place, the problem of the bacchants' costume in a modern production always poses a problem. What should today's maenads wear? The paraphernalia of dappled fawnskins and *thyrsoi*? Fabrics of animal prints were popular in the Sixties and still are. More generally, in an age of sartorial freedom, this outfit is insufficiently bizarre to convey the radical strangeness of these bacchant women under the spell of Dionysus. It remains just that—a funky costume in a play. But what else would achieve the desired effect?

Many other modern directors have tried to solve the problem with little success. For example, I recall Michael Cacoyannis's 1980 production of the play in New York's Circle in the Square. Despite the presence of the great Irene Pappas in the role of Agave, I would have to come close to agreeing with John Simon's cruel description of the chorus's garb. 'The girls', he says, 'were an ethnically mixed group in sluttish costumes whose movements were rather like a floorshow in a medium priced third-world bordello.'[46] Or take a more recent production by the American Repertory Theatre at the Loeb Drama Center of Harvard University (late 1997 to early 1998), which I did not myself attend, although I have seen photographs of the production: 'The Chorus is intriguing,' says one easy-to-please reviewer, 'in their gothic paleface make-up highlighted with red lips, eyeshadow, and long dark red kinky tresses, wearing off-white gauzy ripped dresses and Doc Marten style boots.' (That same reviewer, I should note, also marvelled at the utter lifelikeness of Pentheus' head carried by Agave.)[47]

---

[45] Shephard (1991), 83.

[46] *New York Magazine*, 20 October 1980, quoted in Hartigan (1995), 86.

[47] Quotation from a review of this production by Angel (Wendy Chapman) at www.sceneplay.com/reviews/TheBacchae. Photographs of the costumed actors and certain scenes at www.amrep.org/past/bacchae/html.

The solution of the Dionysus Group was to use nudity itself as a costume and to show scenes of actual disrobing on the stage. Although nudity was not a part of the play at the start of its performance, this is the one aspect of Schechner's production that has left the most lasting impression. From June to November 1968, the female members of the chorus wore red thigh-length chitons and black panties. The men wore black jock straps underneath short pants and T-shirts or went bare-chested. For the birth and death rituals, they undressed down to panties and jockstraps. But, on Grotowski's advice, they gave up what he called a cheap 'striptease' and took the risk of appearing naked in these scenes and in the ecstasy dance (that followed the birth ritual), with invitations to the audience to follow suit.[48] This change also meant that Dionysus and Pentheus in his turn also appeared naked at critical moments. Although the Group had previously conducted practice exercises in the nude, the innovation in the theatre posed substantial risks for actors and spectators alike. It may be difficult, now after so many years, when hardly an eyebrow is raised at public nudity in the theatre or the cinema, to imagine the shock value of unadorned naked bodies, especially those of men. In fact, one of the most notorious responses to this display occurred when the Group was briefly on tour in the Midwest in January 1969 and performed in Ann Arbor at the University of Michigan, where they were arrested and jailed for a night on the charge of 'corrupting the morals of the good people of the State of Michigan'.[49]

Schechner was surprised by the vehement reactions. 'The nudity', he said, 'stirred a storm beyond our expectations. Group members were worried about police records. Students were upset about repression. Legislators spent heat over the twin evils of communism and obscenity—and saw plain connections between the two. Everyone who saw or even read about *Dionysus* had something to say about the nakedness. It is good, it is bad; it is shocking, it is banal; it is necessary, it is gratuitous. Nakedness gets

[48] Schechner in McNamara *et al.* (1975), 92, claims he was always uncomfortable with the women's costumes, which he felt 'were out of a college production of a Greek play'.

[49] Shephard (1991), 201. He gives a detailed account of this conflict between town and gown, 197–201, as does Schechner (1968*b*), 94–6. Previous stops at the University of Colorado and the University of Minnesota also raised a storm of controversy, but the production at these institutions met with generally favourable reviews. See further Shephard (1991), 186–96.

confused for sexuality and sexuality becomes a political matter.
"What is the limit?" people ask. "The limit of what?", I reply.'[50]
Schechner's notebooks for the period, however, record some of
the psychological difficulties faced by the actors in presenting
themselves as so unprotected in exposure to public view. The
risk was 'for each performer to do what is most difficult: be
naked without being either abstract or strip-tease sexual'.[51]
Schechner therefore led experiments in workshop with the
Group in 'exploring the relationship between physical and psychic
nakedness—between nakedness and vulnerability'.[52] For all his
high-mindedness, however, he came to acknowledge that 'the differences among body liberation, serious art, and sex shows are of
degree. They each center on the body: the first as celebration, the
second as symbolic or metaphoric "objective correlative," and the
third as merchandise. And in each there is more than a pinch of
the other two.'[53]

In *Dionysus in 69*, nudity heralded not just a daring exhibitionist
display, but as the mischievous choice of numerals in the title
suggests, it even teased theatre-goers with the possibility of a still
more titillating performance in public space. While this taboo-
breaker never actually took place, one of the major appeals of the
play for many spectators, especially the numerous repeaters, was
the focus on the body. Members of the audience could strip and
join the proceedings; they could reciprocate caresses if the performers invited them to touch. Earlier, I mentioned the Total
Caress sequence, which finally had to be abandoned as too disruptive, even for the ideals of the Performance Group in their encouragement of audience-actor interaction. But available to all was the
voyeuristic freedom permitted to them throughout the performance. The libidinal energies harnessed by the group as aids to their
work as an ensemble might have had a primarily emblematic value
in objective terms—a value that was compromised to some extent
by the fact that some of the actors had already paired off in real life.
But the performative context left the emphasis on exposed sexuality as more than ambiguous, especially in light of the two quite

[50] Schechner (1968*b*), 96. See this entire essay for the significance of nakedness in
his theatrical vision.
[51] Schechner (1973) in Schechner (1994), 116.
[52] Schechner (1973) in Schechner (1994), 117.
[53] Schechner (1973) in Schechner (1994), 115.

drastic changes made to Euripides' script, both of which involved the figure of Pentheus.

In the working out of the contest between Pentheus and Dionysus, it was decided that about halfway through the play Pentheus should be given a chance to escape the god's power. The idea was that if some woman in the audience were willing to have sex with him right there and then, the performance would be over and the god defeated. While this outcome seemed highly 'preposterous', 'this innovation altered the foregone conclusion of the contest between the characters, changing it into a game with high stakes'.[54] As it happened, almost every night a woman did come to Pentheus to extend her help, or at least her sympathy, although, with one exception, it ended when she returned to her place.[55]

A second and even more confrontational use of sexuality was the substitute action chosen for Pentheus' final capitulation to Dionysus in that most sinister scene of *Bacchae*. There Dionysus deflects the Theban king's threats of violence against the maenads on the mountain and instead holds out the temptation to fulfil his repressed voyeuristic desires: 'Do you want to see?' And when Pentheus suddenly assents, he discovers the price: 'Then you must go dressed as a woman.' Transvestism for Pentheus in the Euripidean context meant the surrender of his royal status and masculine identity to undergo this terrible humiliation before being subjected to his final punishment on the mountain. His consent was itself a sign of the Dionysiac madness that overcame him. But in a modern theatre, dressing up in drag was a far less threatening spectacle. It could be experienced merely as a game with campy overtones or a floozy nightclub act. Instead, Shephard and Finley (the original Dionysus) wanted to find a more compelling 'basis for the contest between themselves as actors and as characters in the play'. The decision was therefore made 'to reveal and confront a hidden aspect of our natures, a fear of homosexual-

---

[54] Shephard (1991), 81.

[55] There was one time when the sequence was completed, not by a sexual act, but through a certain emotional energy transmitted to Bill Shephard by a woman in the audience, which liberated him from the entrapment of his situation. As the actor playing Dionysus that evening reported: 'Bill got up and left the theater with the woman. I announced that the play was over. "Ladies and gentlemen, tonight for the first time since the play has been running, Pentheus, a man, has won over Dionysus, the god. The play is over".' Schechner (1970), n.p., and quoted too in Schechner (1971), 60.

ity', which would expose anxieties about their own masculine identities.[56] Schechner puts it more strongly:

Early in rehearsals with Bill Shephard and Bill Finley we had to find an equivalent for dressing in women's clothes. In Euripides, Pentheus is possessed and humiliated, rewarded and destroyed. Shephard suggested homosexuality as the counterpart. It was the most difficult thing he could think of doing in public. The homosexual kiss is supreme revealment and concealment at the same time. Dionysus' purpose works through Pentheus' submission. And both performers taste something that attracts and repels them. Neither is homosexual. To many homosexuals in the audience the scene is titillating. Sometimes, as much from anxiety as from amusement, spectators shout encouragement to Pentheus. Unwittingly, they mortify him as Euripides intended: 'I want him made the laughing-stock of Thebes.'[57]

Today, more than thirty years later, such a scene of homosexual seduction in the theatre would hardly raise an eyebrow in a sophisticated audience. But the sexual liberation of the 1960s did not yet include widespread tolerance and acceptance of homoerotic relations between men, and certainly not if openly acted out in public. Although Pentheus' final acquiescence to Dionysus' demands was relegated off-stage, the god's insistence on giving a graphic description of exactly what he required in the face of Pentheus' abject misery and repeated refusals was a powerful and terrifying moment in the psychological impact of the play. This double emphasis on sex—first, Pentheus' search for a woman, who might liberate him, later followed by his submission to Dionysus—paradoxically both undermined Euripides' vision, yet also in some sense, sustained its latent implications.

The entire premise of Euripides' *Bacchae* relies on the audience's knowledge that Pentheus' suspicions about what the women are doing on Mount Cithaeron are wholly unfounded. The bacchants are not there to indulge in illicit sex, as he insists, but to worship their god and be initiated into his mysteries. They are liberated from their domestic lives at home to experience freedom in the world of nature. This world, as the first messenger tells us, is wholly benign. He sees them first asleep after their dancing, 'all modestly and soberly, not, as you think, drunk with wine, nor wandering, led astray by the music of the pipe, to hunt

[56] Shephard (1991), 82.   [57] Schechner in Schechner (1970), n.p.

their Aphrodite through the woods'. When awakened, he sees
them suckling young animals, weaving garlands of ivy, and miraculously bringing forth water and milk from the ground and
honey from their *thyrsoi* (*Bacchae* 558–713). Only when they are
disturbed by men's intrusions (first, by the local herdsmen and
later, by Pentheus himself) do they turn violent, but still with no
hint of sexual aggression.

Schechner's play, however, insisted that ecstasy and communion with the god must entail a liberation of those very erotic
impulses that Pentheus had initially feared. His Pentheus is com-
pelled to succumb to the god's homoerotic demands as an exercise
in submission and domination (a view that might seem very simplistic today)—but not as motivated in Euripides. There Pentheus
capitulates to achieve his secret desire—to spy on the women,
including and especially his mother, and see for himself what he
fantasized they were doing. This scene (*Bacchae* 811–21) is
retained in the script of *Dionysus*, but it takes place *after* Pentheus
emerges, naked, from the pit with Dionysus (as the equivalent of
having already dressed as a woman) and is followed immediately
by sections of the ensuing dialogue, beginning at 918, 'I think I
see two suns', etc. These dislocations are not incidental. Since
Schechner's entire production was in a sense a voyeuristic display—for audience and actors alike—and Pentheus was already
permitted to act out an opportunity for a heterosexual encounter
in the open, what then did this Pentheus want?

The frame of the original text remains: Pentheus' initial threat to
lead an army against the women and bring them back is repeated
again. The maenads will band together against him; the messenger
speech recounting this scene is retained, although it is spoken
before Pentheus is dismembered. But Pentheus' desire to see the
women on the mountain, even if voiced, has transmogrified into a
desire to belong to the group, which has mocked him, mortified
him, and cast him out. It is ecstasy too that he is seeking in their
company. This is why Dionysus first offers him any woman in the
room to be his, and when this doesn't succeed, the god insists on
the homoerotic encounter as the route to that ecstasy—to 'know'
Dionysus in a quite literal sense.

Pentheus' capitulation was to be followed by the Total Caress,
which I have mentioned several times. Although it ultimately got
out of hand, it was originally designed, as Schechner observed, to

'liberate the energies Euripides describes in the play. And I don't doubt that the old Greek knew of the endless subversions these energies undergo.'[58] Subversive, perhaps, in open advertisement of sexual freedom. But less so, if one considers the subtleties of repressed desire, the broader challenges to political authority, and the power of the supernatural to invade everyday life. I don't think I was aware of these complexities at the time, but Stefan Brecht, arguably the best critic of the play, offers important observations:

The interpersonal games of the hippie are not the languorous devolutions of the id but power plays of the ego. Their dialectical evolution into manifestly destructive aggression (the slaying of Pentheus) thus makes sense psychologically, is intrinsic. But Schechner's production fails to mark the point, so its dialectic seems arbitrary. While Euripides' Pentheus is never converted but overcome (by magic at that), Schechner's is seduced, his super-ego succumbs to his id, he is overcome from within, attains liberation by frank homosexuality, becomes a dionysian. Is Schechner proposing that, authoritarians being latent homosexuals, the state be brought to wither away by seducing those in power? In any event, this brings an entirely new element into the play, for the cause of Pentheus' subsequent downfall is now not the cleverness of the god or his own voyeurism, but the dionysian temper within him which betrays him into the motherly love of women, the ferociously womanly love of his mother. The dionysian endangers not only the state but himself. Also, since Pentheus is no longer Authority, his ensuing dismemberment is not rebellion.[59]

Euripides' play has remained a hotbed of conflicting interpretations.[60] The range of recent scholarly work, which has proliferated in recent years, has not resulted in any solid consensus, despite the genuine advances in our understanding of the play. Is the message of the play deeply conservative, even misogynistic, or is it the contrary, subversive, in challenging normative restrictions of law and order? Is the outcome positive in the triumph of divinity and the establishment of a new cult as necessary to the city? Or, is it negative, in that the price to be paid in the eradication of three generations of the royal family in Thebes is too high? No one today would subscribe to such extremes of position at either end. Rather,

[58] Schechner in Schechner (1970), n.p.
[59] S. Brecht (1969), 160. Stefan Brecht reports on three versions of the performance, which he saw at different intervals. His entire essay is worth reading.
[60] See above, n. 7.

we are attuned to Euripides' deeper irony that the Dionysus of the play finally eludes strict definition, even as he eluded his captor. For Euripides, who returned again and again in this theatre to interrogate the nature of divinity, some irreducible mystery always remains.

Schechner's version might at first glance seem less ambiguous, since the political and social climate that engendered its production ensured that there was little sympathy for Pentheus' position, not even after his terrible end, when he has turned from would-be tyrant to victim in that struggle between himself and Dionysus, not even if the protests of Cadmus and Agave against the god's excessive cruelty remain. To the extent that he still represents a ruler, Pentheus may be viewed as an agent of conservatism and governmental repression, who presents an obstacle to freedom, imagination, and creativity of every kind. Yet the Group's 'message', as conveyed through the personage of Dionysus, was hardly without its contradictions and ambiguities, which Stefan Brecht defines in terms of a vacillation between 'pro-hip' and 'anti-hip' that emerges in Schechner's 'liberal anarchism'.[61]

This hesitation is reflected, first, in additions to the messenger speech that reports the scene in the mountain, which exist in four different versions, and, second, in Dionysus' appearance at the end, both to pronounce his curses against the royal family in Thebes, and then to deliver a final, improvised harangue. One messenger declares: 'What I can't tell you is the reason why anyone, god or candidate, can promise a man joy, freedom, ecstasy. And then make him settle for a bloodbath.' Another one adds: 'You can have some kind of catharsis. I don't mind that. It's the pornography of death I mind.' And still another: 'To act out the prevailing taboos is not to be free, no more than to act out the prevailing totems. To destroy property, to get women, will not set you free . . . .' One of the performers remarked that the Messenger speech was supposed to 'function as a rebuke', but it is not meant to be 'reactionary . . . but only in reference to what is reactionary in the revolution'.[62]

[61] S. Brecht (1969), 159. Schechner defended himself in a letter to the *New York Times*, 28 July 1968: 'Neither the repressive and prurient spirit of Pentheus nor the ecstatic revelries of Dionysus offer a pleasant model for society. The conflict between these tendencies is, however, properly and profoundly tragic.'

[62] Schechner (1970), n.p. These brief quotations hardly do justice to these speeches, which are far longer and more complex than can be analysed here.

The dangers of an 'ecstatic fascism' seem to be expressed here, but the ending of the play with Dionysus triumphant is more disturbing, because that 'fascism' of liberation and violence is not acknowledged. At the same time, the exhortation to revolt against the establishment—'firebomb a cop', 'roast a pig', get 'power, power, power'—which came in many forms, according to the actor and the time of performance, was leavened with a quite macabre humour and a devilish imagination. Before the elections of November 1968, Dionysus announced himself as a candidate for president and each night scattered red, white, and blue buttons, with the legend, 'Dionysus for President.' After the elections, more improvisation was in the making. 'And you, Cadmus . . . you will go to the island of Scorpios. There you will become the bodyguard of Jacqueline Kennedy Onassis and there you will be contracted by the Greek Mafia to make a hit on Richard Nixon, who has decided that Spiro Agnew deserves the job.' Or again to Agave: 'You will leave this garage in expiation of the murder you have done, for you are unclean. You will stop performing, and go back to Bobbs-Merrill. You will become the head of the International Children's Books Department. You will establish yourself in Biafra and teach those children how to read. You will teach them to love America.'[63]

Describing the scene on the mountain with the women armed against Pentheus, one of the actors who played the Messenger quoted Agave: 'We must kill this animal. Remember, violence is as American as apple pie.' This perhaps says it all. Yet only now in reading the accounts by the various performers did I realize what was at stake—beyond the doors of the theatre, or perhaps I had heard it all before. Still, in reviving the memories of that closing scene, I realized too that, strangely enough, I had conveniently forgotten it altogether. It was the rituals and the naked bodies that I remembered best.[64]

---

[63] All quotes from (1970), n.p.. These are only the briefest of excerpts.

[64] I would like to thank Edith Hall for her encouragement and patience.

3

Bad Women

Gender Politics in Late Twentieth-Century Performance and Revision of Greek Tragedy

Helene Foley

Unquestionably, contemporary performances and revisions of Greek tragedy world-wide have responded explicitly and self-consciously to the prominent gender politics of Greek tragedy. Without a doubt, the increased interest in these aspects of Greek tragedy since the late 1960s has reflected or engaged with developments in both the feminist and gay and lesbian movements. The far more interesting question, then, is to locate more precisely the nature and range of the response. This essay will try to look at a selection of responses to and remakings of the Greek texts in performance. Although Greek tragedy has been frequently performed or adapted in many cultures during this period, the response to the gender politics of the plays has been particularly sharp in Japan, the USA, Ireland, and, more sporadically, the rest of western Europe; in each case, the nature of the responses can be partly explained by the cultural context. By contrast, in Africa, for example, comparable performances and adaptations have tended to rely on traditional gender roles, and have made broader political and cultural issues such as tyranny, democracy, racism and tribal conflict, colonialism, terrorism, or emerging contradictions between traditional and modern moral values the central focus.[1]

Let me begin with issues posed by a recent production in New York City entitled *Bad Women*, created and directed by Tina Shepherd, Sidney Goldfarb, and the Talking Band. This new play, performed at the Here Arts Center in June 2002, created an explicitly metatheatrical piece in which two actors and four

---

[1] For Japan see Smethurst (2000) and (2002); for Ireland, McDonald and Walton (2002); for Africa, Wetmore (2002).

actresses playing Clytemnestra, Phaedra, Medea, Agave, Deianeira, and Cassandra performed certain diverging or intersecting aspects and high points of their roles before a chorus of gossiping teenage girls in modern dress holding cell phones. Several of the chorus members later adopted for the moment the roles of daughter figures such as Electra and Iphigeneia; hence they moved from outside to inside the action and even began to direct some of it, taking over this role from an intrusive off-stage voice. The production highlighted moments of doubling in the original myths, such as Medea and Deianeira simultaneously rubbing poisons on different ends of the same huge strip of cloth, followed by Clytemnestra with her (actually his) deadly tapestry and net. It included fragments from tragic speeches by all of the heroines, especially those directed to marriage and the condition of women. Though often colloquial, the use of verse also aimed to elevate the play's language. Shepherd was attracted to what she called the scale and the condensed conflict in these myths through growing up in a heavily Greek community in Massachusetts and studying the originals in college. For her, these plays represent an unapologetic and in many ways contemporary investigation of family values in a large and intense form: 'big and bad'. 'I don't know if I have ever known a woman that is completely Medean in what she does, but I certainly have known a lot who feel what she has felt' (programme notes). The shape of the play aimed to engage the audience and bring them closer to the myths in a fashion parallel to that of its chorus. The distance between audience and the myths was underlined by constant metatheatricality, and yet their combined antiquity and modernity became increasingly vivid and emotionally engaging as the play evolved. Not all of these tragic heroines are well known to US audiences, and, on the basis of random discussion with the mostly young audience afterwards, few but Medea were in fact familiar. What provoked Shepherd, then, to create this fragmented dramatic contact with the past?

Certainly, Shepherd's attraction to the 'badness' of her heroines is pervasive and symptomatic. The same is true for the interest in the explicitly ambiguous gendered positions adopted by many of these heroines, who have attracted not only actresses eager for large, provocative, and challenging roles, but male actors, who, as in this play, are equally eager to take on what they view as some of the major female roles in the Western theatrical tradition. If we add in the seemingly more positive, if also more or less rebellious, figures of Antigone and Jocasta, and the largely innocent suffering women from captured Troy found in several of Euripides' plays, it is by and large the outrageous, courageous, untraditional, and often androgynous female figures—both mothers and daughters like Iphigeneia or Electra—who have been most performed and reworked to heighten the gender issues in these plays on the late twentieth-century stage. On the male side, figures who are facing major crises of identity (especially those involving coming to adulthood), which often involve a sexual dimension, such as Oedipus, Hippolytus, Orestes, or Pentheus, have particularly attracted performances focusing on gender issues. Tolerance for and even delight in the transgressive actions and at times aggressive sexuality of these characters apparently extends beyond what would be tolerated from those of less magnitude and mythic pedigree. As John Fisher, author *of Medea, the Musical* discussed below, has remarked, Medea 'fucks up Jason's whole patriarchal structure too, and then she flies away in her dragon-drawn chariot laughingly maniacally. It's like, *yeah*, that's what you want to do when someone spurns you!... People love this women killing kids... It's weird. Killing kids is not okay! Killing kids is never okay—but for some reason it's okay for Medea. It's an interesting audience phenomenon.'[2]

This essay begins with the remaking or revision of the original scripts and moves on to performance, especially cross-dressed performance, before attempting a brief and highly selective discussion of other gender-related issues that played a major role in US and a few British productions during this period. Revisions of Greek tragedy that responded to the feminist movement have frequently involved giving a more prominent, complex, or sympathetic voice to a female character whose point of view is less central or even silenced in the Greek originals, and have gone so far as to re-envision the gender relations of the originals altogether. (Similar effects can be produced by cutting, newly translating, and staging the original plays.) The aim here has been well articulated by Adrienne Rich, for whom 'revision is an act of looking back, entering an old text from a new critical direction... We need to know the writing of the past, and know it differently than we have ever known it; not to pass on a tradition but to break its

---

[2] Wren (2002), 24.

hold over us.'[3] The revised plays often reduce prominent male roles, and they rarely give a more complex perspective to male figures, such as Jason in *Medea*, or even to secondary figures like children. Important exceptions occasionally occur, however. Sarah Kane's dramatically re-imagined Hippolytus in *Phaedra's Love* (1996), Pasolini's full exploration of Oedipus from birth in his 1967 film *Edipo Re*, Jack Richardson or David Rabe's expanded engagement with the adolescent Orestes (*The Prodigal* (1960) and *The Orphan* (1973/4), respectively), or Per Lysander and Suzanne Osten's children's play, *Medea's Children* (published in English in 1975), which makes Medea's children major players in their parents' dysfunctional family, provide a few examples. I shall start with a brief case study of new dramatic versions of the figures of Jocasta and Oedipus. Here both male and female figures have been radically revised. Although in the original plays these characters are closer to innocent victims than to deliberate transgressors of social norms in acts of revenge or rebellion like Clytemnestra, Medea, or Antigone, they often become in these remakings more deliberately rebellious and transgressive. Again, the same may occur to a less radical degree in performances of the original plays; I stress revision in this paper as a way of articulating these issues visibly for a reader with the opportunity for direct and full access to texts but not to performances. This case study attempts to be more international in scope, if highly selective, whereas the final two sections of the essay, because they include a range of less well known and sometimes very recent productions, focus largely on performances in English that could be documented and context-ualized more readily by a US scholar. Undoubtedly, a study of these same issues made within the context of, for example, other European countries or Japan would uncover an equally rich but different multiplicity of approaches to the same issues.

REVISING OEDIPUS AND JOCASTA

Many modern, post-Freudian adaptations of Sophocles' *Oedipus Tyrannus* enlarge on the gender relations between mother and son and frequently make them more sexually explicit than in the original. Some new versions change the dynamics of Jocasta and

[3] Rich (1979), 35.

Oedipus' relation, giving Jocasta more dramatic space (in this respect Seneca's *Oedipus* may lurk in the background) and cultural authority, even to the point where she becomes both protagonist and chief investigator of the truth. In a fashion seemingly characteristic of the era, however, what is often an explicitly feminist attempt to give a 'silenced' Jocasta a 'voice' in fact entails a greater focus on the sexual power of the maternal body and a privatizing reduction, or transformation of the play's original public implications. Whereas Sophocles' Jocasta advised her husband on state matters and publicly dissolved the quarrel between her brother Creon and Oedipus, these new Jocastas in general have no civic role and in some cases adopt in a new form the Sophoclean queen's refusal to survive a confrontation with the truth. Instead, they demand a new perspective on female sexuality and the value of personal relationships in shaping identity and explore the mother–son rather than the father–son bond. Although much feminist literature has focused on the often reductive or demeaning aspect of the cinematic or literary gaze at women,[4] these plays often ask for a counter-cultural, post-Freudian version of that gaze. This section of the chapter will explore a limited selection of new versions of Sophocles' play in order to understand better the compelling power of its gender relations for a twentieth-century playwright, director, or audience.

The American playwright Philip Freund's *Jocasta* (1970) offered the most complete reversal of the original roles between mother and son. In late nineteenth-century Martinique, the protagonist, Catherine de la Célianne, has married a much older, wealthy man after secretly bearing a child to a black slave on her father's plantation. She believes the child to be dead, but in fact her son Yébé was given by her black nurse to be raised by a childless black couple; he has recently killed the unjust overseer for whom he worked (in fact, his father) due to a dispute concerning his wages and gone into hiding. As the play opens, Catherine, who has been a discreet widow for ten years, has been having a secret love affair with a simple young mulatto and escaped slave. Catherine instinctively recognizes in her naive and marginal lover, known to her as Victoire, not only lover but lost child (121).[5] 'Every lover is a

---

[4] See e.g. de Lauretis (1987).

[5] This and all subsequent references to this play are to the page numbers of the text published in Freund (1970).

child to us, when he bows his head at our breast—I felt that even with my own husband, who was so much older than I was' (163). A middle-aged Frenchman named Paul Pitou arrives to warn Catherine that a slave has been seen entering her house at night. He suspects that her new housemaid is the guilty party, but his concern for Catherine's reputation rests in large part on his long-suppressed love for the beautiful and intelligent mistress herself. Catherine, described as 'a woman of strong character' who 'is as dynamic and aggressive as the period and constraining society in which she lives permits' (107), eventually reveals to Paul first her own affair with the young mulatto and finally the birth of her illegitimate child. At first she pretends that the child was a product of rape, but soon reveals to Paul's horror that her wild attraction for the father was as powerful and to her as 'natural' as her current desire for the son. She rages both against the sexual double standard that permits black women to white men, but denies the reverse to herself, and at her inability to take advantage of the freedom she gained at her husband's death. Escape from male dominance was possible only to the point of creating an isolated all-female world consisting of herself, her old nurse, and the nurse's niece, the new housemaid. She could neither escape to Paris, as she imagined she might, because there was no society for her there, nor build a meaningful independence in the gossip-filled world of Martinique. Yet now she believes that she has faced and accepted herself (125).

In the dialogue that leads to her discovery of the truth, she confronts both her own earlier unwillingness to explore the fate of her child and her nurse's deep anger at her white oppressors. Once she recognizes the truth, she attempts to accept responsibility for her son. Her abandonment of the child led to her son's mistaken attack on his father. 'I thought you or my father had murdered him for my sake—and I was willing to keep quiet and ask no questions. Am I not a murderer too?' (159). Though her maternal desire for her son is now tainted with the savage passion she felt for his father, she at first feels no shame at that desire: 'We want to sleep with the fathers of our children—and we want to sleep with our sons too. If we don't know who our sons are, we are very likely to do it. It wasn't an accident that this boy was born, or that he didn't know his father and mother. God didn't arrange that. We did it ourselves. (*again*) We did it' (162). In the end, however, she cannot accept this iconoclastic view that morality is man-made nor, as a result, her own deed (167).

Though Catherine kills herself and fails to save her son, Paul pronounces her innocent in the closing lines of the play (170). Yet this acceptance of Catherine depends on her self-punishment for violating his deepest masculine convictions. This play creates a protagonist with the intelligence, wilfulness, and resistance to destiny of Oedipus, but her actively chosen partner is more child than man and her rebellious claim to sexuality reverts to self-revulsion. What appears to be a challenge to Sophocles' story becomes a reinforcement of social and sexual destiny, requiring the infantilization or enslavement of the Oedipal figure in order to empower his mother. The sudden and surprising religious thematizing of a guilt that was earlier defined in strictly social terms does not emerge as an intuitively obvious discovery. Jocasta's challenge to the limitations of a female role in the end enslaves her to her own body and to superstition.

The former US poet laureate Rita Dove's *The Darker Face of the Earth* (1996) takes a similar approach, but with different results. Set in antebellum South Carolina, the play makes the Oedipus figure, Augustus Newcastle, the son of the daughter of a plantation owner, Amalia Jennings Lafarge, and Hector, a black slave. As in *Jocasta*, the play deliberately raises questions of female oppression in a context populated with powerful women and weakened or disempowered men. The intelligent and attractive Amalia ('an attractive white woman...who exhibits more intelligence and backbone than is generally credited to a southern belle' (15)[6]), is embittered by being forced to abandon both child and love; she has become a masculinized, even cruel manager of her father's plantation—a role she recognizes as oppressive but feels historically unable to escape. The play's Teiresias figure, Scylla, is both frightening prophet and proponent of voodoo magic. The slave Phebe becomes the plantation's second in command in a slave rebellion. By contrast, Amalia's husband Louis has since the illegitimate birth withdrawn into the study of astronomy; Hector, maddened by the loss of his son, has adopted a solitary life in the swamps; the remaining male slaves show no active resistance to

---

[6] This and subsequent references to *The Darker Face of the Earth* are to the page numbers of the text published in Dove (1996).

their lot. This balance is shattered by the entrance of Augustus, a notoriously rebellious mulatto who was raised and educated by the British captain of a slave ship. Amalia's attempt to tame Augustus leads to a passionate romance that develops simultaneously with a slave rebellion fomented by Augustus, Phebe, and outside conspirators. After Augustus accidentally kills Hector, he discovers his identity during the rebellion. Assigned to kill Louis and Amalia, Augustus performs the first task but cannot go through with the second. Augustus ends the play simultaneously heroized for his role in the successful rebellion and destroyed as a human being.

Amalia, like Freund's Jocasta, rebels against her lot by breaking sexual taboos and surrendering to her body; she too complains about the double standard exercised by the philandering Louis (17). Nevertheless, the bond of shared intelligence, rebellion, suffering, and oppression between herself and Augustus complicates and to some extent equalizes their relationship. Augustus is torn between the struggle for freedom and love (146), as Amalia assuages her own guilt as master through her idyllic relation with her slave. When Amalia discovers and faces the truth, she does not withdraw into Sophoclean silence and hanging. As she reveals his identity to Augustus, she laments the irony of her failed attempt to rescue her much-loved baby from disaster. Then, picking up the knife Augustus drops, she completes his assignment for him. Augustus, who has been educated on Greek myths, earlier tells Amalia he finds them 'a bit too predictable' (84). The forces driving the disaster in this play are social and historical; despite Scylla, divinity plays no role. In addition, the errors and desires that divide and unite Augustus and Amalia also have, perhaps, a greater historical and social plausibility, at least for a modern audience, than in Sophocles' original. At the same time, the greater prominence or visible equality given to Dove's (and in the first respect Freund's) Jocasta figure is bought through a devaluation in the status (if not the intelligence and capacity) of the Oedipus figure. Only, it seems, by making Oedipus a slave (a possibility that lurks momentarily in Sophocles' original (1062–3) before Oedipus discovers the royal identity of the child exposed by the shepherd) can the playwright give Jocasta a more significant subjective role and voice.

Several feminist interpretations of the play have made Jocasta not only the central, but even the exclusive, figure, through whose consciousness the events of the play are relived (on the relative marginalization of Oedipus see also Macintosh, Chapter 12). This trend seems to have begun as early as Martha Graham's dance version, *Night Journey*, in 1947.[7] Graham's dance begins with Jocasta's hanging and unfolds as a reliving of her destiny by the dead Jocasta and a female chorus which amplifies her suffering. A sculpture designed by Isamu Noguchi, suggestive of a bed, occupies centre stage. Oedipus raises Jocasta from this 'bed' and courts her in a ritualized dance (both hold branches) that urges his dominance: he puts his foot on her shoulder, enfolds her in his cloak, and ties her and then himself to the 'bed'. Yet this effort constantly reverses itself in moments where Jocasta herself is 'on top'. When Tiresias intervenes with the truth in this intense sexual relationship, Oedipus blinds himself with his mother's enormous brooch. Jocasta then strips herself of her royal robe and hangs herself with the by-now highly symbolic rope (she is off the 'bed', but the rope now may suggest an umbilical cord as well as fate). As in Freund, this version makes the sexual relation between mother and son central, but eliminates anything that would detract from Jocasta's own experience of the events.

The Belgian playwright Michèle Fabien's dramatic monologue of 1981, *Jocaste*, makes the queen the only figure on-stage. As in Graham, the drama unfolds as a reliving and re-examination of the past by the dead, painfully isolated Jocasta. Above all, this Jocasta breaks her long silence and names herself Jocasta, a woman in love, not queen, widow, wife, mother. 'See Oedipus, your mother is a woman!' Jocasta is woman, not the man of the Sphinx's riddle, not the figure entrapped by Sophocles' narrative. 'Yet one does not gaze upon one's mother when she is a woman. One does not gaze upon a woman when she is a mother' (99).[8] She asks the anonymous stage musician and the audience to look at her death by hanging, an event upstaged by Oedipus' self-blinding in Sophocles' text. For Oedipus seeks himself, not his mother (95), nor the seventeen years of shared peace and contentment of their bed. In the closing lines Jocasta, naming herself again, asks the blind

---

[7] See Graham (1961) for a video record of *Night Journey*, Graham's notebooks (1973), and Leatherman (1966) for further background and discussion. This trend is continued in the recent *YokastaS* by Richard Schechner and Saviana Stanescu, staged at La MaMa, New York in March 2003, sadly too late for a full discussion here.

[8] References are to the English translation in Kourilsky and Temerson (1988).

Oedipus to recognize her as his unchanged lover through the touch of her naked flesh.

In the central sections Jocasta also contemplates the demand of the audience and the play's version of the myth that she kill herself (rather than survive like Oedipus); she claims her traditional death is as much execution as suicide. She too has her relation to the city; she imagines asking the plague to enter into herself, accepting death, and receiving the city's recognition for bearing Oedipus and sharing in the city's cure. Instead, 'the deliverance of Thebes will happen without Jocasta, outside of her—Jocasta outside the walls, outside of love, outside the law' (90).

Fabien's play was staged at the Ensemble Théâtral Mobile in Brussels, then in Paris, and in The Hague; it received the Prix Triennial de Littérature Dramatique in 1987. Hélène Cixous's *The Name of Oedipus: Song of the Forbidden Body* also gives to Jocasta's desiring body the central lyric voice of the text. The play was initially written in free verse as lyrics for a hymnic opera by André Boucourechliev at the Avignon theatre festival in 1978; it was later reworked in English as a dance/theatre/operatic piece in New York entitled *Jocasta* and performed in 1998 by an exclusively female company, Voice and Vision, with music by Ruth Schonthal and choreography by Christine Sang (*New York Times*, 11 June 1998). A major French feminist theorist and writer, whose work has been much translated into English, Cixous aims to recover subjective female experience in a male-dominated culture through a form of 'woman's writing' that decensors her relation to her sexuality and her culturally controlled body. Deconstructing and reconstructing traditional archetypes and myths can form a part of this process.

Cixous's Jocasta must finally escape not fate, but self-denial and the names and identities given her by men.[9] She is initially obsessed with fears of abandonment, due to her father's rejection of her as he went off to die alone. She claims to have known the truth of Oedipus' identity from the first moment, but chooses not to know, and even to claim that their union benefits from the close identity between the two. Refusing to be bound by the demands of patriarchal conventions (including incest and patricide) and language, the passionate, unconditionally loving Jocasta entreats Oedipus to forget the world outside their love and remain in an enveloping primal night/sea/womb world in which the boundaries

---

[9] For further discussion see Pavlides (1986) and Freeman (1998).

between self and other dissolve, the two become one, and gendered and familial (mother, father, child) identities break down. Oedipus, under pressure from the demands of a city imagined as a demanding female (262), the allurements of fame, and his own myth, at first withdraws into guilt and silence. Jocasta's death occurs not by hanging but because she welcomes and gives way to it after Oedipus' withdrawal; she dies in the company of an androgynous Tiresias, who has adopted the form of a desiring young man and transports her beyond life, singing a song with which Jocasta's mother lulled her to sleep as a child. Oedipus arrives too late to accept Jocasta's bisexual redefinition of himself in a utopian space beyond ordinary use of words, binary opposition, divinity, law, possession, and time. 'Nous continue', he says, using a singular verb for the plural 'we'.[10] The text, which refuses a linear narrative and traditional tragic structure, similarly underlines Jocasta's overall rejection of the dominant symbolic order.

Revisions of Oedipus by male artists can also focus ecstatically and defiantly on a passionate mother–son bond, however. Steven Berkoff's *Greek* intertwines class and sexual issues. When his working-class Eddy discovers his identity, he rejects the self-punishment of Oedipus, preferring to sink himself right back into the body of his delightful wife-mother (see further Macintosh, Chapter 12). For Berkoff, liberation from Oedipal guilt is clearly tied to social, political, and linguistic liberation. Along similar lines, in Pasolini's 1967 film version, *Edipo Re*, the representation of the myth in Sophocles' play is prefaced by a modern interlude set in a rural town in 1920s fascist Italy that echoes Pasolini's own past. Here a husband (an army officer) is passionately jealous of his warmly maternal wife and the newborn son who worships her. Whereas the baby first focuses on Jocasta's face in a beautiful, sunny field during a moment accompanied by powerful classical music, the father stares angrily into his son's baby carriage and seizes his son's tiny ankles menacingly during a night visit to his crib. Pasolini's Oedipus later wins the actress playing the mother as Jocasta, accomplishing as well by implication the baby's Oedipal wish. (Laius is played by a different actor in both the frame and central story, but remains a hostile figure throughout.) The queen, who makes only one public appearance (as Oedipus' seductive

---

[10] See Judith Miller's introduction to Cixous (1994), 250.

prize for silencing the Sphinx) in the Thebes of this play, is largely confined to a harem where she childishly plays with other women and otherwise devotes herself to her new husband's bed without (apparently) producing children. Indeed, in this version the couple knowingly make love as mother and son after their discovery of the truth. Pasolini asserted elsewhere, in deliberate response to the Freudian taboo, that the mother–son bond was never meant to be violated or prohibited.[11] Oedipus' final confrontation with Jocasta's desirable nude body (also the audience's first view of it), hanging above their bed, leads to an explosive blinding scene. In this film, even the relation with Oedipus' loving foster parents is developed at sufficient length to enhance the pathos of the hero's double loss of family and country. In the central story, Oedipus is as fascinated by Tiresias' role as androgynous flute-player as by his role as prophet; the film closes with the blind Oedipus, led by Tiresias' assistant in the inner story, Angelo, in a now post-fascist, and less idealized modern location (Bologna, Pasolini's birthplace). The blind, symbolically androgynous young man now plays the flute and goes to his destiny in the field where the baby of the opening scenes first fixed on his mother's face.

Pasolini's Oedipus retains throughout the film visible traces of his youth that we have seen from his first appearance as an adolescent in Corinth: biting the back of his hand at moments of anxiety, losing his temper, and acting impulsively. His obsessive fear of his destiny and the complete complicity of his character and fate pronounced at Delphi predominates throughout this story of self-discovery that is far more elaborated than in Sophocles' original. The Japanese director Suzuki's *Oedipus*, a cut and lightly adapted version of Sophocles, retains more traditional gender roles for Oedipus and Jocasta, but focuses, like Pasolini, almost entirely on Oedipus' self-discovery.[12] The play's political dimensions

---

[11] Petkovic (1997), 54. In the Blue Light Theater's 1998 *Oedipus*, written and directed by Dare Clubb at the Classic Stage Company in New York, the play's naive Oedipus reacts to the oracle by rushing back to Corinth to fulfil it by killing his father and sleeping with his mother, only to discover that he is a foster child. As Merope puts it to Oedipus after the love-making, 'We'll suffer for this, probably, but so what?' The four-hour, exhausting, often parodic epic then followed the hero to Thebes. (As reported in reviews by Ben Brantley, *New York Times*, 12 October 1998 and Vincent Canby, *New York Times*, 18 October 1998.)

[12] This discussion is based on performances at Delphi, Greece, in 2000 and in New York City in 2001.

recede into the background, thus enhancing the familial drama. Creon becomes a figure suggestive of menacing father as well as uncle. His first appearance, behind the central door of the set through a glass that simultaneously functioned as a mirror, made Creon's entry suggest at first the return of a paternal ghost in which Oedipus could, if he were aware of it, see a mirrored older double of himself haunting the palace. Oedipus' first scene with Jocasta takes place on an empty stage, thus enhancing its intimacy. The mother stands above her seated son, visibly embodying for the audience her maternal status and authority. Later, a chorus of three elders is replaced by a group of women in white who are not visible to those on-stage and come from outside the stage building; they suggest a closing-in of divine or psychological forces in a significantly female form. Jocasta's recognition of the truth is expressed by a single, terrifying turn toward the back of the stage. She stands motionless before the mirrored door until her exit. The play ends with Oedipus' self-discovery, and eliminates elaborating on Jocasta's hanging, the blinding, and the final public confrontation with chorus, Creon, and Oedipus' daughters. Oedipus remains the central figure in this version, but by keeping the primal familial realities so visible on stage during the entire search for the truth, the play focuses the audience's attention on the underlying archetypal sexual dynamics.

CROSS-DRESSING IN PERFORMANCE

As in *Bad Women*, a number of performances of Greek tragedy have involved all-male, variously cross-dressed, or more rarely, all-female casts. In cases like Sir Peter Hall's performance of Aeschylus' *Oresteia* at the National Theatre in London in 1981, the choice to echo the all-male casting of the original Greek performance aimed deliberately to underline the 'sex war' that the poet Tony Harrison enhanced in his translation, as the following lines from the chorus's description of the sacrifice of Iphigeneia in *Agamemnon* illustrate:

so a Father can take his own she-child   take her
and kill her   his she-child   his own flesh and blood

The war-effort wants it   the war-effort gets it
the war for one woman   the whore-war   the whore-war

> a virgin's blood launches the ships off to Troy
> Her shrillings   beseechings   her cries   Papa   Papa
> Iphigeneia   a virgin   a virgin
>
> what's a virgin to hawks and to war-lords?[13]

As Harrison put the casting issue in the programme notes: 'Though it is a fact that men played all the parts of *The Oresteia* in 458 B.C., that in itself is not of course sufficient justification for our wish to have an all male company. The victory of father-right over mother-right is the social pendulum of the trilogy. To have women play in our production would have seemed as if we in the twentieth century were smugly assuming that the sex war is over and that the oppressiveness of the patriarchal code existed only in past times. The maleness of the piece is like a vacuum-sealed container keeping this ancient issue fresh.'[14]

In the case of Japanese performances, such as that by the Japanese director Yukio Ninagawa in his 1978 *Medea*,[15] the all-male cast permitted the exploitation of Japanese theatre traditions like Noh, Kabuki, and Bunraku, which not only use exclusively male actors, but have established conventions for different types of roles. Thus the Kabuki-trained actor playing Medea, Tokusaburo Arashi, could shift from the voice and gestures of a trained actor of female parts, or *onnagata*, to those of a male figure in order to express Medea's androgynous shift from beleaguered female to empowered, heroic avenger. This split was underlined when the actor took off his female costume with prominent breasts to reveal a male body dressed in a red robe with a still female face. Overall, the choice to adopt an all-male cast can emphasize visibly that the plays were composed and acted by males for a predominantly male audience and invites the audience to view the plays as about men 'playing the other'—that is, playing out through outrageous female characters writ-large aspects of the self otherwise denied to men[16]—rather than an attempt to capture a female subjectivity. All-female productions, such as that of Cixous's *Jocasta* mentioned above, underline the reappropriation of the texts by female subjects,

[13] Tony Harrison (1986), 195–6.   [14] R.B. Parker (1986), 353.
[15] For extensive information on performances worldwide and further discussion, see Smethurst (2000) and (2002), which elaborate on the play's feminist message, and Foley (1999) and (1999–2000).
[16] See Zeitlin (1985).

whereas the playing of a single male part by a female actor, such as Shiraishi Kayoko, who played Dionysus in Suzuki's *Bacchae*, can be used to draw attention to the god's androgynous nature.

In the USA, however, an important tradition has developed of pointed cross-dressing by male actors to call attention to the actor's female impersonation in revisions of Greek myth and tragedy that range from exaggerated and serious to pointedly camp. In New York, this tradition began with Charles Ludlam, whose Ridiculous Theatrical Company performed his version of *Medea* in 1987, continued with plays written and performed by a former member of the group, Ethyl Eichelberger, and resurfaced in 2001 in Bradford Louryk's one-man performance entitled *Klytaemnestra's Unmentionables* at the Here Arts Center.

Ludlam's Ridiculous Theatrical Company aimed from the mid-1960s to transform 'what is in low esteem into the highest form of expression',[17] to adopt an approach that has been called primitive, strictly non-academic, colourful, outrageous, melodramatic, vaudevillian, parodic, often highly stylized, yet at the same time painful, immediate, and involving. Most of the major female parts were played by gay men, although women were included in the company. For Ludlam, the male actor's playing of the Other is a profound and serious political and theatrical statement. 'For example, certain women have played Camille in modern times and failed because they were asking to be taken seriously.'[18] 'If a man plays Camille . . . you begin to think it is horrible, but in the end you are either moved or won over. You believe in the character beyond the gender of the actor, and no one who has experienced that can go back. In such cases, this theatre is political in the highest sense of influence.'[19] 'Drag is something people are prejudiced against, because women are considered inferior beings. A woman putting on the pants, on the other hand, has moved up. So to defiantly say that women are worthwhile creatures, and that I'll put my whole soul and being into creating this woman and give her everything I have, including my emotions (and the most taboo thing is to experience feminine emotions), and to take myself seriously in the face of ridicule, that's it. That is the highest turn of the statement. It's different than wanting to make women more

[17] Dasgupta (1979), 78.   [18] Dasgupta (1979), 90.
[19] Dasgupta (1979), 83–4.

like men. It allows audiences to experience the universality of emotion, rather than believe that women are one species and men another, and what one feels the other never does. Even the women's movement is based on conflict and anger; my Camille is synthesis, an altogether different tactic.'[20]

Ludlam's *Medea*, written in 1984, condenses Euripides' original into strong, accessible prose and highlights the deliberately foreign, anti-democratic, anti-moderate, anti-fatalistic, intelligent, and unapologetically passionate nature of the heroine. The play closes with a caustically ironic statement that throws cultural prejudices back into Jason's face: 'Why should I feel guilt or shame? I am not responsible for these. I am not responsible for my actions. They were destined before I was born.'[21] Though designed as a vehicle for Ludlam himself, the part of Medea was alternately played after his death in 1987 by two other members of the company, his successor Everett Quinton, and a female member of the Company, Black-Eyed Susan.[22] The Nurse's role, originally written for Quinton, was considerably expanded to include that of a highly dramatic Messenger, chorus, and a frequent companion who reacts and signals pointedly to Medea throughout. This enhanced the audience's open pleasure in Medea's outrageous play-acting for both those on and off stage, including shrieks, evil laughs, dramatic gestures, sudden and witty shifts in mood, and self-conscious irony. This black-gowned Medea is a veritable virtuosa in suffering who relishes her revenge with appealing intensity. The children are played by large dolls, which diffuses the terror of the infanticide, as does Medea's departure seated comfortably in a large dragon that glided past Jason across the stage accompanied by flashing lights.

Ethyl (James) Eichelberger, a classically trained actor who joined Ludlam's company in 1973, eventually moved on to imitate Ludlam by becoming writer and performer of his own shows.[23] He joined the world of Lower Eastside clubs devoted to a

---

[20] Dasgupta (1979), 88.   [21] Ludlam (1989), 813.
[22] According to the introduction by Steven Samuels to Ludlam (1989), xviii, Ludlam was reluctant to play a part that involved killing children. I would like to thank Black-Eyed Susan (Susan Carlson) for her information about this performance. My discussion is based on a video of *Medea* with Black-Eyed Susan as Medea and Quinton as Nurse, available at the Library for Performing Arts at the Lincoln Center, New York.
[23] Parnes (1988), 272.

range of performance art, including transvestite performance in Eichelberger's case marked by its unusual refusal to lip-synch (feign singing previously recorded music) popular songs; instead he wrote his own and accompanied them on the accordion or piano. His performances, like Ludlam's, recycled and reinvented classical material, but were more radically revised, less polished, more presentational, and constantly evolving in performance. There were solo and group versions of many scripts. By displaying a tattoo of himself as a cross-dressed male angel on his back while playing female roles, by his direct conversations with the spectators and asides, his exaggerated make-up,[24] huge wigs, and striking costumes, his fast-paced delivery, his use of film clips, his compressed use of time and space, his gymnastics, songs, and dances, his magic tricks and juggling, Eichelberger purposely discouraged his audience from 'suspending disbelief'.[25]

His first important show, presented at La Mama, Etc on East 4th Street, was a collage of Racine's *Phèdre*, Sophocles' *Oedipus*, and French cabaret in which Eichelberger took all the parts from the chorus to Tiresias. The choice of play was a tribute to the influence of Sarah Bernhardt on his conception of female roles.[26] As Robert Baker's review described it:

He does this—and it's a brilliant tour de force—with the help of various props: a sexy torso sculpture for Hippolytus; a voodoo doll with feathers, chicken feet and large bisexual organs for Tiresias; a kind of strawless scarecrow for Jocasta; various other 'fetish dolls' and milliner's mannequins for the other personae.

He uses voice changes as well, and different bodily poses. But the fascinating thing is the flux between the characters, the way they don't quite change 'enough' between speeches, so that Oedipus and Jocasta get mixed up, or Phedre's identity is jumbled up with that of her maid or even the object of her desire . . . None of this is played camp, ever really played for laughs. It's funny of course, but most of all it's eerie, as is much of Ludlam's own theatre.[27]

Echoing the gay community's fascination with Hollywood idols, Eichelberger's attraction to major female roles in Greek tragedy

---

[24] Jeffreys (1996), vii.
[25] Parnes (1988), 329–30. I am deeply indebted to Joe Jeffreys for providing me with tapes, scripts, and other information. This discussion depends in large part on his work and the earlier dissertation of Parnes (1988).
[26] Jeffreys (1996), 70.   [27] *Soho Weekly News*, 8 December 1977, 70.

and myth (Phaedra, Jocasta, Medea, Klytemnestra, Medusa, Ariadne), and historical queens (Nefertiti, Catherine the Great, Elizabeth I or Mary, Queen of Scots, Saint Joan, Carlotta, Empress of Mexico), represented an opportunity to express his tabooed feminine (emotional, inconsistent, passionate, angry, vain) side in the great roles of the western tradition.[28] 'I chose to be a drag performer ... because I was tired of being a character actor who played weird people, because I know it affects your life. What you play on-stage affects who you are, and at one point I said I only wanted to play the most glamorous, most magnificent, strong women in the world, that have ever been in history. And I do it, and it has turned me into a better person. I play only women I admire ... If I thought I was degrading women, I would stop doing it.'[29] Nevertheless, while his more contemplative Klytemnestra in his 1987 *Klytemnestra: The Nightingale of Argos* mixes an obsessive grief for Iphigeneia with ill-treatment of an Electra she could not love (see Figure 8), the attraction to impassioned 'evil queenery' generally prevails.[30] His Medea begins her opening speech with:

> Am I an evil woman
> tis *you* must be my judge
> listen impartially
> be equanimitous
> then loose the venomous hate from your heart
> spit at the mirror Medea
> the image you see will be yours
>
>   . . .
>
> are we not one tonight?
> fear not the awful truth
> Medea seeks vengeance for you.

Or, as the prologue to *Medea* states: 'It is written that wisdom and passion are not possible together in the same room at the same time, but we promise you passion. You can supply the wisdom later.'

Eichelberger's *Medea* not only focuses, as do all his pieces, on his heroine's point of view before all others, but deliberately echoes the relation of the drag queen to society and takes on larger issues

---

[28] Parnes (1988), 272, 276.   [29] Parnes (1988), 296.

[30] All quotations from Eichelberger's *Medea* are from an unpublished script, courtesy of Joe Jeffreys.

FIGURE 8. Ethyl Eichelberger as Klytemnestra in *Klytemnestra: The Nightingale of Argos* at P.S. 122, New York (1987).

of identity and representation. 'People will strike at one who glitters'; 'I'm an exotic—we're not popular this year!'; 'I tried to be normal, and what did it get me'.[31] Similarly, in *Jocasta, or Boy Crazy*, Eichelberger created a paedophile (Jo/e) attracted to young boys. 'But he was so young, Tiresias, and he was pretty and he liked me,' says a surviving Jocasta in a post-disaster dialogue with Tiresias.[32] She, however, does not wish to hear the prophecy Tiresias has for her, hysterically repeating, 'I don't want to know.'[33] As Eichelberger commented, 'My heart goes out to people who are attracted to children.'[34]

Bradford Louryk's 2001 revival of the Ludlam–Eichelberger tradition in his one-man *Klytaemnestra's Unmentionables* at New

---

[31] Quotations from Parnes (1988), 279.
[32] Jeffreys (1996), 101.
[33] Unpublished audio tape, courtesy of Joe Jeffreys.
[34] Parnes (1988), 293.

York's Here Arts Center both absorbs and changes the tradition of his mentors.[35] The piece (with text adaptations by Rob Grace and directed by Jennifer Wineman) offers a sequence of monologues from Klytaemnestra, Electra, a Fury, Medea, and Phèdre. A bare set includes a bathtub, red drapes, and a dressing table at which Louryk changes wigs and adjusts make-up for each part. While he changes his costume, the audience sees voice-over film-footage of Louryk practising and discussing his own transvestite performance. Other distancing effects include Louryk's visible sideburns, which testify, like Eichelberger's tattoo, to the actor's male identity. Louryk adopts the lip-synching of drag performance but performs to his own voice, thus opening the possibility for tensions between voice and body movement and creating the effect of a ventriloquism in which the performer becomes his own dummy and as well the victim of the larger narrative in which s/he is embedded. For example, the Fury's out-of-control body is deliberately at odds with her voice, which is devoid of the wrath she represents. Louryk insists that he does not give 'a drag performance. It is an exhibition of both the complexity and subtlety of the female body, the female voice' (programme notes). Each character has her own vocal style and physicality. The acting is pointedly non-naturalistic, aiming at a magnitude like that created by Sarah Bernhardt at the Comédie Française.

Louryk's pastiched texts represent an attempt to take ridiculous theatre to a new level of intellectuality and linguistic complexity. Louryk's portrait of a Klytaemnestra paralysed by fear of retribution was influenced by Greek tragedy, Charles Mee's 1994 *Agamemnon*, and Jean-Paul Sartre's *Les Mouches* (as Louryk put it in interview, Klytaemnestra's 'dead white look' is borrowed from Sartre's guilt-ridden heroine with her deathly white make-up); his Electra by Aeschylus, Sophocles, and Euripides, *Les Mouches*, and Eichelberger; his Medea by Ludlam, Heiner Müller, Cherubini's opera *Medea* as performed by Maria Callas, and the story of Andrea Yates, the troubled Houston housewife who drowned her five children in 2001; his Phaedra by Euripides, Racine,

---

[35] I would like to thank Bradford Louryk for an extensive interview and a tape of his performance, which I also saw live. Joe Jeffreys reports that other actors doing imitations of Eichelberger still appear sporadically on both the East and West coasts.

Eichelberger, and Sarah Kane's *Phaedra's Love*.[36] The bathtub, as the site of Klytaemnestra's killing of Agamemnon, Electra's enforced washing of the family's dirty laundry, Medea's infanticide, and Phaedra's suicide, creates continuity between the scenes. Medea's connection with Yates and 1950s housewifery is underlined by her apron, bizarrely marked with a child's red-rhinestone handprint, tinkling spoon earring and a bracelet hung with domestic items (see Figure 9). Electra, psychologically arrested at the moment of her father's death, wears a child's dress that no longer fits. Klytaemnestra's jewellery is formed in the shape of foetuses. Louryk's concern with voice and body offers a performative

FIGURE 9.   Bradford Louryk as Medea in *Klytaemnestra's Unmentionables*, Here Arts Center, New York (2001). Photograph by Emilie Baltz, reproduced courtesy of Bradford Louryk.

[36] Sartre's *Les Mouches*, Cherubini's *Medea* and Sarah Kane's *Phaedra's Love* were first performed in 1943, 1797, and 1996 respectively. Maria Callas first sang Cherubini's *Medea* in 1953.

analogue to the feminist concern discussed above that involves enhancing the 'voice' of marginalized tragic females and locating their subjective presence more pointedly in the desires of the female body; yet it is motivated by different concerns. Louryk argues that his masculine distance from the female role enhances his ability to play the other; female impersonation liberates the male actor by giving him two sexual identities and new modes of self-expression.

These three female impersonators apparently modernize the impulse to 'play the other' very likely present, if in a different form, in the originals. The performance draws attention to the motives for and theatrical opportunities embodied in this projection. In addition, Louryk's performance experiments with the problem of a male actor projecting a non-naturalistic female character through voice, gesture, and mask (he communicates the part far more with body than face), a problem faced in a different theatrical space in Athens as well. In both cases the formal, artificial quality of voice and gesture enhance the audience's focus on the words of the actor and the shape of his complex identity.

Revising Greek myth or drama to serve as the basis of new plays by all-female performance groups was particularly prevalent in the USA in the 1970s and early 1980s: both the Rhode Island Feminist Theater's 1974 *Persephone's Return* and Eleanor Hakim's 1978 musical *A Lesbian Play for Lucy* by Medusa's Revenge in New York used the Demeter/Persephone story. The first examined the mother–daughter bond and rape,[37] whereas the second staged a triangular relation between a butch Athena, a daughter Persephone, and a terrible mother Hecate. The Women's Ensemble of the Berkeley Stage Company's winter 1975–6 *Antigone Prism* explored the performers' personal relation to Antigone's courage and values;[38] Actors' Sorority planned to stage *The Rex Family*, the Oedipus story from Jocasta's point of view, in Kansas City, Missouri, in the late 1970s. In New York City, the Westbeth Playwrights' Feminist Collective presented in January 1975 a *Medea* revised by Gloria Albee that deleted the heroine's murder of her children;[39] Spiderwoman's *Lysistrata Numbah* in 1977

---

[37] Canning (1996), 134–6.   [38] Canning (1996), 178–9.
[39] The typescript is available in the Lincoln Center Library for the Performing Arts. See Van Zyl Smit (2001), 270. The Corinthians kill two of Medea's seven children, however.

focused on male abuse of woman both publicly and privately;[40] Emmatroupe's 1979 *Against Silence* stressed the disruptive effects of Iphigeneia's sacrifice on the mother–daughter relation between Clytemnestra, Iphigeneia, and Electra;[41] the Women's Experimental Theatre performed *The Daughter's Cycle*, which culminated in the play *Electra Speaks*, at the Interart Center in New York from 1977–80; the Split Britches Theater Company created their own version of Euripides' *Alcestis* entitled *Honey, I'm Home* at Hampshire College in 1989.[42] The attraction to Greek sources was in some cases based on a feminist quest to challenge and destabilize myths of origin and formed part of a larger move in feminist psychology to restore psychic health through female archetypes. The mode of creating and performing these pieces was characteristic of feminist theatre at the time. My discussion here will stress the ambitious and best-documented performance by the Women's Experimental Theatre.

The Women's Experimental Theatre (WET), founded by Clare Coss, Sondra Segal, and Roberta Sklar, offered in *The Daughter's Cycle* a theatrical exploration of women in the patriarchal family and the female journey from childhood to maturity. Founded in part out of feminist disenchantment with the sexism of New Left politics in the 1960s and 1970s, the group turned to a collective exploration and deconstruction of the formation and enforcement of gender roles by cultural institutions; it challenged female infantilization and subjugation in the family and the family romance.[43] Borrowing from feminist consciousness-raising techniques, *The Daughter's Cycle* grew out of large workshops that included up to 150 women and aimed to unearth what were felt to be the lost untold stories of women. Although the three founders retained firm artistic control, they perceived audience members as 'acting partners' and aimed to facilitate their self-recognition and change; at the end of each performance the cast and all-female audience members recited a matrilineage in which they named maternal ancestors. Women played all the parts, including the silent male

---

[40] Canning (1996), 168–9.   [41] Foley (forthcoming *a*).

[42] See Curb *et al.* (1979), who comment on the significant role that Greek myth played in US feminist theatre (65) and list feminist theatre groups and their productions. This article cites *The Rex Family*, which was never actually performed.

[43] Unless otherwise noted, my sources here come from the self-description by the group in Coss *et al.* (1980) and (1983).

characters in *Electra Speaks*; the performance was designed for
the female spectator and at least once a week the audience was
exclusively female to provide for the most unfettered possible
response.[44] Part I, *Daughters*, explored the complex and ambivalent mother–daughter relation; Part II, *Sister/Sister*, looked at the
patterns of alliance and betrayal in relations between female siblings in the family context; Part III, *Electra Speaks*, studied
women in the 'archetypal family' of the *Oresteia*, Clytemnestra,
Electra, and Iphigeneia as mother, daughter, and sister, but included a Cassandra, who tries to persuade Clytemnestra that she is
not the 'other woman' but a fellow rape victim, and an Athena,
who as a glib lawyer concludes her defence of Orestes with the
words, 'I tell you if that woman were alive today I'd haul her into
family court.' Overall the play posed the question 'Whose interests
are served by the institutionalized division between women in the
family?'[45] WET's Electra moved tentatively to self-recognition,
separation, speech, and survival through observing the experiences
of mother, sister, and herself. Electra's voice opened the piece
by narrating 'the old story', while the other performers mimed
physical and vocal images depicting the myth.[46] Short scenes
involving direct address, commentary, and repetition followed.
For example, a monologue by Clytemnestra stressed the contradictions of Orestes' relation to herself:

> his mother became his food
>
> . . .
>
> he's turned her into a tit
> A jug a tit a boob
>
> . . .
>
> This baby, this infant, this boy
> has colonized her body . . .
> he eats her at his will.
>
> . . .
>
> he creates his institutions
> religion, family, law
> philosophy education
> at night he sucks her titty
> By day he wreaks his vengeance
> This baby man hates his mommy . . .

[44] Canning (1996), 180.   [45] Coss *et al.* (1983), 241.
[46] Malnig and Rosenthal (1993), 207.

> he thinks she keeps him alive
> he fears her breast is hers . . .
> he fucks her, he rapes his mommy
> he rams it down her throat . . .
> he begs for her forgiveness . . .
> this baby man
> he's just a mass of contradictions
> claims reason for himself
> institutionalizes his hatred
> gives her his seat on the bus
> wages war on Indochina
> and nods off in front of the TV
> and dreams of mommy
> and dreams of power[47]

The all-female cast members enacted male roles, deliberately questioning fixed gender identities.[48] Each performer also assumed Electra's identity at some point, thus defining her as everywoman or everydaughter. In her first attempt to speak for herself Electra announced:

> Electra is trying to speak
> She is not a speaker
> But she has something she wants to say
>
> . . .
>
> she wants to speak
> she eats
> she talks——she eats
> talks eats eats talks
> talk talk talk talk talk talk talk
>
> . . .
>
> she's holding her breath
> she can't speak
> there's probably more she could say

Electra discovered that gaining autonomy does not require devaluation of her mother or idealization of her absent father. After confronting her mother about her surrender to Iphigeneia's sacrifice, or even potentially to the sacrifice of Electra herself, Electra said to her father/the audience: 'I don't know how to be any more. I can either be your daughter or my self. I don't know how to act

---

[47] Parts quoted in Malnig and Rosenthal (1993), 208; Canning (1996), 164–5.
[48] Malnig and Rosenthal (1993), 207.

any more. I used to pass. I used to pass well. I can't pass any more.
I don't know how to talk any more. If you hesitate for one second,
you won't get what you need. Because they don't want that . . .
They want someone who knows . . . If you say what you think,
you're done for . . . If you do this—you're done for. If you do
that—you're done for. I don't know how to act any more . . . '
Finally, she moves tentatively from sorrow to laughter and a new
life:

She tugs	She belches
She lugs	She is passing air
She heaves	She is breathing
She hauls	She signals
. . .	
	She has never done this before
She stands firm[49]	

By 1985, however, Segal and Sklar, the remaining members of the
company, decided to stop performing theatre; contemporary feminists were in their view now confronting different issues involving
race, class, and gender within their own community.[50]

   Both Emmatroupe and WET developed experimental methods
of acting and training actors designed to suit their feminist aesthetic, including Brechtian distancing techniques. WET's Sondra
Segal, for example, spoke and changed expression so rapidly that
her characters became a series of projective masks. WET actors
mixed social role, character, and self in their performance; they
came from a variety of backgrounds and in all shapes and sizes.
They developed exercises to be shared with audiences, including
those that articulated silence.[51] Split Britches, however, brought
the audience into the process of acting and cross-dressing more
aggressively. The group, consisting of Deborah Margolin, Peggy
Shaw, and Lois Weaver, had been assigned to do a version of
Alcestis during a college residency at Hampshire College in 1989.
Honey, I'm Home, their new version, included personal material
that highlighted the production process. At one point Peggy
(Admetus) pretended to forget her lines, and when prompted by

---

   [49] Both quotations in Malnig and Rosenthal (1993), 210.
   [50] Malnig and Rosenthal (1993), 212, and Canning (1996), 209.
   [51] On Emmatroupe see Johnson (1983); on WET, Malnig and Rosenthal (1993),
210, 203, 205; and Canning (1996), 93.

Lois (Alcestis), Peggy burst out with 'I can't take this!...I said I didn't want so many lines. And I didn't want to play a man.' Deb, Peggy, and Lois then sat down on-stage to discuss their roles, their theatrical process, and theatre in general. The play became as much about themselves as about Alcestis, who in any case returned in the final scene not as Lois, but in a new form as the spirit of women who died through male abuse. Reversing normal practice in naturalistic theatre, their feminist theatre made the subtext the text and permitted each actor to develop her own roles. In *Honey, I'm Home*, Split Britches worked with a mixed cast of students. The play's humorous exploration of the social construction of male roles included the incorporation of Muddy Water's 'I'm a Man' into the text; the most 'authentic' male in the cast was the experienced Lois Weaver.[52]

More recent productions, such as *Bad Women* or the play-reading of John Epperson's *My Deah* (*Medea* reset in the contemporary South) at the New York Theatre Workshop in fall 2001, seem more representative of current trends in cross-dressing in US performances based on Greek tragedy. The inclusion of a few male actors playing women in both these performances was neither remarked on nor explicitly exploited in ways that it had been before. Bradford Louryk's insistence on permitting actors the full range of opportunities for performance may be one element here. Another may be a declining focus on gender difference alone in favour of commonalities between the sexes, or on a range of sexual identities that transcend biological gender.

OTHER NEW VERSIONS

Other contemporary productions or revisions of the originals have used Greek tragedy to explore and question different gender issues. Here I shall simply sketch briefly some examples of a range of possibilities. I shall stress recent idiosyncratic performances from the USA and Britain and avoid discussion of the play that has proved most popular as a framework for revision of gender issues in Greek tragedy, *Medea*, as well as multiple new versions and performances of Antigone, Phaedra, and the women in the house of Atreus. Many of these plays have been discussed from this

---

[52] Hamilton (1993), 138–40, 144.

perspective elsewhere, but space is the relevant factor here.[53] Versions of Antigone use her female identity to express a range of cultural, religious, and political resistance; new Phaedras, like Jocasta, explore female social subordination, marriage, and sexuality; revised Clytemnestras still take on politics and maternity. Medea has been used to explore feminist rage (above all in the Irish poet Brendan Kennelly's *Medea*) and female exploitation, and to ground the mistreatment of women as Other historically in racism, colonialism, and class tensions.

Several new versions have approached through Greek tragedy issues relating to women's entrapment in their own beautiful but ageing bodies. Susan Yankowitz's *Phaedra in Delirium*, a new version of Euripides' *Hippolytus* also influenced by Seneca and Ovid, was performed at the Classic Stage Company in New York, 1998. Her modern Phaedra is an ageing woman in her early forties, recently married to a wealthy and successful Theseus. Shortly after their wedding, Theseus has left her on an isolated ranch with her horse-mad and as yet pre-sexual stepson Hippolytus and gone off to philander on an increasingly extended business trip. Hippolytus and Theseus are played by the same actor, so that the son is literally the image of the older man with whom Phaedra fell in love at the time of his first encounter with her sister Ariadne. Age and ageing were as critical to this play as female isolation and oppression by cultural standards and expectations.[54]

Ellen McLaughlin's *Helen*, performed in spring 2002 at New York's Public Theater, was a revision of Euripides' *Helen* that addressed female icons in contemporary as well as ancient society, especially film stars like Marilyn Monroe. The play provokes a more complex understanding of those fascinating figures whom we love to hate and watch self-destruct. McLaughlin's Helen has remained perfectly preserved in an upscale Egyptian hotel throughout the Trojan War (loosely linked with the First World War in this play), attending to her beautiful body in the company of her recalcitrant storytelling maid, but bored and frustrated as she awaits rescue from Menelaus and re-engagement with history. When Menelaus finally arrives he is accompanied by the divinely

---

[53] On Medea see Hall, Macintosh, and Taplin (2000), Foley (1999–2000), Wren (2002), and various articles in McDonald and Walton (2002); on Clytemnestra, see Foley (forthcoming *a*) and on Phaedra, see Foley (forthcoming *b*).

[54] See further Foley (forthcoming *b*)

created image of Helen for which the war was actually fought (in Euripides the image disappears at his arrival). Faced with a choice between the complex real wife and the image, which perfectly lives up to her role, the war-weary Menelaus opts for the image. Too many people have died to make an innocent Helen possible. Helen is left with the option of eternal entrapment in her myth and a life entirely defined by surfaces, or changing her story and becoming a real but anonymous woman who ages and becomes herself a story-teller. The heroine's final decision, not made at the conclusion, will presumably be conditioned in part by her encounters earlier in the play with Io, another mythical sexually harassed victim of divine violence, who stands in part for the world's nomadic female refu-gees, and the goddess Athena, who, like Menelaus, illuminates the futility of wars.

Greek tragedies are inclined to blame female figures for every-thing that goes wrong, in part because women are viewed as funda-mentally less self-controlled than men. In plays like Euripides' *Bacchae*, the entire female population of Thebes is maddened by the god Dionysus and takes off to worship him in the mountains; eventually, the women, including the queen mother, Agave, tear apart the young king Pentheus who has come to spy on their rites. Both Caryl Churchill and David Lan's *A Mouthful of Birds* (pub-lished 1986) and Maureen Duffy's *Rites* (premiered in 1969) offer an enactment of unanimous female violence in their revisions of the *Bacchae*, but claim a new perspective on it. In these plays, Agave and the women become the central characters; female violence is not a myth but a reality. Richard Schechner's revision of *Bacchae*, *Dionysus in 69*, discussed in the previous chapter by Froma Zeitlin, takes a more androgynous approach to its own climactic violence.

In *A Mouthful of Birds*, *Bacchae* serves as a parallel text to scenes of contemporary life; the two worlds converge in the final dismem-berment by the female characters of a young man, Derek, who has put on female clothes. Gradually possessed by resistance to their lives and social roles, by ecstatic dance, by alcohol, love, fear, anxiety, memory, habit, and by Euripides' plot, the women move from asserting their wills (Doreen/Agave says 'no' to an aggressive neighbour) and isolated acts of violence (Doreen slashes a neigh-bour who turns the radio too loud) to full-scale scapegoating. The play reveals the pleasures of violence as well as ecstasy. These 'bacchants' are unwilling to return from their escape 'to the mountain' and all of their lives are changed by this event. As the character Lena says at the conclusion: 'Everyday is a struggle because I haven't forgotten anything. I remember I enjoyed doing it. It's nice to make someone alive and it's nice to make someone dead. Either way. That power is what I like best in the world. The struggle is everyday not to use it.'[55]

Rites, first performed at the National Theatre in London in 1969, finds a group of more or less socially and economically powerless women performing such daily rituals as combing, making-up, and complaining in a public lavatory; they become gradually empowered by and enthusiastic about their artificially segregated, claustrophobic environment. (The audience sees the lavatory built by stage hands before the play begins.) After caring for a woman who was provoked to attempt suicide due to male abuse and surrounding the derelict Old Mother Brown with a threatening dance, the women turn on and dismember a figure in a coat, suit, and short hair whom they interpret as a male spy. It turns out to be a woman. Ada, the lavatory attendant who serves as an Agave figure, has the body thrown down the incinerator and the women hurriedly part ways in conspiratorial silence. The audience itself becomes eavesdroppers or spies on the catastrophic living out of dangerous clichés about gender. Rather than resisting the mis-ogynistic clichés of Greek tragedy, these plays enact and even find pleasure in a politically motivated and highly ambivalent move from passivity to violent female resistance to the status quo. Like many adaptations, *Rites* was explicitly created to offer promising roles to distinguished actresses frustrated by the dearth of them.[56]

Finally, a number of new versions attacked gender issues through the tragedies, but transformed the tone and genre of the originals to mix comedy with serious tragic action. Among the many performances and adaptations of Euripides' *Trojan Women* that aim to evoke contemporary situations in which women and children have become the surviving victims of often futile wars and brutal victors, the adaptation by the American playwright Charles Mee, *The Trojan Women: A Love Story*, alone attempts to take his audience past the bleak conclusion of Euripides' *Trojan Women* and *Hecuba*. The first half of the play borrows from both

---

[55] Churchill and Lan (1986), 70.
[56] Duffy (1983), 26. For further discussion, see Hersh (1992).

Euripides' plays, a range of music, and fragments from popular culture and literature, but concludes with the departure of a cowering, shell-shocked Aeneas and other male survivors for a new destiny. Hecuba makes Aeneas promise to found a society that will ultimately avenge Troy by conquering the Greeks. The final section of the play takes place in Dido's Carthage and offers a new, dramatic version of Vergil's *Aeneid* 4, especially as embodied in Berlioz's 1859 opera *Les Troyennes*. Aeneas and his men are generously welcomed, both generally and sexually, by Dido and her women, in a luxurious spa. The humour and music (e.g. 'When You Wish Upon a Star', 'Dreaming my Dreams with You', 'Our Love is here to Stay', 'Bewitched, Bothered and Bewildered') of these scenes temporarily transform the victims through peace and pleasure. But the war-shattered Aeneas cannot accept this feminized world and decides he must depart for a harsher destiny. Dido refuses to leave with him for this new society (Rome). The play concludes with the betrayed Dido (and in this version Aeneas has deliberately misled her throughout) drowning or nearly drowning her love in a hot tub (the ending is the director's choice). The play flirts, often humorously, with moving beyond a tragic division between the priorities of the sexes, but ultimately fails. If the director chooses Aeneas' drowning, the play ends with a question-mark, since this would ahistorically preclude the founding of Rome; the alternative would deny the reality of the powerful patriarchal aggression and defiant female independence of the first act with its vivid set strewn with piles of shoes, graffiti, and dead dolls.[57] This deliberate effort toward living a civil, humane life, however unrealistic or even illusory, is characteristic of Mee's dramatic interpretation of history and of relations between the sexes.

The play in some sense served as a precursor to Mee's ambitious tragi-comic exploration of male–female conflicts in his play *Big Love*, which is based on the whole of Aeschylus' Danaid trilogy, despite the missing final two plays (the first play, *Suppliant Women*, is preserved). Echoing Aeschylus' plot, fifty (in this case, Greek) women have determined to escape to Italy in a yacht from arranged marriage with their first cousins (Greek-American).

[57] For a detailed description and discussion of the initial 1996 performance at the University of Washington in Seattle, directed by Tina Landau, see Bryant-Berteil (2000). Landau also directed a second staging in the same year at the abandoned East River Park Amphitheater in New York.

They take refuge in a villa, then pressure the owner to accept them as refugees until the cousins arrive to claim them. Only three of the sisters and brothers actually appear on stage as characters and each represents a gender stereotype. Lydia and her fiancé Nikos have the most thoughtful and open approach to the dilemma; he aims to woo her rather than forcing her into marriage. Lydia wants not a separate history of the sexes, but a human history in which men are good to women. Olympia is easily swayed by every form of persuasion and cliché, and is highly susceptible to the commercialized image of the modern nubile woman. Her counterpart Oed is less developed. Thyona is an ardent feminist who thinks little of men in general; her fiancé Constantine insists on the legal marriage contract and is happy to force the women to wed against their will. He persuades the rest. When the women are left no choice but to marry, Thyona persuades them to kill their husbands after the ceremony. All except Lydia do, and she is put on trial and exonerated by the host's wise mother, Bella, for opting for love in a form that may or may not include marriage or other socially approved gender relations. The sisters are to remain as Bella's 'daughters' in a family that includes an unmarried son and a gay nephew; they will escape punishment since society entirely betrayed their appeal for refuge and a real choice. As a whole, *Big Love* exploits clichés about the sexes that are familiar in Aeschylus' original, but satirizes and ironizes them in a context that is anything but naturalistic and often humorous. Two scenes, for example, find first the women and then the men literally throwing themselves on the stage as a group as they express frustration over sex roles and their situation.

Finally, some new versions have changed not only the genre but the gender orientation of characters in order to use Greek myth to explore contemporary issues. John Fisher's 1996 *Medea, the Musical*, a play within a play in the tradition of *Kiss Me Kate*, begins as an attempt to restage the story with a gay Jason; this camp musical will 'create a space for the homosexual on-stage' by having the hero marry 'a straight woman for purely pragmatic reasons' and develop multi-dimensional gay characters.[58] It also critiques the politics of

[58] I would like to thank John Fisher for sharing a script and other materials. Helpful reviews include *American Theater* 13.10 (1996), 7; the *San Jose Mercury News*, 9 August 1996; the *Sonoma County Independent*, 19–24 November 1996; *L.A. Weekly Media, Inc.* (www.laweekly.com/ink/theater-ross.shtml).

gender identity. In fact, the Swiss composer Rolf Liebermann's opera, *Medea*, completed in 1999 and performed at the Opéra Bastille in Paris in February 2002, similarly represented a Jason who tries to escape from the clutches of a dominating, pregnant Medea to a liberating and lyrical love in the arms of Creon, the king's son; here Medea kills the young Creon, not her unborn child. An earlier version was performed in Hamburg in 1995.[59] Originally a 1994 student production at the University of California, Berkeley, Fisher's musical went on to considerable runs in San Francisco, Los Angeles, and Seattle and won numerous awards. Both his and Liebermann's versions begin with the story of the Golden Fleece, which allows us to follow Jason and Medea's relationship from its inception.

In Fisher's musical, which will be my focus here, Jason's fellow male actors and the stage crew are gay, whereas the female cast members are straight. When Paul/Jason unexpectedly falls in love with Elsa/Medea, life and art mix as they begin to challenge gender stereotypes. Paul resists conforming to pressures from the gay community as the two conspire to give a feminist interpretation to the piece. Elsa argues that the play's Medea makes no sense as a woman; why would an intelligent woman fall for a stupid foreigner 'who offers her nothing but a little adventure and the occasional screw' and fail to notice that Jason was gay (20)?[60] Euripides' heroine is in her view a male creation designed for male actors. The new Medea, says Paul to the director, John (Fisher himself), will be neither a stereotyped victim nor bitch, but a woman who makes sense to women as well as men (55). The lovers prefer the version of the myth in which the Corinthians, not Medea, kill the children. John objects that 'the only reason anybody comes to see a production of *Medea* is to watch Medea kill small children'. Besides, he says to Elsa, 'killing your children is a feminist act. It's the ultimate act of self-empowerment. It's like burning your bra.' No, insists Elsa, 'it's a woman hurting herself to hurt the man she loves because he no longer loves her. It's a man's idea of a feminist act' (60). Just before the opening, however, Paul and Elsa begin to revert to sexual stereotype, quarrel, and break up. Having previously derided drag as demeaning, Paul arrives on stage for the

---

[59] *New York Times*, 27 February 2002.
[60] Page numbers are cited from Fisher's unpublished manuscript of the play.

opening night with a red kimono, high heels, and a strawberry blonde wig. In the musical's version of the myth, Phaedra and her beautiful stepson Hippolytus are Aeetes' guests in Colchis. Jason now blatantly pursues Hippolytus. Not to be outdone, Elsa proclaims a passion for Phaedra. The entirely chaotic new version is an unexpected success with a gay audience; Elsa agrees to stay on to 'hold up the lesbian end'. Jason and Medea jointly and absurdly perform a sacrifice of their 'babies', who are two adult males. There are mutual apologies all round at the festive conclusion.

Like *Bad Women*, Fisher's parodies to some extent rely on the audience having sufficient ownership of the myth to appreciate the humorous transformation of the original and reconfirm the active presence of the tradition on the contemporary scene. More generally, current versions build on but ultimately represent a very different response to Greek tragedy from earlier feminist reactions such as Kate Millett's, whose *Sexual Politics* (1970) focused on the dangers of origin myths like that offered in the *Oresteia*, where in her interpretation female subordination and misogyny are justified in a climactic defeat of matriarchy by patriarchy. Sue-Ellen Case went on to argue that Greek tragedy represented male actors in drag who perpetuated negative, dangerous, or unrealistically heroic female stereotypes and crippling binary oppositions between the sexes while suppressing the subjective experience and public participation of real women. Case recommended that the feminist reader read against the texts and resist being coopted by them even to the point of concluding that tragedy's major female characters 'are properly played as drag roles'.[61] Preoccupation with origins has not diminished, but remains in practice less awed and fearful. Recent productions and new versions often embrace the horrific aspects of Greek tragic heroines as part of a necessarily painful, even self-destructive resistance to cultural stereotypes and an opportunity for both sexes to play exciting female roles. Gender politics in these revisions are as in the originals still political, but often more personal or private (e.g. investigations of marriage) and less focused on public issues. Demands for equal recognition and acceptance of female sexuality dovetail in many respects with the characterization of Clytemnestra or Medea

---

[61] Case (1988), 15. For a useful critique and discussion of the issues, see Gamel (1999).

in the Greek originals. This impulse exists side by side with a resistance, as in McLaughlin's *Helen*, to the still prevalent iconization of the female body.

In an era that explored multiple sexualities and socially constructed subjectivities, the non-naturalistic construction of Greek tragic characters now seems more of an opportunity to make gender politics legible than a dangerous impediment. Revisions endow both male and female characters with new subjectivities, voices, and cultural resistances, but the inexorable plot structures of the originals remain to remind the audience of the complexities of this task and the fragilities of their resolutions. Characters no longer achieve recognitions of their 'true' identity but confirm the instability of a self struggling with powerful internal and external forces in a world where gendered identities are actively changing. Many performances now embrace tragic heroines as men in drag. Persistent use of metatheatricality and anachronism neutralizes the scholar-feminists' fear of audience cooptation through traditional dramatic identification with female characters. At the same time, new versions can inadvertently or sometimes self-consciously and comically perpetuate some of the stereotypes they are resisting. In current US street slang, 'bad' can be awesomely 'good'; the same seems at least partly true of the often outrageous representation of gender politics in both ancient and contemporary versions of Greek tragedy.

4

Heracles as Dr Strangelove and GI Joe

Male Heroism Deconstructed

Kathleen Riley

As the sex war's still being fought,
which sex does a myth support?
you should be asking.
　　Tony Harrison, *Medea: A Sex-War Opera* (1985)

INTRODUCTION

Euripides' *Heracles* has not been adapted for performance with great frequency, but its exploration of the problems inherent in the social construction of masculinity, especially our culture's pervasive legitimization of male violence, has led to a new interest in staging the play in the wake of the feminist movement and its critique of traditional thinking about gender. The feminist reappraisal of Euripides' *Medea* discussed by Foley in the previous chapter has been a particularly important factor in the revival of interest in his *Heracles*. The connection was memorably drawn by Tony Harrison in a reference to Heracles as Medea's male counterpart in *Medea: A Sex-War Opera* (1985). The comparison underlines the unfairly different treatment, in both ancient myth and modern media, meted out to male and female filicides:

> He killed his children. So where
> is Hercules's electric chair?
> A children slayer? Or is Medea
> The one child-murderer you fear.

Harrison's drama ends by initiating a shift in media focus from the 'Medea syndrome' to male filicide. Newspaper headlines and front-page reports of mothers murdering their children are projected on a screen, but the final projection, 'which freezes the music and the chorus', quotes a real tabloid newspaper headline,

'A FATHER CUTS HIS 4 KIDS' THROATS', with 'FATHER' crudely underlined in red.[1]

Euripides' tragic figure of Heracles, the father who murders his own family, had indeed not resonated powerfully in the mid-twentieth century, although other aspects of the Heracles myths (especially the labours) did appeal to the German-speaking world. Werner Herzog's first 'short' film, *Herakles* (1962), ironically juxtaposed the mythical hero with a contemporary body-builder. Neither the Swiss playwright Friedrich Dürrenmatt's *Herkules und der Stall des Augias* (first broadcast on Radio Bern in 1954 and staged in 1963) nor Heiner Müller's anti-tragedy *Herakles 5* (written in 1966, although not performed until 1974) had much to do with Euripides. Even Hartmut Lange's Brechtian treatment of the myth in *Herakles*, a study of Stalin performed in West Berlin (1968), which deals with the hero's guilt in general terms, did not centre on the infanticide.[2] Yet directors have now begun to appreciate the importance of Euripides' decision to put at the centre of a tragedy the darkest episode of Heracles' myth, the murder of his wife and children. The concept of the warrior, the trained killer who misdirects his aggression against his own household, has found powerful resonances in our own society, where marital violence and the male child-killer are pressing social concerns, not least afflicting our own 'warriors' in the military forces. The apparent topicality of the issues raised by this hero has been a crucial factor in putting him back on the public stage. The last five years have been the most prolific in the play's entire performance history. In 1998 alone four professional productions of new translations were staged, including two in Amsterdam, one at London's Gate Theatre, and one in Vicenza. Euripides' play was incorporated in Theodoros Terzopoulos's *Heracles Trilogy* (1999), staged in Istanbul, Japan, and Barcelona. In November 2000 an

---

[1] Harrison (1986), 370, 437, 448. The quotation was from *The Sun*, 19 October 1983.

[2] Dürrenmatt's play was revived several times both in the 1960s and subsequently; the text is available in Dürrenmatt (1998), vol. viii. Hartmut Lange, who was the Chief Dramaturg of the Deutsches Theater in East Berlin between 1961 and 1964, moved to West Berlin in 1965. In 1968 two of his plays were staged there together as a diptych, *Der Hundprozess* and *Herakles*, under the direction of H. Heyme (who is also discussed in Fischer-Lichte's chapter, below, pp. 342 and 359). The first play considered the negative side of Stalin, the second the positive. They are published in Lange (1988).

original multi-media interpretation of Heracles' myth, directed by Jay Scheib, was presented in New York's Time Square. Four months later a new German translation of Euripides' tragedy was performed at Theater am Kirchplatz in Liechtenstein, and in August 2002 the National Theatre of Northern Greece staged it in modern Greek at Epidauros.

This chapter tries to put this revival of interest in Euripides' tragedy in historical context by comparing two particularly important adaptations. Amongst other productions staged in the latter part of the twentieth century, *Heracles* has attracted the attention of two major English-language poets with high public profiles, each writing in a historical period of momentous change and uncertainty, who have deployed Heracles' ambivalent heroism as a symbol of the paradoxical condition of masculinity and civilization in their own era. The verse play *Herakles* by the American poet Archibald MacLeish, conceived and produced at the height of the Cold War, and British poet Simon Armitage's *Mister Heracles*, a version of Euripides' tragedy commissioned in the dawn of the new millennium, scrutinize the problematic place of the returned warrior within a domestic and broader cultural context. These two versions, which neatly frame the late twentieth-century period forming the subject of this book, demonstrate clearly how responses to the masterworks of the Greek tragic repertoire evolve and alter with the social and political climate. Their different focuses reveal the drastic shifts in society, culture, and sensibility which had been brought about by social transformations during the intervening decades.

ARCHIBALD MACLEISH'S *HERAKLES* (1965)

Archibald MacLeish (1892–1982) was a poet whose considerable literary achievements ran parallel to a distinguished career of public service and high office. An alumnus of Yale, where from 1911 to 1915 he became well versed in English and classical literature, and Harvard Law School, and a veteran of World War I, his education and early life experiences instilled in him the seeds of liberal humanism, as well as an acute social and political conscience. While many of his early poems were influenced by pioneering modernists like T. S. Eliot and Ezra Pound, and the often quoted final couplet of his own *Ars Poetica* (1926), 'A poem should not mean | But be', was simplistically adopted as a kind of mantra of extreme modernism, MacLeish eschewed the modernist pre-occupation with the private individual's experience and the poet's alienation from society. He believed that ideally poetry should function as 'public speech' and in his own verse and in essays such as 'The Irresponsibles' (1940), which attacked intellectual and literary apathy in the face of international crisis, he advocated what has been called 'his personal commitment to his art, to turn it outward upon the living world'.[3]

MacLeish's role as a public poet was not confined to the promotion of humanist values in his creative work. An admirer of Eleanor and Franklin D. Roosevelt, he became a chief adviser to the President as well as an occasional scriptwriter of Roosevelt's speeches and fireside chats. Among the numerous appointments he held during the Second World War and the immediate post-war period were Librarian of Congress (1939–44), assistant director of the Office of War Information (1942–3), Assistant Secretary of State (1944–5) and assistant head of the US delegation to Unesco (1946). In the 1950s MacLeish devoted himself to teaching and writing and was awarded two of his three Pulitzer Prizes. His public voice, during these years, was raised against the unwholesome climate of McCarthyism and anti-communist hysteria (for example, in his 1952 radio play *The Trojan Horse*). Soon after his verse play *J. B.*, a twentieth-century retelling of the story of Job, which earned him his third Pulitzer, had been successfully produced on Broadway, MacLeish began work on *Herakles*. It took him six years to recast the myth of Heracles and the murder of his sons as a dramatic parable for the atomic age, a contemplation of its wonders and evils. These six years represented one of the most destabilizing chapters of the Cold War in which the world witnessed intensive nuclear experimentation and armament, the thirteen-day Cuban missile crisis in October 1962, the beginnings of the space race, the construction of the Berlin Wall, America's entry into the Vietnam conflict, and the assassination of an American President. *Herakles* is an ambitious response to these events, explained by MacLeish in a letter written to Gerald Murphy on 16 September 1964, just over a year before the world première of *Herakles*:

---

[3] Somer (1988), 121.

I have known for a long time that that myth was our myth . . . Our age like his life is heroic in that highest and most daring sense that we take our meaning from him. For our age is tragic as his life was and as all the heroic ages must be. The deeds are performed, the miracles accomplished, the wonders visited—and there is still the world as it was—the dog as it was, except that the dog is now tied up in the cook's slops in Eurystheus' kitchen . . . It is true tragedy—tragedy to wring the heart: all these tremendous intelligences daring to take space and time and matter apart and to dig deep down under into the eternal dark and returning in triumph to what?

MacLeish retained Euripides' distinctive ordering of events in the Heracles myth. Contrary to the traditional order, in which Heracles had performed the labours as a penance for the murder of his family, Euripides had transposed the murders to the point after the twelfth labour had been successfully accomplished. This bleak alteration necessitates a reassessment of the labours and raises the question of whether they have been nullified or made futile. MacLeish summarized in a programme note the unsettling moral conundrum produced by this chronological inversion:

If the labours come first as they do in Euripides, how do the murders follow? If it is not the murderer of the sons who masters the beasts by way of penance, but the master of the beasts who murders the sons, why are they murdered?

MacLeish added another dimension to this dilemma by replacing the interventionist figure of Lyssa (Madness) with a blinding fit of megalomaniac violence. He thus introduced into his Euripidean framework both the concept of inevitability and a changed notion of culpability, and he formulated these in a way that underlines the ambiguity of the phenomenon he saw as the 'Heracles' of the late twentieth century—our notion of Science:

I felt very strongly then that the myth of Herakles is very much what the modern myth of science has been . . . The myth of Herakles ends with his return from the labors and the discovery that in his wars against the monsters he has destroyed his own sons. This is also the myth of science for us. Science has produced the bombs; science has produced the destruction of the young.[4]

It is significant that MacLeish's reading of the filicide, as a paradigm of the dangerous potential of scientific militarism, is devoid

---

[4] MacLeish in Drabeck and Ellis (1986), 213–14.

of any subtext relating to sexual politics. By contrast, for Simon Armitage, writing in the post-feminist era, the Heracles who is a paradigm of militarism is also necessarily a comment on the way society construes masculinity and the cultural and political authorization of male violence.

MacLeish's *Herakles* opened on 27 October 1965 in Ann Arbor, where it ran for fourteen performances, and was produced by the University of Michigan's Professional Theater Program with the APA (Association of Producing Artists) Repertory Company in the University's Lydia Mendelssohn Theatre. With the establishment of the Professional Theater Program in 1962, the University of Michigan became the first university in the United States to engage a resident repertory ensemble for a long-term contract. Its honorary sponsors included the playwrights Arthur Miller and Thornton Wilder and the actresses Judith Anderson and Helen Hayes. The purpose of the Program was to offer a broad selection of high quality contemporary theatre and to produce a new play each year. It had previously presented the American premières of Behan's *The Hostage* and Shaw's *Man and Superman.* The world première of *Herakles* was part of the Program's fourth Fall Festival, along with three other plays—Hart and Kaufman's *You Can't Take It With You,* Ibsen's *The Wild Duck,* and Beckett's *Krapp's Last Tape.* The production was directed by Alan Schneider, who had previously directed MacLeish's television play *The Secret of Freedom* (1960).

Throughout his career as one of America's foremost theatre directors, Schneider alternated between academic and commercial assignments. While serving as an assistant professor at the Catholic University of America, he directed productions of Sophocles' *Electra* (1943) and *Oedipus the King* (1950). He enjoyed a close association with Samuel Beckett, staging all the American premières of Beckett's plays, beginning with *Waiting for Godot.* He also directed the original productions of all the major plays of Edward Albee and several works by Harold Pinter and Bertolt Brecht. In the cast of *Herakles* were APA members Rosemary Harris as Megara and Sydney Walker as Herakles. It is clear from a letter MacLeish wrote to Richard Burton on 7 August 1965 that casting and initial rehearsals took place at the Phoenix Theatre in New York, with which the APA had an alliance.

The play comprised only one act and had a running time of an hour and fifteen minutes. It opened in the present at the site of the Delphic oracle's ruined temple where three American tourists (Mrs Hoadley, her daughter Little Hodd, and a governess Miss Parfit) had come to explore ancient myth with the aid of a Greek guide. With this contemporary scene MacLeish juxtaposed the tragic dénouement of the myth, so that the modern Americans shared the stage with Megara, Herakles, and the Pythian figure of Xenoclea. The tourists, literally drawn into the myth, watched as Herakles returned in triumph from his labours and demanded from Apollo oracular approbation of his exploits and the deification he had been promised (see Figure 10). The main movements of the play were towards and beyond Herakles' realization that the monstrous 'enemies' he boasted of killing upon re-entering the Theban gate were, in fact, his seven sons come to greet him. In these movements MacLeish appropriated elements of the Euripidean waking and rehabilitation scenes, and transformed the role of

FIGURE 10. Sydney Walker as Herakles and Rosemary Harris as Megara outside the doors of Apollo's temple in Archibald MacLeish's *Herakles* at the Lydia Mendelssohn Theatre, University of Michigan (1965).

Megara into an amalgamation of the Euripidean characters Amphitryon and Theseus.

The high profiles of MacLeish and Schneider led to the production receiving reviews in national newspapers and magazines such as *Variety*, *Life*, *The New York Times Book Review*, and *The Christian Science Monitor*. A common critical reaction was disappointment. There was unanimously high praise for Rosemary Harris's performance, but many critics felt that MacLeish's subject was esoteric and his treatment of it dramatically static. The review in *Variety* (10 November) claimed that the play was 'better to read than see on the stage' and that MacLeish's message was 'lost in a plethora of spoken words too complex in their poetic structure for dramatic impact. The great ideas suffocate in verbiage.' Several reviewers stated their preference for the suspense and tragedy of the original text. This is surprising in view of how rarely Euripides' play had been performed in America or elsewhere.[5] One of the more sympathetic reviews MacLeish's play received was that written in *The Christian Science Monitor* (13 November) by Richard Cattani, who, while acknowledging the difficulties that H*erakles* posed as a piece of theatre (for example, its brevity and lack of action), came nearest to penetrating the play's philosophical core and identifying the precise correlation between the ancient myth and modern reality. Cattani was aware of the importance of the hero's climactic recognition of his crimes to interpreting the meaning of the labours, and of the conflict between heroic and domestic values, which MacLeish had inferred from Euripides' text:

This revealed filicide points to the true assessment of Herakles' labors: grandiose, selfish, tragically delusive. Though he had silenced the dogs at the gates of hell and seized on the golden apples—symbolical of his having overcome the world and become a god—he had failed to overcome the horror of his own heart...*Herakles* presses us to consider the values of decency and family life in an affluent and atomic age wherein labors of Herculean magnitude can so easily entice us to feats of mock-godly grandeur.

Cattani's review, however, betrays unmistakably its pre-1970s date. The play's filicide and uxoricide are conceived by the critic

---

[5] The only vaguely commercial production of *Heracles* contemporary with MacLeish's play was an off-Broadway reading of William Arrowsmith's 1956 translation on 20 February 1959, performed by Qwirk Productions and directed by Geraldine Lust.

as the consequences of a problematic heroism, but without reference to a problematic masculinity or, more generally, to the question of sexual politics.

Although the play's subdued critical reception indicated a cultural climate inhospitable to Greek tragedy, even in modern adaptation, audience attendance in Ann Arbor was encouragingly large,
leading to a strong expectation that the production would transfer
to Broadway. However, the managing director of the Phoenix
Theatre, T. Edward Hambleton, and Alfred 'Delly' de Liagre,
the producer of *J. B.*, were both convinced (almost certainly cor-
rectly) that the play was commercially unviable. Their grounds
were that it was written in verse, it presupposed too much classical
knowledge, and its grim, implacable judgement on the civilized
world was ill-suited to the tastes of the average Broadway theatre-
goer.[6] Yet MacLeish's programme note shows that he believed
absolutely in the modernity and relevance of his play's mythical
hero:

> In our generation the myth of Herakles is closer to the human mind, to the
> imagination of the race, than it has been for thousands of years . . . The
> murders are no longer madness because we know ourselves to be capable
> of more dreadful murders . . . Indeed, the mocking question of our time,
> the question which later generations may think most characteristic of our
> time, is precisely the question of the labors of Herakles.

This conviction led MacLeish to add a first act to the existing
drama and publish the expanded version in 1967. The most important change is the addition of Professor Hoadley, a Nobel
laureate physicist, who is confined to a wheelchair and not dissimilar to the German scientist Dr Strangelove in Stanley Kubrick's
1964 darkly comic science fiction film. Hoadley, accompanied by
his family, has arrived in Athens, 'fresh from his beneficent dis-
coveries'[7] and the Prize ceremony in Stockholm, prior to returning
home to America (1). He has come to Greece, 'the fatherland of his
heroic soul' (5), seeking, like Herakles, oracular guidance at the
conclusion of his labours. The physical analogy between Hoadley
and Herakles is unequivocally drawn in the stage directions where
the Professor is described as 'a huge bulk of a man, strong hands

---

[6] See MacLeish in Drabeck and Ellis (1986), 214.
[7] This and all subsequent references to MacLeish's *Herakles* are to the page
numbers in MacLeish (1967).

straining at the flanges of the wheels' (2). The two characters are also related in terms of temperament and their dichotomous potential as fighters against the monsters that threaten the world. Both men are bullies and share a madness or megalomania with other fictional Cold-War characters such as the demented General Jack D. Ripper in *Dr Strangelove* and the psychotic asylum director Dr Mathilde von Zahnd in the 1962 comedy *Die Physiker* by Dürrenmatt (on whose own play about Heracles see above, p. 114). *Die Physiker* also examines the morals of science in a world increasingly insane and on the brink of nuclear annihilation. Hoadley's sojourn in Greece is born of a desire to revisit the myth of Heracles, which he believes will make meaningful his own labours, in the only setting commensurate to his heroic vision and heroic longing.

This augmented version reflects the date of its genesis in the mid-1960s in its connection between the domestic circumstances of MacLeish's mythical and contemporary heroes. The dysfunctional marriage and constant acrimony of the first act lend it Albee-esque strains. It resembles scenes from *Who's Afraid of Virginia Woolf?* (1962) and *A Delicate Balance* (1966) in which the drawing room becomes an arena for competing familial cruelties. Yet the dynamics of this particular sex war also suggest the influence of Strindberg's *The Father* (1887), which was largely inspired by the nineteenth-century theory that Aeschylus' *Oresteia*, and especially the trial scene in *Eumenides*, described a real historical shift from matriarchy to patriarchy. Strindberg's father is both a soldier and a scientist, but his wife Laura 'undoes the entire construction of the Captain's masculinity. She undoes him as a scientist, and as a father.'[8] Although with less design or efficacy, Mrs Hoadley similarly attempts to undo her husband's male and heroic identity by demeaning and even infantilizing him ('So that's it!—why we came. You wanted | Herakles to play with!' (18)). She is an embittered, waspish, and possibly alcoholic woman, both afraid and disdainful of her husband's hubristic master plan. Although certainly not the creation of a misogynistic writer, her character plainly pre-dates feminist revisionism in the theatre. Within this Strindbergian struggle, however, MacLeish problematizes the male–female opposition. Unlike Laura, Mrs Hoadley is undoubt-

[8] Rosslyn (1998), 188, 190.

edly a victim and ultimately powerless. By reproof and mockery she may challenge the notion of male heroism, but does not succeed in subverting it. Moreover, MacLeish does not present maleness as a straightforward construction, but creates instead images of compromised masculinity: in the words of the crippled professor's Stockholm oration lurks the spectre of the Hoadleys' estranged homosexual son, who represents the sons of Heracles slaughtered in a frenzy of over-achievement, and who has no place in his father's heroic schema, a schema which glorifies

> boundless daring, unknown deeds
> never before attempted, arduous
> undertakings in a room alone,
> impossible discoveries, dreadful weapons
> capable of holocaust, of extermination,
> fire as hot as God's.
>
> (17)

What MacLeish presents is essentially a pre-feminist deconstruction of male heroism, and anything in the play approaching a gender critique remains subordinate to the writer's interest in the myth of science and its implications. Yet, although MacLeish lacks a recognizably political language with which to articulate gender issues, he nevertheless sets up meaningful contrasts between his male and female protagonists that provide the reader with conflicting perspectives on the heroic paradigm at the play's centre. The voices of human despair, reason and enlightenment in the drama are all female. Hoadley's ambition for a world controlled by science, and his intolerance of weakness and imperfection, is perceived by his wife as madness: 'To want the world without the suffering is madness! | What would we be or know or bear | or love without the suffering to love for?' But Hoadley responds that the only thing left to man, and his 'ultimate pride', is, through science, to make a world free from suffering (21–2). Without politicizing the point, MacLeish makes clear throughout the play that it is the two wives, Mrs Hoadley and Megara, and the off-stage effeminate youth, who suffer for this 'ultimate pride', this masculine conception of the heroic.

Hoadley is last seen at the close of Act One roughly handling his wife as he sermonizes on 'human perfection' and the 'triumphant mind'. Resentful of her undisguised loathing of his brave new world, he laughs at her pain as he tightens his grip on her wrist. The denouement, which is played out in Act Two, is revealed only to the women in the party whose prescience is contrasted with Herakles' short-sightedness. As Herakles violently tries to force an answer from the oracle, Megara offers him an alternative to his laborious, heroic existence, but it is not one he can comprehend: 'We need the edge of ignorance to live by, the little, ignorant unknown of time beyond us in the dark that could be anything' (76–7).

The most urgent message contained in MacLeish's *Herakles* concerns the perilous ease with which the selfless monster-killer arrogates to himself godlike powers and prerogatives. MacLeish wrote, 'the great modern myth is not Jesus but Herakles—not God become man but man become God. It is still true that man-become-God is the great contemporary tragedy—dead sons and ruined faith.'[9] His play portrays a situation in which the modern 'Herculean feats' of science and technology are motivated not by altruism, but by an endless need to prove divine capability. In Act One Hoadley, extolling the achievements of his own age, declares, 'We should be gods to know what we know' (13) and talks of atomic weapons, the new instruments of apocalypse, as having a 'fire as hot as God's' (17). It is Megara, at the close of Act Two, who responds to her husband's assertion that 'A man is made for anger' by suggesting that aspiring to godhead entails imitating the sense-less destruction practised by divinity:

> Nothing, neither love nor trust
> nor happiness matters to the will of god:
> it can and down the city tumbles.
> Down the children in the bloody dust.
> Nothing is terrible as the will of god
> that can and can and can.
>
> (88–9)

Implicit in this impassioned protest is the opposition between male and female values. The writer opposes domesticity, compassion, and female suffering to the indifference of the male demigod.

MacLeish's failure with *Herakles* to arrest popular imagination must be qualified. The stage production was the imperfect realization of an unfashionably tragic vision of the world. Part of the

---

[9] In a letter of 18 March 1970 to Karl Galinsky, quoted in Galinsky (1972), 244.

problem was the play's unabashed didacticism, its conceptual strength, which has been seen as a dramaturgical weakness.[10] But the two-act version, which resolved some of the difficulties of the 1965 script, has never been performed, and is ripe for revaluation by a twenty-first-century audience; the relevance of its warning about 'man become God' has been renewed by the ethical debates on biotechnology (especially cloning and stem cell harvesting) and by intensified fears of chemical, biological, and nuclear warfare since 11 September 2001. Any modern staging, however, would demand reappraisal of the text in the light of the feminist revision of gender roles, and recent thinking on male violence, especially domestic violence. Such a production would need to make explicit the relationship between child-murder and problematic masculinity, a relationship only implicit in MacLeish's investigation of modern heroism.

MacLeish's *Herakles* is unmistakably a product of its time, located in a period of transition between different cultural and theatrical languages. It was staged on the eve of the social changes initiated by the women's movement, a corollary of which was a new curiosity on the part of theatre and film practitioners about the male psyche. Just weeks after MacLeish's *Herakles* opened, the English Stage Company first presented at London's Royal Court Edward Bond's *Saved*, a powerful and acutely observed study of the violence endemic in a South London council estate and its aimless young men. The play, which contains an on-stage infanticide, helped to precipitate the abolition in 1968 of the Lord Chamberlain's power to censor plays. It has been frequently restaged since its première, a mark of the interest shown by directors of the feminist and post-feminist eras in the problematization of received notions of maleness and in the relationship between these notions and the social evils of domestic violence and child abuse.

More recently, mainstream cinema has displayed a similar interest in representations of masculinity. In 1993 Susan Jeffords was already observing that 'externality and spectacle have begun to give way to a presumably more internalized masculine dimension . . . More film time is devoted to explorations of [men's] ethical

---

[10] 'As a poet of social consciousness he satirizes more effectively than he dramatizes. . . . Too often he is over-insistent, a shouter and convincer rather than a seducer' (Jaffe (1976), 147).

dilemmas, emotional traumas, and psychological goals.' The central question posed by Hollywood depictions of male heroism since the 1980s has been 'whether and how masculinity can be reproduced successfully in a post-Vietnam, post-Civil Rights, post-women's movement era'.[11] Within this cultural climate, Euripides' *Heracles*, which details the shift from external to internal heroism, becomes an ideal text for the modern enquiry into the problematic male hero, and consequently a powerful piece of social drama.

ARMITAGE'S *MISTER HERACLES* (2001)

These trends in theatre and film have precipitated the recent reversal of fortune in the performance reception of Euripides' *Heracles* detailed at the opening of this chapter. An excellent example of how recent social and cultural developments have influenced, consciously and subconsciously, the modern reading of this ancient play is Simon Armitage's *Mister Heracles*. Born in West Yorkshire two years before MacLeish's *Herakles* was staged, Simon Armitage was Britain's official Millennium Poet and is a prescribed author in the GCSE syllabus. *Mister Heracles*, his first major project undertaken for the stage, was commissioned by the West Yorkshire Playhouse in Leeds where, under the co-direction of Natasha Betteridge and Simon Godwin, it received its world première on 16 February 2001. Explaining his approach to interpreting the original text, Armitage says he 'didn't simply want to contemporise' the ancient drama or update it to a specific point in history:

In *Mister Heracles*, it is as if the whole of human history has occurred within the lifespan of one family. Atomic weapons and spears are spoken of in the same sentence, quantum physics and spinning wheels considered in the same thought . . . No cultural or historical co-ordinates were beyond possibility using this full-spectrum approach.[12]

The play, therefore, incorporates a vast transhistorical compass into which are built many deliberate anachronisms and which was reflected in the stage design and costuming. What gives cohesion

---

[11] Jeffords (1993), 245, 247.
[12] Armitage (2000), viii–x. All subsequent page numbers in the main text of this chapter refer to this edition.

to this chronologically 'full-spectrum approach' is the play's thematic focus.

In his penultimate speech the hero of *Mister Heracles* demonstrates to Theseus that his lineage and life's work constituted a progression towards catastrophe. He declares himself 'a case study, | a living, breathing, one-man case-history' (51). Armitage has said that the play is about what he sees as the 'very strong contemporary theme' of heroism.[13] Central to his reworking of Euripides' drama is the notion which was clearly in the mind of the author of the Senecan *Hercules Furens*, and which was developed in Ulrich von Wilamowitz-Moellendorff's seminal edition of Euripides' text (1889), that the potential for violence is within Heracles from the outset of the play. In the Senecan version the madness may be externally instigated by Juno, but the characters of Iris and Lyssa are excised and what actually precipitates Hercules' downfall is his own nature. Armitage goes further than Seneca in internalizing the germ of violence, while at the same time perceiving a meaning in the violence that extends far beyond the figure of Heracles. He sees the madness and infanticide as the inevitable, if extreme, products of the terrifying capabilities bred by such modern phenomena as virtual reality, relentless acceleration in the speed of technological advances, and systematic desensitization to all forms of violence. More particularly, Armitage's study of heroism has at its core the cultural psychology of militarism and masculinity, and the problem, above all, of trained killers adapting to civilized and civilian society.

From the beginning of the production an overt, although highly eclectic militarism was established through images borrowed and condensed from history and popular culture, and reflecting the fragmented focus of the military in the post-Cold War era. The play opened in outer space where Mister Heracles, an astronaut, gradually floated into view as the title of the play flashed above the stage like the opening credits of a film. At the beginning of Euripides' play the explanation for Heracles' absence is that he is undertaking his twelfth labour, an attempt to abduct Cerberus from the Underworld. In Armitage's version the twenty-first-century equivalent of this *katabasis* (descent) is interplanetary exploration, with Heracles the first man to travel at the speed of

---

[13] In an interview on BBC Radio 4's *Front Row*, February 2001.

light. Dispossessed and anxiously awaiting his return, Megara, Amphitryon, and the three sons of Heracles had the appearance of refugees or prisoners of war whose images are familiar from Second World War newsreels. The setting also gave the impression of a post-atomic apocalypse, an impression supported by the presence of the chorus, who, in modern dress and grimy blue work coats, had the task of cleaning up after the fallout. In the second choral ode the original strophe and antistrophe were adapted in the choreography of twelve songs, performed alternately by the four members of the chorus in a style akin to modern rap music. These songs depicted the labours of Heracles as the exploits of a comic strip hero or a character from the *Boys' Own* annuals.

In preparation for their execution, and at Megara's request, the family are permitted by Lycus to enter their house and exchange their ragged clothes for party outfits. In the production, the boys emerged dressed in kilts, Megara in a party dress and tartan sash, and Amphitryon in tails and campaign medals. They appeared as the proud stock of the army establishment. Heracles, on his return, reinforced this image, assuming again his role as head of a traditional nuclear family within a rigidly hierarchical military community. His costume was a cross between the uniforms of an English soldier and a US air force pilot. King Eurystheus of Argos, who in Euripides' tragedy ordered the labours, has been replaced in this version by a state military organization from which, by his own admission, Heracles is absent without leave. Consistent with his unspecific uniform, this military entity is unnamed and could as easily be NASA as a military battalion. It is clear, at any rate, that unlike Euripides' Heracles, who is an individual and solitary fighter against evil, Armitage's hero operates within an official and organized military culture.

In drawing a contrast between Heracles' initial bluster, bravado, and slightly imperious manner, and the tenderness of his reunion with his family, Armitage has reproduced the breach Euripides also highlighted between heroic and domestic values. He has beautifully rendered into modern verse the moving simile in which Herakles compares his children to *epholkides* (Euripides, *Heracles* 631), little boats towed after a ship:

> All climb into me,
> life will not give out,

> will not splinter me.
> Sail in my slipstream,
> my candle afloat
> and my paper boats.
>
> (25)

Heracles' simple assertion to his family, 'Today is put back' (22), provides both a powerful closure to the traditional homecoming-and-rescue tale dramatized in the play's first half and an effective prelude to the climactic *peripeteia* (reversal) with which the second half begins. Armitage is significantly juxtaposing Heracles' behaviour as an affectionate father and unfailing protector with his celebrated public image as a relentless killing machine.

The sudden appearance of Iris and Lyssa midway through Euripides' play, which interrupts the joyous choral ode celebrating Heracles' rescue of his family (763–814), marks a chilling reversal for which the audience has in no way been prepared. Armitage's robust, almost ribald, interpretation of the ode prepares the audience, in some measure, for the tone and import of the supernatural dialogue, especially when the chorus remarks,

> Goodness has come with years of nurture,
> but willpower and killer instinct too
> are in his nature.
>
> (31)

These lines adumbrate the disaster in that Heracles' 'killer instinct' is the very instinct that Armitage's Madness is able to activate and turn against Heracles. The chorus offers a further, ominous reminder that Heracles' skills as a killer, the skills he will now employ to save his family, have been honed and perfected in his unquestioning service to duty:

> Now, with kith and kin
> to be protected,
> the true Heracles steps forward.
> Now he must kill for himself, not just to order.
>
> (31–2)

In a radical departure from its Euripidean model, the epiphany of Iris and Madness, as staged by Betteridge and Godwin, seemed to parody the James Bond world of glamour and gadgetry and owe something as well to the Cold-War landscape of a John le Carré spy novel. The two characters, as Armitage has drawn them, represent the state military organization which Heracles, by exerting his independence, has snubbed. Unlike Euripides' Lyssa, who 'runs races' into Heracles' heart, Armitage's Madness uses an electronic device that locks onto Heracles' frequency, activating a violence that is intuitive. Significantly omitted from this scene is any mention of Hera, her vengeful purpose, or her initiation of the madness. Nor does Armitage's Madness admonish Iris and Hera, as in Euripides' text (848–54), for proceeding against an undeserving object of Olympian wrath. His Iris explicitly confirms what the chorus had earlier unwittingly predicted, that the efficacy of the method by which Heracles will become mad is entirely contingent upon his predisposition to violence. The 'injection' of madness to be administered to Heracles will multiply 'his sense of being human', which Iris says,

> is fine if he's as meek as a lamb and so on,
> but poor Heracles—a born killer through and through—
> there's no telling what a man like that might do.
>
> (33–4)

The chorus's depiction of Heracles as 'a born killer' establishes for the contemporary audience an immediate association with Oliver Stone's 1994 film *Natural Born Killers*. The film, based on a story by Quentin Tarantino, is an analysis of the mass media's glorification of the culture of violence, and charts the career of two psychopathic serial murderers who achieve the status of legendary folk heroes. Like Stone, Armitage is dissecting the celebrity attached to the perpetrator of violence and the impact on the individual of a cultural psychology according to which violence is the norm.

The symptoms of Mister Heracles' madness reveal Armitage's internalization of his hero's psychosis and explanation of his loss of self as symptomatic of the imperative of violence that has defined his previous existence. In Euripides' text Lyssa describes how she will carry out her commission predominantly in the first person, thus stressing her very physical operation through Heracles, whose mind and body will be consumed by her force. Moreover, Heracles' madness begins to take effect while Lyssa is still on stage, drawing attention to what she is doing to him: 'Look at him!'[14] By contrast, Armitage's Madness, whose concise diagnosis is given in the third

---

[14] Euripides, *Heracles* 867. All quotations from Euripides' own text are taken from the English translation by Barlow (1996).

person, exhibits a clinical detachment. The process of triggering Heracles' madness is not one of violent upheaval (as charted by the Euripidean Lyssa's catalogue of graphic images at 861–71), but involves what Iris describes as an 'electronic adrenalin shot' (32). Madness elaborates on this process:

> The subject feels a flash
> of blinding light, leading to temporary memory loss
> and sometimes a funny turn or possible blackout
> before sense returns.
>
> (33)

This electronic charge will sever instinct from reason and Heracles will act 'as if spell-bound, radio-controlled, or on strings' (34). Madness does not specify the consequences of Heracles' hallucinatory behaviour. Euripides' Lyssa states that she will make him kill his children (865). Armitage's Madness is less precise, although the psychosis will involve a kind of mental 'cinematic replay' of the twelve labours: 'All the past comes spooling through the mind' (34). The chorus also interprets the madness as serial flashbacks to the routine slaughter imposed by the labours:

> Some whirlwind of the mind
> whips up a version of his life
> which he acts out on his own kind.
>
> (35)

Thus, as in Euripides, the hallucination is a parody of the labours and an inversion of Heracles' heroic self. Where Armitage diverges from his classical model is in his suggestion, developed in his reworking of the rehabilitation of Heracles, that the madness and murder are the culmination of a natural progression towards an unnatural act.

In the Messenger's account of the onset of Heracles' madness in *Mister Heracles* there is significantly no English equivalent of the powerful Euripidean phrase 'he was no longer himself' (931) to signal the abrupt transition from sanity to insanity. Similarly, as Euripides' Messenger recounts the physical symptoms of the madness at 932–5, the emphasis is on the metamorphosis and distortion of the normal self—the contorted features, the foaming mouth, and the maniacal laugh—but Armitage's Messenger describes a system in overload, the intensification of symptoms already present, and the easy awakening of a latent psychosis:

> A nerve pumped in the wall of his neck,
> just here, as if the man couldn't swallow,
> and his eyes swelled in their sockets. His veins
> were hot, overloaded.
>
> (37)

Heracles' mad speech, as reported by Armitage's Messenger, is also symptomatic of the heightening of a mentality practised in violence and enslaved to a manic speed of activity:

> Father, this isn't the time to clean the house,
> I have breakthroughs to make, barriers to crash,
> more dirty work to do before I stop.
> No rest for the wicked indeed. No peace.
>
> (37)

The snatches of speech, which in Armitage's text precede the murders of the first two sons, generalize the targets of his rage: 'Here's one I'm killing for the mother state'; 'here's a killing for the greater good' (38). These indicate that the madness has not necessarily been triggered by the most recent events in Heracles' life, but is the inevitable consequence of a culture steeped in violence in which, as MacLeish's play also pleaded, the achievements that advance civilization can also be responsible for its dehumanization and destruction.

In the Leeds production the same actor played the roles of Madness and the Messenger. He was thus the last character to enter the house before the madness erupted and the first to re-emerge in its aftermath. Armitage's adaptation of the Messenger's speech is one of the finest monologues in the play and Nick Bagnall's interpretation of it was a compelling piece of naturalistic acting through which the full impact of the tragedy was conveyed. What Armitage has successfully translated from the original speech is the sense of the ordinary and domestic that is fractured by the onset of madness. His Messenger begins his account by saying,

> It was just happenchance I was present,
> the way that a person walking the beach
> or harbour might be asked to photograph
> a sweet family grouping with their camera.
>
> (36)

From this quiet opening he reconstructs, in steady rhythm, each murder and the mounting sense of his own powerlessness.

Armitage adds an even more sinister element to the original by indicating the pent-up violence beneath the surface of this ideal image of the nuclear family.

At the end of the Messenger's speech the façade of the house was slowly lowered onto the stage to reveal, within a blood-red cavity, the tableau scene of a family living room in which Heracles was asleep and bound amid the carnage he had wrought. This image of 'ordinary suburban horror', identified by Lyn Gardner in her review of the play,[15] found almost simultaneous analogies in two widely publicized real-life incidents of domestic homicide, both occurring in quiet middle-class English suburbia. In Surrey, one week before the opening of *Mister Heracles*, Anthony Smith, a former sergeant-major in the Coldstream Guards, described by family and neighbours as a devoted husband and father who had enjoyed a glittering military career, suddenly, and seemingly inexplicably, shot dead his wife and two small children. Unlike Euripides' Heracles, he then succeeded in killing himself. Gardner mentioned the case in her review of *Mister Heracles*, while another newspaper reviewer asked 'Does the violence of warfare incite soldiers to other sorts of violence?'[16] Six months later PC Karl Bluestone of Gravesend, also remembered as a respected officer and an adoring father, used a hammer to bludgeon to death his wife and two of his four children before hanging himself. In an article which appeared in *The Daily Telegraph* in the wake of this second tragedy, the writers attempted to explain the psychology behind such increasingly common instances of filicide, declaring, 'We stare hard at the neat images of middle-class family life. The ordinariness and decency of the situation are an affront to the imagination.'[17] These men were only two amongst nine British fathers who murdered their children in the space of two years.

What makes Smith and Bluestone offer particularly close analogies to Euripides' Heracles is their role as heroes of modern civilization: Smith had been a member of the Queen's ceremonial guard at Buckingham Palace and had served with his regiment in Northern Ireland, while Bluestone had been part of a tactical unit in North Kent whose purpose was to combat specific anti-social

---

[15] *The Guardian*, 24 February 2001.

[16] Susannah Clapp, in *The Observer*, 25 February 2001.

[17] Elizabeth Grice and Nicole Martin, 'What drives a father to kill his family?', *The Daily Telegraph*, 31 August 2001.

crimes such as vandalism. The disturbing phenomenon of 'civilization heroes' as the perpetrators of domestic violence has also surfaced in America's War Against Terrorism. Between 11 June and 19 July 2002 four military wives were murdered, allegedly by their husbands who were based at Fort Bragg in North Carolina, the headquarters of America's élite Special Forces unit. Three of the men were Special Operations soldiers who had recently returned from service in Afghanistan and, of these, two committed suicide after their wives were killed. Military authorities denied that there was a connection between the killings and the men's service in Afghanistan, but the much-publicized wife murders prompted an investigation into the military's provision of 'reunification training' for soldiers returning from combat deployment, family assistance centres and support groups, and post-deployment counselling. Such cases as these certainly lend powerful and truly tragic force to *Mister Heracles*. Moreover, the fact that fathers as child-killers have increasingly become the focus of both public interest and forensic psychology has helped to make Euripides' shocking *Heracles* a more attractive and stageable proposition for directors and dramatists than in previous decades.[18]

Following Euripides, the rehabilitation of Armitage's hero comprises three main stages: Heracles' waking and the psychotherapy scene in which Amphitryon guides his son towards recognition of his deeds (see Figure 11); Theseus' arguments; and Heracles' final progress from the contemplation of suicide to the shouldering of his fate. In Euripides' play Heracles wakes from his madness uncertain whether he has returned to Hades. The disorientation experienced by Armitage's Heracles, however, is expressed in a military context. He asks, 'Am I captured? Were we overtaken | in battle?' (42) and wonders whether he has been the victim of some form of chemical warfare. On seeing his father nearby, Heracles begs to be freed 'before the enemy returns' (43). When Euripides' Heracles finally recognizes the corpses as those of his wife and children and asks who their murderer is, Amphitryon gives the answer, 'You with your bow and whichever god was responsible' (1135), thereby pronouncing the gods' guilt and Heracles' role

---

[18] See Larry Milner's analysis and use of Euripides' tragedy in his recent large-scale survey of filicide, *Hardness of Heart, Hardness of Life* (2000), which also draws on forensic case studies, international statistics, and other literary representations.

FIGURE 11. Adrian Bower as Heracles and Patrick Toomey as Theseus in *Mister Heracles* at the West Yorkshire Playhouse (2001). The rehabilitation scene, following Heracles' madness and murder of his family.

as the blameless instrument of divine will. In contrast, reflecting the relative absence of the gods from *Mister Heracles*, Armitage has Amphitryon answer pointedly, 'Heracles, you killed them, nobody else' (44), 'Like a man possessed, by his own dark thoughts' (45). This stands in interesting contrast to Amphitryon's straightforward announcement in Euripides, 'You were mad' (1137). Armitage is redefining Heracles' temporary loss of reason and control as possession by an internal force generated by the hero's very mode of existence. Consistent with this reading of the madness is Heracles' admission, 'It came from inside. I was . . . capable' (49).

The role of Theseus in Armitage's play highlights the playwright's perception of the complexities inherent in any attempt to apportion blame for the murders. He is the one character who tries to externalize Heracles' madness and who, at least at first, alludes to workings on a supernatural level. Yet even he soon argues that the madness was inevitable in view of Heracles' lifelong obedience to the destiny which his own heroic attributes had shaped for him:

> All your life you have fallen into step.
> Born musclebound you've thrown your weight around,
> born bright you've cracked the most cryptic of codes,
> born of such birth you've held your head high,
> followed the script exactly as planned.
> So this fall was the most obvious thing
> in the world—it was certain to happen.
>
> (52)

Theseus thus represents for the audience the problem of determining the cause of the violence that has erupted and indicates the necessity of treating the individual psychology as merely part of a complex social whole.

Heracles' two major speeches in Euripides (at 1255–1310 and 1340–93), in which he makes his moral and spiritual journey from an old to a new type of heroism, have been substantially altered and truncated by Armitage in accordance with his own objectives. In the original version of these speeches Heracles protests against the immorality of the gods and their indifference to human suffering. He acknowledges Amphitryon as his 'true' father and renounces Zeus who, he says, begot him to be the enemy of Hera (1262–3). In Armitage's play it is not the enmity of his stepmother, but the expectations created by his divinity that have contributed to Heracles' tragedy:

> Well, father, I have tried to be your son,
> tried hard to be a son of a true man,
> not someone god-like or legendary,
> but it cuts deep. Living up to his name
> keeps driving me on, towards the extreme,
> all part of a bigger push to be seen.
>
> (51)

Whereas Euripides' Heracles, by renouncing Zeus, asserts his humanity, Armitage, like MacLeish before him, goes further in declaring the death of Zeus and dramatizes the dangers of man

becoming God in God's absence. In the first of these final speeches
Heracles concludes,

> I see my life for what it is—a list
> of things accomplished, acceptance speeches,
> records broken, puzzles solved, clocks beaten,
> all in the end without wider meaning.
>
> (52)

Like MacLeish's Herakles, and his Cold-War counterpart Professor Hoadley, Armitage's hero has sought and failed to discover the
ultimate meaning of his labours. In his second speech, however, he
does try to re-evaluate his past achievements in the aftermath of
their tragic culmination. Armitage has amplified lines 1281 ('The
pitch of necessity to which I have come is this') and 1294 ('This is
the pitch of disaster I think I shall reach') of Euripides' text to give
a very different exposition of Heracles' tragic fall and his relationship to Necessity. In the play's most sustained analysis of the
causes of the madness, Heracles recalls, in Theseus' presence,
the process of his gradual desensitization to the act of killing, the
anaesthetizing frequency of the deed, the shift from what was a
trained action to the point where 'instinct and reaction take over'
(53), and the sort of impassivity that can only end in mania. Asking
Theseus if he remembers the first time he killed a man, he assures
him it gets progressively easier (53–4):

> Soon instinct and reaction take over.
> I've loaded magazines without thinking,
> lined up the cross-hairs, beaded a target
> as if I were just pointing a finger,
> then beckoned death by pulling the trigger.
> Along lines of sight, I've followed the trace
> of gunfire passing through armour and flesh,
> seen daylight flashing on the other side,
> seen death blink its eye, and not broken sweat.
> At first it caused a dryness in the throat;
> these days it doesn't even raise the pulse.
> I've killed without giving a single thought
> to the speed of a bullet: one mile
> per second, and spinning for good measure.

Armitage even ascribes to Heracles, during the madness, a degree
of consciousness—consciousness of excitement, something that
Euripides' hero never experiences.

During my crimson rage, here in my house,
when the red mist came down into my eyes,
even though I was cut off from my soul
I remember one thing—feeling alive.
That's how far I've come: only butchery
of those I love most provokes life in me.
Oh, my children and my wife, that your death
were in me all the time, waiting to hatch.

(54)

These extraordinarily acute insights, which Armitage's Heracles articulates into his own psychological condition, have strong resonance for a society that is becoming better educated about the role of post-traumatic stress disorder in the experience of combat veterans. The trauma suffered by Vietnam veterans has been fictionalized in such films as Michael Cimino's *The Deer Hunter* (1978), Hal Ashby's *Coming Home* (1978), and Ted Kotcheff's *First Blood* (1982). Benedict Nightingale astutely began his review of *Mister Heracles* in *The Times* (23 February 2001) by noting the connection made in the play between the Vietnam experience and the madness of Heracles: 'We have all heard of Vietnam vets who, years after the war, have gone on the rampage, sometimes killing their nearest and dearest. For the poet Simon Armitage, Euripides' Heracles is an example of much the same syndrome.'

The resurgence of interest in performing Euripides' *Heracles* coincides with the public impact of Jonathan Shay's highly original study of the symptoms of combat trauma through a comparative analysis of the mutually illuminating first-hand narratives of Vietnam veterans and Homer's descriptions in the *Iliad* of the behavioural phenomena displayed by combatants, especially Achilles. One behavioural phenomenon particularly pertinent to Armitage's reading of Heracles' madness is 'the berserk state', a term used by Shay to designate the warrior's blind and concentrated frenzy:

A soldier who routs the enemy single-handedly is often in the grip of a special state of mind, body, and social disconnection at the time of his memorable deeds.[19]

In the light of vivid reports by Vietnam combat veterans, Shay examines aspects of the five *aristeiai* (heroic killing sprees) on

---

[19] Shay (1995), 77.

which Achaean warriors go in the *Iliad*, and their transgression of 'the ambiguous borderline between heroism and a blood-crazed, berserk state, in which abuse after abuse is committed'. During this state the 'berserker' exhibits attributes that are simultaneously god-like and bestial, the factor common to both conditions being a lack of all restraint:

Restraint is always in part the cognitive attention to multiple possibilities in a situation; when all restraint is lost, the cognitive universe is simplified to a single focus. The berserker is figuratively—and sometimes literally—blind to everything but his destructive aim. He cannot see the distinction between civilian and combatant or even the distinction between comrade and enemy.[20]

The inability to distinguish between friends and enemies, along with the other cognitive inversions of what would 'normally' be described as deeds of courage, inversions symptomatic of the berserk state, are what Ruck is referring to when he describes Euripides' maddened Heracles as 'the ironic antithesis of his own dominant heroism'.[21] The madness of Mister Heracles has notably precise similarities to the martial rage of certain heroes of the *Iliad*, in which *lyssa* and its cognate epithets are used to denote the soldier's possession by blind fury and bloodlust. Moreover, Shay's definition of the berserk state, which is apposite to Heracles' loss of self, also corresponds to the Homeric meaning of *lyssa* (for example in the description of Hector at *Iliad* 9. 237–9).

As Shay demonstrates (and Armitage's hero acknowledges), the potential of the berserk state to recur episodically in civilian life is ever-present and can destroy the victim's ability to function as a responsible citizen in a normal domestic or cooperative environment: 'Unhealed combat trauma . . . destroys the unnoticed substructure of democracy, the cognitive and social capacities that enable a group of people to freely construct a cohesive narrative of their own future.'[22] The explosive potential, which Armitage's Madness actuates in Heracles, has a close equivalent in recent history and in the personal experience related by one of Shay's patients, a veteran of three Vietnam combat tours in tanks:

Every three days I would totally explode, lose it for no reason at all. I'd be sitting there calm as could be, and this monster would come out of me with

---

[20] Shay (1995), 77, 86–7.   [21] Ruck (1976), 60.   [22] Shay (1995), 181.

a fury that most people didn't want to be around. So it wasn't just over there. I brought it back here with me.[23]

Mister Heracles' final speech reads as a dissection of the causes and effects of the berserk state. It is away from the excess of sensation, hyper-alertness and disconnection ('I was cut off from my soul'), which are characteristic of this state, that Heracles realizes he must be rehabilitated:

> I need to go back to the beginning
> get into a calm life, depressurise,
> have a normal heart for half a minute,
> tone it down, tune it to a finer scale
> of living.
>
> (54)

His last words in the play are a prayer that he may 'come down to earth, back to personal space' (57). The need for rehabilitation is eventually acknowledged, but only partly and awkwardly begun. Shay and Armitage provide good examples of how, in the last decade in particular, writers with very different commissions have used the mythology and literature of the ancient Greeks as a tool in their analyses of the problems inherent in the roles designed for men in modern society and especially the military.

At the end of Euripides' *Heracles* the hero discovers a capacity to endure the life that confronts him. As he states, 'I shall have the courage to endure life' (1351). Of greater symbolic importance is Heracles' decision to retain his weapons, the traditional tokens of a less complicated heroism, now grievously laden with new meaning and exacting greater courage and resolve from their bearer. Heracles is able to make this progression through the redemptive power of friendship taught him by Theseus, who bears him off to a new life in Athens. Armitage, however, places far less emphasis on friendship in his reworking of the play's ending. Instead his Heracles exhibits a Senecan independence in the final phase of his rehabilitation. This is also clear from Armitage's explanation that, 'when the gods die, they leave man in control of his own moral identity, and after experiencing his greatest tragedy, Heracles must confront his greatest challenge. We observe the agonising creation of the new kind of superman: one who takes responsibility for his

---

[23] Shay (1995), 33.

actions' (x). The reworked ending, however, does not achieve the impact of the original. Armitage's 'depressurisation' is in no way comparable to Euripides' 'I shall have the courage to endure life', or to his hero's moving refusal to repudiate the 'painful companionship' of his club and bow. In removing the emphasis on friendship, Mister Heracles seems to have gained only half a new understanding. He knows that he 'was born to a way of life | that went into receivership' (51), but has not yet found a substitute. It appears a deliberately disquieting ending, which lacks the muted optimism of humanistic resolve with which Euripides had invested his own reworking of the Heracles myth.

Archibald MacLeish's *Herakles* and Simon Armitage's *Mister Heracles* are a continuation of the process, begun by Euripides in the fifth century, of deconstructing and reinterpreting the heroic and tragic Heracles and identifying, in contemporary terms, the implications of his labours and his suffering. Both writers discovered in Euripides' play a powerful symbol for the uncertainties of their own age as well as a means of formulating, and responding to, questions about the place and nature of traditional male heroism and the cultural legitimization of violence. The decades which separate the two productions witnessed enormous transformations—social, political, and theatrical—which illuminate the differences between them in focus, emphasis, and critical reception. In particular, the women's movement of the 1970s, and the growing conviction that women's status and role cannot be understood without analysing the role of men, have aided the rediscovery of Euripides' *Heracles* in the late twentieth and early twenty-first centuries and profoundly affected our reading of the filicide. Thirty years of social change and theatrical revisionism have enabled Armitage to develop, as central to his deconstruction of heroism, critical gender issues which MacLeish in the mid-1960s could only partially articulate.

Section II

DIONYSUS IN POLITICS

5

Sophocles' *Philoctetes*, Seamus Heaney's, and Some Other Recent Half-Rhymes

Oliver Taplin

I

In 1995 the United States had a President who believed that poetry might be important enough to quote in public.[1] That December, Bill Clinton visited Derry in Northern Ireland, and made a speech which culminated with a full quotation of what have become some of the best-known lines of later twentieth-century poetry in English:

> History says, *Don't hope*
> *On this side of the grave.*
> But then, once in a lifetime
> The longed-for tidal wave
> Of justice can rise up,
> And hope and history rhyme.
>
> So hope for a great sea-change
> On the far side of revenge.
> Believe that a further shore
> Is reachable from here.
> Believe in miracles
> And cures and healing wells.

The phrase 'Hope and history rhyme' even went on to supply newspapers with their front-page headlines at the time of the Good Friday Agreement in 1998.[2] These lines come from near the end of *The Cure at Troy*, subtitled 'A Version of Sophocles'

---

[1] It is reported by Percy (2002), 8–9, that on the wall of his home at Chappaqua, NY, Clinton has a framed postcard from Heaney which says, 'It was a fortunate wind that blew you here.' This is from the closing lines of *The Cure at Troy*, quoted on p. 166 below.

[2] Heaney himself documents some of the afterlife of these lines, citing, among others, Mary Robinson, Dick Spring and Gerry Adams as well as the titles of books by Clinton himself—*Between Hope and History: Meeting America's Challenges for*

Philoctetes', Seamus Heaney's one and only play to date. It was first performed by Field Day Theatre Company in the Derry Guildhall on 1 October 1990, before touring Northern Ireland and the Republic, and finally transferring to the Tricycle Theatre in Kilburn, London, in April 1991.

The passage quoted is not, however, derived directly from Sophocles: the lines are the third and fourth stanzas of a seven-stanza choral 'ode' that is slotted into the play by Heaney. This 'interpolation' comes at the point where in the original Heracles intervenes *ex machina* to stop Philoctetes and Neoptolemus from returning home to Greece instead of going to Troy (i.e. between lines 1407 and 1408 of the Sophocles text). Nearly all of the play up until this moment has been translated in a pretty close and con-scientious way—much closer indeed than most modern versions of Greek tragedy by creative writers. Heaney's most important change—and only major change—from the Sophocles is in the treatment of the chorus at the beginning and the end. In the Greek original Neoptolemus' crew of sailors are rather low-key, both in the quantity and impact of their contributions; and, while unobtrusively worked into the plot, have little to offer in the way of what might be called 'lyric insight'. Heaney replaces them with three women (though the number and gender are not, perhaps, essential). Their words stick pretty close to Sophocles for the rest, except that they are given a kind of pre-prologue before the play proper begins; that they deliver this much-quoted 'ode'; and also immediately after that speak the final 'voice of Hercules', which is treated as an 'expression of recognition which Philoctetes has repressed...the voice of his unconscious' (*Notes*, p. 173; see Figure 12).[3] These two additions at either end of the play are more reflective and self-reflexive than anything in the Sophoclean original; and they include the most controversial and memorable lines in the play. It might be thought ironic that the most notable bits of *The Cure at Troy* are those which are pure, unprecedented Heaney. But, in that they give a civic dimension to the plot of the

the 21st Century (1996)—and by Nadine Gordimer, *Living in Hope and History* (2000). This is in footnote 5 of the very useful publication in McDonald and Walton (2002), 171–80, of notes that Heaney sent to the American director Tony Taccone in 1995 (hereafter cited as *Notes*). See also Denard (2000), 1–2.

[3] Heaney's own voice, pre-recorded, spoke these lines in the American Repertory Theatre production of *The Cure at Troy* in 1996, illustrated in Figure 12.

FIGURE 12. The 1996 ART production of *The Cure at Troy* in Cambridge, Massachusetts. Neoptolemus, holding the bow, cannot bring himself to desert Philoctetes.

play, and in that they deliver some sort of 'sense-making' by a group who have been witnesses rather than agents, they are arguably Greek and authentic in spirit.

'Sophocles has been Field Day's Greek dramatist'[4]: but *Philoctetes* was not an obvious choice. Why *Philoctetes*? And why this non-canonical play in 1990? I shall approach its new potency in recent times by way of a longer perspective on its performance reception. And finally I shall return to Heaney's optimistic—or half-optimistic—ending.

II

Philoctetes emerges from the records of the APGRD database (in summer 2002) as the fifth most performed of Sophocles' seven

---

[4] Seamus Deane in McDonald and Walton (2002), 148.

surviving plays in modern times (with more entries than for *Ajax* and *Trachiniae*). This relatively low rating is hardly surprising: *Philoctetes* is far from a model tragedy. It has a very small cast, and is the only surviving play by any Greek tragedian with no female parts and no overt gender interest. Furthermore it is set on an uninhabited island, or at least an uninhabited part of it, and so it has no civic setting; its chorus (as already implied) has no major set-piece odes; and the central role is taken by a howling, stinking, ragged outcast. It is often said (quite wrongly) that 'nothing happens' in *Philoctetes*: it is true that there is no death, no cataclysmic violence—some say that it is not really a tragedy at all.

The most striking statistics to emerge from the database records are that under 30 per cent (20 out of 74) of registered productions were performed before 1960, and that well over half (42 out of 74) have been put on since this volume's watershed year of 1969. And of the 27 productions in the 1990s, no fewer than 9 were in the form of *The Cure at Troy*. Clearly the 1960s were some kind of turning point in the performance reception of this play, as they were for Greek tragedy as a whole (see Edith Hall's 'Introduction').

There are, nonetheless, some fascinating details that emerge from the earlier records. For a start, it was one of the plays mounted in ancient Greek at the school on Capel Street, Dublin, in the early 1720s by Thomas Sheridan.[5] So the chronological span of this survey begins and ends, strikingly, in Ireland. The three-act French version by Jean-François de La Harpe was mounted at the Comédie Française in 1783, and was a celebrated showpiece for the star actor Talma. Bridging the Revolution, it was frequently revived across the next 45 years: evidently the dilemmas of the play had something to say in Enlightenment France.[6] *Philoctetes* was also one of the very first ancient plays to be put on in modern Greek, when it was staged in Odessa in February 1818. This was an event, both in Greek awareness of the Enlightenment, and in emergent national identity.[7] To close the nineteenth century,

[5] This is R. B. Sheridan's grandfather. See Stanford (1984), 32 with 43; Hall (1997*b*), 61; Hall and Macintosh (2004), ch. 9. So this production should be added to the *Hippolytus* and *Oedipus Tyrannus* in Marianne McDonald's valuable catalogue of 'Greek tragedy in Ireland', McDonald and Walton (2002), 80.

[6] See Mandel (1981), 132–3; Flashar (1991), 40.

[7] See the interesting article reprinted in Spathes (1986), 145–98; also Topouzes (1992), 166–7.

Philoctetes became the basis of a new play by the young André Gide in 1898.[8]

Among the rare productions in the first half of the twentieth century, two stand out for their associations. *Philoctetes* was mounted in ancient Greek by the Harvard Classical Club (founded 1885) in 1933. The director was a junior faculty member, Milman Parry—the most important Homer scholar of the century, who died young in 1935. Odysseus was played by Harry Levin and the music was by Elliott Carter, both at the threshold of distinguished careers. Philoctetes was played by a talented student, Robert Fitzgerald, who went on to become, among other things, a mentor for Seamus Heaney and the (posthumous) dedicatee of *The Cure at Troy*. *Philoctetes* also played its part in the introduction of Greek tragedy into modern Japanese theatrical culture. It was put on in Japanese in the Hibiya Amphitheatre by the Tokyo University Greek Tragedy Study Club in 1962, as one of the hugely popular series of productions directed by Professor Masaaki Kubo of the University of Tokyo. These lie behind the important productions of Greek plays by Yukio Ninagawa and Tadashi Suzuki. All of these varied and scattered productions are, in their different ways, presages and anticipations of the extraordinary 'coming of age' of this play in the closing years of the twentieth century.

III

Much of the crescendo of scholarly re-evaluation of *Philoctetes* during the 1960s and 1970s was centred on Neoptolemus' dilemma. The choice between ends and means, career opportunism versus unworldly integrity, advancement through corrupt company as the alternative to naive ineffectiveness—this life-choice spoke clearly to the times and seemed extraordinarily 'modern'.[9]

---

[8] Helpfully presented and translated in Oscar Mandel's pioneering book (Mandel (1981), 159–78). This little-known volume was something of a path-breaker in reception studies, including the performance reception of Greek tragedy. His erudite section on '*Philoctetes*, 1502–1896' (pp. 121–50) shows how between 1770 and 1880 the play was more of an inspiration for painters and sculptors than for writers.

[9] This aspect of the play made a huge impact on me personally when I first read it in the mid-1960s. Encouraged by Eduard Fraenkel, my very first academic publication was on this play: Taplin (1971)—it starts from the cliché that 'Nothing happens' in *Philoctetes*.

But this was not, in fact, the focus of either of the major interpretations which came from the world of letters in the decades leading up to what proves to be the key year in the reception of this play, 1990.

The most influential work of criticism was undoubtedly the 1941 essay 'Philoctetes: the wound and the bow' by the American literary journalist Edmund Wilson (died 1972).[10] For Wilson (who was much influenced by his Greek teacher at his privileged school in Pennsylvania) the play becomes a 'parable of human character'. Philoctetes' disease, his raving instability, aggravated by a degrading society, is inextricable from his special strength: he cannot have the bow without the wound. Taking a cue from Gide, Wilson sees Philoctetes as the figure of the creative artist, the creative artist as morbid genius; and there is a suggestion that one aspect of his disease is sexual insatiability. In the end the Philoctetes-figure is cured, and his divine gifts are put to the service of his people. How? Wilson's answer is that this happens through the trust and admiration of a guileless young person (Wilson repeatedly calls Neoptolemus a 'boy'). The essay concludes: 'in taking the risk to his cause which is involved in the recognition of his [Neoptolemus'] common humanity with the sick man, in refusing to break his word, he dissolves Philoctetes' stubbornness, and thus cures him, and sets him free, and saves the campaign as well'. The social dimension is for Wilson clearly secondary, however, to the personal. Men of genius are difficult; they need the unconditional admiration of pure young people if their gifts are to be realized and released for the world.

Wilson reached a wide readership, but his essay does not seem to have done much to put *Philoctetes* back on stage.[11] That was more the achievement of a playwright who made a new Philoctetes for the world of the Cold-War era. Heiner Müller (1929–96) was one of the most important—arguably the most important—German playwright of the generation after Brecht. He sought out a variety of ways to express his fiercely ambivalent politics within the heavily policed DDR, and prominent among these was repeated

---

[10] The title essay of Edmund Wilson (1941).

[11] Although Tom Stoppard's television play *Neutral Ground* (Stoppard (1998)), 'based on' *Philoctetes*, was transmitted in 1968. It is a spy thriller set in the Balkans. In Robert Silverberg's excellent science fiction novel *The Man in the Maze* (1969), the Philoctetes figure has exiled himself to the remote planet of Lemnos.

reworking of ancient Greek material (including Prometheus, Heracles, Oedipus and Medea). He worked on his first project of this kind, *Philoktet*, from 1959 to 1964, and published it in 1965.[12] It was first performed (in Munich, not in the DDR) in 1968, and has been staged many times since, especially during the 1970s. It is not easy to gauge how much or how little impact this play has had outside the German-speaking world, but it certainly makes a fascinatingly harsh and anti-sentimental contrast with the works of 1990 which I am going to discuss. Müller has selected the play in order to subvert its humanity, rather than to endorse it.

The language of the play is poetic, yet fierce, abrasive, and disturbing; its plot veers on an unpredictable course between glimpses of humanity and un-illusioned pragmatism.[13] Müller has stuck to the three central characters of Sophocles; but he has no chorus and (of course) no Hercules. His play does not require a knowledge of the Sophocles; and presumably the great majority of those who have seen and appreciated it have not known the Sophocles, or certainly not closely. At the same time, there are a multitude of intertextualities, and many places where the text briefly coincides with the Greek play, sometimes in confirmation of its significance, and sometimes in order to contrast or reject the classic 'model'. Basically the plot takes the same form and sequence as Sophocles', including the pivotal off-stage change of heart by Neoptolemus which brings him to the determination to return the bow to Philoctetes. But throughout the Müller play not only is the language far tougher and more lurid, there are also crucial ways in which the plot is changed and made more 'realistic': *Philoktet* is set in a world where power-politics suffer under no cloak of morality.

For one thing, each of the three protagonists brings with him a large body of manpower, so that military might and not just personal ethics are at stake. Then, for instance, once Neoptolemus has the bow, it does not need the intervention of Odysseus before he sets off to fetch help so that Philoctetes can be dragged to Troy by brute force. Then, the bow is finally returned to Philoctetes, not because Neoptolemus voluntarily gives it, but because he drops it in the

---

[12] For helpful discussions of Müller's *Philoktet* in relation to the Greek raw material, see Kraus (1985); Flashar (1991), 241–4; Hardwick (2000), ch. 4, especially pp. 69–71; Lefèvre (2000); Otte (2001).

[13] I have found the translation by Oscar Mandel in collaboration with Maria Kelsen Fader in Mandel (1981), pp. 223–50, an invaluable help.

middle of a hand-to-hand sword fight with Odysseus. This happens
as the play approaches its closing twists. Once Philoctetes has the
bow back, he embarks at once on preparing a long and humiliating
death for Odysseus. There follows this crucial passage:[14]

PHILOCTETES [*He shoots a vulture and throws it to Odysseus*]
>   Your vulture. Learn from him that which you taught.
>   Eat; he has eaten your kind before;
>   Soon he will dine on you; eat, eat your grave
>   So you can feed your grave after you die.
>   What, friend, you shudder, you do not relish
>   Your work?

NEOPTOLEMUS
>   Nor I mine.
>   [*He picks up his sword and runs Philoctetes through the back*]
>   The first of my dead
>   Are you whose gate to hell gapes at his back.
>   I wish another man had opened it.
>   Pitiful glory, killing a dead man.
>   His blood flows from the belly of his death,
>   But long ago it dribbled from his foot.
>   I have ended both his injury and ours.

ODYSSEUS
>   You proved yourself my quick apprentice.

It is a shocking turn, all the more powerful for its sudden 'killing'
of the Sophoclean plot.

   The two of them begin to bury Philoctetes' corpse, but then
Odysseus realizes that his body can be useful to them at Troy. He
can make up a story about how Philoctetes was killed fighting
heroically against Trojans, and he can thus retain the loyalty of
Philoctetes' men. Neoptolemus, repelled by this cynicism at the
expense of the dead, threatens to kill Odysseus with the bow, but
Odysseus points out that, in that case, he could never retain the
loyalty of even his own men, let alone those of Odysseus and
Philoctetes. The play ends with a telling symbolic exchange of
burdens: Odysseus takes the bow and Neoptolemus carries the
corpse of Philoctetes. As was said in the Prologue (by the actor of
Philoctetes, wearing a clown's mask[15]):

---

[14] I quote the passage, including stage directions, from Mandel (1981),
247–8.
[15] Mandel (1981), 223.

Our spectacle is grim—let me be plain—
It lacks a Message to take home and frame.

What does emerge clearly from the Müller play is that for him the central character is Odysseus, and that Odysseus is the 'winner'. He will win the war at Troy, while Philoctetes' 'cure', so central to Wilson and others, is nothing more wholesome or redeeming than a sudden, brutal stab in the back.

IV

'I remember the end of 1989 when the walls came tumbling down. . . . People walked the streets with smiles on their faces, but there were chill winds blowing already . . . ' These words open the second half of Timberlake Wertenbaker's play *Three Birds Alighting on a Field*, and are spoken by Biddy, the upper-crust English rose with winsome integrity, who is one of the three central characters in a large cast. *Three Birds* was first performed on 5 September 1991, after extensive workshops with Max Stafford-Clark at the Royal Court Theatre, and was revived with changes in 1992.[16] The play—at least, at first glance—is an entertaining comedy of manners in over twenty short scenes. It exposes and satirizes the commercialization and conceptualization of the art market, starting with an 'emperor's-new-clothes' auction where a purely white canvas is sold for over £1 million. It is specifically set in the early 1990s, and even includes a 'new' Romanian who poses as an innocent and impoverished art enthusiast in order to set himself up as a capitalist dealer on the model of the quick-witted and smooth-talking Jeremy. He completely fools the uncompromising painter, Stephen, who has withdrawn from the London art world in anger at its fickle artificiality.

Three Birds is light and amusing, and has none of the darkness and distress of Wertenbaker's explicitly Greek-informed *The Love of the Nightingale* (1988), or of her various translations and adaptations of Greek tragedy.[17] The play nevertheless touches

---

[16] The text in the collected plays of Wertenbaker (1996*b*) has changes from the single-play text of Wertenbaker (1992), above all the omission of two scenes bearing on Philoctetes. Although it is nowhere declared, I believe that the 1996 text is that of the 1992 revival. Unless I indicate otherwise, I shall be quoting from Wertenbaker (1996*b*): the opening quote is from page 411.

[17] Including *The Thebans* (for the RSC in 1991); *Hecuba*; *Dianeira* (Radio 3, 1999). On *The Love of the Nightingale*, there are good observations by Sara Soncini (1999), 73–4.

on several disturbing and far-from-ephemeral matters to do with gender, race, aspiration, failure, and the value (if any) of art. There are also resonances with *Philoctetes*. A girl-friend of Stephen uses him as a nude model for a painting of Philoctetes, and explains the story to him (388–9); he describes London as his 'Troy' (394). And later, when Stephen has been lured back to the metropolitan scene through the naive admiration of Biddy, he says, 'Even Philoctetes must have got tired of his island'—to which it is retorted that most of the victorious Greeks were drowned on the way home (439–40). These are light touches but well worked-in. Indeed, in the earlier version (see footnote 16) there were actually two scenes which explicitly epitomized the Sophocles play, casting Biddy as Neoptolemus and Jeremy as Odysseus. 'Odysseus, I recognize the shape of your words', says Stephen.[18]

Three Birds ends with Stephen's paintings back in fashion, and with his finding a happy artistic and sexual relationship with Biddy. So, it might be felt that the Philoctetes motif is too heavy for such a happy-ending comedy—some critics made this complaint at the time, and the cuts from the text suggest that they were not unheeded. But it does give a fascinating new twist to the Edmund Wilson interpretation. As in his account, Philoctetes stands for the artist whose genius and refusal to compromise isolate him; and the sexual ingredient of the 'cure', which is brought by the young Neoptolemus, implicit in Wilson, is explicit in *Three Birds*, where Neoptolemus is equated with Biddy. It only seems a shame, given Wertenbaker's feminism, that the female Muse serves the male Artist.

V

Philoctetes was in the air around the time when the walls came tumbling down. The APGRD database records no fewer than five productions from 1988, including the powerful staging by the Cheek-by-Jowl Company at the Donmar Warehouse, directed by Declan Donnellan (see Figure 13). And Derek Walcott had been working on his great poem, *Omeros*, for well over two years before its publication in September 1990.[19] Walcott managed to

---

[18] Wertenbaker (1992), 58.

[19] 'For three years, phantom hero, I kept wandering to a voice...', Walcott (1990), 323. Here as in all subsequent references I cite the Faber edition, which has the British rights from Farrar, Strauss & Giroux. It is a shame that, while the

FIGURE 13.   The wound and the bow. In this scene from the 1988 Cheek-by-Jowl production, Philoctetes (Keith Bartlett) refuses the final plea from Neoptolemus (Paterson Joseph) to go to Troy. Heracles, visible in full armour, appears above.

synchronize the promotion of the book with going to see the *Cure at Troy* in Derry in early October 1990—a nice crossing of paths at the centre of this chapter![20] He had, apparently, been encouraging Heaney to write a play,[21] and it may well be that *Omeros* influenced Heaney's choice and treatment of *Philoctetes*. I cannot find any clear evidence that either *Omeros* or *The Cure at Troy* influenced Timberlake Wertenbaker, but it would be surprising if neither did.

Omeros is not a play, and has not been adapted for performance on-stage, although Walcott has given many readings, including most of the poem for BBC Radio 4. It is, nonetheless, a mighty— indeed epic[22]—work of literature, and central to any account of the literary world in 1990–1. So I hope that a diversion to look at its treatment of Philoctetes may be of interest.

Many interleaving and interactive stories, from the present and from the past, are told in *Omeros*. Four are the most important. The first involves three people: the fisherman, Achille (the 'main man'); his friend and rival, Hector, who gives up fishing for taxi-driving; and the woman they both love, Helen. The second is the story of Plunkett, the English sergeant-major, who has 'gone native' in the Caribbean, and of his Irish wife, Maud. Then there are two singletons: the narrator 'I', a cosmopolitan poet from St Lucia, who is suffering a mid-life crisis; and finally, another fisherman and close friend of Achille, Philoctete (also often known as 'Philo'—all the Greek names in *Omeros* are, of course, in the French patois pronunciation).

The importance of Philoctete in the poem is marked by his speaking its very first line, and his being named in the second (p. 3). His wound, caused by the scraping of a rusted anchor hidden in the surf, is introduced on the next page. This opening scene is set after its healing (p. 4):

American edition has a beautiful Walcott watercolour on its cover, the British edition merely has the complacent 'ff' motif.

[20] I owe this satisfying fact to King (2000), 513.

[21] King (2000), 494.

[22] On pp. 12–13, the poet recalls a childhood vision of a black fisherman who 'scanned the opening line | of our epic horizon'. For excellent observations on Walcott's relation to epic, see Gregson Davis in Davis (1997*b*). The authorities cited by Joseph Farrell in Davis (1997*a*), at 249–50, who deny the applicability of the term, seem to have a very blinkered idea of the scope and location of 'epic'.

He does not explain its cure.
'It have some things'—he smiles—'worth more than a dollar.'

What affinities, then, does this Philoctete have with his Greek namesake?[23] Walcott had drawn on the Sophocles play before, in his play *The Isle is Full of Noises* (1982). Unfortunately, this has never been published; but, to judge from a brief résumé, it would seem that it involved some kind of choice between the Odysseus-voices in favour of the commercial and touristic exploitation of the Caribbean against the Philoctetes-voice of old insular integrity.[24] In *Omeros*, on the other hand, there is no equivalent of Neoptolemus nor Odysseus, no choice between home and Troy, and no bow (at least, not obviously). There is just the disabled Philoctete who lives on a volcanic island with his terrible pain: it is the figure and not the play which is woven in by Walcott's eclectic genius.

'... [A]ffliction is one theme | of this work ...' (p. 28). Plunkett has an old war-wound and psychological scars, eventually displaced by his grief for Maud; 'I' is suffering from depression and self-disgust. Philoctete's ulcerous wound is so bad that, howling and stinking, he cannot even participate in fishing forays; he drowns his pain and humiliation in drink at the No Pain Café. Philoctete himself believes his sore to be inherited somehow from the suffering inflicted on his ancestors by their manacles as they were brought on the Middle Passage.[25]

His cure, when it is achieved about three-quarters of the way through the poem, comes from Africa. The salve is a plant whose seed has been brought by a migratory bird, and—in a passage of astonishing power—it is sought out by Ma Kilman, the old 'sybil' who is the keeper of the No Pain Café: she retains some African instincts for her ancestral gods and for natural medicine. The plant's effect is 'homeopathic' in that it both looks like Philoctete's wound and stinks like his wound.[26] As Philoctete is healed and regains his strength and his self-belief, so too the 'I'-narrator begins to feel healed also ('There was no difference | between me

---

[23] There are good observations on the role of Philoctete in Austin (1999), especially 29–34, and Hardwick (2000), ch. 6, especially 102–5, and also Chapter 8 in this volume.

[24] I am indebted for being able to infer even this much to King (2000), 412.

[25] Some key passages on pp. 19, 129 and 248.

[26] I cannot help wondering if there is here a distant echo of the Telephus myth. He was wounded by Achilles' spear, and could only be cured by the weapon that wounded him. In the end, some rust from the spear is applied as a salve.

and Philoctete', p. 245). His cure is then completed by his visit to the healing sulphur-pits of the island in the company of the 'spirit' of Omeros/Homer.

> Then Philoctete
> waved 'Morning' to me from far, and I waved back;
> we shared the one wound, the same cure.
>
> (p. 295)

Even the bereaved Plunkett slowly finds his self-esteem again. Near the end of the poem Ma Kilman, in conversation with the old storyteller, Seven Seas, says,

> '... Philo standing godfather. You see?
> Standing, Philo, standing straight! ...'
>
> .   .   .
>
> Seven Seas sighed. What was the original fault?
> 'Plunkett promise me a pig next Christmas. He'll heal
> in time, too.'
>   'We shall all heal.'
>   The incurable
> wound of time pierced them down the long, sharp-shadowed
> street.
>
> (pp. 318–19)[27]

So the wound and cure in *Omeros* are partly to do with a recovery of personal self-respect, and partly a rediscovery of Africa as a way to expunge the stigma of slavery and ancestral pain. Perhaps there is a trace here of the Sophoclean reintegration of Philoctetes into the Greek heroic mainstream? *Omeros* reflects, in any case, another facet of the longing for healing in the world of the 1980s, newly awake to its old wounds.

VI

The centrality of the wound and the cure is declared in the very title of Seamus Heaney's play. The significance of the wound is explored in the choral 'pre-prologue', added at the very beginning:

---

[27] This seems to be simultaneously an optimistic statement of human endurance and an acknowledgement of the incurable finality of death. It is distantly recalled, perhaps, in a haunting phrase in the third of Seamus Heaney's sequence 'Mycenae Lookout' in *The Spirit Level* (1996): 'I felt the beating of the huge time-wound | We lived inside.'

> People so deep into
> Their own self-pity self-pity buoys them up.
> People so staunch and true, they're fixated,
> Shining with self-regard like polished stones.
> And their whole life spent admiring themselves
> For their own long-suffering.
> > Licking their wounds
> And flashing them around like decorations.
> > > > (pp. 1–2)

But Heaney does not take the obvious and simplistic course of also introducing or interpreting the cure at this stage. For about nine-tenths of the Sophocles original, all the emphasis is on Philoctetes' potential military role at Troy; and it is not until Neoptolemus has established true trustworthiness between them that the prophecy about Philoctetes' cure is introduced (lines 1329 ff., 1378–9). Heaney carefully follows this (72–3). When Philoctetes still refuses, he works into Neoptolemus' response an echo of the opening (74): 'Stop just licking your wounds. Start seeing things.'[28]

In Sophocles, after Philoctetes' intransigent refusal, the availability of cure is reiterated by Hercules (1424, 1437–8). And this is translated by Heaney in the chorus which in *The Cure at Troy* (78–9) articulates the voice in the volcano ('I heard the voice of Hercules in my head'). But in between his refusal and this 'voice' come the celebrated seven stanzas of which the third and fourth were quoted at the beginning of this chapter (p. 145). The second stanza has been as fiercely controversial as the third and fourth have been widely quoted:

> The innocent in gaols
> Beat on their bars together.
> A hunger-striker's father
> Stands in the graveyard dumb.
> The police widow in veils
> Faints at the funeral home.

This is the only place in the play where an allusion to the Troubles in Northern Ireland is so explicit and intrusive that it must be recognized as such. There are other passages which may be heard as direct allusions, for example, 'Are you going to stay here saying no for ever?' (69—cf. the slogan 'Ulster says "No"'), or 'reprisal

---

[28] *Seeing Things* was to be the title of Heaney's 1991 collection of poems.

killings' (79). But these do not need the allusion in order to make proper sense. Of course, references can be read in—but so can they be by any audience-member in any particular—and quite other— context. So, it is interesting that Heaney has more than once expressed regret over this stanza; and it is even reported that he sanctioned its omission in a production in the USA.[29]

Heaney has himself insisted that: '... while there are parallels. ... between the psychology and predicaments of certain characters in the play, and certain parties and conditions in Northern Ireland, the play does not exist in order to exploit them. The parallels are richly incidental rather than essential to the version' (*Notes*, 175). And yet almost everything that has been written about *The Cure at Troy* has dwelt on it as a play for Ireland, a play that is in some sense 'about the Troubles'. There are two main reasons for this, both worth exploring, and both calling for some qualification.

The first is that Heaney's only play to date takes its place as part of the extraordinary phenomenon of the remaking of ancient Greek tragedy in modern Ireland. Marianne McDonald, who has tirelessly explored this, has compiled a list of no fewer than twenty-four plays produced between 1969 and 1999 which draw—some more directly, some less—on Greek tragedy. They include well-known works by authors as various as Brian Friel, Tom Paulin, Brendan Kennelly, Derek Mahon, Marina Carr, and Frank McGuinness.[30] There is in fact such a variety that it is hard to make generalizations that are valid for all, beyond that 'there is something in the Irish air'. Several of the issues adumbrated by Edith Hall in her 'Introduction' to this book apply to many of these recent Irish/Greek plays: gender politics, revenge, individual and state, the use and abuse of power, free choice and determinism. But, as Frank McGuinness has recently emphasized, in response to the suggestion that this is a peculiarly Irish phenomenon: 'No ... It seems to be happening through the English-speaking world, that

---

[29] Wilmer, in Patsalidis and Sakellaridou (1999), 224–5; but he gives no details.

[30] This catalogue of 'Greek tragedy in Ireland' is in McDonald (2002), 80–1. Her own work on the subject is listed in p. 82 n. 1. There are significant additions to the literature on the subject by several other contributors to McDonald and Walton (2002), especially the chapters by Michael Walton and Seamus Deane. Other notable contributions to the subject are Wilmer (1999); Hardwick (2000), ch. 5; Denard (2000); and Richards (2000).

the Greeks are emerging as the dominant international force in our theatre. Possibly because we are living at a time of apocalypse. The strong meat is the diet they want to feed on.' *'Across Europe too . . .'* adds the interviewer.[31]

But *The Cure at Troy* is not just another instance of the phenomenon of 'Greek tragedy in Ireland': it was specifically written for Field Day, to be first performed in Derry and then to tour round towns in both Northern Ireland and the Republic. Field Day was set up in 1980 by Stephen Rea and Brian Friel, and it was soon joined by a group of writers and practitioners, including Heaney himself. It was their belief that, as put in Heaney's own words, 'We could create a space in which we could try to redefine what being Irish meant in the context of what had happened in the North, the relationship of Irish nationalism and culture. We were very conscious that we wanted to be quite independent of the British influence exercised through Belfast and the equally strong cultural hegemony of Dublin.'[32] Field Day put on fourteen productions between 1980 and 1998, nine of them world premières. In addition to *The Cure at Troy* and Tom Paulin's *The Riot Act* (1984), an adaptation of *Antigone*, they would have put on Athol Fugard's *The Island* in 1983, had they not been prevented by the Arts Council of Northern Ireland.[33]

Given that original seedbed, it is not difficult to see some of the local factors which drew Heaney to this particular play. Neoptolemus has to choose between the smooth, political opportunism of Odysseus, that Nobel-class economist with the truth, and the uncompromising purism of Philoctetes. This polarity was, no doubt, even more immediate in the Northern Ireland of 1990 than it is in most places in most times. Then there is the Wound, specifically glossed as a kind of self-pitying fixation (see p. 159 above). And there is the Cure, far less easy to pin down and far less easy to exemplify; but the repeated imperatives of the fourth stanza of the famous lyric (quoted on p. 145)—'So hope. . . . Believe. . . . Believe. . . .'—are clearly saying that this can somehow be achieved.

[31] Long (2002), 280.
[32] Quoted by John Walsh (1990) in the course of an interesting piece he wrote for *The Sunday Times.*
[33] Reported by Deane (2002), 161 n.1 and n. 2—a case of 'British influence exercised through Belfast'? On *The Island* see Hardwick, below, Chapter 8.

While the play was well received originally, and has been repeatedly revived in Britain and in the USA during the last twelve years (see e.g. Figure 12 above), it has not pleased everybody. Those with most commitment to one side in the conflicts within Ireland have least liked its irenic 'uplift', and especially its ending. Marianne McDonald has even entitled one of her characteristically robust nationalist essays 'When despair and history rhyme: Colonialism and Greek tragedy'.[34] Terry Eagleton has objected: 'How, in the north of Ireland context, do you demarcate a resourceful openendedness from shopping all you believe in?' He insists that the stuff about believing in miracles simply does not translate into the realities of Irish politics.[35] Seamus Deane, old friend of Heaney and fellow director of Field Day, does not like the play's evasion of what Troy stands for (this is worth quoting at length):

Troy's 'meaning' in the play's system of political reference is ostensibly clear; it refers to Northern Ireland. But there is the problem that it also refers to a place that is finally sacked and that this prelude to the final battle, which seems to be about a miraculous change, is not in any coherent sense really about an alteration that will bring reconciliation. Instead, it will bring victory to one side and defeat to the other. This can all be dismissed by denying that the play should be mapped precisely on to the Northern Irish situation. But that would, surely, be to say that it can be partially mapped in that way only up to the critical moment. Then the allegory or the reference system can be abandoned. This seems unsatisfactory. It's a way of having your cake and then not eating it. The issue has to be faced.[36]

But in the course of insisting that the 'allegory' should be capable of being fully followed through, what Deane does is to show that the kind of precise mapping onto the Northern Irish situation, which he expects, does not work in his own terms either. In the course of this diatribe, he has to make it sound as though Odysseus stands for the Greeks at Troy (i.e. the Unionists), while Neoptolemus stands for the Trojans (Nationalists). In other words, his starting point—that Troy 'refers to Northern Ireland'—is untenable: the play does not have 'a system of political reference'.

The play does not map completely onto the Irish situation in 1990 (nor today). Once it had survived its original genesis, there was and is no reason to expect it to do so; and, in my view, there

---

[34] McDonald (1997).   [35] Eagleton (1998), 374–7.
[36] Deane (2002), 159–60.

was no reason to expect it to have done so even at the first performance in Derry. I would hold that the same is true of the
tragedies of ancient Greece. They came about at a particular
moment in the history of the city of Athens; but they also had the
strength to survive and outgrow that topical time and place. A key
reason for this resilience is that, instead of being pushed inward
towards enclosure within the terms of local allegory, they were
constantly pushing outwards towards the universal or the univer-
salizable. By reacting against the pull towards 'topical' drama,
Heaney thus achieves something closer to Sophocles than his
critics call for. Heaney is (unlike so many creative artists) concise
and acute in articulating his own artistic purposes: 'by being an
impatient reaction to the burden of dutiful "commentary"-type
drama ("Troubles art"), *The Cure at Troy* seems to me not only a
declaration of a need for the imagination to outface the expectations of the topical but also a proof that it can happily and
"relevantly" do so' (*Notes*, 178).

Of course *The Cure at Troy* did not prescribe any secret formula
that could cure the terrible wounds of Northern Ireland. It could
not, and it should not, be expected to. As the chorus put it:

> No poem or play or song
> Can fully right a wrong
> Inflicted and endured.
>
> (p. 77)

The good that poetry and drama may do in the world is much less
easy to pin down or to assess. And, in so far as it has power, that
power is not limited to only one time or place. Ireland was not the
only festering wound in the world in 1990—no more then than
now. Nor was it the only place where there might be hope for
change for the better. Looking back from 1995, Heaney wrote
(*Notes*, 176): 'I don't think I would have had the gall to do a play
with such a consoling outcome had it not been for the extraordinary events of late 1989.' When Neoptolemus urges on Philoctetes
that, 'This is the summer of the fall of Troy' (p. 73), we might well
hear an echo of the fall of Ceauşescu, the fall of the Berlin Wall.
The Trojan War can be mapped no less significantly—and no less
inexactly!—onto the fall of Soviet-style communism.

Of course, there were downsides already threatening from the
start in 1989, as Wertenbaker's play was already pointing out (see

p. 153 above). A hint of downside as well as uplift may well be there, indeed, in Sophocles' play. Hercules, at the same time as promising victory and glory, warns Neoptolemus and Philoctetes to show piety to the gods during the sack of Troy. Lines 1441–2 say (in Heaney's version, p. 79):

> But when the city's being sacked
> Preserve the shrines. Show gods respect.

One of the most notorious acts of impiety at the sack was Neoptolemus' slaughter of the aged Priam at the altar of Zeus. It might be argued that this is an ominous cloud on the horizon of the bright sky at the end of Sophocles' play, a flaw built into the 'consoling outcome'.[37]

VII

Heaney is a poet, and *The Cure at Troy* is still, to date, his only play. Another reason why he and others have turned to Greek drama in recent years is that it gives a special opportunity to include the power of poetry within a play[38]—'Poetry | Allowed the god to speak' (p. 2) is Heaney's way of saying this.

Yet much of Heaney's version is not notable for its high poetry: on the contrary, it is sometimes complained that the dialogue parts of *The Cure at Troy* are remarkably plain, even pedestrian or unpoetic. It is true that the Greek iambics are put into a rough blank verse, which eschews the kind of verbal colour, striking images, and word-plays that Heaney could easily have produced 'in his sleep', had he wanted to. It is a self-denying plainness of a kind that Brendan Kennelly, or Ted Hughes, let alone Derek Walcott, would find difficult if not impossible. In terms of linguistic and poetic register, the iambics of Heaney's play are, in fact, not at all distant from those of Sophocles. What may not be obvious until it is performed or read out aloud is that it is intensely and consistently *speakable*. Once delivered, it is clear that it is very much not in prose; and also that it is not in a contrived or elaborated or strange language. It is perhaps the most speakable of all

---

[37] I argue this more fully in Taplin (1987).
[38] Frank McGuinness in Long (2002), 280, singles this out as one reason why modern Irish poets have turned to Greek drama.

modern versions of Sophocles in English. It is true that there are occasional homely—or Hibernian—touches that are attractive, for instance (p. 27):

> Life is shaky. Never, son, forget
> How risky and slippy things are in this world.
> Walk gently when the cup's full, and don't ever
> Take your luck for granted.

But too much of this, and it would be a different and more colloquially limited play.[39]

Perhaps the greatest gain of this low-key iambic diction is that it is set off radically against the lyric passages—and that too is very much in harmony with the Greek original.[40] Heaney translates the lyric passages of Sophocles into short-lined stanzas with tight schemes of rhyme or half-rhyme. He does this not only for the lyric dialogue *parodos* (entry song) and for the two fully-fledged choral songs in the middle of the play, but also for the big quasi-monody when Philoctetes is left behind with the chorus, and even for the little lyric snatches during the first big scene.[41] These lyrics are superbly crafted, often remarkably close to the Sophocles, and every word cries out to be heard clearly in performance, whether or not accompanied by music. 'I am afraid I am devoted to the notion of each word being heard clearly by the audience. Bell-bing it into the ear, then carillon to your heart's content' (*Notes*, 179–80). There is no call for apology: the evidence is clear, in my view, that a high premium was put on the audibility of the lyric as well as spoken parts of the original Greek productions.

The 'pre-prologue' (pp. 1–2), which dwells on the role of the chorus and on the strengths and weaknesses of poetry, is expressly metapoetic. It is, interestingly, not in lyric metre but in blank verse. This makes the lyric verse of the crucial seven stanzas

---

[39] In *Notes*, 174–5, Heaney suggests to his American director that the spoken parts of the play should be delivered in whatever English accent is local, including the translation of '*Och*' into '*Aw*'.

[40] Rachel Buxton points out to me that there is a somewhat similar contrast of levels of diction—and of distant closeness to contemporary Ireland—in Heaney's version of *Buile Suibhne*, which he calls *Sweeney Astray* (1983, first published by Field Day).

[41] The passages catalogued are: *parodos* lines 135–218 = pp. 12–15; choral songs at 676 ff. = pp. 37–9 and 827 ff. = pp. 45–7; quasi-monody at 1081–1168 = pp. 59–61; little choral snatches at 391 ff. = pp. 22–3 and 507 ff. = p. 28.

shortly before the end of the play all the more striking when they
suddenly ring out—and suddenly depart fundamentally from
Sophocles (p. 146 above). They too are self-reflexive, but are also
hortatory and incantatory poetry. They begin:

> Human beings suffer,
> They torture one another,
> They get hurt and get hard.
> No poem or play or song
> Can fully right a wrong
> Inflicted and endured.

And, not least, there is that most famous line, in rhyme with 'once
in a life-time':

> And hope and history rhyme.

Although the line is always quoted as so ringingly unequivocal,
there may be a touch of irony here, not uncharacteristic of Heaney:
'hope' and 'history' do *not* rhyme, of course, not by any phonetic
stretch.

This might seem a crafty quibble, but we are dealing with a poet
who devotes great craft to his rhyme and half-rhymes. I think that
this interlocking of rhyme and meaning may also bear on the very
final words of the play. Here Heaney turns three lines of Greek
anapaests (a semi-lyric metre) into two six-line stanzas and a
pendent extra line, all delivered by the chorus (pp. 80–1):

> Now it's high watermark[42]
> And floodtide in the heart
> And time to go.
> The sea-nymphs in the spray
> Will be the chorus now.
> What's left to say?
>
> Suspect too much sweet talk
> But never close your mind.
> It was a fortunate wind
> That blew me here. I leave
> Half-ready to believe
> That a crippled trust might walk
>
> And the half-true rhyme is love.

[42] A double-reference to the watermark in the poet's paper?

So, the play does not end on the major-key resolution of a perfect rhyme, nor with a complete stanza. It ends with the half-rhyme of 'believe' and 'love', which is a true half-rhyme, yet is made hesitant being called a 'half-true rhyme'. Similarly but differently, the 'rhyme' of 'hope' and 'history', which is not a true rhyme at all, may still be half true.

And the chorus is only 'half-ready to believe'. This is surely significant after the ringing reiterated imperative 'Believe...' in the celebrated stanzas (quoted on p. 145). The chorus in a Greek play lives within the play and is never granted an omniscient or definitive status: I would maintain that the same reservation holds for *The Cure at Troy*. Despite all the public recitations (and despite Bill Clinton), 'It lacks a message to take home and frame', as Heiner Müller has it (p. 152).

Heaney has himself sometimes expressed a half-regret that *The Cure at Troy* is too optimistic, that it has too much of what he calls 'uplift'.[43] But, as in the Sophocles, the uplift is not blinkered and is not simplistic. It seems to me that the poet of Colonus and the poet of Mossbawn have both managed to 'suspect too much sweet-talk', while at the same time staying true to the imperative of 'never close your mind'.[44]

---

[43] He is reported by Walsh (1990) to have said, 'If the play has a problem, it is that it is too full of uplift.'

[44] I am most grateful to all three editors—Edith, Fiona, and Amanda—for their various support. I am also indebted to Sandie Byrne, and especially to Rachel Buxton, who has fed me many helpful leads on Heaney and Heaniana.

6

Aeschylus, Race, Class, and War in the 1990s

Edith Hall

SPEAKING THE UNSPEAKABLE

During the Gulf-War bombardment of Iraq in early 1991, hardly any images of the enemy appeared in the western media. When a rare photograph of a dead Iraqi soldier, leaning through the wind-screen of his burnt-out vehicle, was published in *The Observer* (28 February), Tony Harrison wrote 'A Cold Coming'. In this poem the 'charred Iraqi' spoke directly to the poet/narrator. His voice was cynical, unforgiving, full of hate:

> Lie and pretend that I excuse
> my bombing by B52s,
>
> Pretend I pardon and forgive
> that they still do and I don't live ... [1]

By letting the dead Iraqi speak, by imagining his thought pro-cesses, by acknowledging that the targets of the allied forces attacking Iraq were human beings, full of human hatred, Tony Harrison made his British and American audiences think about their countries' foreign policies.

Harrison's Iraqi is quite aware that victors do not want to engage in dialogues with their dead opponents. The ancient Greeks, he says, did not make poems in which Hector, left dead on the battle-field, revealed his bitterness about their conquest of Troy: 'I doubt victorious Greeks let Hector | join their feast as spoiling spectre'. But unlike Homer's Hector, the unappealing Iraqi in Harrison's poem is neither patriot nor hero. He is bitter that he was poorly paid and that everyone in Iraq lived under 'black clouds'. He recalls the torture he practised for Saddam's regime, the looting,

---

[1] 'A Cold Coming' was first published in *The Guardian* on 18 March 1991, and later that year, along with the photograph (by Kenneth Jarecke), in the eponymous collection *A Cold Coming: Gulf War Poems*. In this chapter citations are taken from Harrison (1992), 48–54.

'the Scuds we launched against the Jews'. But ultimately the reader is asked to see little difference between him and his killer, the common soldier on the enemy side, 'some screen-gazing crop-haired boy | from Iowa or Illinois'.

This chapter was completed in the autumn of 2002, a year after the terrorist attacks on the USA on 11 September 2001, and more than a decade after the Gulf War, provoked when Saddam Hussein, who had already incurred international condemnation for his persecution of the Kurds, launched the Iraqi invasion of Kuwait. The eleven intervening years have revealed the horrifying extent of the Iraqi leader's arbitrary exercise of power, repression of ethnic minorities, abuse of human rights, and alleged development of chemical, biological, and now nuclear weapons. As I write a new war between the USA (with or without the endorsement of the United Nations) and Iraq seems increasingly likely. It is important that the reader be aware that the argument in this chapter, the first half of which concerns the 1991 Gulf War, was developed without any knowledge of what happened between the USA and Iraq from late 2002 onwards. This has made it extremely difficult to write and may make it controversial or uncomfortable to read. But feeling on edge may actually be appropriate. For the subject of this chapter is precisely the way Greek tragedy helped audiences in the 1990s cope with political discomfort.

Tony Harrison is a dramatist as well as a poet. In order to address issues his audiences might prefer to ignore he has repeatedly adapted dramatic texts (especially ancient Greek plays), as the type of literature whose features of impersonation and absent narrator lend it to giving voice to the voiceless. Some reviewers objected to the ending of his 1988 stage play *The Trackers of Oxyrhynchus* (inspired by and including the fragments of a Sophoclean satyr drama), when the satyrs metamorphosed into filthy London vagrants. Homelessness, especially of the psychiatrically ill, had become an urgent issue during the 1980s, as a result of the Conservative government's policy of ejecting large numbers of people from hospitals and leaving them to their own helpless devices—a policy entitled, with Orwellian cynicism, 'Care in the Community'. One of the trademarks of the other director to be discussed in this chapter, Peter Sellars, has been even more radical topicalization of the standard repertoire; notorious for his 'social underbelly' versions of Mozart (*Don Giovanni* (1987) was set amongst Harlem heroin addicts), the most politically charged of them all was his 1996 Glyndebourne Festival Opera production of Handel's *Theodora*, which relocated the story of spiritual resistance to state tyranny from fourth-century Antioch to modern America. It was a protest against the American way of capital punishment, as the Christian martyrs Theodora and Didymus sang their final, rapturous duet from the tables onto which they had been strapped to receive their lethal injections.

From their earliest days Greek tragedians had a reputation for saying the otherwise unsayable. Ancient sources record that they were prosecuted for revealing things in the theatre which were too painful, shocking or controversial for their audiences to stomach. There was a tradition that Euripides was prosecuted for showing the respected hero Heracles going mad in a play performed at a public festival: the problem here was the clash between the indecorous content being represented and the decorous civic context. Aeschylus supposedly caused a riot in the theatre with a tragic performance which exposed the secret contents of the Eleusinian mysteries: although many of his audience had been initiated, experiencing the mysteries was an intensely private, personal matter whose discussion in the collective presence of citizens was prohibited. Aeschylus' near contemporary Phrynichus probed a more political wound by putting on a 'historical' tragedy about the Persian king Darius' suppression, in 494 BCE, of the Asiatic Greek citizens of Miletus. Phrynichus was consequently fined for making his audiences weep by 'reminding them of their own troubles'. The Athenians bridled, apparently, at the direct representation of real-life pain and hatred which they or their friends had experienced.[2]

In response to this ancient report, in his *The Labourers of Herakles* (first performed 1995), Harrison himself took the role of Phrynichus. In his *Prometheus*, as the final part of this chapter will argue, Harrison 'reminded us of our own troubles' by discovering in the role of Io a sensitive new avenue by which to approach even the Holocaust—a sore so painful that the legitimacy of artistically representing it all has been seriously called into question. Greek

---

[2] Euripides: *The Oxyrhynchus Papyri*, no. 2400, edited by E. G. Turner (1957). See Foley (1985), 156; the play must have been the *Heracles* discussed in Chapter 4 above by Kathleen Riley. Aeschylus: Aristotle, *Nicomachean Ethics* 3. 1111ᵃ 8–11, with scholia. Phrynichus: Herodotus 6. 21.

tragedy's potential for 'reminding its audience of their own troubles', for permitting the exploration of difficult, painful, or controversial subject-matter, is certainly one reason why it has recently attracted both Harrison and Sellars. The Greek tragedians, especially Aeschylus, have been found to allow the probing of the collective psyche, the political underbelly. Aeschylus has assisted the exploration of the socially distasteful, indeed the *occupation* of ideological territory on the very margins of the publicly acceptable.

Greek tragedy has long been used to say the things *officially* banned from public discourse. Dissidents operating under conditions of censorship have often found its archetypal situations useful disguises for the allegorical expression of dangerous views. The first translation of Sophocles' *Electra* into the English language was a privately circulating royalist attack on Oliver Cromwell (Aegisthus), printed shortly after the execution of Charles I in 1649; Sophocles' *Oedipus* long fell foul of censorship in Britain because of the perceived obscenity of the mother–son sexual relationship.[3] In Greece itself, during the dictatorship of 1967–74, there was a list of eight thousand proscribed titles, including some works by the Greek dramatists as well as modern authors like Samuel Beckett, publication or vending of which was punishable by up to five years' imprisonment. The Aeschylean Prometheus found himself labelled an 'anarcho-communist' and banned in the heart of his ancestral home. Productions of Greek tragedy were also carefully policed under the terms of the junta's circular order to all theatres in Greece, which included the banning of any pieces which could 'disturb public order', 'propagate subversive theories', or 'undermine the healthy social condition of the Greek people'. Some dissident 'allegorical' versions of ancient plays did, nevertheless, manage to escape the censor,[4] and Greek drama, performed outside Greece at events organized to raise awareness of the junta's excesses, played a part in bringing the colonels under

---

[3] See Edith Hall (1999*b*); Macintosh (1995).

[4] See Van Steen (2000), especially 204–8 on *Lysistrata* in 1969; Van Steen (2001); and Van Dyck (1998). Much more recently, Luca Ronconi's production of a Greek comedy, Aristophanes' *Frogs*, was at the centre of a censorship row in Italy in 2002, when it was alleged that Silvio Berlusconi's right-wing government had tried to interfere with the criticisms levelled at it in the production (*La Repubblica*, 20 May 2002).

international pressure.[5] Yet the primary focus of this chapter is something rather less easy to identify than overt or official censorship. What is under scrutiny is the ways in which politically motivated directors have used Greek tragedy to evade the more implicit, unconscious, consensual, and culturally endorsed policing of the represented and the representable.

Future cultural historians may remark on the presence of Aeschylus in the politics of the late twentieth century. On 4 April 1968, for example, one of the darkest moments in modern history, the African-American community heard the news of the assassination of Martin Luther King. They rose in fury in 110 cities. Thirty-nine people died; thousands were injured. Race and class hatred dominated the psychological agenda of America. That night Bobby Kennedy had to exhort the distraught Black ghetto in Indianapolis to the lawful pursuit of justice. Only Aeschylus would do. The climax of his speech was this quotation: 'In our sleep pain which cannot forget falls drop by drop upon the heart until, in our despair, against our will, comes wisdom through the awful grace of God.' Some resonant choral lines of Aeschylus' *Agamemnon* (179–81) were thus implicated in epoch-defining civil conflict. In a cycle of bloodshed reminiscent of Aeschylus' vision of the curse blighting the royal house of Argos, two months later, on the day preceding the opening of Richard Schechner's *Dionysus in 69*, Bobby Kennedy himself lay dead. But Aeschylus' *Agamemnon*, along with its partner plays in the *Oresteia* trilogy, went on to become a crucial element in the living repertoire of the stages of the world, enjoying productions by such theatrical titans as Koun, Mnouchkine, Stein, Hall, and Serban, its complex and ambivalent portrayal of blood feud and judiciary, overlord and citizen, Greek and barbarian, parent and child, man and woman, now speaking louder than ever before to our war-torn modern consciousness.

---

[5] For example, 'An evening of free Greek music and drama', organized in London in early 1970 by the Greek Committee against Dictatorship and sponsored by the British Musicians Union, Fire Brigades Union, and TGWU. The participants included Melina Mercouri, Minos Volonakis, Mikis Theodorakis, Maria Farandouri, Glenda Jackson, Janet Suzman, Joss Ackland, John Williams, and the English Chamber Orchestra. It included Patrick Wymark's recital of the Edict on Censorship (translated by Volonakis) as well as readings from proscribed texts such as *Antigone, Trojan Women, Philoctetes*, and Aristophanes' *Lysistrata*, and *Assemblywomen*. The APGRD holds a copy of the programme.

We can already begin to see how this efflorescence of *Oresteia*s was inseparable from the global historical crisis of its moment—the climax of the Cold War, followed by the fall of the Berlin Wall and western liberal capitalism's compromised 'victory' over its long-time Soviet rival. The *Oresteia* has offered a theatrical site for exploring the decades-long repercussions of international war, the corrosive psychological effect of feuds, and the impossibility of finding a compromise between irreconcilable claimants to political authority. As an APGRD volume devoted to the *Oresteia* will soon argue, the trilogy continued to be performed repeatedly in the 1990s, as the world struggled to discover a new political shape and direction, while western Europe and the USA searched for a new enemy against which to define their own identities, and against the backdrop of the terrible civil wars, war crimes, and reprisals afflicting the nation states which had formerly comprised the communist Soviet Union and eastern bloc.[6]

The undoubted importance of the *Oresteia* has led to the relative academic neglect of the other four Aeschylean tragedies, all of which have been treated to important performances during the last three decades. In East Germany the martial *Seven against Thebes* was given an anti-war charge by the Berliner Ensemble as early as 1969,[7] and a much more recent production lies behind an Italian film exploring the 1995 siege of Sarajevo (see further Michelakis, Chapter 7). The ethnic confrontation depicted in the Aeschylean *Suppliant Women* has also produced realizations emphasizing international politics as much as gender relations within marriage. But the two Aeschylean plays which have enjoyed the most political performances are those which have, since the age of romantics and revolutionaries, always had the most rebellious, oppositional, and sometimes even seditious associations—*Persians* and *Prometheus Bound*:[8] *Persians* was a charter text for French revolutionaries, for the leaders of the Greek War of Independence;

---

[6] See Macintosh, Michelakis, Hall, and Taplin (forthcoming).

[7] Siegrist (1997), 351.

[8] This chapter is not the place to join the Classicists' debate on the authorship of the tragedy *Prometheus Bound*. Richard Schechner himself produced *The Prometheus Project* at the Performing Garage in 1985, which was broadly speaking anti-nuclear. Schechner's Prometheus was an enlightened Iranian both persecuted by the Shah and also rejected by the Islamic fundamentalists. Other radical versions have included William Reichblum's minimalist Noh-influenced *Prometheus Bound* at La MaMa in 1984 (Walton (1987), 375) and Tom Paulin's *Seize the Fire* (1989).

Prometheus Bound was central to the romantic dreams of liberty expressed by Goethe, Schlegel, the Shelleys, Byron, and Marx,[9] and even to the man who originated the term 'communism', a nineteenth-century Christian socialist called John Goodwyn Barmby, who published his views in a monthly magazine he entitled *The Promethean: or Communist Apostle* (1842).

The shape taken by the performance reception of Greek tragedy in the former eastern bloc is slightly different from that in western Europe and the USA. Both Aeschylean 'revolutionary' plays were important in East Germany well before the 1968–9 watershed, partly because of the importance there of the British communist George Thomson's *Aeschylus and Athens*. This classic of Marxist cultural theory (on which see also Fischer-Lichte, Chapter 13, p. 335) was first published in 1941 by Lawrence and Wishart (the publishing house then closely associated with the British Communist Party), but made a bigger impact in German translation in 1957.[10] *Persians* was familiar in 1960s East Germany, where Mattias Braun (a student of Brecht originally from the west) reacted to US aggression in Korea by creating a heartfelt, slang-laden, *Persians* set at a decadent high-society cocktail party. Originally produced in 1960, it was revived several times in different East German locations. *Prometheus Bound*'s longer and more intense love affair with revolutionary socialism was also used (ironically) in the 1960s by Heiner Müller.[11]

It is therefore no surprise that it is these two plays which have produced the most oppositional of all political interpretations in the last decade of the twentieth century, both by directors prepared to criticize not only liberalism's properly approved targets of tyranny and overt racism, but even the economic system of free-market capitalism itself. Their critiques of First World imperialism extend to engaging with the possibility that even adversaries in international warfare, and advocates of socialism in the domestic

[9] See Ferris (2000), 134–57; Hardwick (2000), 128–30.

[10] See Siegrist (1997), 349. The impact of Thomson's work is clear in Ernst Fischer's classic of Marxist literary theory, *Von der Notwendigkeit der Kunst* (Dresden, 1959).

[11] On Braun's *Persians* see Trilse (1975), 150–5; Kuckhoff (1987), 19–20. Heiner Müller's *Prometheus* was published in 1968 but first performed in a Zurich production directed by Peter Stein (1969). See Siegrist (1997), 357–8. *Persians* has recently returned to Dresden, where a version by Durs Grünbein, directed by Niels-Peter Rudolph, opened at the Staatsschauspiel in Dresden in February 2002.

arena, may have legitimate perspectives. Without for a moment wishing to denigrate the achievements of campaigners on behalf of women and ethnic minorities, it must be said that by the 1990s they had won many of their arguments, at least publicly, in the west. The same can hardly be said for the ordinary Muslims and Arabs who objected to US bombardment of Iraq, Libya, or Afghanistan, or, indeed, for the homegrown organized working class. Yet *Persians* and *Prometheus* have produced interpretations which explore the perspectives of people belonging to two of the most unpopular and unfashionable groups in the last decade of the twentieth century—Iraqis and British miners, male members of a largely white and heavily unionized sector of the industrial proletariat. Thus Greek tragedy has been able to offer a powerful medium for directors whose views come from 'dangerous' ground at the very edges of what mainstream (even left-liberal) North American and British ideology deems acceptable.

PETER SELLARS'S *THE PERSIANS* (1993)

Aeschylus' *Persians* has recently (1998) been translated into modern Iranian. The translator, Fuad Rouhani, was an urbane and moderate Iranian citizen, a talented musician, who also translated Plato. He had a distinguished career in international law behind him by the time he was made first Secretary-General of OPEC, stationed at Geneva, in 1960, his tenure of which office was characterized by a naïve but idealistic determination to keep politics and religion out of OPEC. He was a true cosmopolitan. What will really be interesting is to see how long it takes for his translation of Aeschylus' *Persians* to find a performance in his own country. The British tour by Theatre Bazi in 2002, for example, is the first by an Iranian company since the 1979 revolution. It is revealing that the director is Attila Pasyooni, a survivor of anti-idolatry legislation, who worked with Peter Brook on *Orghast* at Persepolis in the long-ago heyday of the Shiraz Arts Festival, before the fundamentalist revolution (see Chapter 1).

It may be a long time before contemporary Iranians perform Aeschylus' *Persians*. But an international cast of actors playing the Iranians' Iraqi neighbours spoke through it in the early 1990s, in a production emanating from the land of Saddam Hussein's deadly enemy, the United States of America. This was Peter Sellars's new version of Aeschylus' *Persians*, written by Robert Auletta, which fundamentally challenged the American image of the ordinary people on the enemy side in the Gulf War.[12] Certain stereotypes of Arabs and Muslims—in particular relating to their perceived sensuality, effeminacy, and irrationality—had been increasingly exposed in the west, at least since the publication in 1978 of Edward Saïd's seminal *Orientalism*, as fictive ethnicities belonging to the now obsolete ideology of imperialism. But the Gulf War showed how easy it was to fill the void, created in the western imagination by avoidance of authentic pictures of an Asian enemy, with conjured images of all Iraqis as inherently hard, tyrannical, cruel, militaristic, and above all terrifyingly *different*. This is what was so remarkable about the challenge to stereotypical thinking posed by the humanized Iraqis of Sellars's *Persians*, which gave voice to the enemy side in a manner similar to Harrison's poem 'A Cold Coming'.[13]

Auletta's adaptation transposed the play's action from ancient Persepolis to modern Baghdad itself. The military disaster portrayed was not the defeat of the Persian fleet by the Athenians in the ancient sea battle of Salamis (September 480 BCE), but the bombing of Iraq by the USA (January–February 1991 CE). Given the opprobrium heaped on this new *Persians* in the USA (as opposed to Europe, where reactions were mixed but generally temperate), it is important to stress at the outset that Auletta's version was not remotely blind to the faults of the enemy. This Iraq was militaristic, despotic, arbitrary, and guilty of imperialist ambitions. The audience was forced repeatedly to remember that Saddam Hussein's conduct as Iraqi president had been absolutely disgraceful—there was considerable discussion of the royal family's vanity (Saddam's mother (standing at the rear of Figure 14) is

[12] Sellars's *The Persians* was first performed at the Salzburg Festival in Austria in July 1993, before being performed at the Edinburgh Festival in August, the Mark Taper Forum in Los Angeles in October, and at the Hebbel-Theater in Berlin.
[13] Of the numerous books on 'Orientalism' inspired by Saïd's work, the most important has been Kabbani (1986). Since Harrison and Sellars, giving a poetic voice to the Islamic opponents of the USA or Israel has become a useful tool for radical artists seeking to go beyond the unquestioning languages of a 'patriotic' war. Bruce Springsteen's lyric *Paradise*, on his 2002 album *The Rising*, juxtaposes the voice of a Palestinian suicide bomber in Israel with an American 9/11 widow. Steven Berkoff's one-man drama, *Requiem to Ground Zero*, which premiered at Edinburgh on 14 August 2002, includes the voice of a suicide terrorist on one of the 9/11 planes.

FIGURE 14.   Martinus Miroto dances the role of the messenger, reporting the disaster at Salamis to his queen, Atossa, in *The Persians*, directed by Peter Sellars (1993).

writing her dead husband's official biography), and emphatic references to Saddam's terrible slaughter of 'tribesmen in the hills, | and others in the swamps', designed to bring to mind the gassing and other persecutions of the Kurds (a people whose desperate plight Sellars has indeed recently highlighted in the German staging of his 2002 *The Children of Heracles*). Far from being concerned about the suffering of the Iraqi people, Auletta's megalomaniacal, exhibitionist Saddam boasts to his mother that he has 'never been so happy' or fulfilled:[14]

> I defied the United States of America!
> The most arrogant people in the world!
> And they could not destroy me!
> This Super Power, as they like to call themselves.

Indeed, the section of Auletta's *Persians* which is most different from that of Aeschylus is the conclusion, which considerably extends Xerxes' relatively short scene in order to explore the ambition, cruelty, and Oedipal motivation of a monstrous man who can put himself above both local and international law, commit acts of desperate cruelty, and even mandate genocide. Auletta and Sellars may have asked their audiences to imagine the condition of the Iraqi people, but they were equally determined to put the Iraqi leader's atrocious conduct under the spotlight.

Aeschylus' *Persians* had always been remarkable because its cast consists exclusively of Persians, the invaders of Athens and their much-hated enemies. It combines a deeply anti-Persian tenor, emerging above all in the vain and incompetent figure of Xerxes, with a striking acknowledgement that Persian casualties must have caused terrible misery, especially to Persian widows and parents. In the 1990s it became an opportunity for Sellars's actors to impersonate the much-hated enemies of the USA and at least *imagine*, for an hour or two, what it must have felt like to be a citizen of Baghdad during the air raids. For some reviewers, even in Europe, this extreme form of topicalization was outrageous. When describing the Edinburgh Festival production, Irving Wardle fulminated in *The Independent on Sunday* (16 August 1993) that this 'dire charade' had 'broken all records in the name of topical relevance'. Certainly Aeschylus' war poetry was radically updated to ram home the Iraqi context. At the end of the first long chorus, the hotel where the earlier part of the production was set was hit by bombs and rockets. Auletta found a grim poetry in the language of the modern military. Instead of chariots, bows, and

---

[14] Auletta (1993), 37, 33, 47, 88.

sabres, the catalogues of hardware in *Persians* speak of the Iraqi's 'Scorpion Battalions', 'Cobra Squadrons'; the lament for the city lists the 'Thousands and thousands of sorties ... | invisible Stealth bombers ... | monstrous B-52's carpet bombing ... | ... | Cluster bombs exploding'. Yet Auletta's free adaptation was absolutely faithful to the emotional register of the original, which above all emphasizes its characters' hatred for the enemy, terror, and longing for the dead.[15]

This empathetic procedure, by which Sellars's audience listened to ordinary Iraqi hatred and agony, was not something much encouraged in other prominent media. (Neither video footage from inside Iraq nor 'embedded' journalists featured in the 1991 Iraq war.) Indeed, it was nearly effaced by the effect of unreality created by CNN's computer graphics and euphemistic terminology of destruction—large sites containing many humans were 'taken out' like icons in a computer game. It was in response to this 'catastrophic collapse of the real' that the theorist of Disneyland and postmodernity, Jean Baudrillard, made his notorious claim in a newspaper article that the Gulf War was so unknowable in the west that, epistemologically speaking, it 'did not take place' at all.[16] Sellars used Aeschylus to reassert that the war not only had taken place, but had hurt real people badly. He was explicit in the programme note that he saw one of the roles of theatre as offering a substitute for journalism, as countering the everyday censorship of human sympathy:

The Gulf War was one of the most censored wars in the history of journalism. The Pentagon carefully controlled the flow of information to the outside world. One of the things we rarely saw on television in this war with Iraq was Iraqis. Dead or alive. The term 'collateral damage' was used to describe dead daughters, wives, mothers and fathers. The human toll was largely discounted or screened out with ideological or commercial filters.[17]

The Darius scene, especially, is a full-frontal assault on its audience's feelings. The audience is informed that 'Metal, flesh, screams have become one', and 'five hundred children a day' are

---

[15] Auletta (1993), 13, 41–2, 20–1. On the distinctive emotional register of the original tragedy see Edith Hall (1993) and (1996), 19.

[16] Baudrillard's article was published in *The Guardian* on 11 January 1991, p. 25, and is reprinted in Baudrillard (2002).

[17] Sellars's programme essay is reproduced at the beginning of Auletta (1993).

dying. Darius takes his wife on a tour of a children's hospital where the electricity has been cut off and mothers rock their dying children because their incubators have broken down. Before he returns to the underworld, Darius provides his wife with a warning to relay to the Americans, sitting 'comfortably in their capitols, | smiling, playing golf, appearing on television | and speaking of their great achievements': his message is simple: the Iraqi experience demonstrates that political power disappears fast and easily.[18]

Equating Iraqi and American hubris, let alone encouraging sympathetic feelings towards Iraqis, was, for many in Sellars's audiences, going far beyond the pale. At the American performances, which took place at the Mark Taper Forum in Los Angeles in October 1993, about a hundred members of the 750–strong audience walked out *every single night*.[19] They did so not just at the beginning of each performance, but over the whole course of it, as if each individual offended person found his or her breaking-point at a different moment in the production. But what they all seemed to find it difficult or impossible to bear was Sellars (or rather his chorus, impersonating people who in reality will inevitably have hated their enemy) actually saying the unsayable: 'I curse the name of America' (37). The audience did not want to be told how much their nation was hated. Even now, at the distance of a decade, or perhaps *because of* the distance of the decade that has included the events of 11 September 2001, the terminology of the chorus's viewpoint on the USA, whom they label 'terrorists', does remain intensely shocking even to a jaded western literary critic like me (33):

> They are terrorists, you see.
> Force always seems to work for them.
> They are experts at applying sanctions—
> to garotte a country,
> cut off its vital life of trade,
> suffocate and humiliate its people...

---

[18] Auletta (1993), 66, 69, 74.

[19] Lahr (1993), 103. There was a much warmer reaction to the production in Europe, especially Salzburg. Sellars is particularly admired in Austria and Germany, for both aesthetic and political reasons. It is no coincidence that the first book-length study of this director, by Gottfried Meyer-Thoss (2002), has been written in German.

Applying the most charged terms in the American political imagination to the Americans themselves, making the Americans the wielders of force and garottes, probing the extreme limits of linguistic relativism, pushing the audiences to discover where the edges of their collective group loyalty and consciousness lay—these are tasks for which Auletta and Sellars found the earliest tragedy in the western repertoire to be especially suited.

Sellars's previous direction of a Greek tragedy was also focused on American foreign policy, although the implied enemy was Latin American rather than Asiatic. *Ajax* (1986) was also written by Auletta and premiered at the Kennedy Center in Washington, before transferring to the La Jolla Playhouse and a European tour. It was actually set at the Pentagon. By implying the context of a senate hearing or a politically charged trial, it confronted the ways in which Sellars believes public speech is policed. This was achieved above all through the use of the deaf actor Howie Seago (who later played Darius in *The Persians*) as Ajax (see Figure 32 in Chapter 15 below). Seago's signing of Ajax's primal pain drew extreme attention to the gap in all the other characters' rhetoric between feeling and its expression. Sellars himself is ready to use the term 'censorship' (rather than, for example, what many people might regard as 'unconscious control mechanisms') to denote the ways in which information and viewpoints are regulated in the American media. His use of deaf signing as stage language owes much to both Robert Wilson's *Deafman Glance* (1970) and Pina Bausch's *Nelken* (*Carnations*, 1982);[20] Sellars thinks that our culture lays too much emphasis on words when in actuality 'Ninety per cent of our communication is non-verbal.' He insisted that Howie Seago, a deaf actor, as the ghost of Darius, was 'simply a great actor' by any standards, and that he put more effort into communication than many who can hear. But, for Sellars, using a deaf actor served other more self-conscious purposes: it underlined the key aim of theatre—the search for common understanding and the undermining of misrepresentation. The very presence of a deaf actor asks the basic question, 'How it is possible for one person to understand another, and where do the *mis*understandings occur?'[21]

---

[20] See L. Taylor (1995) on deaf signing in Bausch and Sellars. The text of Robert Auletta's *Ajax*, along with his notes, several photographs, and a discussion by W. D. King, were published in the journal *Theater* 18 (1986).

[21] Quotations from Pappenheim (1993).

Even before the Gulf War (let alone 11 September 2001), Sellars had been interested in what he believes is mass self-deception, collective misunderstanding. He has said that 'the large-scale newspapers, and particularly television, operate under tremendous censorship' of a consensual and latent nature, a censorship operated by 'a strange faceless collective that makes its decisions without asking anyone'. He seems to think of this collective as consisting of the unelected arbiters and endorsers of appropriate ideology, suitable opinion, fitting sensibility, tasteful sentiment, sanctioned emotion, licensed viewpoint, valorized reaction, and legitimate response. These arbiters, he thinks, are employees of media corporations, working in such places as 'a tall office building on the corner of 57th and the Avenue of the Americas (Sixth Avenue) in New York', where CBS makes its decisions.[22]

Where Tony Harrison's *Prometheus*, as we shall see below, is fascinated by the ways in which the public memory of conflicts and catastrophes is constituted years after the event, Sellars's *Persians* was remarkable for the (relative) immediacy with which he used ancient theatre to comment on contemporary politics. Sellars is fascinated by the interface between high art and the making of contemporary history in media devoted to current affairs. Shortly before *Persians* he was involved in the news-driven operas of the 'post-minimalist' composer John Adams, including the diplomatic comedy *Nixon in China* (1987) and, more significantly for the current argument, the 'terrorist tragedy' of 1991, *The Death of Klinghoffer*. Sellars conceived the idea of an Iraqi *Persians* while working on the premiere of *Klinghoffer*, which told, in the style of a passion-play, the terrible story of the 1985 hijacking of the Italian cruise ship *Achille Lauro* by four Palestinian commandoes, and the brutal killing of the wheelchair-bound Jewish-American passenger Leon Klinghoffer. The connections Sellars drew between Aeschylus' *Persians* and the topical East–West confrontation portrayed in *Klinghoffer* seem to have been two-way, since commentators remarked on the 'Greekness' or 'almost Attic formality' of its dramatic style.

During the *Klinghoffer* rehearsals the Gulf War broke out, and Sellars was struck by the similarities between the scenes he saw on CNN news and those which he was staging. But what he found

---

[22] Sellars (1989), 90.

painful was awareness of what actually was *not* being shown, as a
result of the US embargo on Iraqi reactions to the war and, indeed,
on Iraqi subjectivity altogether. He said at the time of *Persians*:

> I have come to think of theatre now as almost an alternative information
> system—what can't be shown on television can be said on-stage. In Amer-
> ica the war in Iraq was shown with no Iraqis at all—dead or alive. So, in
> this evening, we're saying come and meet a few![23]

In the programme note he argued along similar lines, that TV
images of war launder and censor the daily death toll. 'One of the
possible reasons for theatre to continue to exist in our technological
age is as a kind of alternative public information system that is able
to partially humanise the denatured results of our vaunted and
costly objectivity.' As Michael Billington observed, these views
are important not so much for their specific and controversial
referent—the Gulf War—as for their general truth: television has
turned each one of us 'into a spectator of global conflict whereas
theatre still has the capacity to shock us into moral awareness'.[24]
You do not have to agree with Sellars's stance on American foreign
policy to see that he is exploring the potential of Greek tragedy to
deepen and develop our moral capacities as world citizens at the
dawn of the new millennium.

Greek tragedy has recently proved fertile territory for the exploration of its relationship with journalistic film footage and
photography, news programmes, and documentaries, including
those recording the current American–Islamic conflict; this is
demonstrated in Michelakis's discussion of Nikos Koundouros's
The Photographers, based on *Antigone* (Chapter 7). Sellars is also
concerned about the way that other American art forms—especially commercial cinema—create the culture that licenses the
current shape taken by American foreign policy, especially the
tolerance of bombardment, with its high risk of extensive civilian
casualties. The chorus say they are being terrorized by

> . . . real American made monsters—
> Rambo, The Terminator,
> torn from their Hollywood homes . . .
> fantasy screens . . . and set down upon us . . .
> given permission for a true killing spree . . .

---

[23] Pappenheim (1993).   [24] Billington (1993).

breathing bullets . . . the true American way . . .
The pounding blood force of their bloody country . . .[25]

The hyper-masculine American heroes played by Sylvester Stal-
lone and Arnold Schwarzenegger, who use terror as they police the
world with their armouries of automatic weapons in the name of an
ill-defined notion of individual freedom, the type of heroes criti-
cized in recent versions of *Heracles* (see Riley, this volume), are
here blamed for reinforcing in their audience of American citizens
the ideology which can uncritically support the bombardment of
Iraq. Sellars has also said that Greek drama simply had to be
instituted because every citizen of Athens needed training in how
to participate in a democracy, how to decide whom to vote for, how
to distinguish liars from truth-tellers, and how to administer justice as a juror. This director perceives a real problem in American
culture, where citizens are expected to be responsible participants
in a democracy and to act on juries when their 'only training is
Rambo and *Hill Street Blues*'.[26]

TONY HARRISON'S *PROMETHEUS* (1998)

If Peter Sellars's *The Persians* showed its audience what it was like
to an 'enemy without', a bombarded Iraqi, Tony Harrison's first
feature film, *Prometheus*, is frank about an 'enemy within'—or,
more precisely, about northern English working-class people
facing life below the poverty line. It is inspired by the Aeschylean
tragedy and is throughout informed by its dialogues and confron-
tations. The screenplay at one point even quotes the ancient tragedy in ancient Greek: Hermes' first apostrophe to Prometheus
(*Prometheus Bound* 976–8) is in Harrison's version addressed with
contempt and malice to miners descending a mineshaft.[27] The cast
includes familiar figures—Kratos, Bia, Prometheus (a former shop
steward with the National Union of Mineworkers), a chorus of
Oceanids, Hermes, Io—but with the important addition of some
extra miners, a small miner's son, and his mother and grand-
mother.

One of the reasons Harrison likes film is that 'the cinema screen
can give heroic stature to the most humble of faces . . . an essential

---

[25] Auletta (1993), 45.   [26] Sellars (1989), 93.   [27] Harrison (1998), 18.

requirement in a film where the most unlikely wheezing ex-miner is slowly made to represent Prometheus himself'.[28] Walter Sparrow delivers an unforgettable performance as the spokesman for Harrison's unlikely heroes, an old shop steward for the British National Union of Mineworkers, who in due course turns into Prometheus. Harrison's film draws epic inferences from the land-mark conflict in British post-war socio-economic history. Twice in the early 1970s, under Edward Heath's Conservative government, the National Union of Mineworkers had brought Britain to a near-standstill by striking in protest against sudden pit closures. In both 1972 and 1974 the country was forced to work a three-day week in order to economize on energy consumption. The strikes improved miners' pay, conditions, and status, and the Conservatives never forgave them. The Right Wing's new warrior, Margaret Thatcher, returned to power in 1983, after defeating Argentina, 'the enemy without', in the Falklands War. Her priority was now the defeat of the 'the enemy within'.

In early 1984 the National Coal Board threw down the gauntlet by announcing the closure of twenty pits (in the event far more than that have closed down). The closures would necessitate making over twenty thousand men redundant, removing the income from hundreds of thousands of British people in mining and allied industries, and destroying dozens of communities across the poorest regions of Wales, Scotland, and North-East England. The miners went on strike. Although Harrison's *Prometheus* is set in its own 'present' of the 1990s, their strike is signalled as the point at which Kirkby, the northern English community the film portrays, was thrown into crisis; an early image is the Old Man's coal carving of a figure in Promethean pose captioned 'Striking Miner, 1984'.

In defending the mining communities, Harrison has accepted into art heroes even less acceptable than the destitute vagrants who become the heroes towards the end of *Trackers*. It is one thing for a poet to support oppressed causes which have been legitimized by mainstream western liberal ideology, such as women and ethnic minorities, in whose name countless produc-tions and adaptations of Greek tragedy have emerged over the last three decades. It is quite another to make any kind of heroes out of

---

[28] Harrison (1998), xxii.

the white male working class, especially the National Union of Mineworkers. In reality the NUM at the time of the strike was a diverse and conflicted organization, boasting principled family men, intransigent ideologues, really brave moral heroes, decent moderates desperate for a quiet life, hotheaded youths spoiling for a fight, grey-headed sages, scabs, and secessionists in unequal proportions. Its leadership was split between those who proposed keeping the mines open and those for whom the point of the argument was the right to dignity, work, and remuneration, not necessarily the right to dangerous work in the unhealthy conditions of the mining industry. Yet these ordinary, hardworking, proud, community-minded, argumentative, and increasingly desperate men were almost universally portrayed during the strike as dangerously violent hooligans and thugs; the right-wing press insinuated that they were in league with Libya and the Soviet Union (a ludicrous claim in the UK, where communism almost completely failed to take root in the working class). Even mainstream media unquestioningly set about discrediting Arthur Scargill, the hardworking president of the NUM, whose greatest crimes were political shortsightedness and a lack of charisma, by implying that he was a corrupt, avaricious bully, and even a national traitor.

A constant theme in Harrison's work has been the inaudibility in our culture, and especially in 'high' artistic culture, of the voices of the working class. In *Prometheus* the boy thoughtlessly lights a fire with his father's archive of newspaper cuttings on the pit closures, destroying even the last memorials of the miners' subjective experiences. In another important symbolic moment the Promethean fire bestows on the miners of Kirkby not only an audible voice but the capacity to speak in verse. Hermes is deeply suspicious of poetry, because 'Poets have taught mankind to breach | the boundaries Zeus put round speech', and indeed, the miners, imprisoned on a cattle truck, lose their customary dialectal habits and become extempore poets themselves.[29] This charming, humorous scene is a wonderful antidote to the silencing and gross misrepresentation of the miners during and since the strike. At the time the footage on news programmes showed hardly any miners' faces. There was,

---

[29] Harrison (1998), 33. On this aspect of the film see the perceptive comments of Hardwick (2000), 133–4.

however, a brief row about the media presentation of the so-called Battle of Orgreave on 18 June 1994. The early evening BBC newscaster reporting the shocking confrontation between mounted police and pickets at Orgreave Colliery sat in her studio underneath a photograph apparently depicting a miner kicking a policeman's head. This was an unrepresentative image since 51 miners were injured in comparison with fewer than 28 policemen. Every other television channel was saturated with frightening images of miners, except for the independent-minded 'minority' Channel 4 News at 7.00 p.m., on which the anchor Peter Sissons interviewed the chief police constable of South Yorkshire with commendable scepticism. But despite the efforts of Sissons and a few other newspeople of similar professionalism, neither the miners nor their leaders ever had the remotest chance of fair representation. They displayed emotional strain, swore publicly, had strong accents, unfashionable haircuts, unglamorous clothes, few media contacts, and absolutely no experience in the manipulation of public opinion. They inevitably lost the public relations war before the strike had even begun.

A couple of courageous individuals did seek to give the miners an immediate hearing: Richard Hines quickly organized a Sheffield-based TV documentary *Cole not Dole* (1984), and Peter Cox's *The Garden of England* (1984) was a documentary (subsequently a play) about a Kentish mining community resulting from a National Theatre Studio Workshop. But both achieved only marginal exposure and disappeared fast. The nearest the miners got to a sympathetic hearing in mainstream media was a song by the activist songwriter Billy Bragg. His indignant lyric 'It Says Here', on his 1984 album *Brewing Up with Billy Bragg* (which reached the Top Twenty during the strike), explicitly complained about the one-sidedness of the press coverage of trade union matters: 'those who own the papers also own this land . . . When you wake up to the fact | That your paper is Tory | Just remember there are two sides to every story'. But even this briefly voguish song neither offered positive images of the miners nor gave them a voice.

Indeed, the victims in this epochal conflict remained virtually silenced in the public imagination until the mid-1990s, when the Berlin Wall had safely fallen and the mining industry in Britain had been decimated. Tens of thousands of people who never

impinge on the collective consciousness still live in the former
mining communities—they are now very poor, suffer increasing
levels of petty crime and addiction, attend failing schools, and
possess nearly worthless real estate. It is in this context of almost
total silencing, erasure by non-representation, that Harrison's
cinematic treatment of the miners' strike needs to be appreciated.

Illumination can be gained from comparison of *Prometheus*
with three films which share its subject-matter and are nearly
contemporary with it. Mike Figgis's one-hour documentary *The
Battle of Orgreave* (2001) finally allowed the mining families involved in that confrontation to relate it from their own perspective.
A realist (but ultimately escapist) attempt to tell the miners' tale,
which has enjoyed relatively wide circulation on account of the
presence of Ewan McGregor as the male love interest, is Mark
Herman's 1996 *Brassed Off*, the fictional story of the Grimley
Colliery band. This film is curiously optimistic in its message,
which implies that working-class people are so resilient that they
can heroically weather with a wisecrack even wholesale removal of
their livelihood. Stephen Daldry's moving *Billy Elliot* (2000), on
the other hand, portrays an eleven-year-old working-class boy's
desire to study ballet. Its context is strike-bound Easington, one of
the toughest colliery towns in County Durham. Billy's father and
brother are miners, daily attending the picket line. The film is
broadly sympathetic to them (although critical of their construction of masculinity). But its message is ultimately about an individual's ability to transcend his class origins and tribal culture;
Prometheus, on the other hand, which shares a similar focus on a
young miner's son, is about all humanity's collective need and
desire to transcend its own tragic history. The shift from the
individual to the collective, from the specific to the general (in
the terms of Aristotle's *Poetics* 9, from the historical to the philosophical), is made precisely by grafting the particular struggle of
the British miners onto the transhistorically significant ancient
Greek myth. It is this fusion which constitutes the total originality
of the film. Harrison has tried to forge a new cinematic language,
based on myth, which can also accommodate the figuring of the
real and contemporary. This mythic language is one which can
represent and be spoken by gods and miners alike. It is unique.
Through the special diction of poetry everyday people speak and
their environment is illuminated: Harrison believes that 'film

and poetry have a good deal in common', and poetry can 'enter the inner world of people in documentary situations'.[30]

Harrison's creative labours included the collection of materials. The film attempts to offer a true memorial to the British miners and their past: Harrison had originally planned to create a theatrical performance of *Prometheus Bound* on a slag-heap in Yorkshire. But when it became clear that all the pits would close down, he visited them, collecting signs and equipment which physically appear in the film. In order to create his authentic documentary situations, he also collected vast amounts of information, carefully pasted into a series of notebooks. They include newspaper and magazine cuttings about the mining industry (especially accounts of accidents with high death tolls), images of Prometheus from ancient Greek vases to the high temple of capitalism constituted by the Rockefeller Center, sketches, photographs, and postcards. The terrible legacy of pollution left by heavy industry is as prominent a topic in the notebooks as in the film, whose landscapes make bleak visual poetry out of derelict cooling towers (see Figure 15). Some

FIGURE 15. A menacing Hermes (Michael Feast) revels in industrial pollution in Tony Harrison's film *Prometheus* (1998).

[30] Harrison (1998), xxiii.

words are written out in the notebooks for contemplative purposes: on p. 563 of Notebook 3, Harrison has simply written 'Spreng-bombe—high explosive bombs', 'Vernichtungsfeuer—annihilat-ing fire', and 'Vernichtungslager—extermination camp'. These terms underlie one of the film's least noticed achievements, the way it uses resonances from classical poetry to find a poetic voice in which to address the most challenging of artistic topics, especially for a non-Jew—the subjectivity of victims of the Holocaust.

Others have used Greek tragedy to explore particularly sensitive aspects of the Second World War, for example the viewpoint of German soldiers as presented through the myth of Oedipus in Rainer Simon's film *The Case for Decision Ö* (1991), on which see Michelakis in the next chapter. But the representation of the Holocaust itself has become the most notorious controversy in critical theory and postmodernist thought. It has been argued that any kind of fictive construct is disrespectful to what was all too horribly true, that art must transform memory (which in the case of the Holocaust is an extremely dangerous process), that non-survivors should not write about the Holocaust, that its themes should not be made available to a general and especially to a non-Jewish audience, and even that it can never be legitimate for non-Jews to attempt to represent the Holocaust at all.[31] Others have simply viewed the topic as too horrific or too irrational to be even imagined, let alone expressed, and that the only rational reaction to such 'ineffability' is a reverential silence.

Critics have debated the relative strengths and weaknesses of different aesthetic modes in negotiating the moral and cognitive minefield posed by the murder of millions—truthful memoir, documentary, docufiction, realist fiction, parable, fable, con-sciously distortionist cartoon, comic grotesque, allegorical fantasy. But in *Prometheus* Harrison evades selecting any single aesthetic mode. He combines a more realist 'documentary' strand (for example, in the picture of pilgrims' candles at Auschwitz), with a symbolic and surrealist mode created by powerful audiovisual events, such as the screaming miners being melted down in a German foundry. With these he interweaves a third strand

---

[31] For succinct overviews of these questions see Friedlander (1992), 1–21, and especially Schwarz (1999), 1–42. For a different perspective see Clendinnen (1999). On issues facing film directors dealing with the Holocaust see the remarks of Insdorf (1983) and Avisar (1988).

consisting of narrative patterns, perspectives, and active interventions derived from the ancient tragedy, slightly reminiscent of the allusive use of myth in Primo Levi's 'The Canto of Ulysses', which also revolves around hell fires, added in 1958 to *Survival in Auschwitz*. Harrison's answer to representing the Holocaust is aesthetic pluralism plus Aeschylean tragic myth. This is well illustrated by one part of the Auschwitz sequence. The 'realistic' approach along the railway track is accompanied by the composer Richard Blackford, who sings a lament in the persona of a Jewish cantor. The power and solemnity of this moment is shockingly disrupted by the arrival of the contemptuous Aeschylean lackey Hermes, who violently snuffs out the candles left by Jewish pilgrims and snarls a speech to camera explaining why: 'Fuhrer Zeus' hates 'These candles that can help them cope | with history and lack of hope.'[32]

In *Prometheus Bound* Io is viciously persecuted, half turned into a cow, and sent on a lonely journey eastward by a vindictive divinity. Her 'leaping' entrance, tortured by the gadfly, followed by her agonized account of her eviction from ancestral home and homeland, constitute one of the most extraordinary treatments of a persecution victim's subjectivity anywhere in ancient literature. It makes the matter of being transformed into an animal, and treated like one, emotionally plausible. It is this aspect of Io's role in the ancient tragedy to which Harrison has so brilliantly responded. His Io is pursued across Europe by 'Poor KRATOS and his sidekick BIA', who 'miss the swastikas of yesteryear':

> They've come to Dresden and they've sighed
> for the good old days of genocide.
> How they've yearned to reinstate
> the furnace as a people's fate.

Io's desperate, wordless journey extends through several sequences. She is eventually arrested with great brutality by Kratos and Bia, who hurl her into the cattle truck. They use cattle-prods to force her into the abattoir, where the camera studies her slaughter, the disgusting industrialization of death and the processing of her carcass, which is finally cremated.[33]

In the abattoir sequence Harrison has therefore put the Aeschylean cow-metamorphosis to the most sombre possible use. Since he has written about the experience, as a child, of watching documentary

---

[32] Harrison (1998), 61.   [33] Harrison (1998), 45, 78.

newsreel of the extermination camps and the Holocaust, it is possible, as Froma Zeitlin suggested to me, that Harrison had unconsciously absorbed images from the dreadful Nazi propaganda film, *Der ewige Jude* (1940), which he tells me he has certainly seen; this includes a horrifying episode showing the kosher slaughter of animals, in concealed slow motion, to convey the idea that Jews are barbaric in their treatment of animals and therefore deserve similar treatment. Be that as it may, in Io's frantic but wordless agitation, movingly portrayed by the athletic Fern Smith, Harrison has created images suggested by the Aeschylean mythic drama to forge a medium of representation weighty enough for its subject-matter, capable of conveying extreme pain on an individual level, but avoiding any hint of sensationalism or voyeurism. Harrison has said specifically that his Io's experience is a poetic-cinematic attempt to convey the subjectivity of a Holocaust victim. He wants his viewers to see, with brutal literalness, what it means to be turned into a cow (or into a human treated like a cow) destined for a death chamber.

But Io also necessitates the use of a *female* figure, the extended evocation of the terror of an individual woman, terror conveyed through the performer's physical body and animal noises (the emotional force of which gained much from Fern Smith's own committed vegetarianism), rather than through the inherently inadequate medium of words. This acts as a reminder that fewer women than men actually survived the selection for the gas chambers because they were thought less valued as skilled labour—a fact that has been used to explain why there have been many more male writers of Holocaust memoirs.[34] More than half a century after the Holocaust, Harrison thus finds in Greek tragedy potential for speaking about some of the most unspeakable acts in human history, for making the millions of invisible victims of the gas chambers slightly more visible. We may never be able to look directly at the Holocaust's naked, ugly face, but the shocking force of Io's death certainly exempts Harrison from the charges of trivialization and disrespect often levelled against artists representing the Holocaust.[35]

[34] Schwarz (1999), 5.
[35] Langer (1995), 3. Aeschylus has also been used by Jewish writers when addressing the issue of the Holocaust. The 2003 production in Tel Aviv of Rina Yerushalmi's *Mythos*, a Hebrew version of the *Oresteia*, made clear references to the Holocaust in the depiction of mass graves at Troy.

FACING THE UNFACEABLE

In 'A Cold Coming' Tony Harrison's dead Iraqi has a face where
the dead flesh forms a 'dumb mask like baked dogturds'. That
poem is published in a collection of war poetry entitled *The Gaze of
the Gorgon*. The culturally pervasive connection between the idea
of the mask and the idea of death is always dialectical: in ancient
Greek thought the gaze of the Gorgon, the archetypal mask-head,
was literally lethal because it turned the viewer into stone.[36] But
Greek tragedy is also a masked art, and wearing a mask can,
paradoxically, also permit the viewing of the unviewable: as
Nietzsche put it in *The Birth of Tragedy*, Dionysiac art compels
us to gaze into the horror of existence, yet without being turned
into stone by what we see.[37] In the programme note to the National
Theatre *Oresteia* for which he was translator, Tony Harrison famously developed this Nietzschean idea by suggesting that the
Greek tragic mask allows its wearers to keep their eyes open in
situations of extremity, just as a visor allows a welder to look into
the flame (see further Wiles, this volume p. 255). This powerful
simile is suggestive for the function of the genre as a whole. To
attend a performance of a thoughtfully directed Greek tragedy can
be to assume a kind of aesthetic mask through which we can bear to
contemplate situations of extremity.

This idea is similar to one of the most brilliant arguments
Aristotle proposed in defence of all mimetic art, including drama:
artistic representations of reality are educative precisely because
they allow us to contemplate horrific things 'which cause us pain to
witness in reality' (*Poetics* 4. 1448[b] 10–12). Aristotle cites the
examples of disgusting creatures and human corpses. We can't
bear to look upon the corpses of the Iraqis our own soldiers and
pilots have killed, nor on our own angry poor we have created by
class war and unemployment, and have great difficulty even imagining an art form adequate to the representation of the subjectivity of the millions of dead victims of the Holocaust. But through
the familiar, ancient, formal lineaments of Greek tragedy, by

---

[36] See above all the influential essays 'Death in the eyes: Gorgo, figure of the
Other' and 'In the mirror of Medusa', in Vernant (1991), 111–50.

[37] '... wir werden gezwungen, in die Schrecken der Individualexistenz hinein-
zublicken—und sollen doch nicht erstarren', from *Die Geburt der Tragödie*, section
17, English translation adapted from Nietzsche (1993 (1872)), 80.

peering, at first cautiously, through its mask, even the pain on which our lives and society are predicated, even the countless forgotten people whose suffering we have permitted can be briefly remembered, be rendered faintly visible and audible, at least for a little while. Theodor Adorno may have said that writing poetry after Auschwitz was barbaric, but he qualified this by also saying that 'suffering has as much right to expression as a tortured man to scream'; at the height of the Vietnam War, Walter Kaufmann argued that the value of tragedy lies in its 'refusal to let any comfort, faith, or joy deafen our ears to the tortured cries of our brethren'.[38] In the 1990s, through Aeschylus, real screams have just about been heard through the world of postmodern signs, computer generated images, and iconic news footage used by the media which constitute our psychological environment.

What lends the significance to Sellars's and Harrison's productions of Aeschylus is their ideological edginess. This is revealed in the tone of many of the reviews, which tend to mask political disagreement under aesthetic complaint. It is instructive to compare the enthusiasm of the general response to a successful version of another Aeschylean tragedy, *Suppliants*, which has shown how 'politically correct' opinions can be so diluted as to take the visceral punch out of Greek tragedy altogether. Charles Mee's *Big Love* (on which see Foley, Chapter 3) is an amusing sex comedy, but, according to Rush Rehm, it 'turns Aeschylus into a chocolate for the knowing bourgeoisie... happy to consume culture that is wacky, well-pedigreed, and watered down'.[39] Neither Harrison nor Sellars is unaware of the problem inherent in using elite western art to represent non-elites and non-westerners. The father in *Prometheus* has a healthy working-class disrespect for the classical books which have been central to the education and culture of his masters, and Sellars is convinced that an important theatrical event can make effective waves far beyond the cosy world of the performance context: 'The most important nights in the theatre were seen by only a tiny fraction of the population and yet they have passed into the history of the world.'[40] Nor is either Sellars or Harrison unaware of the danger of defusing issues by looking at them through art, of the ambivalence of their own role in applying

---

[38] Adorno (1966), 362; Kaufmann (1968), 182.   [39] Rehm (2002), 111.
[40] See O'Mahony (2000), 7.

salve to liberal consciences. The cynical charred Iraqi says to the narrator of Tony Harrison's 'A Cold Coming','That's your job, poet, to pretend | I want my foe to be my friend.' Sellars, meanwhile, fears that radical theatre can easily become just another fashionable pursuit for the comfortable classes: he said in his acceptance speech for the Harvard Arts Medal 2001, delivered 5 May 2001, that 'the arts have been placed to one side as the decorative phenomena, as the dessert, as the thing that comes later, the option, the entertainment for a bored leisure class'. But he remains committed to *trying* to make the arts play a central role as 'the actual way in which the most difficult things on the planet can be faced and shared, in which we find the language with which to speak of the unspeakable, in which we can actually describe to each other the most difficult things we're facing'.[41] In the summer of 2002, as he was preparing to stage his adaptation of Euripides' *The Children of Heracles*, he explained why he believes he is so 'obsessed' with Greek drama: 'I'm way more interested in democracy than I am in theater.'[42]

What distinguishes Sellars and Harrison is not just that one is primarily an opera director and the other a poet, that one has directed Aeschylus on-stage and the other on screen, nor that one is American and one English, nor that one is a bourgeois Harvard graduate and the other working-class in origin. It is more important that for Sellars radical politics can still have an optimistic agenda, while Harrison is apparently more convinced of the impossibility, in the light of human history, of maintaining an affirmative perspective. Harrison's *Prometheus* is a howling lament for the death of aspiration, for the end of the dream of utopia offered by socialism; his charred Iraqi in 'A Cold Coming' warns the poet against assuming that a collective and progressive global sensibility is possible:

> Pretend I've got the imagination
> to see the world beyond one nation.[43]

---

[41] The text of Sellars's speech is available on the Harvard website, www.fas.harvard.edu/~spectrum/2001/may/sellars_speech.pdf.

[42] Lecture delivered at the international Symposium on the Contemporary Performance of Ancient Greek and Roman Drama, held at the J. Paul Getty Museum on 20–23 June 2002. The APGRD holds a transcript of the lecture.

[43] On *Prometheus* as a lament for the end of utopian thinking see Edith Hall (2002); on Harrison and affirmative thinking see Rowland (2001).

Yet Sellars is too young, too idealistic, or too obstinate to relinquish the hope of a multi-ethnic 'world beyond one nation', and he imagines it through the inspiring form taken by his casts. He uses performers to transcend the ethnic and national barriers, so vividly recreated in his *Persians*, which allow human beings unflinchingly to drop bombs on each other's children. The cast impersonating Iraqis in his *Persians* included an African-American actor, a Hispanic, and the composer Hamza El Din, who has fused Arabic and Nubian musical traditions with a western conservatory training, and with study of the Japanese *biwa* in Japan. He has produced an astonishing sound that wordlessly articulates the idea of a global language.[44] Sellars' choreographer Martinus Miroto, who movingly danced Aeschylus' messenger speeches (see Figure 14), is an Indonesian specialist in Javanese classical dance who studied in Germany with Pina Bausch.

The question facing us, therefore, is whether Africans, Asians, Americans, Australasians, and Europeans can learn to live together and collaborate like Sellars's cast members, or whether we are doomed to the horror of the global war envisaged by Harrison's Hermes in a speech so prescient it now seems strange that it was ever excluded from the final version of *Prometheus*.[45]

> We're immortals. We can wait
> for mortals to disintegrate.
> Waiting's the policy at present
> waiting, say for Cross or Crescent
> to clash in Crusade and *jihad*.
> Now that would make Zeus really glad.

[44] Hamza El Din's music for the play was recorded and released on an album *Available Sound: Darius* by Lotus Records in 1996, and was nominated for the prestigious Preis der Deutschen Schallplatten Kritik.

[45] Notebook 3, p. 628. I am extremely grateful to Tony Harrison for allowing me to consult the Notebooks, and to all the following for their frank discussion of aspects of this difficult chapter: Robert Auletta, Fiona Macintosh, Jon Marcus, Richard Poynder, Christopher Rowe, Froma Zeitlin. This chapter is dedicated to the memory of Margot Heinemann, and to the former mining families of Maerdy Colliery, South Wales.

7

Greek Tragedy in Cinema

Theatre, Politics, History

Pantelis Michelakis

INTRODUCTION

Two decades have passed since the publication of the pioneering studies on cinema and Greek tragedy by Marianne McDonald (1983) and Kenneth Mackinnon (1986). Their work has helped establish film adaptations of Greek tragedy as an autonomous study focused on a body of films aesthetically diverse but thematically related (Mackinnon), best represented by the work of two directors of international renown, Pier Paolo Pasolini and Michael Cacoyannis (McDonald). In the last twenty years, the number of films on Greek tragedy has grown steadily, with the involvement of heavyweight names from the worlds of cinema, poetry, and the novel. Since the early 1980s more than thirty new film, television, and video adaptations of Greek drama have appeared.

Greek directors have produced an average of one to two such films a year,[1] including Babis Plaitakis's *Summer of Medea* (1987) and Nikos Koundouros's adaptation of Sophocles' *Antigone*, entitled *The Photographers* (1998). In Italy, Mario Martone made *Rehearsals for War* (1998), based on Aeschylus' *Seven against Thebes*, and *A Place on Earth* (2000), drawing on Sophocles' *Oedipus Tyrannus*. In England, Don Taylor translated and directed the *Theban Plays* for the BBC (broadcast in September 1986), while more recently Tony Harrison wrote and directed *Prometheus* (1998). In Denmark Lars von Trier made a film of Euripides' *Medea* for Danish television (1988). In Germany Rainer Simon directed a film around Sophocles' *Oedipus Tyrannus* entitled *The Case for Decision Ö* (1991), and Jean-Marie Straub and Danièle Huillet produced a film of Sophocles' *Antigone*

---

[1] Kyriakos (2002), 126–68, 239–41.

(1992). Outside Europe, Woody Allen drew on the story of *Oedipus Tyrannus* in two of his films, *Oedipus Wrecks* (1989) and *Mighty Aphrodite* (1995). Amy Greenfield made an experimental film adaptation of *Oedipus at Colonus* and *Antigone* entitled *Antigone/ Rites for the Dead* (1990). Another Oedipus film was made by the Colombian Jorge Alí Triana, entitled *Edipo Alcalde* (*The Mayor Oedipus*, 1996). To this body of film adaptations a number of films of modern stage productions should be added: not only video recordings of and about productions such as those of the *Oresteia* by Peter Hall, Peter Stein, and Karolos Koun, recordings which were edited, broadcast on television, and/or made commercially available on video in the early 1980s; but also feature films, for instance Hugo Santiago's reworking of the 1986 stage production of Sophocles' *Electra* by Antoine Vitez (*Électre*, 1990) and Catherine Vilpoux's film version of *La Ville parjure ou le réveil des Erinyes* (1999), based on a modern rewriting of Aeschylus' *Eumenides* by the feminist writer Hélène Cixous (on whom see also Foley, above, Chapter 3).

This long but by no means exhaustive list of recent films demonstrates beyond any doubt that, since the publication of the studies of McDonald and Mackinnon, the landscape of film adaptations of Greek tragedy has changed significantly. It is the purpose of this chapter to explore some of the ways in which that landscape has altered, and propose some ways in which the shifts in focus and direction manifested in these films can be related to the distinctive and always interrelated aesthetic and political contexts of the 1980s and 1990s.

The growing body of film adaptations of Greek tragedy can, for example, be examined in the light of a renewed interest in film and cultural studies in the relationship between cinema and other art forms, especially theatre. In the last couple of decades numerous publications have appeared in the area of film adaptation. It is especially the work that has been done recently on popular film and TV adaptations of Shakespeare (a very popular and thematically adjacent field), and on heritage drama, that has prompted a reconsideration of adaptation as a theoretical and methodological issue.[2] Rejecting the legitimacy of concepts such as fidelity and authenticity, scholars have come to question two assumptions

---

[2] Jackson (2000); Vincendeau (2002).

which often underlie studies of adaptation, namely the transcendental character and uniqueness of the written word (whether a theatre script or a novel), and the inevitable dependence and inferiority of its re-presentations.[3] The kind of adaptation that a film projects is conditioned by factors much more complex than the comparison between film and original. It involves and is mediated by multiple linguistic, audio-visual and cultural codes. Adaptation is not only, or primarily, about the relation between a film and the text it is based on—even though the study of important narrative shifts between the original and the adaptation can be very illuminating. It is also about the context within which a film is produced and consumed, the values and needs which legitimize its engagement with and valorization of a canonical text, and those which define a certain kind of adaptation in opposition to another. The translation from one art form to another raises a number of issues which could be called collectively the sociology of adaptation: issues of genre, spectatorship, intertextuality, heritage and history, and authorship. It is through such channels that one may hope to recover the meanings that Greek tragedy has acquired in late twentieth-century cinema, and to understand the complex processes that contribute to the politicization of the classical past on screen.

One specific aspect of adaptation which is of special importance for the reception of Greek tragedy in cinema is that of the relationship between cinema and theatre. This is a relationship which goes all the way back to the end of the nineteenth century and the emergence of cinema as a medium and art form.[4] Theatre has always been very important for cinema on a practical and institutional level, not only in terms of thematic choices and narrative techniques but also in terms of actors, directors, and audiences. Since the 1950s the interaction between stage and screen has also attracted the theoretical attention of cinema theorists and practitioners. Brecht's theory of the epic theatre and Artaud's theatre of cruelty, but also the theoretical writings on stage and screen by André Bazin and Walter Benjamin, have had a profound impact on both film analysts and European avant-garde directors, including those of the French Nouvelle Vague and the New German and

---

[3] Cartmell and Whelehan (1999); Naremore (2000).
[4] e.g. Brewster and Jacobs (1997).

Greek Cinema.[5] It is no coincidence that Brecht and Artaud's impact on cinema theory and practice can also be traced in film adaptations of Greek tragedy—especially if we consider that some of the anti-realist trends characterizing avant-garde theatre are the product of direct engagement with Greek tragedy.

A full-scale examination of recent adaptation in films of Greek tragedy is beyond the scope of this chapter. There is no room here for a full theoretical exposition of the many facets of adaptation and the relationship between cinema and theatre. What I intend to do is to explore issues revolving around two basic premises or assumptions. First, many recent film adaptations of Greek tragedy engage self-consciously and systematically with the success of Greek tragedy in contemporary, especially avant-garde, theatre. Second, this interest of film directors in theatre is in accordance with and can be set in the context of a more general search by film directors for a cinema aesthetics, which runs counter to the realism of the 'classical' Hollywood industry and which focuses on political, cultural, and historical issues and processes rather than on the individual as a psychological entity and moral agent. It is within this double framework and with the help of selected examples (rather than through a full-scale examination of my material) that I will attempt to explore some of the issues that recent film adaptations of Greek tragedy raise regarding intertextuality, spectatorship, and the interaction between politics and aesthetics, industry and art.

STAGE AND SCREEN

Filmed theatre is a well-established phenomenon in cinema and, especially, in television and video.[6] The first films of Greek tragedy, like those of Shakespeare, were recordings of stage productions, either in a studio or in their original setting.[7] Since the 1950s, and especially in the last twenty years, the theatre films of Greek tragedy have incorporated not only recordings of stage productions, but also documentaries and adaptations; to these can be added films which, although not based on staged productions, adopt theatrical settings, acting methods, and narrative

---

[5] For an overview see Roloff and Winter (2000).
[6] See, for instance, the excellent collection of essays in Picon-Vallin (2001).
[7] Mackinnon (1986), 43–50; Michelakis (2001), 242–3.

techniques. Mackinnon devoted a whole chapter of his 1986 book to films made in the 'theatrical mode', examining their formal similarities with theatre. In this section I would like to look at films which self-consciously draw attention to their relation with avant-garde theatre, films which celebrate their subjective and selective engagement with theatrical spectacles while also reinventing in cinematic terms the political power of avant-garde theatre to explore and question the realities inhabited by its spectators.

One of the earliest and most radical films of this kind is Brian De Palma's *Dionysus in 69* (co-directed with Robert Fiore and Bruce Rubin), based on Richard Schechner's acclaimed stage production of the same name (see also Zeitlin, above, Chapter 2). One of De Palma's first projects, the film is characterized by what was later to become a trademark of his directorial style, the split screen.[8] The spectator is presented with two views of the theatrical spectacle, taken with hand-held cameras, that reveal different and often unexpected perspectives of the theatrical spectacle and which convey a sense of documentary realism. The filmed spectacle captures the fluidity and fragmentation of the spatio-temporal boundaries of the performance and, especially, the increasing interaction between actors and spectators which concludes with the final triumphant procession of Dionysus and his followers into the street, and the literal bursting of theatre into reality. The split screen and the hand-held camera offer two modes of viewing that complement each other. The documentary mode of the camera promises unmediated access to a reality beyond the screen, a reality that is nonetheless constructed, as it is both less complete than the view of the spectator in the theatre and at the same time more intrusive since it goes beyond the physical capabilities of the theatrical spectator. Similarly, the split screen both reinforces the immediacy of the filmed subject and at the same time acts as a reminder of the impossibility of objectively viewing the reality of the stage. In other words, the film is made in a documentary mode while also challenging the illusion of cinematic objectivity. As one of the earliest experiments of the young De Palma, *Dionysus in 69* testifies to the shaping of a new avant-garde aesthetics of filmmaking, an aesthetics for recording not simply theatre but reality at large, to be further explored and perfected in his subsequent

---

[8] Bouzereau (1988), 26–7; Bliss (1983), 26.

feature films. It raises important questions about cinema and its ability to construct fiction, represent reality, and encompass radicalism. It is no surprise that this radical new cinema is born in its encounter with a powerful stage production which, as Zeitlin and Hall show in this volume, is itself the product of one of the most transgressive and turbulent, but also liberating moments of postwar American culture and society.

Another film that reworks a radical play and transposes its politics onto the screen is *The Perjured City, or the Awakening of the Furies (La Ville parjure ou le réveil des Erinyes)*, made by Catherine Vilpoux in 1999. The film is based on a stage production of Hélène Cixous's play of the same name,[9] performed by the Théâtre du Soleil in Paris and across Europe in 1994–5. The play, written in 1993–4, is a modern rewriting of Aeschylus' *Eumenides* and focuses on what is probably the greatest medical scandal in the history of modern France, the transfusion of contaminated blood over a prolonged period of time with almost no penal consequences for the medical and political authorities involved. Drawing on blood contamination as a social problem but also as a metaphor for the malfunctioning of the collective body of French society, the play becomes an examination of the clash between true justice and codified law which lies at the core of ancient and modern democracies, and points towards the need for accountability on the part of the modern state and its medical and political representatives.[10] The film version not only heavily abridges and edits the six-hour-long stage production, but reworks it by including news footage, newspaper cuttings, and law-court testimonies of haemophiliacs. These are either inserted as intertitles or superimposed over the recorded theatre spectacle. The extra-theatrical material is adduced in a form which makes it apparent that it can be considered to be evidence in the legal proceedings enacted in the on-stage court, but also commentary on the relevance of the spectacle for the contemporary reality within which it is produced. The film captures and juxtaposes segments of the theatre production and the reality to which it refers, whereas the credits of the film self-consciously identify this juxtaposition as memory: the theatrical spectacle, we are

---

[9] Published as Cixous (1994).
[10] See further Fort (1997) and (1999); Noonan (1999).

told, is 'remémoré' for the screen. The concept of memory, so important for Vilpoux's postmodern cinema aesthetics but also for Cixous's and Mnouchkine's feminist politics and commitment, sets the tone for the various processes that mark not only the creation of the film from Mnouchkine's theatrical spectacle, but also the creation of Cixous's play from ancient and modern traged-ies. The film thus ambitiously reconstructs both the play and its stage representation and, in addition, the dialects of the relation-ship between the staged play and reality, through the selection, combination, and juxtaposition of narrative segments. The illusion of the seamless recording of a staged event is broken down and reassembled as cinematic memory. Vilpoux's film-memory points to a strategy for representing the radicalism of a stage performance different from that of De Palma's split screen. Yet, both directors draw on the documentary quality of cinema, to remind us that cinema does not reproduce reality but interprets it, engaging with it selectively.

If Vilpoux and De Palma self-consciously explore the process through which a radical reading of Greek tragedy is transposed from stage to screen, a similar exploration is undertaken by direct-ors who draw on theatre rehearsals. Of course, documentary foot-age from theatre rehearsals is often used for television programmes which commemorate or, otherwise, celebrate an acclaimed stage production by providing behind-the-scenes information. Examples of this kind of use of rehearsal footage include the work around Karolos Koun's productions of Greek tragedy and comedy by Mimis Kougioumtzis—*Chronicle* (1970), *In memoriam* (1972), and *Before the Performance* (1982). Peter Hall's produc-tions have also attracted this type of response, in Channel 4's production *The National Theatre of Great Britain at Epidaurus: The Oresteia* (1983) and, more recently, in Ben Phelan and Dirk Olson's *Tantalus: Behind the Mask*, documenting the prepar-ations for Hall's production of *Tantalus* at Denver in 2000. But far more intriguing are films in which documentary footage from stage rehearsals becomes a metaphor for the creative processes involved in the reception of Greek tragedy on the modern stage and screen.

A film whose fictional narrative centres around such a process is Mario Martone's *Rehearsals for War* (*Teatro di Guerra*), made in Italy in 1998, which includes narrative footage from the rehearsals of the 1996 production of *Seven against Thebes* by Martone and his theatre company, Teatri Uniti. The film is set in 1995, during the civil war in the former Republic of Yugoslavia. It revolves, in semi-autobiographical manner, around the members of an avant-garde Neapolitan theatre company, New Theatre (Teatro Nuovo), rehearsing for a production of Aeschylus' *Seven against Thebes* to be mounted in Sarajevo. The documentary character of the stage rehearsals is in a way lost in the fictional narrative of the film, but it is also reasserted as the film draws on the Meyerholdian training techniques and the commitment to the political role of theatre, which informed Martone's 1997 stage production of Aeschylus' play. Documentary material, useful to Vilpoux for reconstructing the dialogue between a theatre production and its social environment, provides here the subject-matter for an artistic reworking of the stage production.

The interaction between cinema, theatre, and reality is omnipresent in *Rehearsals for War*. The film ends with the cancellation of the plans for putting on *Seven against Thebes* in Sarajevo, as the director's contact in the besieged city is killed. Reality invades theatre and changes its path. The open-endedness of the film narrative is very much in accordance with Martone's on-going interest in Greek tragedy. In fact the porousness of art, its constant interaction with reality, is at the centre of Martone's theatre and cinema.[11] The published screenplay, accompanied by an extensive introduction in the form of a diary, further supports this sense of continuous interaction between art and reality, a sense of work in progress, providing as it does glimpses into the production of both the stage version and the subsequent film.[12] The film, like the published screenplay, functions as a diary, a testimony to an on-going exploration or journey. The openness of Greek tragedy to the world reappears in Martone's next film project, entitled *A Place on Earth* (*Un Posto al Mondo*, 2000): documentary footage from Martone's controversial stage production of Sophocles' *Oedipus Tyrannus*, which featured a chorus of immigrants, is here incorporated into archival news footage concerning wars, persecutions, and famine in order to reflect on the phenomenon of immigration and on the need for western societies to accommodate difference.

---

[11] O'Healy (1999); Rascaroli (2003).   [12] Martone (1998).

De Palma's split screen, Vilpoux's memory, and Martone's re-hearsals constitute three different narrative stratagems for re-pre-senting in cinema the constant and fragmented interaction between Greek tragedy, modern stage, and contemporary reality. Another film that focuses on rehearsals and unfinished projects to engage with the politics and socio-economics of stage productions of Greek drama is Babis Plaitakis's *Summer of Medea*. Made in Greece in 1987, the film is about the French protagonist and Greek director of a production of Euripides' *Medea* in personal and professional crisis. Their project comes to a premature end half-way through the rehearsals, incapacitated by the clash of two different world-views as well as the failure to secure a state subsidy for the production. At the end of the film the leading actress, marginalized both linguistically and culturally, flies from Greece like Medea in the chariot of the Sun; the 'Jason' figure of the director-husband, meanwhile, is left behind, to reflect on the premature death of his brain-child, the production. The film is set in an unfinished arts centre, a deserted concrete building ex-posed to the midsummer sun, a telling metaphor for the ambitious and ultimately doomed project that is never to take off at all. *Summer of Medea* uses Euripides' play in a metatheatrical—or rather metafilmic—way to explore the clash between a star and an auteur, and to play out the drama of lack of funding.

It is illuminating to compare *Summer of Medea* with an earlier film made about Medea in the 1970s, which also focused on the rehearsals for a stage production. Jules Dassin's *A Dream of Passion* (1978) starred Melina Mercouri. It drew on a stage production of *Medea*, directed by Minos Volonakis in 1976, to show the psychological, social, and institutional mechanisms through which Greek tragedy becomes relevant and appealing to modern audiences. For instance, the film featured the protagonist making the acquaintance of a real infanticidal mother in order to under-stand better the theatrical role she is playing, and also the recording of the stage rehearsals by a crew of the BBC. The film concluded in an optimistic tone with the rehearsals successfully completed and the stage production triumphantly opening at the ancient theatre in Delphi. *A Dream of Passion* showed the flirtation of elevated culture and theatre with the world of popular culture and the media, celebrating the possibilities that cinema and televi-sion provide for the dissemination of Greek tragedy. This was an optimistic view of the potential of Greek tragedy to appeal to the mass media and their audiences, a view from which later films step back. *Summer of Medea* provides an ironic take on the creative processes involved in staging Greek tragedy, on both personal and institutional levels. In *Rehearsals for War*, on the other hand, the meaning of Aeschylus' *Seven against Thebes* for the actors and their world emerges through commitment to the political role of avant-garde theatre *in opposition to* the institutional framework of state subsidies and the distortion of reality by the mass media.

TRAGEDY, HISTORY, POLITICS

The first explicitly political readings of Greek tragedy in cinema were those by Pier Paolo Pasolini in the Italy of the late 1960s. The radical cinema of Pasolini is as much a product of the time that gave birth to Schechner's *Dionysus in 69* as the result of the polit-ical preoccupations and intellectual vision of a Marxist film poet. Like Schechner's theatre, Pasolini's cinema marks the beginning of the use of Greek tragedy to address modern issues full-frontally, not just by analogy but through direct references to the world of the spectators—and even through the fusing of narrative compon-ents and tropes which blur the literary, artistic, chronological, or other boundaries separating Greek tragedy and the modern world. In Pasolini, the politicization of the classical past emerges through its encounter with the geographical and cultural 'other' of Africa and the Third World. This is true for *Edipo Re* and *Medea* where the political and cultural clash between Afro-Asian and European codes (visual as well as aural) becomes a constitutive part of the narratives about Oedipus and Medea. But it becomes even bolder in *Notes for an African Oresteia* (*Appunti per un' Orestiade Afri-cana*, 1970), where the fictional mode of the previous films gives way to the pseudo-documentary style of a narrative in which the *Oresteia* serves as a hermeneutic tool, an exemplary text with which to think about the political birth of post-colonial Africa. The legacy of Pasolini's politicized Greece can be traced not only in Italy, to the films of Liliana Cavani and Mario Martone, but also to geographically and aesthetically diverse films such as Tony Harrison's *Prometheus* and Jorge Alí Triana's *Edipo Alcalde*. In the most ambitious among recent film adaptations of Greek tra-gedy the classical past becomes a tool for self-conscious political criticism and analysis: it serves to make sense of important historical junctures or cultural phenomena and allows for a stereoscopical examination of Western civilization as a whole, embarking on the exploration of ideas such as history, democracy, and progress.

One of the modernist directors who has drawn on Greek tragedy in order to reflect on historical processes is Theo Angelopoulos in his *The Travelling Players* (1974).[13] The film, produced a few years after the director's return from the revolutionary Paris of the late 1960s, presents Greek tragedy as a narrative grid onto which one of the most critical periods of modern Greek history is woven. The intergenerational conflicts of Aeschylus' *Oresteia*, and especially their civic resonances, are mapped onto the life of a modern Greek theatre group whose members are named after the tragic heroes. We follow them over a period of twenty years, which includes the German occupation during the Second World War as well as the dictatorship which preceded it and the ensuing civil war. The film was shot towards the end of the regime of the Colonels, and if it escaped their censorship it was because it dealt with the classical past, subject-matter which was often thought to be beyond suspicion. As a tool for political resistance, the adapted plot of the *Oresteia* offered a pessimistic commentary on the contemporary world of the Colonels' regime as well as on Greece's recent past: the theatre of history, viewed through the cycle of violence of the *Oresteia*, provided a tragic spectacle which questioned the concept of progress and the possibility of escape or change.

In Rainer Simon's *The Case for Decision Ö* (1991), the ancient tragedy of Oedipus is superimposed on another modern tragedy set in Greece during the Second World War, this time presented from the point of view of a team of German soldiers. The film is set near Thebes and focuses on the shooting of a film of Sophocles' *Oedipus Tyrannus* by a German squad, set against the larger background of war. The film explores the relationships between art and politics, the personal and the collective, domination and resistance. The young German soldier who plays Oedipus is presented with his role scene by scene. His gradual realization of Oedipus' tragic situation takes place along with the realization of his own position as a German soldier in occupied Greece, in the theatre of war. The

---

[13] The screenplay is published in Angelopoulos (1997), 103–202.

German team is eventually trapped in an ambush by the Greek
partisans who hover menacingly over the narrative of the whole
film: the shoot-out with which the film ends re-enacts Oedipus'
encounter with Laius, the inevitable encounter of the individual
with history. However, the encounter of the individual with his
destiny marks the end of his story, not the beginning. The soldier
playing Oedipus dies along with the director and the rest of the
squad. *The Case for Decision Ö* has a tragic dénouement where
innocence cannot guarantee redemption.

The story of Oedipus, and the issue of the individual and his or
her responsibility vis-à-vis historical processes beyond their control, are of special importance for post-war Germany. The film
is based on a screenplay by Ulrich Plenzdorf, written in 1986,
which draws on a Cold War novel by Franz Fühmann entitled
König Ödipus exploring the issues of guilt and responsibility of a
society which strives to come to terms with Nazism and the Second
World War.[14] Yet the production of the film by the Eastern
German studio DEFA in 1991 gives the narrative an added layer
of meaning. The film was made just two years after the collapse of
the German Democratic Republic and provides a glimpse of the
intensive self-questioning which followed the fall of the Berlin
Wall and German reunification.[15]

The Photographers, made by Nikos Koundouros in 1998, is set in
an imaginary Islamic country ravaged by civil war and oppressive
warlords, and invaded by western news reporters. The film is
about the clash between the west and Islam, the western media's
self-indulgent depiction of scenes of violence, but also the exploitation of such scenes for the promotion of Islamic fundamental-
ism.[16] The film focuses on men hungry for power and spectacle
(both eastern warlords and western photographers), meeting with
female resistance. The 'chorus' of the photographers, with their
cameras menacingly pointed towards heaps of corpses, contrasts
sharply with the 'chorus' of local women looking on in silent
protest. The role of Antigone is split between two characters
played by the same actress. One of these characters is a woman
who buries her brother against the will of the local warlord, and the

---

[14] Plenzdorf (1988), 289–329; Fühmann (1968), 219–302; cf. Riedel (2000),
381–2.
[15] Kersten (1991); Schenk (1991).   [16] Kyriakos (2002), 141–4.

other is the only female photographer in the film, who takes the side of her Islamic *Doppelgänger*. Burial becomes an act of resistance, a sign which negates the spectacle of male cruelty set up by the Islamic despot for the consumption of western journalists and spectators. The film revisits the political, religious, and sexual aggression embedded in language and gaze, and explores alternative modes of communication which transcend cultural barriers and resist the commodification of violence and suffering, blending feminism with pacifism. Koundouros had previously drawn on the narrative of Sophocles' *Antigone* for his stage production of *Antigone: A Cry for Peace*, produced at the border between Greece and the former Republic of Yugoslavia in the course of the Balkan war in 1994. *The Photographers*, produced after the Balkan war, relocates Sophocles' play to a region which was soon to become the theatre of the war against terrorism.

In two of the most ambitious films of the 1990s, Greek tragedy provides the subject-matter for reflecting upon twentieth-century Europe and western civilization in general and in large-scale terms. In 1992 Jean-Marie Straub and Danièle Huillet, two of the best-known auteurs of European cinema, produced a film version of *Antigone*, provocatively entitled *The Antigone of Sophocles after Hölderlin's Translation Adapted for the Stage by Brecht* (*Die Antigone des Sophokles nach der hölderlinschen Übertragung für die Bühne bearbaitet von Brecht*). The title invites the spectator to reflect on the multiple layers that the film incorporates, the plurality of voices that it is made to express.[17] The complexity of the process of filming Greek tragedy is at once acknowledged and confronted (see Figures 16 and 17), just as the idea of authorship is both questioned (through the proliferation of authors) and at the same time asserted. A similar effect is achieved in the case of the film *Prometheus* by the British poet Tony Harrison (1998) through the ambitious simplicity of the one-word title.[18] From the title alone it is impossible either to contextualize its action or make assumptions about its authorship. It invites the merging of myth and tragedy, of ancient and modern readings of its subject. Straub and Huillet carefully select and draw attention to the segments of the past they

---

[17] See further the perceptive analysis of Byg (1995), 218. The screenplay is published in Straub and Huillet (1992).
[18] Published screenplay in T. Harrison (1998).

FIGURES 16, 17. Two photographs of Astrid Ofner as Antigone in the film *Antigone*, directed by Jean-Marie Straub and Danièle Huillet (1992). The second image shows Danièle Huillet's hands.

chose, in such a way that meaning is created through the coexistence and constant juxtaposition of different authors and texts. Harrison, on the other hand, absorbs influences and incorporates them in a narrative whose challenge to the spectator is not to reconcile but to unravel its threads. The two films are worth considering at greater length, not least because their radical politics and modernist aesthetics feed into each other with exemplary consistency.

Friedrich Hölderlin's translation of *Antigone* was published in 1804, the very year that Napoleon upgraded himself from First Consul to Emperor, putting despotism forcefully back on the European political agenda and striking a severe blow against the ideals of the French Revolution. It is no wonder that Hölderlin's anti-classical translation, reflecting the violent theatre of politics in his own time, attracted Brecht's attention on his return from exile in the USA to Europe in the aftermath of the Second World War. In Brecht's adaptation of Hölderlin's translation, performed in the Stadttheater at Chur (Switzerland) in 1948, Creon is involved in an imperialist war against Argos, whereas Polynices has become the enemy because he abandoned the war. It is in this version, with Creon as an imperialist aggressor recalling Hitler, and with war and violence as a plague from which humankind cannot escape, that Straub and Huillet turned to *Antigone*. The layers of history and political experience incorporated in their text and signalled in their title are therefore several and complex. The stage version, viewed as a preparatory exercise before the production of the film, opened in post-unification Berlin during the Gulf War (1991). Straub dedicated it 'to hundred thousand—or more; we don't even know—Iraqi dead that we have murdered'.[19] The film version is not as explicit in its references to the world of the spectators, but it is equally polemical in its criticism of contemporary culture and in its questioning of the power of humankind to progress.

Harrison's *Prometheus* is similarly ambitious in setting out to explore the legacy of the industrial revolution in the post-communist Europe of the 1990s. For all its differences from the Straub and Huillet *Antigone*, it too draws on Romanticism and Marxism as two of the most important chapters in the cultural history of modern Europe. For Harrison, Shelley's romantic

[19] Straub in Giavarini (1992), 40.

Prometheus Unbound (1820) is a landmark among modern readings of the Aeschylean Prometheus, not least because it reflects the sadness of its creator at the fate of the French Revolution and the failure of Europe to sustain change and to progress. The other landmark in Harrison's reading of the modern reception of *Prometheus* is the association of the Titan with the triumphant but ultimately destructive history of twentieth-century socialism. In the grand narrative of his film, Harrison brings together Shelley and Marx to examine issues such as the Holocaust, unemployment, and pollution (see Hall, chapter 6, above). If Straub and Huillet painstakingly revisit and combine selective readings of Greek tragedy, Harrison engages with more diverse discourses.

The political radicalism of the two films is manifest not only in their intertextual references but also in the stylization of their language and photography. In *Antigone*, the clash between Antigone and Créon is articulated in terms of different mentalities, ideologies, sexes, and ages, but also as a conflict between acting methods and pronunciations. The role of Creon is played by Werner Rehm, a professional actor, whereas Antigone is played by a first-time actress, Astrid Ofner. A similar contrast is achieved in *Prometheus* with the visual and linguistic juxtaposition between the culturally elevated Hermes of Michael Feast, dressed in a silver suit (see Figure 15 in Hall, Chapter 6, above), and the uneducated, shabby Old Man, played by Walter Sparrow. In *Antigone*, not only are Hölderlin's and Brecht's verse forms upheld with the utmost attention, but Straub and Huillet further stress the stylization of Hölderlin's language by training their actors to stop at the end of each line, often with a simultaneous cut from one take to another.[20] The fact that the Greek verse itself cannot be precisely reconstructed does not prevent Straub and Huillet from experimenting with the possibilities of reconciling rhythm and dialectics, form and meaning. On the other hand, in Harrison the formalism of his rhyming verses and its contribution to the rhythm of the film as a whole seek to provide a modern equivalent of the effect of the Aeschylean original rather than a symbolic reproduction of its effect (except, of course, in Hermes' brief quotation from the tragedy, addressed in ancient Greek to the miners descending

---

[20] Straub and Huillet (2001), 116–20.

the mineshaft).[21] If stylization and rhythm have a (pseudo-)historicizing effect in Straub and Huillet, the same features in Harrison's film relate to the world of Greek tragedy only by analogy. In both cases the quest for rhythm brings cinema closer to the stylization and confrontational character of ancient tragedy but also back to its own roots, the silent films of the early twentieth century, rediscovering the tension between mechanical repetitiveness and artistic harmony.[22]

Antigone is set throughout in the ancient theatre of Segesta in Sicily, and it is shot from a single point of view challenging the cinematic convention of the moving camera. Straub and Huillet's camera explores the possibilities of the point of view of the theatrical spectator, yet it also redefines the theatrical experience by being located at one of the two stage entrances, taking a position that the theatre spectator cannot really occupy.[23] The point of view of the theatre spectator is also challenged by the static chorus of four elders, who face the actors with their backs constantly turned towards the auditorium, holding a position that the chorus of a stage production would try to avoid. In *Antigone*, then, the theatrical space of the ancient theatre is broken down and reassembled as cinematic. In *Prometheus*, on the other hand, the stylization of Greek tragedy is rediscovered through the bold combination of landscapes of modern tragedies, from sites prominent in the collective memory of the spectators, such as Auschwitz, to completely neglected (or forgotten) sites such as the factories of Copsa Mica in Romania and the coalmines of Yorkshire in England.[24] The spectacle of history consists of a succession of tragic landscapes, complete with Prometheus' golden statue raising its fist in a posture of defiance. One of the scenes which shows most clearly how the plot of the film (*story*) establishes a symbolic relation with the grand narrative of the twentieth century (*hi-story*) is the sequence in the derelict cinema where the Old Man, accompanied by Hermes, watches Prometheus' journey on screen. The cinema is a metaphor for the world of the Old Man, a metaphor for his polluted environment, poisoned lungs, and failed ideology, but also a site of imagination, memory, and resistance: in his desire to punish the

[21] *Prometheus Bound*, 976–8; T. Harrison (1998), 18.
[22] Cf. Byg (1995), 215 and 225–6; T. Harrison (1998), xxv–xxvii.
[23] See the excellent analysis by Byg (1995), 226–9.
[24] Michelakis (2001), 252–3. See e.g. Figure 15 in the previous chapter.

gods, the Old Man ignites a pool of petrol on the screen which, after burning down Hermes, consumes the statue of Prometheus and the Oceanids as well as the cinema and the Old Man himself. Throughout the film Harrison celebrates, and at the same time deconstructs, the power of ideology and resistance.

The self-destructive defiance of the Old Man, and the way he melts down Hermes and Prometheus' statue, can be compared with Antigone's death and its consequences for Créon with which Straub and Huillet's *Antigone* ends. Both films promote a sense of closure poised between utter annihilation and triumphant liberation. Both Straub and Huillet and Harrison put forward a vision of art as a medium for resistance, a vision which runs counter to the commodification of contemporary cinema and culture and which challenges the concept of history as a linear, progressive, civilizing force. *Antigone* and *Prometheus* transcend the personal to focus on wider processes, where individuals are not characters with whom to engage emotionally but Brechtian symbols to reflect on and think with. What structures the two films is not a neo-Aristotelian action-packed and goal-oriented narrative but a post-Hegelian dialectic, the clash between opposing forces without the promise of resolution, redemption, or progress. In their different thematic preoccupations and stylistic preferences the two films testify to the diversity of modernist cinema, but also to its participation in debates about modern history and culture and its debt to radical theatre and poetry.

CONCLUSION

I have argued that a considerable number of recent film adaptations of Greek tragedy should be located in cultural and institutional contexts standing outside and apart from those of mainstream commercial cinema. The appropriation of Greek tragedy by art cinema is by no means restricted to the films or the issues I have explored above. It can include other recent films both from Europe, such as Lars von Trier's medieval *Medea* based on a screenplay by the father of Danish cinema Carl Dreyer, and from the Americas, for instance Jorge Alí Triana's *Edipo Alcalde* in a screenplay by one of the most famous poets and novelists of Latin America, Gabriel García Márquez. Moreover, it could be complemented by a separate study of the reception of Greek tragedy in commercial cinema, from Jules Dassin's *Never on Sunday* (1960) to Woody Allen's *Mighty Aphrodite* (1995) and Walt Disney's animated *Hercules* (1997, directed by John Musker and Ron Clements). Here I have attempted to show how a group of aesthetically and ideologically diverse films, which are however all politically committed, are also all concerned with issues relating to the popularity of Greek tragedy on the modern stage and to the self-definition of avant-garde cinema in opposition to mainstream Hollywood productions. Such issues include reflections about the role of cinema and the media in contemporary society, the socio-economics of and interaction between cinema and theatre, the role of seeing and remembering in contemporary art and culture, and the revisiting of critical moments of the West's recent past and present. From such films we learn nothing about the original context of Greek tragedy but a great deal about the modern environments which have sanctioned it and which have given it new meanings. The cinematic reception of Greek tragedy provides glimpses of the tragedy of history and the history of tragedy. The pluralism and heterogeneity of these films defy any simplistic comparison between adaptation and original, encourage a re-evaluation of classical texts for the power of their readings, and make the spectator self-conscious about his or her own interpretations and about seeing as a complex and subjective activity.[25]

[25] My research for this paper has been facilitated by the kind help of Angelo Curti, Laura Rascaroli, Jean-Marie Straub, and Amanda Wrigley, as well as the support of the following institutions: Progress Film-Verleih, Hildesheim University Library, Hölderlin Archive of the State University of Stuttgart, and the Arts and Humanities Research Board. I'm very grateful to Edith Hall and Fiona Macintosh for stimulating discussions and their valuable comments on the penultimate version of this chapter.

8

Greek Drama and Anti-Colonialism

Decolonizing Classics

Lorna Hardwick

INTRODUCTION

In the theatre of the last three decades Greek drama has assumed major importance as an arena for the articulation of anti-colonialist ideas and as a forum for the exploration of post-colonial debates about the relationships between cultural and political identities. My approach to this problematic and sometimes inspiring topic is based on an exploration of practice—in poetry, in theatre, and in the development of self-reflexive cultural criticism. I shall not be addressing directly the huge outpouring of theoretical writing about imperialism, colonialism, and post-colonialism. There are, however, some aspects of my framework that I had better state at the beginning. I am concerned with the sometimes paradoxical relationship between Greek drama and anti-colonialism of various kinds. I use the term 'colonialism' in its broadest sense to include modern variants and to cover domination through educational, ideological, cultural, and economic means as well as by physical force. Colonialism almost always operates with the complicity or active participation of elites among the colonized, and the continuing role of these after independence raises special problems which Greek drama has played a considerable part in addressing. My subtitle is 'Decolonizing Classics'—and it turns out that decolonizing is both adjectival and verbal, communicating a role for Greek drama as a catalyst for change. By this I imply the transformative role of drama—its ability to reshape awareness and change perceptions.

I will be discussing recent drama which has grown from or been performed in Caribbean and African contexts. Of course, Greek drama's importance in the colonial and imperial context is by no means confined to these areas—in Eastern Europe, for instance, it has been significant in the struggle to develop free political and cultural identities and to resist imposed ones.[1] In Ireland, Greek drama has been a major player in cultural and political struggle.[2] In Scotland Greek drama is being promoted as a forum for encouraging new forms of democratic consciousness (in the work of the company Theatre About Glasgow, for instance) and has been subtle in its questioning of easy distinctions between colonizers and colonized (theatre babel's *The Greeks*, 2000, especially David Greig's *Oedipus*).[3]

Colonialism takes different forms and each colonial history is different—as Seamus Heaney has put it, 'in current post-colonial conditions. . . . the more people realise that their language and their culture are historically amassed possessions, the better'.[4] A defining feature of post-colonial literatures has been a post-colonial awareness of and resistance to continuing colonialist attitudes, including cultural forms and pressures as well as ideologies. This issue raises (at least) three main problems:

1. *The relationship between the masses and the neo-colonial elite.* This has been explored by a number of writers, most influentially by Frantz Fanon.[5] This area may include—as Seamus Deane has suggested—constructions of nationalism which reinforce the notion of the 'colonized other' and occlude differences between indigenous socio-political groups—'Nationalism, cultural or political, is no more than an inverted image of the colonialism it seeks to replace . . . The assumption that it shares with colonialism is the existence of an original condition that must be transmitted, restored, recuperated, and which must replace that fallen condition which at present obtains.'[6] In African and Caribbean contexts the problem may raise itself not only through nationalism but also in concepts of 'Négritude' or black essentialism. Similar criticisms to those of Deane have been developed in an African context by Fémi Òsófisan.[7] This matrix of issues is often expressed in debates about cultural as well as political identity and may also reflect ambivalent attitudes about the role of the intellectual and the artist. Awareness

---

[1] See Hardwick (2003*b*).

[2] See Taplin, Chapter 5 above, and Hardwick (2000), ch. 5.

[3] See Hardwick (2003*a*) and Hardwick (forthcoming) for discussion of post-colonial responses to Greek drama in colonizing countries.

[4] *The Sunday Times*, 26 July 1998.   [5] Fanon (1967*a*) and (1967*b*).

[6] Deane (1991), xxv.   [7] Òsófisan (1999*a*).

of these post-colonial power relationships underlies various attempts to revise models of neo-colonialism away from an emphasis on race and ethnicity and towards an exploration of class and other social groupings. Critics such as Stuart Hall have stressed that identity is not a matter of (re)discovery but of production, a retelling of the past. Thus cultural identity may involve 'becoming' rather than 'being'.[8]

2. *The force of colonialism as a constraint on mind and thought both before and after independence.* This aspect has been explored by Ngũgĩ wa Thiong'o, who attacks imperialism as a destroyer of culture, an inducer of shame for names, systems of belief, languages, lore, art, dance, song, sculpture, colour. His belief in the importance of culture in power struggle is exemplified in his use of the phrase 'barrel of a pen' to convey the desired effect of his writing.[9] I shall argue that the refiguration of Greek poetry and drama has played a significant role in the fight back against colonization of the mind, as well as in protest against oppression.

3. For those analysing and writing about these phenomena, a further complication is the charge that African and Caribbean writers have been subjected to a new wave of colonialism because of the imposition of a western theoretical straitjacket in criticism of their writing and theatre practice (i.e. that the label 'post-colonial', which has often been applied to them, actually impedes cultural freedom and growth). Partly for this reason, I shall try to let the writers referred to speak for themselves and will draw on their critical writings as well as their creative work. (Problems 1 and 2 still remain of course.)

Overall, I hope to show that refiguration of Greek drama since the late 1960s has played a significant role in decolonizing the minds of both colonized and decolonizers and that the implications for future perceptions of Greek drama are equally radical. The diversity of material can be shown by an initial focus on two contrasting instances of refiguration of Greek drama in the Caribbean area. From these it is clear that we are engaging with very different histories—not just histories of colonialism and imperialism, but also with the poetics of migration, the migration of performances, and the cultural politics of reception and criticism.

---

[8] For discussion and short bibliography, see Gugelberger (1991). See also Rutherford (1990) and S. Hall (1990).
[9] Ngũgĩ (1983), (1986), and (1993).

GREEK DRAMA IN THE CARIBBEAN

In 1968 the Cuban playwright Antón Arrufat made a translation into Spanish of Aeschylus' play *Seven against Thebes*. This version, *Los Siete contra Tebas*, was awarded the Casa de las Americas Drama Prize, but although published the play was then ignored. In 2001 the play was republished after the Cuban government awarded Arrufat the national literary prize. The initial award of the Casa de las Americas Drama Prize was made by a panel of dramatists from Spain and Latin America, but a minority of two issued a statement of disagreement. This was because they felt that the play was defeatist because its theme of fratricidal struggle sent out an unacceptable message to Cubans at the time.[10] In other words, the conflict between Eteocles and Polyneices could and would be interpreted as referring to contemporary Cuba. The situation was quite complex. The former dictator of Cuba, General Batista, had ruled the country through intermediaries following a military coup in 1933 (the so-called 'sergeants' revolt') until he was himself elected President in 1940. At the next election he was defeated and went into exile in Florida. In 1952 he engineered a second coup and became dictator, propped up by wealth from casinos and gangsterism. The regime became increasingly brutal, with secret police notorious for torture and murder. Fidel Castro landed a small force in 1956, and by the end of 1958 Batista and his entourage fled to the Dominican Republic. (He died in Spain in 1973.) After Castro took power, the government of the USA declared an economic embargo against Cuba and about half a million Cubans left Cuba for Florida, where they formed the core of an anti-Castro movement, encouraged by the US government. In 1961 Cuban exiles supported by the USA invaded Cuba at the Bay of Pigs, where they were defeated. Castro sought support from the Soviet Union, and in 1962 the Cuban missile crisis climaxed in confrontation between the USA and the Soviets. After the Soviet Union backed down, Castro tried to challenge US influence across Latin America, but by 1968 this strategy was seen to have failed, and its icon Che Guevara had died in Bolivia.

---

[10] Arrufat (1968). Similar criticisms have been made against Greek drama in modern Ireland, because of the concern with the effect on audiences of a preoccupation with cycles of revenge. See Hardwick (2000), ch. 5.

In the text of the play, published by the Union of Writers and Artists, there was an 'official' preface which denounced the play because it was said to argue for dialogue with the Cubans in the USA (a different and more explicitly political point than the Casa de las Americas Prize jury dissidents' charge of being dismal). The conflict between Eteocles and Polyneices was thought to be too resonant with the ongoing conflict between the Cubans in Cuba and in Florida. In his version Arrufat chose to include the character of Polyneices (Polinices)—like Racine in *La Thébaïde, ou les frères ennemis* (1664), which also explores the idea of power-sharing—and to include an *agon* (debate) between the two brothers. This is rather similar to the *agon* in Euripides' *Phoenician Women* and highlights differences in the attitudes to power repre-sented by the two men. Modern ideological differences were em-phasized in the Cuban version, with Eteocles distributing wealth among the population and Polinices centralizing wealth within the ruling group. The Messenger was replaced by two spies and the Theban Champions were individualized as characters, with their social positions indicated in the text (e.g. schoolteacher, farmer, merchant).

After its publication, with the damning preface, the play 'disap-peared' until 2001 when it was republished with a new preface. Its world premiere took place in Glasgow in November 2001 in an as yet unpublished English translation by Mike Gonzalez staged at the Ramshorn Theatre (University of Strathclyde) by Actual Theatre Company, directed by Susan Triesman and Steve King. This company aims to present experimental theatre and to exam-ine new ways of approaching classic texts. The production used a non-specific setting—a red banner, rather than the Cuban flag, was used as an emblem.[11] The costume of the chorus of women evoked images of women in conflict zones—Central America, Eastern Europe, Palestine. They were given specific characters and relationships with the Champions. The Champions were de-personalized in one choral ode, wearing three-quarter coloured masks and forming a tableau round another of Arrufat's new features, the soothsayer or bird of war spirit, who wore a white

---

[11] Information is taken from the documentation prepared by Alison Burke for the database of the Open University research project, the *Reception of the Texts and Images of Ancient Greece in Modern Poetry and Drama* (www2.open.ac.uk/Classi-calStudies/GreekPlays.

bird mask. The programme notes (by Mike Gonzalez) invited the audience to judge for themselves what response Arrufat was offering to the Cuban experience and added, 'it seems particularly significant to be presenting this play about the resolution of conflict by violent means when Afghanistan is being bombed daily . . .'.

This example shows that interpretation of Greek drama is fluid. Even in the responses to Arrufat's original version when the setting was thought to be specific to Cuba, the formulations of unease differed—from the general pessimism about the theme of fratricide to allegations of encouraging peace-making with exiles. This ambivalence of response is characteristic of politically interventionist refigurations of Greek drama. It can be seen in Eastern Europe during the period of domination by the Soviet empire and in France during the domination by the Third Reich.[12] Furthermore, the staging is crucial in 'translating' the Greek play into modern consciousness. This is demonstrated in the Glasgow version, which widened the application from the specific place and circumstances of Cuba in the late 1960s to turn-of-the-century concerns with conflict resolution. Protest which is suppressed in one context can be revived and refigured in another.

My second example from the Caribbean region is much more widely known and raises a rather different set of issues. The Nobel Prize-winning St Lucian writer Derek Walcott has been at the centre of critical debate concerning his literary reworking of classical referents and his sometimes abrasive relationship with post-colonial cultural politics. In the context of the histories of colonialism, Walcott's work and its reception point to a number of features which recur in various forms in other writers:

EDUCATION

Walcott was the son of a teacher. At St Mary's College, Castries, which he attended from 1941 to 1947, he received an education developed and delivered by a colonial system and which included study of the canon of English literature and of Latin. Nevertheless,

---

[12] For discussion of successive phases of resistance and use of Greek plays as countertexts on the Czech stage, see Stehlíková (2001), which includes a list of productions. For debate surrounding the staging of Anouilh's *Antigone* in 1944, see J. Parker (2000).

this was not without variations. In his autobiographical poem *Another Life* (1973), he acknowledges the influence of a Catholic teacher expelled from Ireland, while in *Omeros* (1990), the narrator or 'I' figure refers to the barber's shop, 'a kind of schoolroom in which both the literature and world events were discussed . . . on their varnished rack, The World's Great Classics read backwards in his mirrors' while 'toga'd in a pinned sheet', the narrator used to quote from them and discussed world events.[13] Formal and informal education may have had in common the assumption that discussion of literature and large social issues went together, but the snapshot of the informal scene shows its contrast with the pinions of the formal 'toga'd' education.

Walcott's education placed him among those who experienced the 'elation of discovery' through both the patois of the street and the language of the classroom. They 'could lead two lives: the interior life of poetry, the outward life of action and dialect. Yet the writers of my generation were natural assimilators. We knew the literature of Empires, Greek, Roman, British, through their essential classics.'[14] Seamus Heaney has remarked on the way in which 'Walcott didn't divest himself of what are, in one way, the marks of the conqueror, in another way the resources of the English tradition. His negotiation between poles, the exterior pole of literature, London and the world out there, and the inner pole of the Caribbean—it kind of interested me, that balance.'[15] This brings me to the second significant aspect of Walcott's situation in respect of colonialism.

DOUBLE CONSCIOUSNESS

These ironies and negotiated balances underlie the concept of double consciousness which has been explored by critics as an expression of the Trans-Atlantic cultural dynamic created in the African diaspora, notably by Paul Gilroy in *The Black Atlantic* (1993). In the context of the Caribbean, black intellectuals and

[13] *Another Life*, pt. 3, 104–6, in Walcott (1986), 143–294; *Omeros* (Walcott (1990), 71).

[14] *What the Twilight Says* (1970), collected in Walcott (1998), 4. Of course there were also obviously ironic aspects of colonial education, as in the singing of 'Britannia Rules the Waves . . . Britons Never, Never, Never Will be Slaves' discussed by Olaniyan (1995), 94–5.

[15] Quoted in Corcoran (1998), 260.

artists can both be part of western culture and be critics.[16] In Walcott's work, this double consciousness is reinforced by his awareness of his own mixed-race background and by the diversity of cultures among which he was brought up. The expectations of critics in respect of this double consciousness have diverged from his own, with a particularly barbed effect, which is evident in his own critical essays as well as in the reception of his work.

CRITICAL RECEPTION

Until quite recently criticism of Walcott's work has been shaped by discussion of its cultural politics. Initially his poetry was often attacked for its supposedly Eurocentric orientation; subsequently, critical approaches have been based on theorizing about post-colonial literatures, and critics have conceded that Walcott does engage with many of the preoccupations of post-colonial criticism—for example, divisions in Caribbean society—and more broadly with the claim of literature to occupy a space outside concerns with the history of colonialism and racial struggles.[17] Walcott's fluid exploration of the Odyssean predicament bypasses the oppositional polarized structures which were central to Arrufat's version of the *Seven against Thebes* and which lend themselves much more obviously to exploitation in debates about resistance, oppression, and political witness. Walcott's stance against backward-looking and reductionist cultural politics is, of course, central to his poetic and dramatic practice. It is also stated polemically in prose in some of his critical essays.

CRITICAL ESSAYS

Of these works the most important for the current topic are 'What the Twilight Says', 'The Muse of History', and 'The Antilles: Fragments of Epic Memory' (the most recent). These are collected

---

[16] A parallel type of double consciousness exists in the work of Tony Harrison, whose poetry and drama is both the product of a privileged middle-class education and a means of criticizing it. Harrison's critique of colonialism also exhibits the double consciousness of one who writes from within a colonizing society in order to critique it. See especially his play *Phaedra Britannica* (1975), published in T. Harrison (1986), and in his representation of Anglo-Egyptian power relations in *The Trackers of Oxyrhynchus*, staged at Delphi in 1988 (published as T. Harrison (1990)).

[17] For detailed discussion, see Thieme (1999), ch. 7.

under the title *What the Twilight Says* (1998). In 'What the Twilight Says' (1970), Walcott confronted the multiple affirmations of identity offered by mixed-race Caribbean experience:

in our self-tortured bodies we confuse two graces; the dignity of self belief and the courtesies of exchange . . . for the colonial artist the enemy was not the people or the people's crude aesthetic which he refined or orchestrated. The enemy was those who had elected themselves as protectors of the people, who urged them to acquire pride which meant abandoning their dignity, who cried out that black was beautiful like transmitters from a different revolution without exploring what they meant by beauty . . . their rough philosophies were meant to coarsen every grace, to demean courtesy, to brook no debate, their fury artificially generated by an imitation of even metropolitan anger.[18]

This passion underlies Walcott's rejection of a poetics based on affliction or desire for revenge and also his rejection of the idea that a return to original roots is possible—whether African, European, or indigenous.[19] The futility of a return to African roots is explored with devastating effect in the *katabasis* in his epic poem *Omeros*. In this sequence the Caribbean fisherman Achille makes an imagined reversal of the Middle Passage and returns to Africa. In a variation on Anticleia's failure to recognize her son Odysseus in *Odyssey* 11, Achille's father has forgotten the name he gave him. In a reversal of Homeric identities, to his ancestor it is Achille who is the ghost—'Are you the smoke from a fire that never burned?'—for in the African context he never existed. The searing final sequence in the episode tells why. 'The raid was profitable.' Achille witnesses the African slave raiders and the purgatory of the Middle Passage which brought his ancestors to the Caribbean.[20] Walcott is equally ruthless in his subversion of the notion of Eurocentric cultural roots. Classical referents play a developing role in his earlier poetry, but their force is restricted by their association with empire—Greek, Roman, British. In this phase of his work, classical referents are a sign of a double consciousness which recognizes both the assimilationist impact of classical texts on colonized peoples because of their appropriation by the colonizers,

---

[18] Walcott (1998), 27–31.
[19] The poetics associated with this rejection exemplify the cross-cultural hybridity of Walcott's conception of post-colonial poetics: see further Ramazani (1997).
[20] *Omeros* (Walcott (1990)), bk. 3, chs. 25–8. For detailed discussion of the sequence and its affinities with Homer, Virgil, and Dante, see Hardwick (2000), ch. 6.

and also the capacity of writers to use the texts and referents to create new works. Therefore, in effect, their impact is to transform double consciousness into a more pluralistic and multi-layered awareness. In 'Sea Grapes' (1976), a poem which is concerned with personal as well as cultural aspects of consolation, Walcott imagined fluidity of identity—'schooner beating up the Caribbean | for home, could be Odysseus'. However, the elision could not bring inner peace—'The classics can console. But not enough.' Consolatory powers are, for Walcott, limited if confined to the classical past—the 'stones' of the ancient world may turn out to be simply stone heads rolling in the dust—'They were shipped to us Seferis, | dead on arrival' ('From This Far', in *The Fortunate Traveller*, 1981). The allusion is to the theme of the broken statues of antiquity, explored in the context of the relationship between past and present by the Greek poet George Seferis, especially in the sequence *Mythistorema*.[21]

James McCorkle has explored the dual resonance when this image is applied also to African customs lost during the slave trade.[22] In his Nobel Lecture, Walcott described how fragments or sherds from epic and from Greek and Roman culture could be reassembled and redesigned to create a multi-faceted consciousness: 'And this is the exact process of the making of poetry, or what should be called not its "making" but its remaking . . . the process of poetry is one of excavation and of self-discovery.'[23] Walcott denies that there is a retreat into nostalgia involved in the crafting of a poetic voice from the materials of (sometimes colonial) traditions. He sees language itself as 'a place of struggle'.[24]

EMANCIPATION FROM COLONIALLY APPROPRIATED CLASSICAL REFERENTS

The key move here has been Walcott's perception that the culture and society of the ancient Aegean was not westernized European.

[21] For text and translation of *Mythistorema* (1st edn., Athens, 1935), see Keeley and Sherrard (1982). Seferis (1900–71) won the Nobel Prize for Literature in 1963 and spoke out strongly against the censorship imposed by the Colonels' Junta after the coup d'état in Greece in 1967.

[22] McCorkle (1986), especially p. 9.

[23] 'The Antilles: Fragments of Epic Memory', Nobel Lecture (1992), in Walcott (1998), 8–9.

[24] Interview in *Partisan Review* (1990), discussed in Terada (1992), ch. 3.

He created a correspondence between the Caribbean and the ancient sea-borne *koine* culture of the eastern Mediterranean:

The Greeks were the niggers of the Mediterranean. If we looked at them now, we would say that the Greeks had Puerto Rican tastes . . . Because the stones were painted brightly. They were not these bleached stones. As time went by, they sort of whitened and weathered, the classics began to be thought of as something bleached-out and. . . . distant.[25]

This insight about ancient Mediterranean culture is supported by academic research—for example, Sarah Morris's book *Daidalos and the Origins of Greek Art* (1992), which discards traditional periodization and recasts social and ethnic dimensions. Morris argues that *koine* culture was more determined by craftsmen, technicians, and the entrepreneurs who commissioned them than by political constructs assumed from other and later cultures. Daidalos becomes an emblem of the interface between the European and oriental aspects of this culture. In this way Walcott removed Caribbean creativity from being seen as a provincial branch of European culture seeking acceptance, and took it outside the terms defined by another tradition.[26] This has implications for the framework within which most critics have discussed his work.

CRITICS' GENERALIZATIONS ABOUT WALCOTT'S WORK

Critical generalizations about Walcott's work and its relationship to post-colonial theoretical approaches have focused on two key claims.[27]

1. Walcott's work erodes binary oppositions of race and culture.
2. It exemplifies a poetics of migration.

Both these points are useful as starters but I want to argue that they do not go far enough. Walcott does not merely erode simplistic binary oppositions, he actively seeks and explores commonalities (which are not the same as multiculturalism or pluralism, both of which emphasize difference). Furthermore, his development of a poetics of migration is informed and energized by the

---

[25] Quoted in King (2000), 504.
[26] A dilemma formulated by King (2000), 505.
[27] Discussed in Thieme (1999).

understanding that ancient culture, too, is migratory and iterative. His practice exemplifies the point, and builds on the way in which ancient culture underwent a diaspora of its own as it became progressively detached first from its origins and then from the colonizing nations and classes who had appropriated and refigured it, but who gradually ceased to have a use for it.

Both these two extensions of conventional critical analysis depend on sensitivity to Walcott's increasingly subtle use of classical referents, most especially in *Omeros* and in the theatre work that closely followed it—*The Odyssey: A Stage Version* (1992).[28] An overview of the play, which follows quite closely the episodic structure of Homer's epic, which Walcott read in Rieu's 1946 prose translation, shows that in important respects it functions as a performative commentary on Walcott's perceptions of the relationships between Greek and Caribbean culture.

Walcott's extensive theatre work, which spans over thirty years, has seen him (according to Renu Juneja) 'consistently trying to represent the particularities of West Indian experience and the West Indian psyche. As a poet he sometimes leaves this territory, but never as a dramatist.'[29] Outside the Caribbean Walcott is better known as a poet than as a dramatist. However, his work over thirty years as a dramatist and director, including an influential time with the Trinidad Theatre Workshop, developed approaches to the interaction between European forms and Caribbean traditions which eventually culminated in his dramatization of the story of Homer's *Odyssey* in the early 1990s. During the earlier period, Walcott experimented with song, dance, and acting styles based on Caribbean movement and speech. For instance, he was strongly aware of the disjunction between the promotion of Carnival as a tourist attraction and its role as a distinctive art-form which in Juneja's words 'transformed the colonially-imposed impoverishments of spiritual and material resources into something rich and wonderful'.[30] The attraction felt by Walcott for folk tales and the potential of the epic of a cultural journey came together in his choice of the *Odyssey* as the basis for a stage play. The work brought together his commitment to Caribbean art-forms and the accommodation with western European culture

[28] Published as Walcott (1993).
[29] Quotations from Juneja (1992), 236–66.
[30] Juneja (1992), 236, commenting on Walcott (1998), 23–4.

which he had crafted in his poetry, while the choice of epic over tragedy enabled him not only to work through the episodes of a cultural and psychological journey but also to side-step the binary oppositions of tragedy.

Walcott's incorporation of diaspora voices and cultural practices in *The Odyssey: A Stage Version* emphasizes a poetics of cultural fluidity and interaction rather than polarity and difference. The play is permeated by the language of the blues singer and the Creole. A black storyteller provides the narrative framework. In the figure of Billy Blue, Walcott both gives a shaping voice to twentieth-century black consciousness and improvises on the theme of the travelling bards of Homeric Greece. The blues carry the memory of the past (including slavery and exile) but their virtuosity is a phenomenon of contemporary culture, creating their own language and modulations and engaging a new community of listeners. The figure of Eurykleia, too, draws on aural and oral memories but resists reduction to a stereotype and exploitation as a political emblem. Again, Walcott achieves this by subverting both Homeric and modern discourses. The speech rhythms and impact of Eurykleia's role are at least partly dependent on Caribbean culture and on the resonances of the ante-bellum plantation culture of the southern states of the USA. It is she who is the 'cradle' both figuratively in terms of memory, like Billy Blue, and literally—'to me and to my father you have been slave and nurse' (I. xi. 9).

The modern Caribbean thus replaces the ancient Mediterranean as the springboard for cultural dialogue. Convergence is drawn out from the ritual settings through which the adventures of Odysseus are presented. This is so not only in the Carnival settings (see Figure 18 for the association between Carnival and the figure of Circe), but also in the descent to the underworld which is brought about by the performance of an African-Caribbean Shango rite in which Walcott's 'African-Greeks' (as he has referred to them) sacrifice and set out boundaries in terms of Shango ritual, asking their ancestors for health, protection in agriculture, and success in crucial ventures. (The Kele cult in St Lucia includes a variation on this practice in which polished stone axes are arranged in a ritual formation.)

In the Rehearsal Text of Walcott's play the audience heard word-play on the association of black and female victims: 'Troy

FIGURE 18. Photograph of Circe's carnivalesque entrance in Derek Walcott's *A Stage Version of the Odyssey*, directed by Gregory Doran for the Royal Shakespeare Company (premiered at The Other Place, Stratford-upon-Avon on 2 July 1992). 'You'll learn more than the others. The swine I keep penned' (Circe, Act I, Scene xii).

was all smoke, we could hear its black women wail.'[31] So 'blackness' does not have a limited ethnic or geographical dimension; it is rather a signifier of commonality of suffering and surely underlies Walcott's major change from Homer in his stage version, when an assertive Penelope rails at Odysseus' culture of revenge which has brought about the slaughter of the suitors. She then prevents the hanging of the maid. With Greek as with Caribbean culture, Walcott does not tolerate an unexamined nostalgia for return to origins or roots. His Odysseus has to adapt in order to face the future.

Thus the play both opens up the cultural provenances from which performed and written texts may be 'read' and emancipates Homer's epic from association only with the bleached stones of an ancient, and lost, Greece. Walcott's poetic and theatre practice, brought together in his version of the *Odyssey*, liberate Caribbean literature from the effects of the colonization of mind and art. As Grace Nichols has put it in 'I Is a Long-Memoried Woman',[32]

[31] Rehearsal Text 1. 25, held with other documentation relating to the production in the Royal Shakespeare Company archive at Stratford-upon-Avon.
[32] The title poem of her collection *I Is a Long-Memoried Woman* (1983).

> I have crossed an ocean
> I have lost my tongue
> From the roots of the old one
> A new one has sprung

GREEK DRAMA IN AFRICA

The histories of interaction between Greek drama and colonialism in Africa are as varied as, and yield examples comparable to, those found in the Caribbean—the drama of resistance, of partial consolation, and of hybrid affirmation. My first example is from francophone North Africa. A 1966 production of Sophocles' *Electra*, translated by the director Antoine Vitez, was performed in a Roman theatre in Algeria, newly independent from France. The adaptation and its reception is of particular interest because the production was not specifically directed at the Algerian situation. In fact, making Greek plays contemporary and emphasizing their relationship with current situations was a strategy specifically rejected by the translator/director (he also rejected archaeological and primitive/exotic approaches). He did, however, assert that the director is the ultimate translator.[33] In this case, although the director set the play at a critical distance, alienated from the present, its implications for power, conflict, and colonization of Electra's personal, social, and political space struck a vein in the audience. The director recalled, 'The miracle of Babel was accomplished. The whole audience recognised in the *Electra* their nation humiliated for 25 years, subjected to colonial rule, restored to life when hope seemed lost.'[34] Their response introduces into this discussion the claim of the audience to be the ultimate translator, the arbiter of the resonances of the performance. It shows that the less obviously 'political' Greek plays can figure equally powerfully in the registers of post-colonial cultural politics and that the theatre of affliction, with its *alter ego* the celebration of revenge, is a dramatic counterpart to the poetics of affliction discussed in relation to the Caribbean. It also exemplifies the powerful role of the metropolitan in theatre (this production originated in Paris;

---

[33] Documented in Vitez (1995) and (1997); for discussion see Wiles (2000), 190 and 233 n.

[34] Translation quoted in Wiles (2000), 192.

other examples to be discussed below were commissioned by or
premiered in European or American cities).

In the second half of the twentieth century, when it was progressively freed from colonial rule, West Africa became a key area for
adaptations of Greek plays. Two of the premières took place in the
west and other performances were subsequently staged there.[35]
Several of the adaptations of the early and middle 1960s raise
important questions about the role of traditional African theatre
and African politics in the refiguration of Greek drama. Some
demonstrate close links with Caribbean, Black British, or American theatre as well as with cosmopolitan audiences. J. P. Clark's
Song of a Goat reworks aspects of Aeschylus' *Agamemnon*. It was
first performed in 1962 at the Mbari Centre, directed by Wole
Soyinka, and was later staged at the Commonwealth Festival of the
Arts in London in 1965. Kamau Brathwaite's *Odale's Choice*,
refiguring Sophocles' *Antigone*, had its first performance at the
Mfantisman Secondary School, Saltpond, Ghana, in 1962. It was
also staged in Kenya and Nigeria and was performed by the Trini-
dad Theatre Workshop in 1973, directed by Derek Walcott.
Brathwaite had returned to Africa from the Caribbean and worked
as a government education officer in newly independent Ghana.
His work is characterized by the use of 'nation' language, drawing
together African experience and the Caribbean. Efua Sutherland's
Edufa responded to themes in Euripides' *Alcestis*. It was first
performed at the Drama Studio, University of Ghana, in 1962.
Ola Rotimi's *The Gods are Not to Blame* explores the themes of
Sophocles' *Oedipus the King*. It includes lines spoken or sung in
Yoruba and is often thought to provide an allegory for the fighting
in the Biafran War. It was first performed in 1968 by Rotimi's
Olokun Acting Company.[36]

---

[35] The impact of some of these productions both in African and in western
performance has been researched by Felix Budelmann (for further details see
References). For discussion of Rotimi and Soyinka see McDonald (2000).

[36] For the published texts of these plays see Clark (1961), Brathwaite (1967),
Sutherland (1967), Rotimi (1971). *Song of a Goat* was revived in 2001 in Lagos (at
the Muson Centre and on tour), directed by Ahmed Yerima, as part of a new project
re-examining Nigerian classical drama. *Edufa* was revived by Falaki Arts in British
Council sponsored performances in February 1999 in Nairobi, Kenya, and in New
York in 2002 by African Arts Theatre. *The Gods are Not to Blame* has been staged in
the UK on a number of occasions, the British premiere being at the Everyman,
Liverpool, in 1989 by the Talawa Theatre Company.

The play *Tegonni, an African Antigone* by Fémi Òsófisan (who like Soyinka and the classicizing poet Christopher Okigbo studied at the University of Ibadan in Nigeria) is of particular interest because it refigures the Sophoclean model in a nineteenth-century context that addresses racial and imperialist issues and also develops a critique of modern power struggles. It dramatizes the story of a Yoruba princess who is going to marry a British army officer in the late nineteenth century at the time when the British were annexing territories in Africa. Òsófisan explored the implications for racial attitudes and personal courage and also, in following the practice of drawing on traditional mythology as a means of reconsidering contemporary realities, developed an analogue for the struggles for power between military regimes and pro-democracy movements in modern Nigeria. The first version of the play was commissioned and produced by Theatre Emory of the Emory University, Atlanta, Georgia, USA, in autumn 1994 as part of the theatre department's Brave New Work project.[37]

The plays of Òsófisan and other West African dramatists provide a broader context to the work of Wole Soyinka. This corpus relates closely to the major themes which have been developed in this discussion. Three in particular are important—personal educational history, the syncretic relationship between African and Greek theatre, and the role of theatre in critiquing neo- and post-colonial situations. Soyinka is the son of teachers. His mother came from a family of teachers and activists in the women's movement. She was the granddaughter of a Christian priest who played a significant role in Yoruba politics and in 1905 preached in St Paul's Cathedral in London. Soyinka was educated at an elite institution, Government College, Ibadan, and from 1952 studied English, Greek, and History at University College, Ibadan. In 1954 he went to the University of Leeds (like Ngũgĩ wa Thiong'o and Tony Harrison), and subsequently wrote and taught in London.[38] In 1960, the year of Nigerian independence from Britain, he returned to Nigeria and in Lagos and Ibadan staged *A Dance of the Forests*, a revised version of an earlier anti-apartheid play *The Dance of the African Forest*. This play challenged

---

[37] The version published in Òsófisan (1999*b*) is that presented in 1998 at the 50th anniversary of the University of Ibadan at the University Arts Theatre, directed by Òsófisan.

[38] Source: Gibbs (1986), 1–17.

expectations about the future of the country and in particular examined the tensions between the nationalist élite's desire for power and its apparent encouragement of tribalism. It also raised issues about the future direction of Nigerian theatre in English. Significantly, the play exploited the story of Troy in a debate about the justification of war. The debate was set at the court of a corrupt king at the time of the Ghana and Mali empires, but with many characters recognizable by the current generation. Intellectuals (a frequent butt of Soyinka's satire) were called in to rationalize the war. The Historian says:

> Be quiet soldier! I have the whole history of Troy. If you were not the swillage of pigs and could read the writings of wiser men, I would show you the magnificence of the destruction of a beautiful city ... would Troy, if it were standing today, lay claim to preservation in the annals of history if a thousand valiant Greeks had not been slaughtered before its gates and a hundred thousand Trojans within her walls?[39]

Soyinka was politically active and imprisoned in the late 1960s because of his criticism of the Gowan military regime and his campaign for a ceasefire in the war against secessionist Biafra. Subsequently he spent five years in virtual exile in Europe. It was during this period that his *The Bacchae of Euripides: A Communion Rite* was commissioned by the National Theatre in the UK and staged in August 1973 at the Old Vic in London. Two aspects of the play are of particular importance. First, the adaptations made from Euripides emphasized the theme of slavery. A second chorus was added, an ethnically mixed group with a black Leader (to ensure authenticity in the 'hollering' style required for the Leader's solo). The play explored a scapegoat ritual in which a slave was selected for flogging. The stage directions specified a set lined by the skeletal bodies of crucified slaves. Pentheus' tyrannical aspects were brought out and Dionysus' conflict with him resulted in the liberation of the slaves, who eventually joined the Maenads in celebration. This has often been described as representing the development of a play canonical in the European tradition as a form of anti-colonial discourse, but of course it also drew on the Greek tradition of using the chorus to give a voice to marginalized groups.[40] Thus the commissioning, creation, and

---

[39] Soyinka (1967), 57–8; Ngũgĩ (1972), 62.
[40] See above, Chapter 1, pp. 23–4.

staging of the play embody a structure of double consciousness at every level. There is also a double consciousness in the way Soyinka filters the action through the rituals associated with the Yoruba deity Ogun, god of metals, creativity, the road, wine, and war, and his use of lines from traditional praise chants as well as lines closely following Arrowsmith's 1959 translation.[41]

Soyinka is also the author of an essay 'Through the Mysteries of Ogun to the Origin of Yoruba Tragedy'; in interviews and critical writings he has challenged the notion that tragedy originated in Greece—'what are they talking about? I never heard my grandfather talk about Greeks invading Yorubaland' (1988). In *Myth, Literature, and the African World* he has also argued that black Africans were submitted to a second wave of colonialism in having their practices subjected to an intellectual version of western hegemonic practice, which situated the main debates within European thought and neglected the theories and cultures of the colonized countries.[42] The volume also includes an important essay on 'Drama and the African World View' in which Soyinka denies that divergences between a traditional African approach to drama and the European are those of opposition between creative individualism (European) and communal creativity (African). Instead, he asserts that the divergence is between the western compartmentalizing habit of thought—separated myths—and the African sense of interconnected space. Soyinka has been attacked by critics in Nigeria and elsewhere for his African version of humanism and for his emphasis on traditional ritual and myth, which has sometimes attracted the charge of 'nativism'.[43] However, others argue on the other side, recognizing Soyinka's rejection of 'Négritude' and analysing the historicist aspects of his adaptation of Euripides, especially in the challenging exploration of the relationships between African tradition and colonialist culture.[44] It is noticeable that it is Soyinka's use of classical referents and adaptations that is

---

[41] See the Introduction to Soyinka (1973), vi.

[42] Soyinka (1976), 'Preface', x.

[43] For discussion see Crow and Banfield (1996), 93–5, and Broich (1997). Broich denies Soyinka's *Bacchae* status as post-colonial writing because of its use of ritual tribal sacrifice which, along with the Yoruba elements in Rotimi's *The Gods are Not to Blame*, he regards as 'nativist'. This echoes Edward Saïd's use of the term in Saïd (1993), 275–8. In his discussion Saïd relates 'nativism' and its African context to the issues raised by Seamus Deane in respect of nationalism (see pp. 221–2 above).

[44] See Okpewho (1991).

crucial in holding the balance between historical and essentialist approaches in his work and, in the case of *The Bacchae of Euripides: A Communion Rite*, of promoting dialogue between these.

From study of Soyinka, then, I would pick out two rather contrasting points. The first is the sometimes ambivalent status of creative drama for which metropolitan European theatre and audiences are the patrons, showing perhaps an enthusiasm for the exotic which is then subverted by the ironies arising from the author's double consciousness. The second is that the intertextuality of Soyinka's theatre questions the kind of compartmentalism which regards either Greek or Yoruba tradition as prior.

Discussion of African refiguration of Greek drama must also acknowledge the impact of theatre in Southern Africa. The reception of Greek material in South Africa before the end of apartheid shows that productions such as the Cape Performing Arts Board's staging of an Afrikaans performance of the *Oresteia* in 1981 were watersheds because of the way that the non-traditional staging (for South Africa) brought the notion of creating a just society home to the audience. Sophocles' *Antigone* was, of course, used as a springboard by the Serpent Players, a group of black actors based in New Brighton (a township outside Port Elizabeth) and closely associated with the actor, poet, and playwright Athol Fugard. It was the cancellation of a planned performance in 1965, because of the imprisonment of the leading actor Norman Ntshinga on Robben Island for political activities, that inspired *The Island*, a collaboration between Athol Fugard, Winston Ntshona, and John Kani, first performed in 1973. The play became an icon for its denunciation of the brutality and injustice of the apartheid regime. It is a play of particular historical specificity—enhanced by Nelson Mandela's role as Creon in the Robben Island performance on which it draws.[45] Yet it has also been performed at other junctures—for instance in Barbados in the spring of 1994, when it not only marked events in South Africa but is also documented as challenging actors and director to understand their own histories in their relationship to the colonial history of the Caribbean and to confront the interventionist role of the (white European) director.[46]

---

[45] Nelson Mandela refers in his memoirs (Mandela (1995), 541) to the effect of the role on him—'[Creon's] inflexibility and blindness ill become a leader for a leader must temper justice with mercy.'

[46] Source: Leyshon (1999).

The supposedly 'final revival' of the play with Ntshona and Kani was staged in London and toured in the UK and Europe in 2002 (see Figure 19).

The Island is a play which can be said to have been a catalyst for political as well as theatrical change. Perhaps for that very reason it has also attracted criticism for being hijacked by middle-class white liberals—in South Africa and elsewhere. Originally a countertext, it is said to have been domesticated into the dominant discourses of European tradition, marginalizing African tradition and practices. *The Island* has been followed by consciously interventionist and culturally hybrid versions of Greek plays, including *Medea* directed by Mark Fleishman and Jennie Reznek with the Jazzart Dance Theatre (1994–6).[47] This production had the specific aim of constructing an alternative ideology to that of apartheid or African nationalism and of promoting a political and artistic aesthetic which valued cultural diversity and exchange. The spoken script was multilingual, including Xhosa, Tamil, and Afrikaans as well as English (which was spoken by Jason without an Afrikaaner accent). The production was praised for its stunning physical theatre and for its openness to black theatrical forms of expression. Yet, it was also thought to perpetuate racial stereotypes by some critics who thought that Jason was represented as the white rational male with Medea as the black, female, sensual and barbaric 'other'.[48] This raises very interesting questions about the difficulty of translating this particular play across cultural and temporal divides.[49]

The aim of translating Greek literature into the languages of the new South Africa is being taken a step further by Richard Whitaker's new translation of the *Iliad*. One aim of the translation (of which in 2002 about half had been completed) was to remedy deficiencies in the language and outlook of the Anglo-American translations, which Whitaker perceived as remote from the speech and language of South Africans. Another aim was to realize the

---

[47] Performed in Capetown, Grahamstown, and Johannesburg, also on a European tour.

[48] Discussed by Banning (1999).

[49] Witness the problems with anachronisms of social values when other modern versions have recently been attempted. The most successful production I have seen in the last few years, the Oxford University Classical Drama Society staging in 2002, directed by Nat Coleman, was actually in the original Greek and retained the ancient setting.

FIGURE 19. John (Kani) and Winston (Ntshona) prepare for the Robben Island performance of *Antigone* in *The Island* which premiered in 1973. This photograph was taken at the 1995 revival at the Market Theatre, Johannesburg. 'There'll come a time when they'll stop laughing, and that will be the time when our Antigone hits them with her words' (John, Scene ii, in response to Winston's reluctance to dress up as a woman).

potential of Southern African English as a hybrid language (for it has assimilated vocabulary from many of the region's languages, including Bushman, Khoikhoi, Zulu, Xhosa, and Afrikaans) and thus to replace the apartheid policy of linguistic isolation with a contribution to the construction of a new South African identity which is inclusive of difference. Such developments seem to point to the validity of the critical notion that cultures have within them periods of fracture and change, even to the point of trauma, which can nevertheless result in new strengths. The aim of Whitaker and others is to use Greek material to identify commonalities (such as the affinities between Greek and African traditions of gift exchange) through which apparently divergent cultures and political histories may engage in dialogue.[50] Whitaker's project serves as a specially constructed textual analogue to Walcott's performative approach to Homer as a source for the affirmation of cultural hybridity.

In conclusion, what can be made of this extremely disparate collection of examples of the ways in which Greek drama has had such a catalytic role in such varied colonial histories? Of course there is the nowadays rather bland but nevertheless important point about the flexibility of Greek drama, its capacity to seem both familiar and alien, to always embody that critical distance which can transform audiences' perceptions of themselves and of the Greeks (see above, Chapter 1, pp. 41–2). This accounts perhaps for the role of Greek drama in awareness-raising and in the theatre of intervention and witness, especially in the face of censorship and repression. However, Greek drama has also been a means of creating new perceptions, new theatrical practices, and new literatures. A point frequently made by post-colonial theorists is that hybridity in culture merely masks power relations and may reaffirm colonial oppression in opaque ways. A study of refigurations of Greek drama demonstrates the contrary. These reveal the fragmentation of the ideologies of political and cultural oppression and have provided a commentary on different aspects of liberation from the colonization of the mind. At the same time, in working in this fluid way, refiguration has pointed up different histories of

---

[50] For a summary of Whitaker's aims and progress to date, see Whitaker (2002). Part of the translation is available on request by writing to the author at whitr@ humanities.uct.ac.za

colonialism and the different educational and artistic histories of the practitioners. It is probably too soon to make a judgement about how far this is part of redressing the balance of cultural power and how far it signals a realignment of the cultural affiliations of Greek poetry and drama. Nevertheless, it is salutary to reflect on the implications for Greek drama of Ngũgĩ wa Thiong'o's assertion (in the context of pressures on African culture) that pride in language, lore, art, dance, song, sculpture, and colour can be retrieved from colonialist repression.[51] Certainly in the process of refiguration which has taken place in the Caribbean and in Africa, Greek drama has been removed from a narrow context of association with imperial and colonialist appropriation and the associated cultural and political practices and values. It has, in fact, followed a threefold process of political engagement which is characteristic of diaspora communities:

1. self-emancipation from slavery (i.e. resistance to final appropriation, of whatever kind);
2. achievement of civic participation (in new contexts);
3. creation of an autonomous space in which to develop politically and culturally (a theatre of transformation).

The capacity of Greek drama for stimulating and communicating double consciousness and for liberating practitioners and audiences (including European and American audiences) from colonization of the mind has aligned it with the insights of postcolonial dramatists and poets. Some of these have, in their creative work, stripped away easy assumptions about the 'western identity' of ancient Greek culture. In this sense I would argue that Greek drama has not only been a decolonizing force, it has itself been decolonized.[52]

---

[51] Crucial to the claim are the new essays on 'Freedom of Expression' and 'Culture in a Crisis' in the second edition of *Writers in Politics* (Ngũgĩ (1997)).

[52] An earlier version of this chapter was given as a lecture at the Oxford Archive of Performances of Greek and Roman Drama in February 2002. The constructive criticisms and comments of participants gave me much food for thought, now and for the future, and I thank all concerned most warmly.

Section III

DIONYSUS AND THE AESTHETICS OF PERFORMANCE

9

The Use of Masks in Modern Performances of Greek Drama

David Wiles

The appeal of Greek tragedy today stems not just from its content, its handling of themes like women, war, and democracy, but from its formal properties which present a unique challenge to modern actors and directors. Though the most obvious aspect is the chorus (on which see Zeitlin, above, Chapter 2, and Fischer-Lichte, below, Chapter 13), I have chosen to focus this chapter on the mask. In the period with which this book is concerned, the most prominent practitioner who has placed mask at the centre of his understanding of Greek tragedy is Sir Peter Hall, who declared in a recent interview on BBC Radio 3 (*The Verb*, 6 April 2002): 'The mask is absolutely central to doing Greek drama at all. As far as I'm concerned, I would never do a Greek play without a mask.' Although there is much in Hall's practice that I find regrettable, I am entirely at one with his premise, most fully articulated in one of the Clark Lectures he delivered in Cambridge in January 2000, that art depends upon form, that masking is a paradigm for under-standing all aspects of Greek theatre, and that the historical con-vention of the mask made Greek tragedy both aesthetically satisfying and socially efficacious. The mask separates both actor and spectator from the emotions expressed in language, and thus makes the playing of those extreme emotions possible. It encour-ages the actor to break away from a dominant naturalistic style of acting.[1]

I intend to develop a broader cultural and historical view of the mask than Hall does. In order to understand the achievement and potential of the mask in modern performance, it is essential to see it in a wider context. Masks are almost ubiquitous in non-western cultures. The western and Islamic worlds are unusual in regarding the mask as a mode of concealment, not a mode of revelation and

---

[1] Peter Hall (2000).

transformation. It seems to be a correlative of monotheistic religions that they want human nature to be single, not multiple. The one god who sees and knows everything is naturally hostile to the idea of disguises. Non-western masks are often bound up with the idea of possession, when one of the many divine forces in the cosmos enters a human being through the medium of the mask. In medieval Christian drama, masks were worn by the actor playing God and more crucially by devils, because the wearer needed to keep his own human identity separate from the divine. Human characters were played unmasked, because the souls of human beings are always visible to God. In polytheistic masking cultures, the boundary between human and divine is more fluid. Masking survived in the Christian tradition within a carnival context, for carnival was an indulgence in paganism, anticipating the arrival of Lent and the putting away of sinful things. Festive masking, thanks to its association with feasting and wine, was long identified with the ancient worship of Bacchus. The *commedia dell'arte*, the solitary major form of masked theatre that has flourished in the west subsequent to the Renaissance, is rooted in carnival practices. Harlequin descends from the French *Hellequin*, Hell's king—the devil.

After Christianity came the intellectual Enlightenment of the eighteenth century which privileged feeling, or sentiment, as the necessary antithesis of reason. The source of feeling was for a while located in the famous Cartesian pineal gland just behind the eyes. The idea of this gland, postulated by Descartes in the 1640s, was discredited, but the assumption remained that the seat of thought and emotion lies somewhere inside the brain. It follows from this assumption that emotions can be discerned most directly through the face, the area closest to the brain. An Enlightenment culture obsessed with the quality of individual feeling had no time for the theatrical mask. If Harlequin survived in the theatre, this was because he functioned as the carnal alter ego of the sensitive passionate lover. The masked face signified that he represented the principle of the ungoverned body.

Masks of other kinds re-entered western theatrical culture with the coming of modernism. Some of the most exciting twentieth-century masked experiments are associated with the Cabaret Voltaire, the famous Dada cabaret in Zurich during the First World War. This was a convergence of dancers (like Laban), visual artists, poets, and theatre people, all concerned to disrupt received notions of artistic form. The collective madness of the Great War underlined the fundamental irrationality of human beings, and opened people's eyes to a different sense of the human being. In Dada, art was pushed away from the representational towards the abstract. The influence of African masks on the cubists at this time is well known, and how was the actor to render the human face *à la* Picasso, if not through the mask? In the intellectual domain, psychoanalysts had demolished the inner sanctum of the human soul, leaving the ego as a mere façade concealing chaos. The cabaret traditions of puppetry and shadow mime all helped push the Dadaists towards the development of mask-work. They found that the mask helped them in their search for primordial essences, like the essence of sound behind the semantic meaning of words. What they discovered was that when they put on painted cardboard masks, aggressively modern creations that dimly recalled Greek theatre, these masks helped them do madder and madder things, freeing them from their rational bourgeois selves. I quote Hugo Ball, the driving force behind the cabaret: 'The masks simply demanded that their wearers start to move in a tragic-absurd dance.'[2]

One route by which masks entered the modern theatre, then, was through the innovations and philosophy of a radical avant-garde. The other major route that we can trace leads back to Jacques Copeau, the French director who set up his training school after the First World War. Copeau rejected both the rhetorical neo-classicism of the Comédie Française, and the low-key naturalism of André Antoine, and sought to recreate the bare trestle stage of the *commedia dell'arte*. Masks were fundamental to his process of training. The ideal of the bare, empty stage led to the development of a bare, neutral mask, which was to be the starting point for building a character *ab initio*. The line from Copeau leads both to the influential mask and movement training developed by Jacques Lecoq in Paris, and via Michel Saint-Denis, Copeau's nephew, to London and the work of Peter Hall. I find these genealogies interesting, because theatre practices are not transmitted through books but through sustained personal contact. Masks have been far more significant in twentieth-century actor training than they

---

[2] Ball (1974), 64; on cabaret, see Segel (1987).

have been in twentieth-century performance. The tradition derived from Copeau and Lecoq sees the mask as a tool that takes the actor back to the beginning in order to cast off personal idiosyncrasies, and to rediscover how to use the body. The prevailing assumption is that the performer of western theatre can discard the mask when he or she has acquired these skills. Mainstream theatre today still relies on the face, and on the dismal premise of 'method acting' that good acting is essentially about being oneself.

More recently, other routes have also led us to the mask: the rediscovery of folk traditions, exposure to eastern theatre, and the development of the mask in therapy. I shall return to these later in order to show how they have expanded the possibilities for masked Greek theatre in the present. First, however, I shall set out a historical context for the use of masks in Greek theatre before the watershed years of the late 1960s that have been identified by the editors of this volume.

The seminal production in the early twentieth century was *Prometheus*, performed in the ancient theatre at Delphi in 1927. The American director Eva Palmer-Sikelianos was married to the Greek writer, philosopher, and political idealist Angelos Sikelianos. She spent all her inherited wealth to create a festival that included both *Prometheus* and a competition in Greek gymnastics. The masks which she used are exhibited in the Sikelianos museum in Delphi, and were briefly exhibited at London's Theatre Museum; the APGRD holds an ancient film clip with extracts from her production. The masks are objects of beauty, Hellenic rather than grandiose in the Roman manner.[3] It is likely that the great stage designer Edward Gordon Craig would have approved. Craig called, in 1910, for the revival of the Greek mask—not in the form of antiquarian replicas, but works created by artists.[4] Eva and Angelos were great admirers of Goethe, who experimented with Greek masks at the start of the nineteenth century,[5] but the fundamental philosophical influence on the production was Nietzsche, who proclaimed in 1872:

Prometheus, Oedipus and so on—are merely masks of that original hero, Dionysus. The fact that a divinity lurks behind all these masks is the major

---

[3] The best source of images is Palmer-Sikelianos (1993).
[4] See Craig (1983), 126.   [5] Flashar (1991), 52.

reason for the typical 'ideality' of those celebrated characters that has so often raised astonishment.[6]

The different masks, says Nietzsche, betoken the dismemberment of Dionysus into a collection of individuals. This conception justified presenting the chorus unmasked, for their individuation did not need to be marked. Behind Nietzsche lay the fundamental influence of Plato: not only the idea that art pursues the ideal, but also the identification of drama as a form of dance. Where Aristotle in his *Poetics* paired drama with epic, Plato in his *Laws* paired theatre with gymnastics, an activity of the body.

The wearing of masks in Delphi was tied to a metaphysical conception of human existence. Human beings were considered to have an organic relationship to the divine, and to the earth; individuation was a bourgeois concept that was felt to be destroying the world. Angelos Sikelianos spoke of how the masks 'achieve a communion between this gigantic myth and modern souls'.[7] When Eva Palmer-Sikelianos writes about her use of masks, she does so in connection with architecture. She maintains that the enclosing circle of the Greek theatre created a unity between actors and audience, subsumed by a greater harmony: 'This psychological phenomenon of unity realized outside of themselves was accentuated . . . by the use of masks.' The masked actor was oblivious to the spectators, who were in any case above eye level in the Greek theatre, and this removed self-consciousness, and the temptation to smirk and play for effect. 'There existed nothing for each individual actor but himself and the god he was worshipping.'[8] So, lost inside the darkness of the mask, the actor could lose him or herself in the emotions of the text, and the audience would have to find a way of communing with these visionaries.

This emphasis on the experiential qualities of the mask has its obvious dangers: the actor who fails to think about the audience risks losing its attention. Those who did not come to commune could quickly feel excluded. In England at this time, the most important experiments were those of Terence Gray, who presented Greek plays using masks and dancers in the classical-style Cambridge Festival Theatre.[9] Gray, alas, had enemies, and almost all records of his work were destroyed after his death. I pass

---

[6] Nietzsche (1993), 51.   [7] Cited in Fotopoulos (1986), 34.
[8] Palmer-Sikelianos (1993), 222–3.   [9] Cave (1980).

therefore to Paris, where the most important figure is Cocteau, interested in the mask because he wanted to integrate different art forms. His experiments with ritualistic masks in *Antigone* encouraged Stravinsky to work with him on his oratorio *Oedipus Rex* in 1927. Their conception was that the masks should turn the actors into statues, archaeological relics from long ago. These masks uttered a dead language, Latin, uniting the ancient qualities of sound and image. Stravinsky, having in earlier works integrated his music with vigorous ballet, now used the mask to eliminate or minimize movement. This was not the rite of spring but the rite of winter. The mask in this production was not something that animated the body, but something that betokened immobility and death. For theatre, the potential of this conception was plainly limited.

Eugene O'Neill was another in the 1920s who dreamed of a new kind of acting and a theatre of masks. He called for masks in one draft of *Mourning Becomes Electra*, but thought better of it. 'The classical connotation was too insistent,' he wrote. 'Masks in that connection demand great language to speak.' He had no easy answer to the problem of reconciling naturalistic American speech with the heroic classical mask. By 1932 he regretted his lack of resolve, feeling that masks would have served to bring out the deep psychological forces at work, the life-and-death drives that send the characters to their deaths.[10] It is hard to imagine how this new vision could actually be realized. Psychoanalysis owes everything to Greek mythology, and separating the psychic dimension from the historical connotations of the form would have been a difficult undertaking.

With the waning of the modernist impulse, the desire to experiment with masks seems to have passed. The experimentation of Eva Palmer-Sikelianos must be seen in the context of a generation that interested itself in the ideal of the primitive, and in the roots of performance in the body. Appia, Meyerhold, and Isadora Duncan were amongst the many who related theatricality to the expressivity of the body. The coming of Stalin, the depression, and the rise of fascism are amongst the factors that put a brake on experimentation. Theatre became increasingly rooted in the word rather than the body, and preoccupied itself with moral and philosophical

[10] O'Neill (1961), 69.

debate, or musical entertainment. Two major post-war experiments stand out. Tyrone Guthrie's *Oedipus Rex* was performed on the revolutionary thrust stage in Stratford, Ontario, in 1955. Guthrie's interest in masks was linked to his experiment in Greek-style architectural form. Guthrie recognized that when the audience surrounds the actors, it ceases to be voyeuristic and detached, and participates in a kind of ritual. He wanted the audience to commune with Oedipus in his agony, and his ideal of communion harks back to Nietzsche.[11] The anti-individualist philosophy of the 1920s idealists remained, but the deep emotional commitment behind that philosophy had I think gone by 1955, the metaphysics now drained of their politics. The text was that of Yeats (on which see also Worth and Macintosh, below, Chapters 10 and 12), another of the great pioneers of the 1920s who fused dance, drama, and poetry, though he never directly applied those techniques to Greek theatre; paradoxically it took a great poet to create a language that seemed to have no poetry, a language that emerged from within and did not seem to be imposed on the mask from without. The design of the production rested on the now discarded assumption that Greek actors wore raised cothurni and high masks. The symbolism was straightforward: Oedipus was an Apolline solar figure, gold clad, with rays rising from his crown. The white of Tiresias betokened death, and his mask suggested the birds which he as a prophet consults. The designer's sketch (Figure 20) evokes the hieratic nature of the performance, and its stately quality of movement. The convention of the mask made the body more god-like, but not more energized. As Fiona Macintosh has pointed out, *Oedipus* with its links to the psychoanalytic tradition was the key Greek tragedy at the turn of the century.[12] Guthrie's production, based on old-fashioned archaeology, looked backwards rather than forwards.

Another influential production of the same year was Jean-Louis Barrault's *Oresteia* in Paris. Student experiments at the Sorbonne had kept the tradition of the mask in play. For Barrault, who worked in the physical theatre tradition of Copeau, the mask was a means of activating the body. 'Even one's toes rediscover their

[11] Davies *et al.* (1955), 113–15. The APGRD holds a copy of the filmed record of this production.
[12] See Macintosh (forthcoming *b*).

FIGURE 20.   Tanya Moiseiwitsch's costume sketch for the character of Tiresias in *Oedipus Rex*, directed by Tyrone Guthrie (1955).

personality, the muscles of the abdomen find their *raison d'être*, the body regains its whole theatrical function . . .'[13] He used close-fitting three-quarter leather masks with mobile hair that harked back to the African origins of voodoo. The production was not so well received as Guthrie's, and it is interesting to reflect on why it failed. Whilst Guthrie played to a Greek-style auditorium, Barrault was tied to a proscenium theatre (see also Hall, above, Chapter 1, pp. 27–8), and his stage setting was a traditional representation of symmetrical Greek architecture. The style of acting doubtless seemed anomalous. It may also be that audiences were not ready for an intercultural interpretation of the ancient world, one that discarded the old statuesque and rhetorical style of French classical acting. It may be that actors trained in playing Racine were not able to adjust to the style required by the masks. Roland Barthes in an influential review attacked the dishonest exoticism of the production, arguing for a more Brechtian approach to the classics.[14] Yet when we look at the masks today, their exoticism seems much less obvious, their Hellenic references more apparent, because our own conventions of representation have shifted in Barrault's direction.

In the 1960s the most important innovations came from the left-wing Greek director Karolos Koun. Koun ransacked the modern Greek folk tradition in search of masks for Aristophanes, and was very successful in creating carnivalesque productions that seemed to draw Aristophanes out of popular culture. His project was to rescue the classics from a social and cultural élite, and give them back to the people. Tragedy was more problematic, since there was no resource equivalent to folk culture, but he found inspiration in Brecht, who used masks in several productions of the Berliner Ensemble as an alienation device. Koun's most celebrated productions of tragedy include *Persians* (1965, 1976), *Oedipus* (1967), and the *Oresteia* (1980). He evolved the convention of the tragic half-mask, which was borrowed by several subsequent Greek directors. These masks are essentially a negative, cutting out individuality from the face, rather than a positive statement. They had a political dimension insofar as they countered the pre-eminence of the star

---

[13] *World Theatre* (1957), 277; see also Barrault (1961).
[14] Barthes (1972). On Barthes's personal experience of Greek theatre, see above, Hall, Chapter 1, pp. 38–9 and n. 68

actor, giving primacy to the dramatic narrative. They were helpful also in fostering a sense of ceremony within the play, and ceremonial suited the festival of Epidaurus, which became a central component in Greek theatrical life after it was opened to groups other than the National Theatre in 1975. Masks have been particularly popular in Greece, partly because they suit outdoor performance conditions which make facial expression hard to discern, and partly perhaps because they position modern Greek culture as a bridge between east and west, past and present. Koun's half-masks are functional items, because they are simple to make and wear and cause no problems of audibility. But there is an unresolved tension between the alienating, political conception of the mask, and the ceremonial conception. The visible mouth and hidden eyes leave spectators constantly aware of the Brechtian dialectic between actor and role. Yet they also invite the spectator to imagine that the actor has vanished into an ancient ritual.

In western Europe and North America, the approaches of Guthrie and Barrault seemed to be a dead end. Neither found a style capable of unlocking new possibilities in the text. The mask did not provide an obvious way forward. The title of this volume identifies Richard Schechner's *Dionysus in 69* as a landmark which epitomizes the new thinking of the Sixties, and the ruthless discarding of bourgeois tradition. The trademark of that production was its cult of nudity, and the principle of the mask is the antithesis of nudity. Schechner idealized nudity not only as a symbol of new sexual values but also because nudity was associated with authenticity, with the removal of social barriers between individuals, with the intimacy of actor and spectator, and with the discarding of external theatrical form in favour of content.[15] In the asexual nakedness cultivated by the Polish director Jerzy Grotowski in the 1960s, we see the same spirit of the age at work. The revival of the mask had to await the passing of the Sixties quest for authenticity, and a new postmodern Zeitgeist which declared that authenticity was unachievable, that no utterance could ever be rooted in a centre of selfhood, that form was content. Now new meanings could only be created through assembling fragments from the past. Against the background of this new mindset of the 1980s, the mask again became a relevant convention.

---

[15] See the discussion of nakedness in Schechner (1994), 87 ff.

Peter Hall's masked *Oresteia* of 1981 was a new departure, and he followed up this production with *The Oedipus Plays* (1996), *Tantalus* (2000), and *Bacchai* (2002). Hall's philosophy is liberal humanist, and emphatically secular, and thus he has no truck with the modernist assumption that masks matter because they are the thing that tied Greek theatre to religious ritual. Barrault was under the sway of Artaud's conception of ritual, but by the 1980s ritual was out of fashion. Hall has nevertheless systematically promulgated a mystique of the mask, speaking of the mysterious effect it has on the wearer, releasing primal emotions. Through promulgating the idea of possession, something that takes place not on stage but in the rehearsal room, Hall keeps the religious, shamanic sense of the mask alive. Rejecting the functionalist argument that the mask was primarily intended to aid visibility and acoustics, Hall has developed an aesthetic, formalist rationale for the mask, claiming that all art is a kind of mask. Tony Harrison, translator of *The Oresteia*, accepted this thinking completely, though he gave it a more political edge with his statement that the mask allows us to keep our eyes open in situations of extremity, just as a visor allows the welder to look into the flame.[16]

Hall's formalism seems to dispense him from the task set out by Barthes in his challenge to Barrault:

To perform a tragedy by Aeschylus in 1955 has a meaning only if we are determined to answer these two questions clearly: what was the *Oresteia* for Aeschylus' contemporaries? What have we in the twentieth century, to do with the ancient meaning of the work?[17]

Hall lays himself open to attack on ideological grounds. His *Bacchai*, for example, used the Afghan *burka* as a striking stage image, a frame for the masked face, but made no attempt on a conceptual level to relate the oppressive patriarchy of Pentheus to contemporary relations between western and Islamic countries. A formalist is entitled to respond, however, that Barthes's questions are unreasonable. How can one tell a priori what Aeschylus' plays meant?

---

[16] National Theatre programme note to the *Oresteia*. On Harrison's simile see further the final section of Hall, Chapter 6, this volume, p. 194. The masks for the *Oresteia* were designed by Jocelyn Herbert, on whom see also Worth, below, Chapter 10, pp. 274–5. Herbert continued to collaborate with Harrison, notably in his *Prometheus* (1998). For the masks she designed for the Oceanids in that film see Figure 4 in Chapter 1, above.

[17] Barthes (1972), 65.

And if we already have a politically correct understanding of the present, what more can we learn by engaging with Aeschylus? On such a basis, Barthes's political agenda might be dismissed as a thing of the past.

Hall's method has brought him considerable success, with the general public rather than theatrical and classical cognoscenti, and the powerful impact made by his masks has undoubtedly played a large part in this. His masks draw on Greek iconography, as those of Palmer-Sikelianos did in the 1920s, and also on the principle of neutrality or blankness, which allows the audience to concentrate on language, and to use their imaginations to project emotions onto the face. Guthrie used wild Etruscan images from Rome, Koun wasn't interested in classical authenticity, and Barrault's masks had distinctive sculptural features: none exploited the power of emptiness, which must be the fundamental lesson that Hall learned from Saint-Denis. The photograph of Agave holding Pentheus' head (see Figure 33 in Chapter 15, below) demonstrates the power of a vacant face to express an unspeakable emotion. Hall uses masks that cover the whole head, a mode which eliminates the Brechtian dialectic, and encourages the actor to feel a complete loss of self. His *Oresteia, Oedipus Plays*, and *Bacchai* were all designed for the Greek-style Olivier theatre, and transfer to Epidaurus, in accordance with Hall's recognition that space is another element of Greek form. Frontal delivery is a characteristic feature of Hall's style, which results in a strong communication of the narrative to the audience, but weak relationships between characters.

The greatest weakness of Hall's productions stems from a contradiction in his working method thrown up by his conception of the mask. He as a director cannot give instructions to an actor in a mask, because the masked actor loses his ego and can only function as a character. The priority which Hall gives to the text and to the rhythm of the verse means that the actor has to rehearse for a long time with script in hand, which is also difficult in a mask. It follows that most of the rehearsal has to be undertaken without masks, and the mask assumed at the last minute. The final mask may also not be ready until late in the rehearsal period. This means that the actors have very little time to adjust their movements to the dynamic shapes of their particular mask, and learn how to control their bodies in regard to the audience's focus on the relationship of mask and head. The insistence on frontal delivery makes it hard for actors to exploit the play of light on the mask, restricting its animation. The exceptional abilities and experience of Greg Hicks, who has acted in all four productions, have allowed him to overcome these limitations to a significant extent, but other actors tend not to exploit fully the possibilities of the mask. Hall's productions have the hieratic quality of Guthrie's work, rather than the physical fluidity of Barrault, because the mask functions as talisman rather than tool. Hall is more attentive to textual nuance than Guthrie was, but less attentive to choreography and tension between actor and chorus. Ultimately in Hall's productions the text drives and the masked body has to follow where it is taken. There is no Platonic equipoise of mind and body, poetry and gymnastics here: the function of the mask is rather to obliterate body so the mind and the word can triumph.

Hall's later productions replicate, in essentials, a method of work developed for *The Oresteia*. The seminal masked production of the 1990s was *Les Atrides* (1990–2), comprising the *Iphigeneia at Aulis* and *Oresteia*, performed by the Théâtre du Soleil under the direction of Ariane Mnouchkine (see Figure 21). This production decentred the text in a way that caused many English critics misgivings, and developed a French tradition of physical theatre transmitted by Copeau, Lecoq, and Barrault. While Hall's productions are controlled by a beat that emerges from the words, the music in Mnouchkine's work came from a more improvisational interplay between actors, musician, and language. Mnouchkine has described the mask as the 'core discipline' of the Théâtre du Soleil 'because it's a form, and all forms constrain one to a discipline. . . . No content can be expressed without form.'[18] She is like Hall a formalist who will not allow form to be seen as the vehicle for an essential meaning or content. Her work expresses the new spirit of the Nineties through its attention to gender, through its concern with the mind–body relationship, and above all through its interculturalism.

Mnouchkine demands that actors should 'write with the body'. Hers is, at least in principle, not a patriarchal theatre driven by director, language, and written text, but a feminist theatre that turns on collaborative creation, and on creating with body rather

---

[18] Williams (2000), 109.

FIGURE 21. Nirupama Nityanandan as Iphigénie and Simon Abkarian as Agamemnon in *Iphigénie à Aulis* from *Les Atrides*, directed by Ariane Mnouchkine (1990).

than dislocated mind. By starting the cycle with *Iphigénie à Aulis*, she refocused the Aeschylean story on a female protagonist, and it must have been the French psychoanalytic tradition that drew her to this body of myth (see also Macintosh, below, Chapter 12). Aeschylus' deployment of dance, music, and ceremony made him the most appealing dramatist for her purposes. Mnouchkine adopted for *Les Atrides* an eclectic eastern style drawing principally upon Indian theatre, and her decision to use make-up masks alludes to Indian practice. The photo brings out the dynamic relationship of stillness and movement in the production. The vibrant energy of Iphigenia and the morbid gloom of Agamemnon are expressed through the body, not the face. It was a matter of aesthetic principle that there should be no visual reference of any kind to classical antiquity, and this helped ensure a complete escape from the dead hand of classical acting. The intercultural approach emphasized the cultural otherness of the ancient world. Whereas Hall tends to imply that the performance of Greek theatre is self-justifying because the plays are part of his cultural inheritance, Mnouchkine implies that engagement must start from a recognition of difference. She has undoubtedly opened a new line of approach. On a much smaller scale, the work of Thiasos Theatre Company, directed by Yana Zarifi and based in London, exemplifies the possibilities that have been made available. One Thiasos project, for example, involves the staging of *Hippolytus* using Balinese Topeng masks.[19] Each mask provides an inherited system of movement. Zarifi is interested in exploring how dance, an aspect of Greek form which Hall conspicuously ignores, may become the key to theatrical expression.

I pass now to the twenty-first century, and will describe two programmes of research that use the mask to explore new possibilities. Michael Chase, director of the Mask Studio in England, is a maker of masks who also directs productions using his masks. He staged a one-hour *Oresteia* in Stroud in 1990, and Seneca's *Oedipus* in Stourbridge in 2002. His interest in the Greek mask developed from an interest in the therapeutic mask and the relationship between the mask and psychological archetypes. His interest in archetypes drew him to the *Oresteia*, while the poetic qualities of Ted Hughes's translation drew him to *Oedipus*. His holistic

---

[19] The Thiasos *Hippolytus: A Dance Drama* was first performed in 1998.

thinking has been deeply influenced by the ideas of Rudolf Steiner, and the creative line thus leads us back once more to the modernists of the early twentieth century, and the concern of that age to reconcile the material with the metaphysical world. Steiner built a theatre in order to perform his own mystery plays, and his practice was informed by his wife Marie's pursuit of eurhythmy, a blending of recitation and movement. Steiner described very sensitively the relationships between particular vowel sounds and particular configurations of the body.[20] Steiner also maintained that the five branches of Greek gymnastics should be the basis of actor training, and Chase accordingly uses these exercises as the basis for creating sounds that fully engage the whole body. The masks which he has developed allow the voice to resonate, and to enhance the phonic attributes of the poetry. Using Steiner's principles, Chase uses the mask as a vehicle for integrating sound and movement via the breath. His work addresses one of the fundamental problems in Hall's project. Because the *Oresteia* masks created problems of audibility, Hall has subsequently concealed microphones inside his masks. The actor can thus articulate with perfect clarity, but has no need to fill his or her body with breath in order to do so. This results in a lack of energy, and a mismatch between the body of the actor and the dramatic poetry which Hall so values.

Chase evolved his acoustical masks after reading about the work of the Greek mask-maker Thanos Vovolis, whose masks were used in a production of Aeschylus' *Suppliants* at Epidaurus in 1994, and exhibited in London in 1996. He conducted a four-day workshop on Aeschylus' *Persians* at Royal Holloway College, University of London, in 2002. Vovolis examined images of classical Greek masks and concluded that the shape of the mouth related to primary vowel sounds. By a different route, he arrived at the same principle that the mask is a means of integrating body and text. Whilst Chase's creative roots lie in rough-and-ready street theatre, Vovolis's ideals are closer to what Brook terms 'holy theatre'. Artaud was an important inspiration for him. His work with actors draws on yogic methods in order to create a depth of breathing that will allow the dome of the mask to resonate. He is an uncompromising idealist who makes intense demands on the performer, and

[20] R. Steiner (1960).

for this reason his work has not been taken up by mainstream directors. The masks themselves are objects of great beauty, their Hellenic form containing a hint of Noh masks. Vovolis has a ceremonial conception of performance that is more eastern than western, and his understanding of the mask strikes at the heart of the western tradition of performance. He aims at breaking down the division of mind and body, using the mask to create a state of internal and external emptiness. The convention of the mask is related to the convention of the chorus, which also involves an abandonment of ego. Whilst Hall builds an ultimately debilitating mystique around the idea that the mask possesses the wearer, Vovolis speaks of discipline and technique. The long-standing western idea that the mask is a mode of concealment, or a tool for the expression of character, yields to the principle that the mask exists in order to effect the metamorphosis of the actor.

Vovolis's particular interest in Aeschylus may be explained by the importance of the chorus, the power of the poetic language, and the primacy of myth over character. Like Chase, Mnouchkine, Hall, and Barrault, he finds in Aeschylus a dramatist whose formal demands invite a reappraisal of conventional approaches to acting based on the development of character and moral argument. I am not sure if I have succeeded in addressing the question put to me by the editors of this volume: why since 1969, and more particularly since the 1980s, have productions of Greek theatre formed such an important part of the repertory? I have tried to furnish an answer in terms of an ongoing theatrical quest. A lot of the most creative work in theatre in recent years has taken place in the realm of physical theatre—that movement which perhaps owes most to Grotowski, and aims to root performance in the body of the actor. The quest is to find a way of making theatre which roots perform-ance in the body, but does not at the same time throw out the great western tradition of the text. It is a quest to unite the political theatre of the 1950s and 1960s with the metaphysical tradition of Artaud. A classicist might see this as a quest to hold on to the materialist, text-based tradition of theatre rooted in Aristotle, whilst embracing Plato's idealist conception of theatre as a mode of religious dance. Greek theatre, and particularly Aeschylus, offer a way of uniting these binary opposites. The linked and defining conventions of chorus and mask constitute a form that makes this union of opposites possible. The goal has not been reached: what I have tried to tell is the story of an ongoing, utopian quest for a goal that will never be fully attainable.

I have portrayed the 1920s as a hugely creative period, when radical formal experiments were possible. Visual artists, dancers, and theatre practitioners were keen to converge. That creative wave ended with the depression and oppression of the 1930s. European theatre reverted to the neoclassical assumption that Greek theatre was a source of great stories that needed to be retold. Giraudoux, Sartre, Anouilh, and others, particularly in France, saw the Greek world as a source of stories for playwrights to adapt, just as Corneille and Racine had done three centuries before them. The intellectual energy lay in the challenge of Marxism, and the metaphysical dimension of Greek theatre had no force. This volume is probably right to argue that *Dionysus in 69* opened up a new era. With Schechner, we see the human being as ego, as mere psyche, being stretched on the one hand towards the human being as a naked physical body, on the other hand towards the human being as part of a collective process.

We have in important respects, I think, reverted to the body-based and metaphysical thinking of the 1920s, but there have been important changes. That decade valued Greek theatre because it was primitive and ritualistic. The African mask was an emblem signifying the primitive, indicating why the ancient mask needed to be recovered, and why it could lead us to understand the roots of our being. We now have a different understanding of why the African mask haunted the post-colonial imagination. We realize that it is ethically intolerable to dismiss the colonized other as primitive. Barrault stood on the cusp of this change in western consciousness. Theatre practitioners today are more interested in the highly codified, ancient, and sophisticated performance traditions of the east, which show up the emotional poverty of the logocentric west. Shifting global economics have no small bearing on this process, as does the failure of Newtonian science to explain the material universe. We are looking at large cultural shifts. We can no longer speak in the mystical manner of Sikelianos and the rest of that post-Nietzschean generation about communion with some universal world spirit. Postmodernity reduces us to quoting fragments of historical and geographical cultures which we know we can never fully apprehend. Nevertheless the postmodern angst about what is reality, what is self, what are we but the play of surfaces, takes us back to the mask by another route.

As a theatre historian rather than a classicist, it does not trouble me to maintain that the Greek dramatic tradition is no longer important in the theatre because it is a repository of great texts, great words. Greek theatre matters in the theatre today because it is a powerful form, a form that is a basis for continuing creativity. The most important productions of Greek theatre that I have seen have been in Romanian, French, Russian, German, modern Greek, Japanese—hardly ever in English. When I recall these productions, the whole question of language seems irrelevant. When I use the term 'form', I mean partly a set of dramatic situations, but more crucially the enabling devices of chorus, encircling *theatron* (which in Greek literally means 'place for viewing'), and mask. The chorus matters because it offers a transpersonal understanding of the world that is best expressed through the body. The auditorium matters because it imposes a collectivist rather than detached mode of viewing. The mask matters because it frees us from a philosophically discredited obsession with interiority. By blotting out the face, the mask paradoxically reintegrates the body and makes it an instrument capable of embodying rather than reciting a text. Greek theatre has proved to be a form that allows us to address these fundamental concerns.

Greek Notes in Samuel Beckett's Theatre Art

Katharine Worth

The title *Dionysus since 69*, referring as it does to the fortunes of classical drama over the last three decades, also points to the only modern playwright whose work is discussed in this volume. 1969 was the year when Samuel Beckett was awarded the Nobel Prize in Literature. The works for which he received the renowned, international award, including *Waiting for Godot* and his other plays, have given his name a unique resonance in modern theatre, equal to that possessed by Aeschylus and his fellow playwrights in classical times. It seems appropriate, then, to consider what kind of interest Beckett had in classical drama and to examine the theatrical styles he developed which have helped to create a climate favourable to the great revival of interest in ancient theatre during the last thirty years or so.

Links between Beckett and his classical predecessors were recognized in the Nobel presentation speech made by Karl Ragnar Gierow of the Swedish Academy. He brought the ancient Greek theatre into the same space as the twentieth-century playwright when he spoke of Beckett's ability to produce a 'positive' response ('fellow feeling, charity') from a black 'negative' of human suffering and degradation. There was a theatrical precedent for this complex process, he suggested, in 'the accumulation of abominations in Greek tragedy which led Aristotle to the doctrine of catharsis, purification through horror'.[1]

This was a perceptive linking. Beckett is the modern playwright above all others who has recreated (in his own terms) not only much of the theatrical stylization—scenic, musical, poetic—of the ancient Greek theatre, but also something of its spirit. He has restored to theatre a metaphysical dimension through situations

---

[1] The quotation is taken from the English translation of the speech published on the Nobel website, www.nobel.se/literature/laureates/1969/press.

that might seem to deny its existence: the issueless waiting for Godot, for instance, or the unanswered prayers of *Endgame*. He differs from the usual practice of the Greeks—and draws audiences into his own kind of cathartic experience—by having no formal separation at all between the comic and tragic elements in the theatre. He could almost be seen as making a point about this when he describes *Waiting for Godot* (on its title page) as 'tragicomedy'. It is his own way, a modern way, but it often runs close to the ancient tracks. The frequent classical allusions in his plays often convey a playful postmodern enjoyment in mixing things up. Pozzo amuses, for instance, with a neat running together of Greek and Roman when he declaims over Lucky, loaded with the luggage he can't put down unless commanded: 'Atlas, son of Jupiter', instead of 'Atlas, son of Zeus'.[2]

There is plenty of evidence in Beckett's published and unpublished writings for a serious interest in classical mythology and drama. One of his early notebooks in the Beckett Archive at Reading University (known as the 'Whoroscope' Notebook) has pages of notes on Greek playwrights and legends, seemingly intended as a 'fixing' of knowledge.[3] They are enlivened by quirky marginal jottings, as when he asks himself, 'How would you like to have been Thespius' fiftieth daughter?' He was evidently tickled by the story of Thespius, the king who offered his fifty daughters to Heracles as reward for the hero's help in ridding the land of a marauding lion. The reward could be taken either on successive nights or one. Who but Beckett would have been struck by the idea of imagining himself the fiftieth daughter?!

Classical notes are sounded in the early (as yet unstaged) play, *Eleutheria*,[4] markedly in its title which has the Greek rather than the English version of the word 'Freedom'. The name of the central character, Victor, also leans toward the classical with its hint at a hero in classical mode. The young man who answers to the

---

[2] Beckett (1986), 30. All subsequent references to Samuel Beckett, *The Complete Dramatic Works*, appear in brackets after the citation in the text.

[3] The 'Whoroscope' Notebook (MS 3000) is in the Beckett Archive of the Beckett International Foundation at the University of Reading. There is no pagination for the Notebook. (Photocopy, pp. 74–6).

[4] *Eleutheria* was published after Beckett's death in 1995 in the original French. The English translation, *Eleuthéria*, published in the same year, added the accent which makes the title look slightly less Greek. Page references here are to the English-language edition (Beckett (1995b)).

name in the play might appear somewhat more of an anti-hero, ironically withdrawn as he is, indolent and inward-looking. Yet this so modern Victor curiously connects himself with the ancient, heroic world, if only in a dream. He is shown at the start of Act III waking from an apparent nightmare, muttering cryptic words:

> a thousand ships—the towers—circumcised—fire—fire.[5]

The shade of Aeschylus hovers there for a split second, merged perhaps with that of Christopher Marlowe, who fixed an Aeschylean image forever with the ecstatic reaction of his Doctor Faustus to the apparition of Helen of Troy: 'Was this the face that launched a thousand ships?'

The allusion to ships and fire will also call up, for those familiar with Aeschylus' *Agamemnon*, the opening scene of that play, with the Watchman waiting for the beacon fires that will signal the victory of the Greek army. This was the great force which famously set out for Troy with a thousand ships. The Watchman's tedious waiting for the return of Agamemnon to Mycenae has dragged on for a year. Not so long as the waiting for Godot but similarly suggestive of hope long deferred. The fire motif in the play is linked to the long waiting, though it also acquires a strange new significance toward the end of the play when the enslaved Cassandra, shortly to be massacred along with the man who has enslaved her, feels her prophetic powers stirring. 'What fire comes upon me?', she cries, in her painful ecstasy (Aeschylus, *Agamemnon* 1256).

Victor's inner, imaginative powers might be envisaged as having some connection with those of Cassandra. But the covert allusions to the Aeschylean vision are not taken far in *Eleutheria*. It was in the play which beat it to the French stage in 1953 (both were considered for production by Roger Blin) that the potent image of 'waiting' found its apotheosis. *Waiting for Godot* looks out in many directions, but one of these is surely toward Aeschylus and the Greeks. It seems curiously apposite to this discussion that a reason for Blin's choice of play rather than *Eleutheria* was the smallness of its cast.

'Fire' imagery was also to figure in *Happy Days* (1961); of which more later. But before that play was written another Greek

---

[5] Beckett (1995*b*), 125.

tragedian, Sophocles, had made his way into Beckett's theatre. At the start of *Endgame* (1957 in French, 1958 in English) we are invited to recall the anguished cry of Oedipus as he begins to realize that the stranger he killed on his journey to Thebes was his own father, Laius, and that a terrible doom must be approaching (Sophocles, *Oedipus Tyrannus* 813). At this point in his version of *Oedipus Tyrannus*, W. B. Yeats struck a high tragic note:

If this stranger were indeed Laius, is there a more miserable man in the world than the man before you?[6]

It was just these words that Beckett would have heard when, as an undergraduate at Trinity College, Dublin, he saw performances of Yeats's *Oedipus* plays at the Abbey Theatre, Dublin, in 1926 and 1927.[7] In *Endgame* he plays a sardonic variation on the commanding Yeatsian line. *His* blind protagonist, Hamm (both sufferer and Teiresias-like 'seer') pushes Yeats's rhetorical question towards the absurd:

Can there be misery—(*he yawns*)—loftier than mine?
(93)

Then he answers himself with a wry allusion to a past that did once allow for grand statements about personal misery:

No doubt. Formerly. But now?
(93)

'Formerly' might refer to either Sophocles or Yeats. There is an added twist of irony here, for in his version of Sophocles' play Yeats had very deliberately aimed at a kind of modernity, a sense of 'now' rather than 'then'. For the performance at the Abbey Theatre in 1927 he reworked his first script, *Sophocles' King Oedipus*, to make it more spare and colloquial, more completely as he described it on the title page: 'A Version for the Modern Stage'.

Beckett took that modernizing process further, moving it closer to parody. The self-mocking word 'loftier'—and, especially, the yawn—effectively undermine high rhetoric. But Hamm's answer

---

[6] Yeats (1982), 498.
[7] In the revision of his *Sophocles' King Oedipus* (1926) for performance at the Abbey Theatre in 1927, Yeats severely cut the long outpourings of Oedipus and the chorus towards the end of the play, having in mind the needs not only of the audience but of the actor playing Oedipus, Frank McCormick.

to his own question—'No doubt. Formerly. But now?'—brings the possibility of a tragic mood a little closer, with its suggestion that, for all the intellectual distance we may feel between ourselves and the Oedipus of Sophocles and Yeats, we can't help but ask the same tormenting questions, feel our own suffering as uniquely terrible. Strikingly, when Beckett later revised the passage in question he made a notable deletion: the undermining yawn.[8]

There is much more that could be said about such direct debts and influences, but the focus of the discussion that follows is on the remarkable stage effects which, as I see it, indicate Beckett's natural, deep affinity with certain kinds of ancient Greek theatrical stylizations. These are, in the order I shall consider them: number of speaking parts; severe physical restraints on actors; messengers; mask-like effects; chorus; music and dance.

SPEAKING PARTS

Eleutheria excepted, there are no more than three speaking actors engaged with each other conversationally in any scene on Beckett's stage. The restriction has a formal, deliberate look that recalls the three-actor convention of classical tragedy, particularly in the first two performed plays, because in *Waiting for Godot* five actors, and in *Endgame* four are on-stage together for quite long stretches, yet no more than three at a time ever talk together.[9]

In *Godot* the Boy talks only in the presence of Vladimir and Estragon and for the most part only to the former. Pozzo's slave, Lucky, is silent throughout the play except for his extraordinary outburst of speech in Act I (40). That is not 'talk', however. It is an essentially solitary, self-standing 'think' commanded by his master. This master–slave relationship (the word 'menial' is used in the text) is another link with classical theatre. Such a prominent cross-class relationship is of course central to many Greek tragedies (including Phaedra and her nurse in *Hippolytus* and Oedipus and the old Theban shepherd in *Oedipus Tyrannus*) as well as to all

---

[8] Beckett's cutting of yawns in *Endgame* was recorded in copies of the Grove Press edition (New York, 1958) following his experience of directing the play in Berlin (1967) and London (1980).

[9] *En Attendant Godot* was first performed in France in 1953, and as *Waiting for Godot* in London in 1955; *Fin de Partie* was first performed in London in 1957, and as *Endgame* in New York in 1958.

ancient comedy from Dionysus and his slave Xanthias in Aristophanes' *Frogs* onwards. In Act II of *Godot* Lucky falls totally silent: he is said to have become dumb. The mysterious visitation increases tension around this strange figure and also, I think, insinuates the possibility that the unseen space into which he will always disappear is somehow beyond language, perhaps even the space from which Godot might appear. But, of course, Godot never does, unlike the classical deities who do often make their way from their remote Olympian regions on to the stages of ancient Greece.

In *Endgame* similarly strict rules seem to apply to the numbers of actors conversing. Nell, seen as a night-capped head in a dustbin, talks only to the other night-cap, Nagg (during their conversation Hamm is silent, save for one interjection; Clov off-stage). Nagg is allowed into talk with the other pair only after Nell falls silent altogether, having died in the dustbin (103; 116–20). Again, this is a disturbingly active silence.

SEVERE PHYSICAL RESTRAINTS

More spectacularly disturbing are the harsh bodily constrictions Beckett places on his actors: dustbins (in *Endgame*); wheelchair (in *Rough for Theatre I*); the mound of *Happy Days* where Winnie is buried, up to her waist in Act I, to her neck in Act II. *Happy Days* drew comparisons with the *Prometheus Bound* attributed to Aeschylus by a French critic (in *Le Monde*) when the play was given at the Théâtre de l'Odéon, Paris, in 1963.[10] It's not hard to see why. In both plays the central character is brutally immobilized, unable to take a step across the stage. And each is marooned in a remote, inaccessible region where there seems little hope of company arriving to break the terrible isolation.

Prometheus is in that last respect the luckier of the two. He does have visits; other legendary figures appear during the play, eager to tell their own stories. They provide him, as also the audience, with desperately needed dramatic relief and variety. Winnie has scarcely any relief of that kind. True, she has Willie. But she has to work hard to get any kind of response from him: he is the quintessential taciturn male. And for almost the whole of Act II

---

[10] *Le Monde*, 31 October 1963.

he is absent from the scene, reappearing only for the finale, his slow, fantastic climb towards her up the mound. So Winnie has to make company for herself, as when she tells of visitors who did come her way; an unprepossessing couple who gaped at her and said unhelpful things like 'What's she meant to mean?' Beckett could be thought of as seeing how far he could stretch the conventions of Greek tragedy to give a modern slant on the dramatic possibilities in static characters and long speeches. Winnie's 'speech', with minimal help from Willie, has to sustain her—and us the audience—for the whole play.

Underneath the obvious differences between the two plays, notably Beckett's comic/tragic mix, there runs something similar: the sense of an enigmatic power ordaining the awful situation. The Greek audience knew this power was Zeus; at the start of the play they saw his servant, Hephaestus, chain Prometheus to the rock. But questions remain: why this suffering? Prometheus was the benefactor of mankind. He gave them fire. Beckett has his fire motif too, in the playful form of a parasol which startlingly goes alight and is magically whisked away, blazing. Welcome theatre fireworks for the audience, but a dire portent too: Winnie loses her one protection against the distressing heat. She turns the loss to a metatheatrical joke. The sunshade will be there again tomorrow, she promises the audience (154). But it is a loss all the same. A woman is being ruthlessly stripped of comforts and drawn down into the earth by some irresistible force. Like Prometheus chained to his rock, she expresses both the helplessness of humanity and its indomitable will to survive and express itself.

MESSENGERS

The classical kind are very explicit about the news they bring, whether good or, more usually, bad. They tend to be long-winded like the messenger in *Seven against Thebes* who from line 375 onwards lists at great length the accoutrements of every one of the seven attackers. Beckett's messengers are just the opposite: sparing of speech or speechless and profoundly ambiguous, maddeningly so in *Godot*, more hopefully in the later television play, *Ghost Trio* (first broadcast on BBC2, 17 April 1977). In both these the messenger is a young boy, which immediately makes a difference to a viewer's response (see Figure 22). The youth of the boy

F I G U R E 22.   The Boy in *Die Geister Trio*, broadcast by the German
television channel Süddeutscher Rundfunk (SDR) (1977).

who appears at the end of each act of *Godot* suggests both innocence and a kind of finality. It's not possible to get any further by
questioning this speaker. Vladimir tries hard on each of the two
occasions when the Boy brings word that Godot won't come tonight: it will be tomorrow. But only the questions within a child's
reach get answers. The big one, about the nature of Godot, stays
closed. Still, there has been a message of a kind. And Vladimir and
Estragon remain on stage, sending out the subliminal message that
the inscrutable messenger will return, the questioning continue.

The messenger in *Ghost Trio* communicates without speaking at
all. He is silent throughout his brief appearance, as too is the
solitary man, clutching a cassette, to whom he appears. An off-
screen voice tells us at the start that the man ('F' in the text) is
waiting for someone: he thinks he hears 'her' (the working title of
the play was 'Tryst'). What we, the viewers, hear at intervals—and
presume he does—are faint strains of Beethoven's music, the famously mysterious and haunting Largo from his fifth Piano Trio,
commonly known as the 'Ghost' Trio.[11]

[11] Opus 70 No. 1 in D major.

The music sets an emotional or spiritual tone within which the waiting man exists—whether he is aware of it or not. He looks out of the window and door: sees only rain through one; a long, grey corridor through the other. His expression remains set—until the second opening of the door. This time someone is there: a young boy in rainwear who doesn't speak, simply looks with bright attentive eyes. Then he very slowly shakes his head twice, producing also, in the BBC original production of 1977 (supervised by Beckett), a faint smile.

F returns to his cassette and sits bowed over it, face concealed by his hair. It might seem that nothing has changed; yet a change is preparing. In the production of 1977, as the ethereal music of the 'Ghost' Trio reached its mysterious climax, the camera searched out the hidden face of Ronald Pickup's F. He raised his head and a ghost of a smile was seen. A slight gesture, both enigmatic and meaningful, it could suggest that the mute message was not entirely negative but somehow consoling; or perhaps that a long-sought epiphany had been achieved. A messenger had spoken, without words, from some infinitely distant space.[12]

MASK-LIKE EFFECTS

I move now to one of Beckett's most spectacular echoes of classical theatre: his mask-like effects. Though as a playwright he loves the human face and writes wonderfully for it, he also likes to give it highly stylized treatment, moving it further from the personal, achieving a kind of distance and strangeness which allows the face to speak for more than itself. We can trace the process at work in the television play *Eh Joe* (1966).[13] First we see Joe's face in a superficially realistic context and from a commonplace perspective. It is the face of a man, viewed full-length, who is moving about his room, drawing curtains, looking everywhere, including under the bed to make sure he is alone; then finally

---

[12] *Ghost Trio*, written in 1975 for BBC Television, was produced by Tristram Powell, directed by Donald McWhinnie, and transmitted on 17 April 1977, in a programme called *Shades*, along with...*but the clouds*... and *Not I*. Beckett attended rehearsals and advised on the filming. Later in 1977 he directed the play for Süddeutscher Rundfunk at Stuttgart.

[13] *Eh Joe* was first broadcast by BBC2 on 4 July 1966. The text is published in Beckett (1986).

sitting on his bed. At that point a woman's voice 'starts in' on him, telling him things he doesn't want to hear and working up to a mesmeric story; the suicide of a girl whom, says the voice, he had loved but callously abandoned. At intervals the camera closes further in on the listening face, removing it from its day-to-day context, until, at the sombre climax, there is no context; just the face alone, painfully registering the full misery of the story that has been told—and the listener's share in it.

When Patrick Magee played Joe, the silent, anguished face, completely filling the screen, took on the effect of a tragic mask, with its uncanny power to make us surmise the depths beneath its surface.[14] To get the full effect of this illusion in Beckett's play we do of course need to see the whole series of shots in ever deepening focus, leading into the final still. But Magee's face in the last disturbing close-up has something of the commanding and sug-gestive boldness we associate with the masks of the ancient Greek theatre.

That is still more true of the play called *Play*, which premiered in German in July 1963, and then in London, in English, in April 1964. This was the first British production of a play by Beckett to be given by the National Theatre Company (then using the Old Vic theatre). It was also, most probably, the strangest set ever to be seen in a British theatre. In empty space three heads in urns gaze 'undeviatingly front' throughout, able to speak only when the spotlight falls on them, and never to each other (see Figure 23). Beckett wanted their faces to be 'so lost to age and aspect as to seem almost part of urns' (307). Anyone who saw it, as I did, will know how brilliantly Jocelyn Herbert, the designer, met this demand (on Herbert's famous later designs for masks for Greek tragedy see this volume, pp. 30–1, fig. 4, and 255 n.16). Billie Whitelaw, then playing her first Beckett role, has amusingly described the horren-dous make-up, the pancake of white, sludgy brown, and slimy green, and how bits tended to flake off during performance.[15]

---

[14] Patrick Magee played Joe in a production directed by David Clark which Beckett gave me permission to record for educational use in 1972. I lodged a video copy with the Beckett Archive in the library of Reading University.

[15] Whitelaw (1995), 80; see also Herbert (1993), 98–9. This production of *Play* formed half of a double bill with an adaptation of Sophocles' *Philoctetes*. See Stephens (1964), 52.

FIGURE 23. Billie Whitelaw, Robert Stephens, and Rosemary Harris as the heads in urns in Samuel Beckett's *Play* (London, 1964).

In his stage direction Beckett added the rider: 'But no masks' (307). It's a negative that suggests a positive preoccupation. Ancient Greek masks were evidently on his mind since he needed to make clear that what he wanted was a subtle variation, a mask-like effect of flaking and peeling, imposed on the human face but not supplanting it. I recall an uncanny sense that the urns had almost swallowed them, but that something stronger was driving them to assert their individuality, even though it could only happen through these painfully bitter memories.

The most astonishing of all Beckett's mask-like effects is in *Not I* (1973). Here most of the actor's face has been blotted out, leaving only the mouth visible. Detached in this way, it becomes a disturbingly separate entity, no longer part of the whole but the whole; not a mouth but a dominating stage object, Mouth by name, out of which pours a desperate stream of words. There builds up the story of a wretched life in which the speaker seems totally immersed, though she or 'it' pushes away first-person narrative in periodic shrieks of '. . . what? . . . who? . . . no! . . . she! . . . ' (377, 379, 381, 382). The visual focus on the writhing mouth, high in the air above stage, is strange and very new. Yet it calls up thoughts of something strange and very old. The great mouths of some ancient theatre masks define the human face and character in sweeping lines that both conceal and reveal. Which is what fundamentally happens in *Not I*.

CHORUS

In the adaptation of the play for television the character named Auditor was cut from the play so as to give the whole screen to Mouth. This character, a dimly visible but potent presence in the stage original, was also raised above stage level, though less startlingly so than Mouth. The attention of the mute shadowy figure was entirely fixed upon that disembodied feature high above us all. In this way, as in staying silent throughout, Auditor was close to us the audience and thus, it might be said, functioned as our representative, a kind of chorus, in fact. As was commonly the case with the ancient chorus, this one is powerless to intervene. At the points where Mouth repudiates involvement in the story she is telling, Auditor throws out his/her arms in 'a gesture of helpless compassion' (375). It could be thought of as representing exactly our own situation as audience; our helplessness, and also, it might be surmised, our pity. Sadly, this modern variation on the chorus was easier to cut from its original context than any of its classical ancestors would have been.

A chorus that can't be cut figures in *Play* (319). As prelude to the two parts of the action, before and after the lowering of the lights, the three speakers—M, W1 and W2—mutter key lines all together (307–8, 312, 317, 318). What they say should be 'largely unintelligible' (307, Beckett's stage direction). It surely will be so on first hearing although, even then, we will probably catch key words or phrases:

> 'get off me', 'a shade gone', 'darkness best' 'mercy'.

We will hear these again, maybe half-recognize them, in the narratives spoken as solos by the adulterous trio, the man and two women who have been ruthlessly separated as heads in urns. A tentative understanding of the choral murmurings opens up, but it is not enough. Beckett tells us that, and gives us an extraordinary opportunity to go further by having the whole play (running time 20 minutes) repeated word for word. On the second round the almost 'unintelligible' chorus can't but yield more of its meaning. Now we can pick up and fill out the broken phrases from our startlingly recent memory of the solo narratives which gave us both the scraps themselves and their revealing context.

By the end of the repeat the choric gabble has become painfully understandable. We can recognize it as a desperate physical expression of the difficulty in being 'together' which torments the man, his wife, and his mistress. Yet the three do in a way come together, if only in their agitated choric outpourings. And in the second phase of their ordeal, when they go 'down' into another dimension of consciousness, we may sense each moving, if unwillingly, a little closer to the others; perhaps trying to be more aware of them, more ready for change in themselves. 'Change' is the key word, coupled with 'mercy', which emerges from the chorus following the dimming of the light:

> W 1
> W 2   [*Together*].   Mercy, mercy—
> M   To say I am—
>   When first this change—.
>
> (312)

In his note on the final 'Repeat' at the end of the text Beckett himself used the word 'chorus' of the three actors speaking all together. But it hardly needs such a pointer for an audience to recognize links with the traditional chorus of antiquity. So unlike it in many ways, above all in the grimly enforced separateness of the speakers, the babblings of Beckett's trio create strong choric moments, and in the end help to open up the underlying pattern of the play.

MUSIC AND DANCE

To recall the chorus in Greek drama is inevitably to think of music and dance. It might surprise some that these are crucial elements in Beckett's theatre also. In two of the radio plays music is in fact a full-blown character—named Music—with marked personality traits (*Words and Music*, BBC Third Programme, 13 November 1962, and *Cascando*, BBC Third Programme, 6 October 1964). In the stage and TV plays music has figured intermittently since Vladimir sang a lullaby to Estragon in *Godot* and Clov sang in the French original of *Endgame* the song he only 'wants' to sing in the English version.[16] Beethoven's Fifth Piano Trio is central to *Ghost Trio* and the last seven bars of Schubert's *Lied, Nacht, und Träume* to *Nacht und Träume*.[17] *Happy Days* tantalizes us with an actor promising to sing, and finally rewards us with Winnie's incongruous and touching rendering of *The Merry Widow* waltz. This might almost be thought of as a Euripidean monody, which in the ancient theatre was almost always sung by an isolated, suffering feminine heroine.

Music leads into dance and here there are two extraordinary dramatic highlights, one at the very start of Beckett's writing for theatre, the second towards the end. First, Lucky's dance in *Godot*. Pozzo offers Vladimir and Estragon a treat on classical lines. His slave ('menial' he calls him) will perform for them. What would they prefer—for him to dance—or think? They have opposite preferences, so Estragon suggests: 'Perhaps he could dance first and think afterwards, if it isn't too much for him.' 'By all means' says Pozzo, 'It's the natural order' (38). This could well be taken as a glancing allusion to the history of ancient theatre, beginning with the singing/dancing chorus and moving to dialogue, character, and thought.

The dance is grotesque, ungainly, monotonous. It usually draws laughter from the audience in the auditorium, stimulated by

---

[16] Beckett (1986), 64; for *Endgame* see the 1957 French original, published by Les Editions de Minuit, 95.

[17] See Worth (1998), and, more generally, Worth (1990).

comically disappointed reactions from Vladimir and Estragon as the audience on stage. In his production of the play at the Schiller-Theater in Berlin in 1975 Beckett brought out to the full the comic element in the episode of the dance and the stupefyingly interminable 'think' which follows it. Is there a touch of Aristophanic grotesquerie here? There might come to mind Philocleon in *Wasps*, struggling to get free of the netting in which he is enmeshed. Pozzo tells the stage audience that Lucky calls his dance 'The Net'; 'He thinks he's entangled in a net.' The entanglement is grimmer here, however, and closer to the fatal net in Aeschylus' *Oresteia*. The wretchedness of Lucky is too pathetic to be taken just as farce: it brings the dance, along with the 'think', into the Beckettian mode of tragicomedy.

Yet Lucky's stage ancestry often seems to reach back to antiquity. His entry as a slave on the end of a rope, loaded with luggage which he can only put down on Pozzo's orders, has something in common with the overloaded 'carriers' in Aristophanic comedy: the Boeotian straining his back under a huge load in *Acharnians*; Xanthias riding on a donkey but carrying the luggage on his own shoulders in *Frogs*. It's a well worn situation, Xanthias reminds his master as they bandy quips at the play's opening. They need to get a joke out of it—or what will be the point of his carrying all the bags himself? But it will be hard to get a really new joke since 'there's a baggage scene in every comedy'. In Beckett's tragicomedy a new 'baggage' joke appears, in subtle, darker form but still recognizable as linked to the comic theatre of Aristophanes.

Similar links connect the other characters to different forms of classical comedy. Vladimir and Estragon enjoy much physical and verbal knockabout in Aristophanic mode, as in their fooling with boots and dropped trousers. Pozzo's braggartism, on the other hand, could be seen as connecting him with the *Miles gloriosus* ('swaggering soldier') of Plautus. Directors do sometimes give him a military look, as Peter Hall did in his 1997 production of *Godot* at the Old Vic Theatre.

At the other end of the œuvre, the television play *Quad* (1982) consists entirely of dance, or 'mime', as Beckett called it.[18] In the

---

[18] Under its original title, *Quadrat 1+2*, the play was transmitted by Süddeutscher Rundfunk in 1982. Later that year (16 December) it was transmitted by BBC2, under the title *Quad*.

Theatre. This was a remarkable tribute to Beckett's continuing power to attract and influence.

Likenesses, real or perceived, between Beckett's stylizations and those of other cultures such as the Noh theatre of Japan have stimulated much theatrical activity. When invited some years ago to contribute to a collection of essays on Yeats and the Noh, I added Beckett to my discussion of these 'enigmatic influences'. He had not expressed any particular interest in the Noh, yet it seemed to me that there were resemblances. His plays too could often be thought of as 'ghost' plays in the concern with grief and loss, and their offer of mysterious comfort from some remote psychic region; a type of catharsis. *Ohio Impromptu* has this in common with *Sumidagawa*.[23]

The impact of Beckett in Japan in 1960 interestingly stirred up in Tadashi Suzuki new fascination with his own indigenous theatre of Noh and Kabuki.[24] From there his interest moved to the theatre of ancient Greece and he became celebrated for his striking productions of Greek tragedies from *Trojan Women* in 1974 to *Oedipus Rex* in 2000. This kind of progression has not been uncommon. Beckett has accustomed the imagination of audiences and practitioners to an uncompromising non-naturalistic style, with elements of the absurd, open to music, giving weight to silences, fusing poetic force and colloquial comedy. And looking out to remote psychic dimensions. It is not surprising that directors who have felt the pull of Beckett take also to Greek tragedy. Peter Hall, who first directed *Godot* in English, has shown the way and others have followed, most recently JoAnne Akalaitis. She first attracted widespread publicity with her 1984 production at the American Repertory Theatre in Cambridge, Massachusetts, of *Endgame*, set in a derelict subway (and not approved by Beckett), but has more recently directed Greek tragedy, notably *Trojan Women* for the Shakespeare Theatre in Washington DC (1999).[25]

From *Waiting for Godot* onwards Beckett was tapping a well of ancient use while opening up the modern theatre to the startlingly new. Elliptical and veiled, compared with the many open quotations from the Bible and Shakespeare, the classical allusions in Beckett's plays feed into a technique of audacious stylizations

[23] See Worth (1990).   [24] See Allain (2002), 18.
[25] See Hall, Chapter 1, 'Introduction'.

that often, as I have been suggesting, point to the theatre of antiquity. That theatre has been given a subtle extension of life within Beckett's theatre—and a wider one through the influence of his theatre on audiences and practitioners.

All Beckett's stage plays except *Eleutheria* were filmed in 2001, opening up for potentially vast audiences a spectacularly new kind of modern theatre. It is one that invites them to look out to a theatre that is very old, the spectacular theatre of the ancient Greeks.

11

Greek Tragedy in the Opera House and Concert Hall of the Late Twentieth Century

Peter Brown

One does not go to a past work of art for the past but for the
present.

Sir Michael Tippett[1]

About a hundred new musical versions of Greek tragedy have
been performed in the last thirty-five years. Many of them will
suffer the usual fate of operas and never be performed again, and
even their composers are for the most part not household names.
But they are among the leading composers of their generation(s),
and they have been inspired by ancient drama in a remarkable
variety of ways. Some have shown a sustained engagement with
Greek tragedy in a succession of works, and it is also noticeable
that several (such as Gavin Bryars and John Buller among English
composers) have turned to Greek tragedy for their first venture
into operatic composition. Some have been attracted by the similarity of ancient dramatic conventions to those of modern opera,
some by the differences. Most have derived their inspiration directly from ancient drama, some through intermediaries such as
Racine. Altogether they provide evidence for the wide geographical spread of the influence of Greek drama: the following pages
will mention composers from Australia, Austria, Belgium,
Bulgaria, China, the Czech Republic, England, Finland, France,
Germany, Greece, Hungary, India, Italy, Lebanon, Morocco,
the Netherlands, Poland, Romania, Scotland, Spain, Sweden,
Switzerland, the United States, and Wales.

In order to draw attention to the extent of this influence, this
chapter is essentially a reference list. I have no illusion that it is
complete, but it is as complete as I have been able to make it at the
time of writing (and I have deliberately included only a sample of

[1] Tippett (1980), 232; (1995), 217.

the settings of small portions of text). One thing that immediately stands out is that the tragedies most frequently chosen for setting by composers are also those that have been most frequently performed in the theatre in the late twentieth century; only *The Trojan Women* has been relatively neglected by composers. *The Bacchae* and *Medea* have been popular, as have plays about the House of Atreus (not least its women). There has been more interest in Antigone than in Oedipus, and also some interest in Jocasta; but operas about Oedipus have been some of the most strikingly inventive works of this period on the operatic stage altogether.

Some of the operas have followed an ancient text very closely (sometimes even in the original language), others have strung together fragments of text (sometimes a mixture of ancient and modern texts) with no attempt at linear narrative development: the presentation of the hero or heroine is fragmented into a sequence of scenes each representing the character's psychological state, and sometimes the character is further fragmented by being portrayed by more than one performer. (See below on, for example, the *Medea* operas of Dusapin, Blumenthaler, Dittrich, and Guarnieri, or Nono's *Prometeo*.) Orchestrally, it is striking how many composers have used mainly wind instruments, and how sparing they have been in their use of violins. Some have incorporated motifs derived from the surviving fragments of ancient Greek music; more commonly, composers have been influenced by the music of Africa or the Far East in their attempts to convey something of the ancient culture depicted in the texts.

I shall not illustrate all these points systematically. Nor shall I discuss works by composers such as Harrison Birtwistle and Iannis Xenakis in which the influence of Greek drama, Greek myth, and ancient musical theory has been manifest in a more general way. In particular, Birtwistle's *The Mask of Orpheus* (1986) is one of the leading operas of this period inspired by ancient Greece, but it is not based on surviving Greek dramatic texts.

BACCHAE

Dionysus came to the late twentieth century operatic stage before 1969, in Harry Partch's *Revelation in the Courthouse Park* (1961) and Hans Werner Henze's *The Bassarids* (1966). In the former, scenes from *The Bacchae* set in ancient Thebes alternate with parallel scenes set in a Midwestern town in the 1950s on the occasion of the visit of a rock star called Dion, a character reminiscent of Elvis Presley with a band of fanatical female followers, whose arrival is celebrated by a brass band, majorettes, and clog dancers. *The Bassarids* is firmly set in the ancient world, but Euripides' text has been recast with some freedom by W. H. Auden and Chester Kallman (who had earlier collaborated on the libretto for Stravinsky's *The Rake's Progress* and for Henze's *Elegy for Young Lovers*). In this version, Pentheus is a monastic ascetic: in the opening scene we learn that he is spending the first days of his reign in a retreat, praying and fasting; later he tells his old nurse Beroe that he has resolved to 'abstain | From wine, from meats, | And from woman's bed, | Live sober and chaste | Till the day I die!' He issues an edict not only denying that 'the Father | Of the Gods had carnal knowledge | Of Semele, daughter of Cadmus, | And begot a child upon her' but more generally proclaiming it as blasphemy to assert 'that the Immortal Gods | Do lust after mortals and strive | Jealously for their favours'. As in Euripides' play, he believes that Dionysus 'Is but a name | For the nameless Nothing | That hates the light', his worship an opportunity to 'do, | Do, do, do the forbidden | Shameless thing'. As Henze himself has said, the work raises questions 'relevant to us and also to the years around 1968: what is freedom, what is lack of freedom? What is repression, what is revolt, what is revolution?'[2] The questions are raised by Euripides, but Auden and Kallman have recast the text to bring out Pentheus' repression both of himself and of his citizens in ways that strike more twentieth-century chords. Partch (who used his own libretto) more obviously criticizes the American society of his day, with its 'religious rituals with a strong sexual element' and 'sex rituals with a strong religious element' (as he put it). 'I was determined to make this an American here-and-now drama, which, tragically, it truly is', he wrote.[3] But it was by modelling his work on Euripides' play (including, at the end, Agave's discovery that the head she holds is not that of a lion but of her own son) that Partch was able to bring out the full force of the tragedy.

---

[2] This and the quotations from the text are taken from the libretto and CD booklet issued with the recording by Musica Mundi on 314006.
[3] Partch (1991), 244–6.

Partch and Henze can both be seen as foreshadowing the flower-power years that were to follow, though their themes were already relevant at the time of their composition (and indeed earlier: it is surely no coincidence that *The Bacchae* started to become a popular play in the theatre during the twentieth century, a century in which sexual repression and sexual liberation were major obsessions of the western world; and operas had already been composed on this subject by Egon Wellesz (*Die Bakchantinnen* (1931)—a recording was issued in 2001) and Giorgio Federico Ghedini (*Le Baccanti* (1948, revived in Milan in 1972))). The next operatic version of *The Bacchae* known to me is *The Black Bacchants* by Roy Travis (1982, to his own libretto), which includes traditional West African dance rhythms and instruments. But it was particularly the 1990s that saw a succession of operatic versions of *The Bacchae*, starting with a Swedish version of Euripides' text set to music by Daniel Börtz and directed by Ingmar Bergman, performed in Stockholm in 1991 and subsequently broadcast on Swedish television. This project was a collaboration between Börtz and Bergman from the start, and they had many discussions of how it would work in the theatre during the year and a half that it took Börtz to write the music. Bergman has described the chorus as 'missionaries or anarchists or terrorists', and the fact that there are twelve of them in addition to the chorus-leader is seen by the composer as suggesting some similarities between Dionysus and Christ.[4] (But the chorus remain women, each designated by a separate letter of the Greek alphabet and given a separate identity.) The contrast between the power of the gods and the vulnerability of humans is clear, particularly at the end, when Dionysus strikes Agave to the ground. But the opera is above all a psychosexual drama played out between Dionysus and Pentheus: Dionysus is sung by a mezzo-soprano, strikingly similar in appearance to Pentheus (both dressed in black, and with blonde hair, though Pentheus has a beard until he shaves it off on dressing as a woman). The music is for the most part discreetly subordinate to the text, and many key passages are spoken (including the lengthy narratives by the Herdsman and the Messenger and the scene in which Dionysus takes full control over Pentheus). An added visual

---

[4] See the CD booklet for the recording by Caprice on CAP 22028:1–2.

element is the dancing figure of Thalatta ('The Sea'—the reason for the name is not clear).

A more fully operatic version is John Buller's setting of the original Greek text (see Figure 24), performed in London in 1992 by the English National Opera (though this too seems sparse in comparison with Henze's music). The setting is very sensitive to the meaning of the words, and Buller wrote it partly in reaction against *The Bassarids*, since he felt Auden and Kallman had done a disservice to Euripides by rewriting the text. But it was an unexpected choice for performance by a company whose normal policy is to stage operas in English; since it is also their policy not to use surtitles, a work in ancient Greek had some obstacles to overcome, and not all the reviews were favourable (in spite of the addition of an introductory narration of the plot in English and the fact that Dionysus sings in English at points where he manifests himself as a god). The orchestration contributes to the presentation of the characters: Dionysus, for instance, tends to be accompanied by glockenspiel, celesta, or harp, Pentheus by brass, and the three-part women's chorus by wind instruments. Buller was aware of the contemporary resonances of the play, and he knew about the performance of *Dionysus in 69* in New York. 'But', he said, 'what really drew me to the play is its metrical structure. The rhythms of the words themselves are composed like music. That's why I've set it in the original Greek.'[5] He made some use of surviving fragments of ancient Greek music and also reused some material from his orchestral piece *The Theatre of Memory* (1981), which had been inspired by the structure and metres of Greek tragedy. In order to give the title of the work an ancient Greek appearance, he spelt it *Bakxai* (*x* being the ancient Greek letter normally transliterated as *ch*).

The very next year (1993) saw another production in London (directed by David Freeman), this time with the choruses sung in ancient Greek set to music for a female chorus by Iannis Xenakis. (Börtz and Buller too had been faithful to Euripides in having an all-female chorus, though in general it has not been unusual for composers to use a traditional four-part mixed chorus in their settings of Greek tragedy, even when they are otherwise following the original text quite closely.) Two further Greek composers to

---

[5] In conversation with Malcolm Hayes in the *Sunday Telegraph*, 3 May 1992.

FIGURE 24. Sarah Walker as Agave holding the head of her son Pentheus in John Buller's *Bakxai*, directed by Julia Hollander for the English National Opera at the Coliseum (1992).

set the play have been Theodore Antoniou (1995) and Arghyris Kounadis (1996). I regret that I have been unable to hear any of these versions at the time of writing.

The most recent version of *The Bacchae* to receive its première was in fact composed in the 1930s in Berlin by Edwin Geist. Since Geist's father had been Jewish, his music was proscribed by the Nazis, and he himself was shot by them in Lithuania in 1942, having moved there in 1939 on marrying a Jewish woman from Kaunas. But his friends managed to rescue his papers, and his opera *Die Heimkehr des Dionysos* ('The Return of Dionysus'), to which Geist had not put the finishing touches, resurfaced in 2000 and was performed in Vilnius in June 2002. The libretto (by Geist himself) is a very free version of the story of Pentheus, in which (for instance) Agave plays no part: Pentheus kills himself at the end on realizing that he has failed to come to terms with the Dionysiac in himself. It is not hard to imagine the resonances for Geist, as he composed this work in the 1930s, of the autocratic and repressive Pentheus portrayed in the earlier scenes.

MEDEA

The most popular operatic Greek heroine of the last thirty-five years has been Medea. There have been operas based on Euripides' or Seneca's play by the American composers Jonathan Elkus (1970) and Ray Edward Luke (1979), the English Gavin Bryars (1984, revised 1995), the Australian Felix Werder (1985), the Greek Mikis Theodorakis (1991), the Australian Gordon Kerry (1993), and the American Douglas Anderson (2000). The *Médée* of the Hungarian Andor Kovách (composed in 1960 and performed in 1967) was based on the play by Jean Anouilh. The German Bernd Alois Zimmermann had been working on an operatic version of *Medea* at the time of his death (1970). The New York Metropolitan Opera commissioned a work on this subject in the 1980s from Jacob Druckman (who had already included music from the Medea operas of Charpentier, Cavalli, and Cherubini in his orchestral work *Prism* of 1980), with a libretto by Tony Harrison. This opera too was left unfinished on the composer's death in 1996, and only the overture and one scene have ever been performed. But Harrison has published the libretto under the title *Medea: A Sex-War Opera*; it was performed as a play in

Edinburgh and London in 1991–2 (together with the manifesto of the Society for Cutting up Men), and it is included in Harrison's *Theatre Works 1973–1985*, published by Penguin Books.

Of these operas I single out for discussion Gavin Bryars's *Medea*, which grew out of an invitation from Robert Wilson to write the music for a production of Wilson's adaptation of Euripides' play; in the event the proportions of speech and music shifted, so that the work became an opera (Bryars's first), with only some spoken passages. It was an immediate success and marked a decisive step in Bryars's development as a composer. The text is mainly a translation of Euripides' text into modern Greek, but substantial portions are in French (since the first complete version was performed in Lyons) and other parts in ancient Greek or English. In some scenes, the effect of using different languages is to increase the distance between the characters. Bryars's researches into ancient Greek music encouraged him to use a large body of tuned percussion and few brass instruments, and he also decided to dispense with violins and oboes (using saxophones where oboes might have been expected). The vocal writing is much influenced by Richard Strauss, whose writing for female voices was a particular source of inspiration for Bryars, but much of the drama lies in the pulsating ostinato rhythms in the orchestra. Bryars and Wilson regarded Medea as a rational woman, cool, detached, and fully in control of her actions.

In the operatic version of Henry James's *The Aspern Papers* by Dominick Argento (1988) Henry's poet Jeffrey Aspern has become a composer, and the papers sought by a scholar after his death have been changed from love letters to a Medea opera that has been suppressed by his mistress, the diva for whom he had composed it. Parallels are drawn between Jason's treatment of Medea and Aspern's of his mistress, and at one point the story of Medea is sung while performers act it out in dumb show.

Pascal Dusapin's setting of Heiner Müller's *Medeamaterial* was commissioned for performance in a double bill with Purcell's *Dido and Aeneas* in Brussels in 1992 and thus uses a baroque orchestra (though the style of the composition is not baroque). The work is essentially a solo lament, but the autistic schizophrenia of Müller's Medea is conveyed partly by giving some of her words to a quartet of singers: 'she becomes a kind of five-headed octopus', as the composer has put it. Rolf Liebermann's *Freispruch für Medea* ('Acquittal for Medea') is based on the novel of the same name by Ursula Haas, in which Jason leaves Medea not for Creon's daughter but for his son; a two-act version was performed in Hamburg in 1995, a revised three-act version in Bern in 2001 and then in Paris in 2002 as a tribute to the composer, who had been a legendary director of L'Opéra in Paris in the 1970s and had died in 1999. The work is notable for its use of a gamelan orchestra (a traditional Indonesian percussion orchestra).

Volker Blumenthaler's chamber opera *Jason and Medea/Black Enshrouds Red* (1996) incorporates portions of Euripides' play as well as texts by Homer, Ovid, Grillparzer, and others.

The Hebei Clapper Opera Troupe of Beijing performed *Medea* in the style of the traditional Hebei Clapper Opera in 1998, giving over 200 performances, mainly in Europe.

Paul-Heinz Dittrich's 'scenic music' *Zerbrochene Bilder* ('Shattered Pictures', 2001) set texts relevant to Medea by Heiner Müller (including his *Medeamaterial*), as well as texts by Paul Celan and Edgar Allan Poe.

There have been two successful musicals, John Fisher's *Medea, the Musical* (1994) and Michael John LaChiusa's *Marie Christine* (1999). Fisher's is a hilarious and complex work, partly managing to turn the story of Medea and Jason into a comedy (with Phaedra making an unexpected appearance as Medea's aunt), partly showing the tribulations of a theatre director who plans to stage Euripides' play as a gay-empowerment musical. (It is discussed in more detail towards the end of Helene Foley's chapter in this volume.) *Marie Christine* is a more straightforward adaptation of the story, in which the Medea-figure is a Creole woman from New Orleans in the 1890s, trained in voodooism by her mother; she leaves home with a white sea captain who is subsequently prepared to abandon her in the interests of his own political ambitions. (Similar updatings of the story are found in earlier theatrical versions of *Medea*, notably from the 1930s.)

On a smaller scale, Dimitri Terzakis set part of Euripides' text for soprano and ensemble in 1966, Iannis Xenakis set portions of Seneca's *Medea* for male chorus and ensemble in 1967, and Jean Delysse composed a cantata about Medea in 1976. Ronald Calta-biano wrote a composition for soprano and twelve players called

Medea in 1980. In addition, several composers have written music for versions of *Medea* as a ballet or incidental music for productions of Euripides' or Seneca's play.

Finally, October 2002 saw the première in Venice of the complete version of Adriano Guarnieri's *Medea* (earlier versions and extracts had been performed from 1991 onwards), a multi-media work incorporating video film and live electronics as well as soloists, chorus, and orchestra; the part of Medea was shared between three singers, including the rock singer Antonella Ruggiero, and there was no continuous narrative but rather a portrayal of Medea's anguish in a variety of ways. The composer describes it as 'a complex work which poses radically the problem of what kind of dramaturgy is possible today'.[6]

THE HOUSE OF ATREUS

The House of Atreus has also been popular, inspiring such a steady stream of such varied compositions that I shall list them in chronological order in Appendix 1 (pp. 305–7), adding brief comments there on some of the works. Here I comment a little more fully on the works of two leading Greek composers, Iannis Xenakis and Mikis Theodorakis.

Xenakis's engagement with the *Oresteia* began in 1966 when he was invited to compose the music for Alexis Solomos's production of the trilogy at Ypsilanti (Michigan) as part of an ill-fated project to build a Greek theatre there. He subsequently selected the main numbers to form a suite for concert performance, to which he added *Kassandra* in 1987 and *La Déesse Athéna* in 1992, in each case stipulating that the new work should be included in future performances of his *Oresteia*, although *Kassandra* and *La Déesse Athéna* can also be performed as separate works. The work sets selected passages from the trilogy in ancient Greek; the main *Oresteia* suite is for mixed choir (originally also for children's choir), the other two works for a baritone soloist who moves with virtuoso rapidity from high falsetto to low baritone notes. *Kassandra* sets passages from her scene with the chorus in *Agamemnon*, the soloist singing each role alternately; *La Déesse Athéna* sets 28

---

[6] From a paragraph about the work by the composer published on www.teatro lafenice.it/calendario2002/note/.

lines from *Eumenides*. The combined duration of these works is about one hour, and between them they cover most of the main events of the trilogy, though in a fragmentary way and in a form designed for concert, not staged, performance.

Theodorakis's *Electra* was the second of three large-scale operas based on Greek tragedies that he wrote in the 1990s, coming between his *Medea* and *Antigone*; in 2002 he added a comedy, *Lysistrata*. He dedicated *Medea* to Verdi, *Electra* to Puccini, and *Antigone* to Bellini, and the works combine some of the idioms of grand opera with music derived from Greek traditions (including earlier compositions by Theodorakis himself): in the first act of *Electra*, for example, Electra's invocation of the gods of the underworld is based on a traditional lament for the dead found in the Mani; and in the course of the Tutor's description of Orestes' alleged death the chorus at one point sing a passage in the style of Orthodox church music. The influence of Puccini may be seen in the way the orchestra sometimes doubles the soloists' vocal lines, but in general he is the dedicatee rather than the model for the composition. For *Medea* and *Antigone* Theodorakis wrote his own libretto in modern Greek, based on the ancient Greek texts; for *Electra* he used a libretto by Spyros Evangelatos based on a translation of Sophocles' play. In his notes for the first production, the composer stated that he saw the chorus as representing the law of nature and Electra as having been chosen as the agent of the laws of universal harmony, contrasted with the disharmony within the palace;[7] he brings this out in his orchestral writing from her first appearance. But the work ends with Orestes and Pylades dragging Aegisthus indoors to be slaughtered, while Electra urges them to kill him quickly; the chorus tells us that the House of Atreus has now been freed from its sufferings, but the orchestra invites us to think rather of the drama of the revenge killing, and it is hard to feel that universal harmony has been restored.

One striking feature of the list in Appendix 1 is that it ends with three American composers (Reynolds, Fisher, and Simpson) who have all been working on versions of the entire *Oresteia*. They all embarked on these works before 11 September 2001, but the

---

[7] Unpublished notes cited in an account of the work by Gail Holst-Warhaft at www.mikis-theodorakis.net/gh_elektra.html.

ever-relevant theme of justice and revenge has acquired a new sharpness for them and their audiences since that date.

THE TROJAN WAR

Agamemnon's Trojan victims (apart from Cassandra) have attracted less attention, but mention should be made of Michael Tippett's *King Priam* (1962), a work based largely on Homer's *Iliad* but with the focus shifted to Priam and his family. There are many references to Greek tragedy in Tippett's writings, and he said that the portrayal of Hecuba in this opera was based on Euripides' *Hecuba* and *The Trojan Women* rather than the *Iliad*.[8] The influence of Aristotle's *Poetics* has also been detected in the way primarily epic material has been recast in dramatic form, though Tippett probably never read that work at first hand.[9] (The account of Paris' early life in Act I is based on material that we know to have been used by Euripides in his *Alexandros* (an alternative name for Paris), but only fragments of that play have survived; it was originally performed in the same group of plays as *The Trojan Women*.)

There has been, as far as I know, no recent setting of *Andromache* or *Hecuba* (though 2002 witnessed the first staged performance of Bruno Rigacci's *Ecuba*, which had previously received a concert performance in 1951, and Jonathan Darnborough is composing a *Hecuba* to be performed by the Oxford Girls' Choir in 2004). But the American Margaret Garwood's one-act opera *The Trojan Women* enjoyed some success when it was first performed in 1967, and it was revised in 1979. The Polish Joanna Bruzdowicz composed a musical tragedy based on the same play, *Les Troyennes*, performed in Paris in 1973 and combining modern instrumentation with tapes of African and Asian instruments.

Aribert Reimann's *Troades* was performed in Munich in 1986; Reimann had been a child in Berlin during the Second World War, and his experiences there have obvious relevance to his choice of this play to adapt. His libretto is based on the German translation by Franz Werfel, written in 1913 and frequently performed on the German stage from 1916 onwards; Werfel adds pathos to Euripides' text at many points. Reimann's score has at the beginning the

---

[8] Tippett (1980), 227; (1995), 213.   [9] See Pollard (1995), especially ch. 3.

motto 'Krieg ist Wahnwitz' ('War is madness'), words spoken by
Cassandra in Werfel's translation but not in fact included in the
libretto. Reimann is another composer who eschews violins and
includes a variety of wind and percussion instruments. His opera
lasts two hours, without a break, and the main roles are the female
roles of Hecuba, Cassandra, Andromache, and Helen, each well
differentiated in the vocal and orchestral writing. The high point is
Cassandra's scene, which lasts twenty minutes.

The Trojan Women also formed the basis of the first part of Nigel
Osborne's three-part opera *Sarajevo* (1994), which grew out of the
composer's experiences in the Balkans, where he has become very
much involved in musical education; and an operatic version by
the Finnish composer Jani Sivén was performed in Helsinki and
Berlin in March and April 2002. In addition, Dimitri Terzakis
composed a work for high voice and organ based on *The Trojan
Women* called *Der Hölle Nachklang II* ('Echo of Hell II') in
1992–3.

THE HOUSE OF OEDIPUS

The House of Oedipus has been less popular than the House of
Atreus, but I list eighteen works in Appendix 2 (pp. 307–9) of
which ten are versions of *Antigone* and eight are about Oedipus
and/or Jocasta.

Of the *Antigone* operas, in Ton de Leeuw's the focus is more
exclusively on Antigone than in Sophocles' play, partly because
hers is the only solo role (the parts of Ismene, Creon, and Haemon
being sung by the chorus and other parts omitted altogether), and
partly because the work ends with her departure to her tomb;
Creon's tragedy is hinted at only in his confrontation with Haemon. In other respects, however, her role does not dominate:
Creon is on stage for more of the play, and his confrontation
with Haemon is at the heart of the work. The text is de Leeuw's
own translation into French of portions of Sophocles' text. The
composer believed that on one level 'the protagonists are pawns in
a struggle taking place on a plane far beyond their individual
existence . . . Their actions are not so much regulated by autonomous deeds as by reactions to circumstances . . . It is not the subjectivity of the individual that is central, but his general human
condition which is shared by all.' De Leeuw was much influenced

by oriental musical and theatrical traditions, and the musical style is by western standards deliberately undramatic ('The emphasis lies neither on the dramatic build up nor the elaboration of psychological processes')[10], though there is a clear contrast in the styles of Creon and Antigone, particularly in the final scene, where Antigone has far more flowing melodic lines. Like many others in their settings of Greek drama, de Leeuw is sparing in his use of stringed instruments, composing for woodwind, horns, trombones, percussion, synthesizer, piano, two 'cellos and double bass.

Theodorakis's libretto for his *Antigone* uses material from nearly all the other Theban plays as well as Sophocles' *Antigone*, so as to convey the whole story in one work. It seems that he was particularly keen to bring out the theme of civil war in the early scenes of his opera, since that has obvious resonances for any Greek composer and for Theodorakis personally. The work ends with a scene reminiscent of the closing scene of Verdi's *Aida*, with the lovers singing together in the heroine's tomb. In this case it is the ghost of Haemon with whom Antigone sings her duet, since he has already killed himself; he is visible to the audience but not to her. Separated though they are, they both repeat over and over again the opening of the choral ode about the power of love: 'Love invincible in battle . . . ' (Verdi and Theodorakis had in fact both been anticipated by Tommaso Traetta in his *Antigona* of 1772, in which Haemon has somehow found a back way into Antigone's cave while still alive: after they have sung a love duet, Creon relents just in time to order their release, and the opera ends with fifteen minutes of joyful wedding celebrations. An excellent recording of this work was issued in 2000.)

Three versions of the Oedipus legend deserve particular mention. *Gospel at Colonus* is one of the most remarkably creative adaptations of Greek drama that there have been, and one of the most popular: it won a prize as the Outstanding Musical of the 1983–4 season, and it ran for several months on Broadway in 1988. It sets *Oedipus at Colonus* as a prayer meeting in a black Pentecostal church and is thus very unusual in combining Greek tragedy with Christianity. The mixture of beliefs is not altogether coherent, and it is not always quite clear whether we are witnessing a dramatic

---

[10] Quotations from the CD booklet for the recording on NM Classics 92036.

performance or a prayer meeting. But the ending works particularly well, with the Preacher delivering a sermon which gives the
narrative of how Oedipus answered the call from God and vanished from sight, and then the closing hymn: 'Now let the weeping
cease | Let no one mourn again | The love of God will bring you
peace | There is no end.'[11] One factor in the success of the produc-
tions was the involvement of Clarence Fountain and the Blind
Boys of Alabama, the group that helped to put Gospel music on
the map; their involvement is proof enough of the enduring relevance of Greek tragedy, and the success of *Gospel at Colonus*
shows that a work which uses many of the conventions of opera
can have great popular appeal if conceived and performed with
sufficient panache.

Rihm's *Oedipus* combines portions of Sophocles' *Oedipus Rex*
(in Hölderlin's German translation) with quotations from a fragmentary work by Nietzsche about Oedipus ('Oedipus: The Last
Philosopher Talks To Himself') and also quotations from the
Ödipuskommentar by Heiner Müller. The orchestra consists of
wind and percussion instruments, with no strings, until the
moment when Oedipus blinds himself on stage, at which point
two solo violins start playing music that conveys Oedipus'
agony. The extracts from Hölderlin's text are fragmentary, but
the sequence of the play is followed. The effect of the whole
depends partly on the visual differentiation between the dramatic
sections based on Sophocles and the 'monologues' and 'commentaries' based on Nietzsche and Müller. There are also flashbacks in
which earlier events such as Oedipus' murder of Laius are acted
out in dumb show with orchestral accompaniment. Much of the
visual presentation is prescribed by the composer in the score,
including a number of lighting effects. But the score does not
prescribe what is reported to have been one of the most powerful
effects in the original production: at the moment of Oedipus' self-
blinding the spectators found themselves too blinded by unbearably bright lights.[12] Rihm is one of Europe's leading composers;
Oedipus and *Die Hamletmaschine* (also first performed in 1987,
and based on Heiner Müller's play) were his two major operas of
the 1980s.

---

[11] Breuer (1989), 55.   [12] Flashar (1991), 282.

Figure 25. Quentin Hayes as Eddy, among policemen, with Helen Charnock as Wife and Fiona Kimm as Mum in the background, in Mark-Anthony Turnage's opera *Greek* (1988).

Turnage's *Greek* (his first opera) was a triumphant success at the first Munich Biennale in 1988, and its première there was followed by performances at the Edinburgh Festival in the same year (see Figure 25); in 1990 it was performed by the English National Opera in London and also broadcast in a production specially devised for BBC Television. The opera is an abrasive setting of an abrasive text, and it was not to everyone's taste (not surprisingly, as it was an angry work by an angry young man); but it has come to be seen as one of the most important operas of the late twentieth century. It is composed for small but sometimes remarkably noisy forces: four singers each take on several of the main roles, and the orchestra has seventeen players (with no violins). The writing is in turns violent and lyrical, and it displays a wide variety of musical influences, including jazz, rock, and the theme from ITV's *World of Sport*. It appears to have been the contemporary political relevance of Berkoff's play (discussed by Fiona Macintosh in the next chapter) that appealed to Turnage; he even upset Berkoff by making the work more openly political and overtly anti-Thatcherite than the original play had been (but also by including a scene in which Eddy, the Oedipus figure, masturbates). Turnage had been reluctant to write an opera at all, regarding it as an elitist and old-fashioned art form. But the work was important in his development as a composer, just as *Medea* was in that of Gavin Bryars. (By coincidence, both composers make prominent use of saxophones.) I have found no evidence that Turnage cared about the relationship of his work to Sophocles' play, and indeed he has said that he was not particularly interested in Greek mythology.[13] But it remains true that a major work incorporating a variety of late twentieth-century popular musical influences was based indirectly on the most famous of all Greek tragedies.

PROMETHEUS

Prometheus has attracted an experimental three-act opera *Prometheus' Torch* by the Czech composer Jan Hanuš (1965: the mythological subject is expressed through dance and pantomime, while Prometheus himself in a parallel operatic setting is an atomic scientist defying the rulers of a modern state); operatic versions by Carl Orff (1968, setting the original Greek text in nine scenes, with long passages of intoned declamation), and by Meyer Kupferman (1978, in five scenes each telling the story in its own way, partly in German and partly in English); an opera-oratorio *Prometheus Bound* by the Bulgarian Lazar Nikolov (composed 1963–9, performed 1974), and a chamber opera so far unperformed by the Polish Bernadetta Matuszczak (composed 1981–2); George Couroupos's *Hermes and Prometheus* (1971), a setting of one scene from Aeschylus' play for two actors and nine instruments; a cantata *Prometheus Bound* by the same composer (1979), for actors, female chorus, and ensemble; and a cantata *Prometheus* by Theodore Antoniou (performed 1984), for baritone, narrator, mixed choir, and orchestra.

---

[13] Clements (2000), 18.

Luigi Nono's *Prometeo* (first performed 1984, revised version 1985), regarded by many as his finest achievement, has a libretto by the philosopher Massimo Cacciari in ancient Greek, Italian, and German that incorporates passages from Aeschylus' *Prometheus Bound* and also from Hesiod, Sophocles, Euripides, Herodotus, Hölderlin, and Walter Benjamin. The libretto is a collection of fragments, and Nono's setting fragments them still further, rendering the words for the most part impossible to perceive as words. There is no continuous narrative, and no scenic representation (although the work was first conceived as a theatrical project). Nono designated the work a 'tragedia dell'ascolto' ('aural tragedy'), a succession of sounds appealing to the ear and not the eye, and Prometheus for him represented above all the power of thought. The work contains many experiments in the production of sounds with the help of live electronics, sometimes testing the limits of audibility, and it requires intense concentration; the revised version lasts over two hours. It has been described as a 'vast post-theatrical hymn to inwardness'.[14]

OTHER WORKS

The last operatic versions of *Alcestis* known to me were Louise Talma's in 1962 and Ton de Leeuw's in 1963. But Phaedra has inspired a chamber opera *Syllabaire pour Phèdre* ('Spelling-Book for Phaedra') by the Moroccan-born Maurice Ohana (Paris, 1968); Sylvano Bussotti's *Phèdre* (1988); and a televised opera *Ode to Phaedra* by George Roumanis (1995). Bussotti's opera retains the same cast of characters in a succession of different historical settings: Act I takes place in ancient Greece, Act II at the Hôtel de Bourgogne in 1677 on the occasion of the first performance of Racine's play, Act III in Paris in the twentieth century. The point is to emphasize that the same human passions are found in a variety of historical contexts. Benjamin Britten's *Phaedra*, one of the last works he composed, is a setting of selections from Robert Lowell's translation of Racine's play; it was written in 1975 and first performed by Janet Baker at the Aldeburgh festival in 1976,

---

[14] David Osmond-Smith, in Holden (2001), 634.

less than six months before the composer's death. Earlier in 1976 George Rochberg's monodrama *Phaedra* (for mezzosoprano and orchestra), using the composer's own libretto also based on Lowell's translation of Racine, had been performed in Syracuse, New York; and Naji Hakim's cantata *Phèdre*, a setting of two scenes from Racine's play, was performed in London in 1998.

Jonathan Elkus's one-act opera *Helen in Egypt* was performed together with his *Medea* in 1970. John Eaton's opera *Heracles* (based on Sophocles and Seneca) was performed in Indiana in 1972; and Ján Zimmer's opera-pantomime *Hérakles* (composed from 1972 onwards, and influenced by Bertolt Brecht as well as ancient Greek drama) was broadcast on Czech television in 1987.

Param Vir's *Ion* is based on a libretto by David Lan that follows the plot of Euripides' play closely. It was performed in an incomplete semi-staged version in 2000, and fully staged performances of the complete work have been announced for 2003.

CONCLUSION

Throughout this period there has been a continuing tradition of performances of earlier operas, such as the *Medea*s of Charpentier and Cherubini, Traetta's *Antigona*, Strauss's *Elektra* and Stravinsky's *Oedipus Rex*. Incidental music for staged performances continues to be commissioned from leading composers, particularly in Greece (though Harrison Birtwistle's music for *The Oresteia* (1981) and *Bacchai* (2002), both at the National Theatre in London, should also be mentioned). There have been many settings of small portions of text, including John Eaton's *Ajax*, a composition for baritone and orchestra, performed in 1972; Iannis Xenakis's *A Colone* (from *Oedipus at Colonus*, 1977); John Buller's *Kommos* (1982), setting some lines from Aeschylus' *Persians*; and Dimitri Terzakis's *Passionen* of 1977–8, which includes texts from *Prometheus Bound* and *Oedipus Tyrannus*, as well as texts from the Gospels, liturgical texts, and testimonies from Nazi concentration camps. (Several other settings of excerpts from Greek plays have been mentioned above.)

On the lighter side, P. D. Q. Bach (the pseudonym of Peter Schickele) has followed his cantata *Iphigenia in Brooklyn* with the 'dramatic oratorio' *Oedipus Tex* (1988), in which Oedipus is a cowboy ('The moral of this story is, of course: | Don't love your mother, pardner, save it for your horse'). There have also been operas based on Greek comedies, such as the *Lysistrata*s of Emil Petrovics (1962, in Hungarian, first staged in 1971) and Mikis Theodorakis (2002). But it would be beyond the scope of this volume to explore those.

I end by picking out some productions from the year 2002, some of which have been mentioned above, to show how there continue to be both new works and premières of older works:

March	Première of Jani Sivèn's *Trojan Women* in Helsinki
April	Première of Mikis Theodorakis's *Lysistrata* in Athens
May	First staged performance of Bruno Rigacci's *Ecuba* (1950) at Brooklyn College
June	Première of Edwin Geist's *The Return of Dionysus* (1930s) in Vilnius
July	Première of George Couroupos's *Jocasta* at Delphi
August	United Kingdom première of Georges Enescu's *Oedipe* (first performed in 1936, and telling the entire story of Oedipus from birth to death, incorporating both of Sophocles' Oedipus plays); this was a concert performance at the Edinburgh Festival, which also saw a staged production of Igor Stravinsky's *Oedipus Rex* by the Canadian Opera Company, directed by François Girard, in which the plague ravaging Thebes was equated with HIV.
October	Première of Adriano Guarnieri's *Medea* in Venice.

By the time this book appears, Lyons should have seen the première of Michèle Reverdy's *Médée* (with a libretto based on Christa Wolf's *Medea-Stimmen*) in January 2003, and Washington DC should have seen the first full production of Andrew Simpson's *Agamemnon*, and Brussels the première of Pierre Bartholomée's *Oedipe sur la Route* ('Oedipus on the Road', based on the novel of this name by Henri Bauchau), both in spring 2003.

Greek dramatic opera is well and truly on the road.

Appendix 1: Works about the House of Atreus

I take 1965 as an arbitrary starting point, and I omit some student productions also known to me.

1965   Ildebrando Pizzetti (Italy), *Clitennestra* (2-act opera)
          Monic Cecconi-Botella (France), *Les Visions Prophé-tiques de Cassandre* (cantata)

1966   Iannis Xenakis (Greece), *Oresteia* (music drama for choir and ensemble)

1967   Felix Werder (Australia), *Agamemnon* (1–act opera, re-vised 1977, based on Gilbert Murray's translation of Aeschylus)
          Dimitri Terzakis (Greece), *Clytemnestra* (for soprano and ensemble)
          Marvin David Levy (USA), *Mourning becomes Electra* (3–act operatic version of Eugene O'Neill's play)

1967–9   Iain Hamilton (Scotland), *Agamemnon* (1–act opera, re-vised 1987, 1989; unperformed)

1967–70   Jani Christou (Greece), *Oresteia* (opera, left incomplete on the composer's death in 1970)

1968   Daniel Jones (Wales), *Orestes* (opera, broadcast on BBC Radio)
          Pascal Bentoiu (Romania), *Iphigenia's Sacrifice* (radio opera)

1969   Leonidas Zoras (Greece), *Elektra* (opera)

1971   Havergal Brian (England), *Agamemnon* (1-act opera, first performance, on the occasion of the composer's ninety-fifth birthday: composed 1957, and conceived as an introduction to Strauss's *Elektra*, in the belief that it provided necessary background information for the audience of that work. Similarly, Brian had thoughts in his eighties of writing an opera that would combine *Oedipus at Colonus* with *Antigone*, in the belief that *Antigone* could not be understood on its own; he made some progress on this but never completed it.)[15]

[15] Source: correspondence with Robert Simpson in the Havergal Brian Archive at Keele University.

Margaret Anne Wheat (USA), *The Eumenides* (for orchestra, chorus, and electronic tape)

Doug Dyer (librettist, USA), *Blood: From the Heart of America* (musical version of the *Oresteia*, with Orestes as a returned Vietnam veteran)

1972 Michael Adamis (Greece), *Orestes* (for baritone, percussion, and tape)

Francis Routh (England), *The Death of Iphigenia* (for soprano and ensemble)

1973 Elizabeth Gomm (England), *Clytemnestra's Argument* (choral composition)

1974 Elizabeth Gomm (England), *Orestes' Argument* (choral composition)

Peter Wishart (England), *Clytemnestra* (opera)

1978 Aurel Stroe (Romania), *Les Choéphores* (music-theatre piece for radio)

1980 John Eaton (USA), *The Cry of Clytaemnestra* (1–act chamber opera, loosely based on Aeschylus' *Agamemnon*, but showing the events mainly from the perspective of Clytemnestra in seven linked scenes, including flashbacks to Iphigenia's childhood, visions of events at Aulis and Troy, and a dream foreshadowing her murder of Agamemnon on his return)

1983 Aurel Stroe (Romania), *Agamemnon* (music-theatre piece for radio)

1984–5 Conrad Cummings (USA), *Cassandra* (opera, subsequently withdrawn)

1986 Aurel Stroe (Romania), *Eumenides* (music theatre piece for radio)

1987 Iannis Xenakis (Greece), *Kassandra* (for baritone, psaltery, and percussion)

1990 Nicholas Zumbro (Greece/USA), *Kassandra* (opera, based on *Agamemnon* and *Trojan Women*)

1992 Iannis Xenakis (Greece), *La Déesse Athéna* (for baritone and ensemble)

George Couroupos (Greece), *Pylades* (1–act chamber opera, a free adaptation of excerpts from the *Electra* plays of Euripides and Sophocles)

1993   Liza Lim (Australia), *The Oresteia* ('memory theatre (opera) in 7 parts' for soloists, dancer, and ensemble, based mainly on Tony Harrison's translation of *Agamemnon*, but quoting some passages from the *Oresteia*, and also a fragment of Sappho's poetry, in the original Greek)

1994   Rhian Samuel (Wales), *Clytemnestra* (for soprano and orchestra)

1995   Mikis Theodorakis (Greece), *Electra* (2–act opera)

1997   Roger Reynolds (USA), *The Red Act Arias* (for chorus, orchestra, narrator, and computer-processed sound; the first work in a large-scale project called *The Red Act Project* that includes *Justice* (see 1999 below); the third major section will be called *Illusion*)

1998   Garrett Fisher (USA), *Agamemnon* (music drama for 2 soloists, chorus, 2 dancers, and ensemble) (The composer has since been working on a larger opera based on the entire *Oresteia*, with the working title *The Dream of Zeus*.)

1999   Roger Reynolds (USA), *Justice* (for soprano, actress, percussionist, and computer-processed sound; see 1997 above)

2001   Andrew Simpson (USA), *Agamemnon* (1–act opera, workshop production; a fuller production is scheduled for March 2003. This is the first part of a complete *Oresteia*-trilogy: the composer has completed the second part (*The Offerings*) and plans to complete the trilogy with *The Furies*.)

Appendix 2: Works about the House of Oedipus

1963   Lyubomir Pipkov (Bulgaria), *Antigona '43* (opera setting the story of Antigone in the context of the antifascist struggle during the Second World War)

1967   William Russo (USA), *Antigone* (opera)

1968   Roy Travis (USA), *The Passion of Oedipus* (2–act opera)

1971   Reginald Smith Brindle (England), *Death of Antigone* (chamber opera)

1973   Meyer Kupferman (USA), *Antigonae* (1-act opera-monodrama based on Hölderlin's translation of Sophocles)

1974   Josep Soler Sardà (Spain), *Edipo y Yocasta* (2–act opera)

1983   Lee Breuer and Bob Telson (USA), *Gospel at Colonus* (2–act staged oratorio)

1987   Wolfgang Rihm (Germany), *Oedipus* ('music theatre' in 21 sections)
          József Soproni (Hungary), *Antigone* (3-act opera based on Anouilh's play)

1988   Mark-Anthony Turnage (England), *Greek* (2–act opera based on Steven Berkoff's play)

1991   Ton de Leeuw (Netherlands), *Antigone* ('music drama' in 3 parts)

1992   Charles Chaynes (France), *Jocaste* (3-act opera, based indirectly on Euripides' *Phoenician Women*. By making Jocasta central to their presentation of the Oedipus legend, Chaynes and his librettist Jacques Lacarrière hoped to bring out her role as an innocent victim of forces beyond her control, thus making her stand for 'all those women who have been humiliated, despised, or ignored, victims of man's insanity and selfishness', as Lacarrière puts it. Chaynes writes: 'her presence discreetly underlines the role of women and their problems in modern society, ensuring that the myth remains a completely topical issue'.)[16]

1993   Dinos Constantinides (Greece/USA), *Antigone* (3-act opera)

1998   Theodore Antoniou (Greece/USA), *Oedipus at Colonus* (opera)

---

[16] Quotations from the CD booklet for the recording by Disques Chamade on CHCD 5633/34.

1999	Mikis Theodorakis (Greece), *Antigone* (2-act opera)
	John Eaton (USA), *Antigone* (1-act opera)
2001	Zbigniew Rudzínski (Poland), *Antygona* (opera)
2002	George Couroupos (Greece), *Jocasta* (lyric tragedy for actor, soprano, bass, men's choir, and instruments)

RESOURCES AND ACKNOWLEDGEMENTS

McDonald (2001) has a 'Partial list of operas and demi-operas based on classics, including historical topics' on pp. 243–338 and also includes chapters on *Gospel at Colonus* and on Theodorakis's *Medea*.

Otherwise, I have found the following works particularly helpful: Flashar (1991), Sadie (1992), Warrack and West (1992), Reid (1993), Poduska (1999), Holden (2001).

Commercial recordings have been issued of many of the works mentioned in this chapter, though they are not all easy to obtain; Poduska's list is a very useful starting point. I am very grateful to concertmusic@mindspring.com for help in tracking several down and for drawing my attention to others of which I had been unaware. I have also received much help of various kinds from (among others) Theodore Antoniou, Rowena Harrison (Pollard), Gail Holst-Warhaft, Rena Parmenidou (for Mikis Theodorakis), Andrew Simpson, Vladimir Tarasov, James Wood, Nicholas Zumbro, the Havergal Brian Society, and the following publishers: Oxford University Press, Schott, and Universal Edition.

Section IV

DIONYSUS AND THE LIFE OF THE MIND

12

Oedipus in the East End

From Freud to Berkoff

Fiona Macintosh

In 1975 the distinguished German playwright and director Heiner Müller suggestively commented: 'In the century of *Orestes* and *Electra*, which is upon us, *Oedipus* will be a comedy.'[1] That Müller should refer to 'the century of *Orestes* and *Electra*' being 'upon us . . .' is startling. For although the first part of the twentieth century can boast some notable adaptations and revivals of the ancient plays centred upon the House of Atreus, it is not really until the final part of the century (from 1980 onwards to be precise) that Orestes and Electra could be said to have dominated the repertoire.[2]

In this sense, Müller's observations in 1975 might be considered prescient rather than pertinent, especially since the twentieth century as a whole—and especially the first half of the century—is more generally regarded as the century of Oedipus. Of course, it was Freud's insights into Sophocles' *Oedipus Tyrannus* in chapter 5 of *The Interpretation of Dreams* (1900) that played no small part in securing the pre-eminence of Oedipus in the western theatrical repertoire; and Freud guaranteed that Oedipus and his complex became not only a commanding presence in high-intellectual circles, but also a familiar household name throughout the entire century.

However, in the late twentieth-century theatre where the *Oresteias* hold sway, it is in fact hard to find major productions of Sophocles' *Oedipus Tyrannus*. The ancient play that the Renaissance privileged as Aristotle's paradigmatic tragedy has been losing its central position within the mainstream performance

---

[1] Heiner Müller, *Projection 75*, cited by Innes (1993), 201.
[2] The three productions of the *Oresteia* from 1980–2 by Karolos Koun, Peter Hall, and Peter Stein provided the watershed. See Macintosh (1997), 34–18, and Wrigley (forthcoming).

repertoire in favour of plays which lend themselves more obviously to contemporary social and political concerns. In addition to the political readings of the *Oresteia* in the wake of the burgeoning democracies in the former Eastern bloc, other Greek tragedies with strong suffering women or gender concerns—notably *Medea, Antigone, Trojan Women,* and *Bacchae*—have similarly enjoyed a new prominence in the theatre.

What I want to do in this chapter is to provide some kind of explanation for what has clearly become a kind of dethroning of Sophocles' protagonist from the mid-1960s onwards. Whilst Freudian psychology was both prominent and entrenched within theatrical discourse by the 1950s and 1960s, it became evident by the 1970s within society at large that Freud's theories were no longer immune from close critical scrutiny. Indeed in clinical practice, it was the Kleinian psychoanalytical model, in which the mother replaces the father as the focus for exploration, which began to eclipse Freudian orthodoxy. The parallel developments within the theatre, with *Oedipus Tyrannus* losing its central place to the *Oresteia* (in which legal rights to the child are hotly contested), may well be understood in terms of the struggle elsewhere between Freud and Klein.[3]

About this time French academic discourse began to refigure Oedipus with reference to the ambiguities in the designation *tyrannos* (the Greek term originally meant 'the ruler who comes from without' or 'the ruler who has not inherited by birthright', but came to subsume some of the connotations associated with the English word 'tyrant'); and late-1960s versions of Oedipus in the theatre similarly went on to dethrone the 'King' of the (especially) nineteenth-century title in new and dislocating ways. Pasolini's film version set a sentient (rather than cerebral) Oedipus within the arid landscape of North Africa (1967); whilst the Nigerian playwright Ola Rotimi refashioned Sophocles' protagonist against the backdrop of the internecine struggles of the Biafran War (1968); and the most striking recent versions and productions of

---

[3] On Kleinian ascendancy, see Chodorow (1978), Spillius (1983), Benjamin (1988), and Hughes (1990). When Luce Irigaray proclaimed in her first manifesto *Speculum of the other Woman* that the murder of the mother and not the father was the founding act of western civilization (referring, inter alia, to Aeschylus' *Oresteia*), she was summarily dismissed by Jacques Lacan from her teaching post at Vincennes. See Ellmann (1994), 23.

the play in the west have included black heroes from minority groups (one thinks of Lee Breuer's *Gospel at Colonus* (1983); Rita Dove's *The Darker Face of the Earth* (1996) and David Greig's recent adaptation of Sophocles' tragedy in Glasgow (2000)).[4]

Berkoff's *Greek*, which premiered at the Half Moon Theatre in London on 11 February 1980, contributes to the process of dislocation with its East End context and its thoroughly demotic protagonist. Berkoff's highly controversial and often deeply shocking re-engagement with the myth went on to inspire a major postmodern opera by Mark-Anthony Turnage in 1988 (see further Brown in the previous chapter of this volume). In many ways Berkoff's version gestures towards an earlier, parodic Oedipal tradition that includes both Heinrich von Kleist's *The Broken Jug* (1808) and J. M. Synge's *Playboy of the Western World* (1907), in which comic anti-heroes either unwittingly enact the Oedipus pattern in bawdy and bathetic key (as in the German play) or pretend to an act of parricide in order to enhance their own otherwise insignificant stature (as in the Irish version). *Greek* may well be situated within this parodic tradition, and could readily be invoked in support of Müller's claim that the Oedipus of today demands recasting in the comic mould. But what makes Berkoff's radical reworking both representative and striking is not so much its generic mutation, as its defiant refutation of both Sophocles and Freud. In this sense, and perhaps not surprizingly, the post-Freudian Oedipus turns out, in its assault on the ideology of authority, to be no less Oedipal than its forebears.

THE FREUDIAN OEDIPUS AND THE NINETEENTH-CENTURY STAR-SYSTEM

That the Freudian Oedipus is as much a product of the nineteenth-century star-system in the theatre as he is a product of Freud's own clinical observations is clear. The impact on the young Freud of the French tragedian Jean Mounet-Sully in the title role is documented by Freud's biographer, Ernest Jones.[5] Mounet-Sully's Oedipus was conceived in part within the neo-classical school of

---

[4] On Pasolini and Dove see also Foley, above, Chapter 3; on Rotimi and Greig see also Hardwick, above, Chapter 8).

[5] E. Jones (1953), 194.

French acting with its dependence on a translation by Jules Lacroix cast in rhymed alexandrines and with its marginalized chorus of four; but, with its blinded on-stage Oedipus, the production broke new ground in the French tradition (both Corneille (1659) and Voltaire (1718) had omitted this scene on grounds of taste, in marked contrast with the English version by Dryden and Lee (1678), which had revelled in the horrors of both the blinding and the mother–son incest).

There are clear parallels between nineteenth-century theatre architecture and the Freudian psyche generally; and here in the Comédie Française production of Sophocles' tragedy, the marginalized chorus and the dominant, isolated, suffering hero in many ways reflect the Freudian bipartite divisions of the mind. Comments from Mounet-Sully show that the actor was either well aware of Stanislavski's work in Moscow or was at least working along similar lines. When Mounet-Sully describes the rehearsal process as a stripping off of the layers of self and text, he is of course anticipating the parallel that Freud so eloquently expresses between the experience of watching *Oedipus* and the practice of psychoanalysis.[6] If Freud found the source of his psychoanalytical theory in Sophocles' treatment of the Oedipus myth, it is hardly surprising that Mounet-Sully's interpretation of the role made such an impact on him when he saw it in Paris in 1885. When Mounet-Sully included *Hamlet* in his repertoire in 1886, one is tempted to infer that it was his performance that prompted or possibly confirmed Freud's linking of the Sophoclean and Shakespearian tragedies in relation to his theory of the Oedipus complex.

In many ways when the English star actor John Martin-Harvey appeared in the role of Oedipus in the Max Reinhardt production in January 1912 at Covent Garden, he too continued that tradition (however Max Reinhardt's Nietzschean-inspired Dionysiac chorus injected a new threatening 'id' into the equation). But it was, perhaps, the English version of 1945, with Laurence Olivier in the title role, that could be said to have continued the essentially Freudian–Mounet-Sully line. In the Yeats translation (where the chorus is also marginalized), Olivier gave a consummate

---

[6] On a Freudian reading of nineteenth-century stage space, see Green (1979), 1–5, and Wiles (2003). For Mounet-Sully's theory and method, see Macintosh (forthcoming *b*).

performance as the lonely hero pushed beyond the bounds of normal human endurance. When Olivier's Oedipus discovered the truth about himself, he emitted his (now famous) primal scream (in direct imitation, we are told, of the wailing of ermine entrapped by the barbarous practices of huntsmen). For the critic Kenneth Tynan, Olivier's Oedipus cried 'a new born baby's wail': Freud's Oedipus was here in 1945 crudely wrenched anew from his mother's womb.[7] That it was this moment from the production in particular that entered the annals of British theatre history, is perhaps not surprising. For Olivier's 'wail' not only anticipates the Beckettian scream (see also Katharine Worth in this volume, Chapter 10); it also recalls Kleinian psychoanalytical theory, in which the first and crucial trauma occurs on the departure from the birth canal.

OEDIPUS DETHRONED

By the 1950s the star-system had nearly run its course after a hundred or so years of theatre history. Not only did the increasing influence of French theatre practitioners within the English theatre, notably through Michel Saint-Denis and George Devine, introduce a context that demanded change; such cross-cultural perspectives also promoted fertile ground for new work that challenged the hero-centred plays in the traditional repertoire. Arthur Miller's seminal essay 'Tragedy and the Common Man' had appeared in the *New York Times* on 27 February 1949, seventeen days after the opening of *Death of a Salesman*, which had embodied the demotic theory. And by the late 1950s even the stars began to respond to the changes: Olivier's record of the very real difference he felt in the part of Archie in *The Entertainer* in 1957 is significant in this regard.[8]

In many ways the last major twentieth-century *Oedipus Tyrannus*, Tyrone Guthrie's production entitled *Oedipus Rex* in Stratford, Ontario, in 1955, was conceived in marked opposition to the Olivier production, and to the fading star-system itself. Guthrie had resigned from the management of the Old Vic over Olivier's

---

[7] For Olivier's Oedipus, see Shellard (1999), 3–5.

[8] See Olivier's claim, cited in Rebellato (1999), 80–1: 'I began to feel already the promise of a new, vitally changed, entirely unfamiliar Me [...] I now belonged to an entirely different generation.'

decision to mount Sophocles' tragedy in a double bill together
with Sheridan's *The Critic* (another sop, one might infer, to the
ego of the formidable star); and although Guthrie similarly used
the Yeats translation, for him it was the mythopoeic nature of
the text that mattered. Indeed, that Guthrie is in some senses
engaged in the process of downgrading the star is perhaps nowhere
better evidenced than in his designs by Tanya Moiseiwitsch,
which included vast expressionist masks (see Wiles in this volume,
Chapter 9).

By the 1960s the star-system in the theatre was well and truly
spent, and heroes and heroism in the wake of the plays of Osborne
and Wesker seemed in Britain, at least, irrelevant if not fake. The
ills of society, as they were perceived by the Angry Young Men and
their adherents, stemmed from the failure to yoke thought with
feeling: muted middle-class emotions were to be challenged out-
right in the new open forum of vital drama, where fervent responses were to underscore all political and social discourse. And
there was a concomitant hostility to what was considered French
'intellectual' drama (a hostility which was not inseparable from
British anti-European feeling at a time when the threat of declining
Empire led to a form of cultural chauvinism across the board).[9]

BERKOFF'S FOREBEARS

However, whilst some of the plays by the French philosopher
dramatists may indeed have run the risk of dissociating thought
from feeling, French theatre in general was becoming increasingly
concerned with exploring new realms of feeling. And if British
actors of the 1950s and 1960s were given ample opportunities
to test their verbal dexterity, they still acted from the head up.
French theatre, by contrast, was being increasingly informed by
directors who demanded that acting involve the whole body: the
Cartesian divide was now to be overcome by what was essentially a
Freudian mind and body unity in performance (see further Wiles,
Chapter 9).

Steven Berkoff had trained in the essentially cerebral English
performance tradition, but he had also received training in mime
from the school of Jacques Lecoq. Berkoff was in many ways

[9] Rebellato (1999), 142–5.

uniquely well-placed in his generation of actors to achieve this desired unity of mind and body. As a faithful adherent of the theories of the French director Antonin Artaud (he claimed that whilst the English had merely flirted with Artaud before their flings with Brecht and, subsequently, Grotowski, he alone had remained faithful to him[10]), Berkoff subscribes to the Artaudian notion that theatre should provide a site for the revelation of a pre-rational heightened reality. And like Jean-Louis Barrault (Artaud's disciple of the 1960s), Berkoff aims for a psycho-physiological unity: what Berkoff cynics might term as his visceral, 'in yer groin drama'.

That Artaud and Barrault are aiming to convey in the theatre what, in psychoanalytical terms, would be classified as the realms of the unconscious as well as the conscious mind (the id as well as the ego), is abundantly clear. And so when Berkoff uses Freudian terminology in his critiques of the contemporary theatre, it is not fortuitous: he bemoans the absence of British directors imaginative enough to enter 'the interior of man's soul' (his subjects, equally Freudian, are always male and semi-autobiographical);[11] and elsewhere in his autobiography we learn that theatre should be 'closer to Freud than to the political columns of the *Daily Rant*' (5).

For Berkoff, however, there is a deeply political dimension behind his espousal of Barrault's ideal of 'Total Theatre'. If there had been a clear hierarchy in the hero–choral divide in the Oedipus productions of Mounet-Sully and Laurence Olivier, the ensemble performance is seen by Berkoff as the aesthetic correlative to the classless society. Berkoff, the young working-class Jewish actor from the East End, found the pecking order of the 1950s Royal Court and the RSC totally alienating; and when he set up his London Theatre Group in 1968, it was in large measure to counter the essentially class-based hierarchy that pervaded the star-system in London theatrical circles. And when he chooses to write a play inspired by the Greek model, it becomes clear that the chorus for him (in marked contrast to those star-dominated forerunners) is integral to the action: Berkoff's Oedipus and his chorus are one, as the chorus serve to amplify the emotional strains of the protagonist (341).

[10] Ned Chaillet in *The Times*, 16 February 1980.
[11] Berkoff (1996), 243. All subsequent references to *Free Association* appear in brackets in the text.

FREUD AND OEDIPUS AND *GREEK*

Berkoff's choice of Sophocles' *Oedipus Tyrannus* for updating can also be traced to the interests of his forebears. The key chapter in Artaud's *Theatre and Its Double* (1938) is entitled 'Theatre and the Plague', in which he argues that the theatre should seek to (re-) present the plague from which the audience will emerge either dead or purged. And not only was the plague a recurrent trope in Artaud's own theoretical and practical works, he was also drawn time and again to plays with incestuous relationships (notably Ford's *'Tis Pity She's a Whore*, Shelley's *The Cenci*, and his own play *The Spurt of Blood*), in which the ideology of patriarchal authority is challenged. When Artaud's principle English disciple, Peter Brook, staged an ancient play, he not surprisingly chose the *Oedipus* (albeit Seneca's, in Ted Hughes's version (1968)). And as a deep admirer of Brook as well as of Artaud, Berkoff's own choice of the Oedipus legend begins to seem inevitable; and in *Greek*, we find verbal echoes of Hughes's text, which are testimony to that genealogy.

In Berkoff's case, furthermore, there is no attempt to disguise the autobiographical reasons that inform his choice of Oedipus as chosen subject. Berkoff's formation of an ensemble company had been informed by psychological as much as political needs. His various accounts of the company's experiences on tour and in rehearsal reveal that, for Berkoff, the actors had become his surrogate family (283); the family he never had, because although his mother was caring and involved, he remained unable to make contact with his cantankerous and distant father. So now writing his version of Sophocles' play, he confesses he is able to use it 'as a mask for [his] own feelings and ambitions' (2).

Berkoff explains that it was important for him not to take the part of Eddy in *Greek* (unusually for Berkoff, he did not appear in the play until the 1988 revival at the Wyndham's Theatre, when he was too old for the part of Eddy and so appeared as the father); instead he wanted the necessary distance to be able to 'analyse' the material that was far too close to his own life experiences (as the material is, he says in the Author's Note to the printed edition of his play, for many other young men, who in turn identify with his protagonist). Towards the end of Berkoff's autobiography, Oedipus is held up as the representative protagonist:

What did Oedipus tell us except the torments inside the mind of man? Torments of the soul. Show me a tormented man . . . You tell me where I can see this on stage and I will run, since I too am a spectator at the feast. (390)

For Berkoff, as for Artaud and Barrault, the star has been replaced with the archetype of Jungian psychology. This is Oedipus/Eddy as Everyman; and as Eddy becomes narrator and participant in his own drama, very often veering from past, present, and future in the course of one speech, the multiple levels of reality within the play mirror (as Freud saw in the Sophoclean tragedy) the process of unravelling that constitutes the psychoanalytical method in practice.

Indeed, Berkoff's vision is pure Freud in its delight in laying bare Eddy's consciousness. The moment of recognition in Berkoff's play comes during Eddy's stepfather's account of how the young toddler was discovered. The pivotal moment in the play similarly draws on the nautical imagery used in Sophocles' tragedy. However, it also recalls both Klein's archetypal birth trauma and the birth mimes in the work of Barrault (in *As I lay Dying*), Grotowski, the Living Theatre and Richard Schechner (in *Dionysus in 69*—see Zeitlin above, Chapter 2, and especially Figure 7).

DAD tells how London's Tower Bridge opened up 'to allow the steamers' funnels through like some big lazy East End tart from Cable Street opening her thighs . . . '[12] (see Figure 26, which reproduces the poster from the Wyndham's revival in 1988). And with the Bridge's opening, it reveals carefree East Enders on deck enjoying a Sunday outing down the river moments before their Southend steamer gets blasted to smithereens by an unexploded bomb, scattering limbs and torsos to the wind. From the debris and confusion, a toddler is miraculously pulled to safety:

when all had gone and dawn arose we saw what seemed a little doll clinging to a piece of wood but on closer butchering revealed a little bugger of about two he were, struggling like the fuck and gripping in his paw a greasy old big bear, which no doubt helped to keep him up. We threw the bear back in the slick, and lifted the toddler out all dripping wet and covered in oil looking like a darkie so, no one about we took him home and washed him . . . (136)

---

[12] See the text in Berkoff (1994), 135. All subsequent references to this text of the play appear in brackets after the quotation.

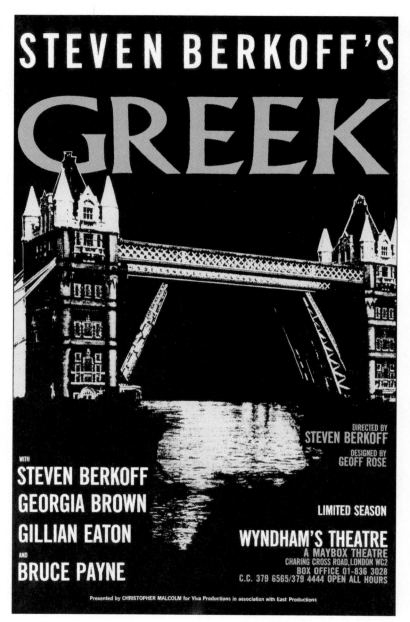

FIGURE 26.   Tower Bridge 'like some big lazy East End tart from Cable Street opening her thighs'. Poster from the revival of Steven Berkoff's *Greek* at the Wyndham's Theatre (1988).

Eddy's arrival in his surrogate family is, like Oedipus' in Sophocles, really a rebirth into another world; but Eddy's new world is a
terrifyingly solipsistic one. That sex and language are intimately
interconnected in Berkoff's Freudian-informed world is underlined by the images of masturbation that recur in this first dis-
junctive part of the play.

In the first scene, Eddy's expository narrative is punctuated by
disconnected platitudes from his family, strongly reminiscent of
the Absurdist exchanges of both early Pinter and Edward Albee.
And whilst Berkoff gives over much space in his autobiography to
a detailed account of his deep admiration for Albee's *Zoo Story* (in
which he appeared to great acclaim at Stratford East in 1965—pp.
270–6), it is no doubt significant that the few terse references to
Pinter are of a personal rather than professional nature (Berkoff
literally followed in the theatrical giant's footsteps, being a few
years below Pinter at Hackney Downs Grammar School in
London). In this sense Berkoff's own Oedipal tussles with Pinter
are here in *Greek* being played out on a formal level in the harsh
East End verismo of the interchanges between the family members
at the beginning and end of the play.

After Eddy has left home following DAD's warnings about the
prophecy (here uttered by two different fortune tellers ten years
apart at the local fair), he enters into the Artaudian world of the
plague—where images of 1970s' disaffection, violence, and wanton
destruction meet with and anticipate 1980s'-style repression by
the authorities. That Eddy as repressed and isolated individual is
no more than a callous observer of his environment is underlined
by his account of a vicious racist assault on the tube, during
which 'the kicking lent a rhythmic ritual to my thoughts which
were beginning to get formed to take some mighty fine decisions
that would shoot me on my path to riches and success . . . '(113). At
this stage in his life, Eddy can only glimpse the Artaudian
heightened reality (here couched albeit in highly sexist fantasies
of priapic conquest), before he is rudely awakened into 'the
seething heaving heap of world in which I was just a little
dot'(113).

Eddy's arrival at the mythological crossroads—here Skidrow
(aka Heathrow) Airport—involves a crisis of identity that is underlined by Berkoff in a deftly enacted choral improvisation. The
Family as chorus provides an accompaniment of airport sounds

and noises to a syntactical muddle, in which we hear a clear allusion to that other Oedipal play, which depends on linguistic confusions, Synge's *Playboy of the Western World*:

All this confused me/who needs to go/do I, do you, do he/I decided to stay and see my own sweet land/amend the woes of my own fair state/why split and scarper like ships leaving a sinking rat/*I saw myself as king of the western world*/but since I needed some refreshment for my trials ahead, I ventured into this little café/everywhere I looked... I witnessed this evidence... of the British plague.

(113–14—my emphasis)

As the German Romantic poet Friedrich Hölderlin said of Sophoclean death scenes in general,[13] the words here in Berkoff's play are truly deadly in the scene of Eddy's (Ted Hughes-meets-Batman) onomatopoeic parricide:

[*They mime fight*]

EDDY.	Hit hurt crunch pain stab jab
MANAGER.	Smash hate rip tear asunder render
EDDY.	Numb jagged glass gouge out
MANAGER.	Chair breakhead split fist splatter splosh crash
EDDY.	Explode scream fury strength overpower overcome
MANAGER.	Cunt shit filth remorse weakling blood soaked
EDDY.	Haemorrhage, rupture and well. Split and cracklock jawsprung and neckbreak
MANAGER.	Cave-in rib splinter oh the agony the shrewd icepick
EDDY.	Testicles torn out eyes gouged and pulled strings snapped socket nail scraped
MANAGER.	Bite swallow suck pull
EDDY.	More smash and more power
MANAGER.	Weaker and weaker

[13] Hölderlin (1970), vol. 2, 456 (from his observations on *Antigone*). On the subterranean impact of Hölderlin's reaction to (and translation of) Sophocles' *Antigone* see also Michelakis, this volume, Chapter 7.

EDDY.   Stronger and stronger
MANAGER.   Weak
EDDY.   Power
MANAGER.   Dying
EDDY.   Victor
MANAGER.   That's it
EDDY.   Tada.
WAITRESS.   You killed him/I never realized words can kill.

                                                    (116–17)

Eddy's subsequent sexual union with the waitress/mother brings with it a new, liberated, and elevated diction, and eventually new economic benefits without any gross exploitation of others, as their greasy café thrives under its new fecund management. However, ten years on in Act II, Eddy is forced to encounter the other face of womankind in the form of the Sphinx (revealingly played by the same actress who plays his wife/mother). The Sphinx is the Kleinian anti-/stepmother, accusatory not loving; and here in Berkoff, she is also a kind of eco-warrior Gaia, whose lot is to preside over the anti-generative state (where sex peep-shows provide light relief and abortion clinics terminate would-be geniuses (123)), which has come about because of the pollution and oppression at the heart of Eddy/Everyman.

If Eddy, like Sophocles' Oedipus, is both the instrument of hope and the source of destruction, he differs from his forebear in his act of defiance in the final moments of the play. According to Berkoff, Eddy possesses a 'non-fatalistic disposition'; and in a chillingly bold act of defiance, his protagonist interrogates both Sophocles and Seneca (and especially Hughes's Seneca), as well as Freud in his refusal to give up his ideal wife, even if she is his mother (see Figure 27). As Michael Billington commented in his review in the *Guardian*, 15 February 1980, Linda Marlowe as wife-mum at least made incest 'understandable'.

Eddy vacillates between following convention and following instinct:

Oedipus how could you have done it, never to see your wife's golden face again, never again to cast your eyes on her and hers on your eyes . . . What a foul thing I have done, I am the rotten plague, tear them out, scoop them out like ice-cream, just push the thumb behind the orb and push, pull

FIGURE 27. Linda Marlowe making incest at least 'understandable' in
Steven Berkoff's *Greek* at the Half Moon Theatre (1980).

them out and stretch them to the end of the strings and then snap!
Darkness falls. Bollocks to all that ... (138)[14]

This Oedipus prefers incestuous union with his mother to violence
and destruction: 'it's love I feel it's love, what matter what form it
takes ... ' (139), Eddy utters, thereby not only illustrating the
complex, but ultimately denying the need for its very existence.

    This daringly optimistic and celebratory ending gestures in many
ways towards the Yiddish theatre enjoyed by Berkoff's grandparents in London's East End of the late nineteenth century. But if the
carnivalesque ending of *Greek* recalls Yiddish theatrical traditions,
its moral bearings lie elsewhere. Eddy's radical moral relativism is,
of course, very far removed from the Sophoclean model, in which
the erotic implications of the mother–son union are scrupulously
avoided. It is far too from the world of Freud's Vienna, where such
feelings could only be repressed and never fully expressed. Eddy's

    [14] Cf. T. Hughes (1969), 51: 'his fingers had stabbed deep into his eyesockets   he |
hooked them gripping the eyeballs   and he tugged | twisting and dragging them
with all his strength   till they | gave way ... | ... | there were rags of flesh strings
and nerve ends | still trailing over his cheeks   he fumbled for them | snapping them
off   every last shred ... '

final speech takes us instead towards that chillingly amoral universe of Jacobean tragedy; and more specifically to Giovanni's (anti-patriarchal) advocacy of brother–sister incest in Berkoff's favourite tragedy, *'Tis Pity She's a Whore* (itself a distant relative of Euripides' lost tragedy of brother–sister incest, *Aeolus*[15]).

By the end of the play Berkoff has succeeded in some senses in dragging us through the Artaudian plague and forcing us to emerge either purged or dead, according to one's levels of toler-ance. It is generally acknowledged that Berkoff's highly exhilar-ating physical theatre paved the way for companies like Théâtre de Complicité, who made their mark in the late Eighties and Nineties; but it is equally the case that plays such as *Greek* anticipated in important ways what has come to be known as the 'In yer face' drama of the late 1990s, which uses sex and violence to plumb and probe the emotional depths of both dramatic subject and audience alike. Plays such as Sarah Kane's *Phaedra's Love* (drawing as it does on both Euripides' *Hippolytus* and Seneca's *Phaedra*) pay more than a passing nod to Berkoff, as they celebrate a world in which the taboo of incest no longer pertains.

Moreover, in a world in which the traditional definitions of 'parenting' are constantly under review, in which traditional rites of passage and the gaps between generations are blurring, where the practice of IVF may well bring with it a decrease in the status of biological parents, we can readily envisage more than one way in which Berkoff's refutation of both Sophocles and Freud might be deemed path-breaking. Oedipus is still crucial, it seems, but in strikingly non-canonical ways. Finally, and perhaps most signifi-cantly, as Berkoff's version joins the other post-Sixties versions of Sophocles' tragedy in showing the *tyrannos*-outsider and his name play now re-sited on the margins of modern society, it may well be that Aristotle's paradigmatic tragedy has now assumed a different kind of importance in the repertoire, at the very same time that Classics as a discipline has lost its traditional centrality and is starting to return with new vigour and new forms from surprising new contexts (cf. Hardwick in this volume, Chapter 8).

---

[15] I am indebted to Edith Hall for pointing out that Ford's ultimate source, via Italian Renaissance tragedy, is the poetic epistle of Canace to her brother Macareus in Ovid's *Heroides* 11. This, in turn, was based on a Greek tragedy, the lost *Aeolus* by Euripides, which was in antiquity notorious for its articulation of extreme moral relativism. See E. Hall, 'Childbirth and family crisis in ancient drama' (forthcoming).

13

Thinking about the Origins of Theatre in the 1970s

Erika Fischer-Lichte

SEARCHING FOR ORIGINS

One of the reasons why Greek theatre has become so prominent in the last three decades is that the theatre has been informed by some significant theoretical and scholarly trends which emerged from the intellectual crisis of the 1960s. In 1972, for example, there appeared two anthropological studies of sacrificial ritual, René Girard's *La Violence et le sacré*, and Walter Burkert's *Homo Necans*. Both used evidence from ancient Greece to explain the practice of sacrificial ritual, and even traced the origins of Greek tragedy to ritual practice. At the same chronological point many experimental German directors turned to Greek drama, especially Klaus Michael Grüber and Peter Stein, whose *Antiquity Projects* at the Berlin Schaubühne were produced in 1974 and 1980 respectively. This chapter explores the relationship between the academic and the theatrical manifestations of interest in ancient Greece and asks why this interest sprang up in the Seventies.

This new focus on ancient Greece, in both academe and the theatre, needs to be seen in historical context. The search for origins had not been high on the agenda of the Humanities or Social and Natural Sciences in the earlier decades of the twentieth century. Nineteenth-century scholars, on the other hand, had been obsessed by it, and it is little wonder that in Classics the question of the origin of theatre—which at that time meant European theatre or, more precisely, ancient Greek theatre—featured prominently. Philologists and archaeologists alike pursued it thoroughly and with great enthusiasm. In 1839 the Greek Archaeological Society started excavating the Theatre of Dionysus at Athens, and there was enormous anticipation and excitement about the results. Not only the scientific community but also the larger public, consisting of the educated middle classes, waited impatiently for any study dealing with the origins of ancient Greek theatre, and greedily devoured every new publication on the subject.

In 1872 a new book appeared on this subject written by a young Classics scholar, Friedrich Nietzsche, who hoped it would help him qualify for a Chair in philosophy. The book, entitled *The Birth of Tragedy out of the Spirit of Music*, was not greeted with enthusiasm, however. Indeed, it caused a scandal in the Classics establishment. It did not qualify its author for the professorship for which he had hoped; instead, it cost him his reputation as a philologist and all his students at Basel University (except for one Law student and another of German Literature). It was the greatest possible failure.

What can have seemed so scandalous about a book which, by its very subject, would seem to have fitted perfectly into mainstream contemporary concerns? First and foremost, it was the statement that ancient Greek theatre originates in the Dionysian principle, which is manifested in and enacted by a chorus of satyrs, the original dithyrambic chorus. It is this principle which annuls individuation, changes individuals into a state of ecstasy, and transforms them into members of a dancing, singing community—a community in which the boundaries separating individuals are dissolved. This idea meant a slap in the face to an age in which there was a cult of the individual. The shock it caused was not even softened by the other concept Nietzsche formulated in the study, the idea that tragic theatre only comes into being as long as the Apollonian principle, the principle of individuation, is also included: it is from the collision of both principles that tragic theatre arises.

This collision not only aims to annul individuation, but is emphasized by another scandalous statement:

Greek tragedy in its oldest form dealt only with the sufferings of Dionysus...all the celebrated characters of the Greek stage—Prometheus, Oedipus and so on—are merely masks of that original hero...this hero is the suffering Dionysus of the mysteries, the god who himself experiences the suffering of individuation...This suggests that dismemberment, the true Dionysiac *suffering*, amounts to a transformation into air, water, earth and fire, and that we should therefore see the condition of individuation as the source and origin of all suffering and hence as something reprehensible.[1]

[1] Nietzsche (1993), 51–2.

It can thus be concluded that Nietzsche connected the origin of Greek theatre with a very particular ritual: the ritual of dismemberment.

That which in 1872 seemed frivolous and even sacrilegious—relating Greek tragedy, then revered almost like a holy scripture, back to archaic ritual—had become more acceptable by the turn of the century. Twenty years later, in *The Golden Bough* (which first appeared in 1890), the anthropologist James G. Frazer argued that a ritual of death and resurrection, a ritual of dismemberment, can be found in all cultures and is a universal rite. Jane Ellen Harrison, a Classical scholar and the leading spirit of the so-called Cambridge Ritualists, set out to prove that ancient Greek theatre—tragic as well as comic—originated in such a ritual. In *Themis: A Study of the Social Origin of Greek Religion* (1912) she tried to offer evidence in support of her claim that there was a pre-Dionysian ritual in which the Spring Demon (*eniautos daimōn*) was worshipped. An ancient *Ur*-ritual of this kind seemed to explain the reason why similar structures in which a deity underwent dismemberment, death, and resurrection, in a pattern corresponding to the annual cycle of seasons, could be found in many different religions—such gods include Osiris, Tamuz, Adonis, Orpheus, and Persephone. The Dionysian ritual, accordingly, was an offshoot of the ancient sacrificial ritual to the Spring Demon. The dithyramb (hymn to Dionysus) was created in the Dionysian ritual and tragedy developed from dithyrambic poetry. Thus ancient Greek theatre originated in an ancient sacrificial ritual, in the ritual of the *eniautos daimōn*.

Harrison's theory was much discussed, challenged, and refuted. Although it resembles Nietzsche's theory, it was taken seriously rather than being dismissed as scandalous. After the First World War, Jane Harrison abandoned the question of ancient Greek theatre's origin altogether and dealt with other subjects. The question seemed outdated and no longer of general interest. It was addressed only by a few specialists, who could not count on any great public resonance, even within their own disciplines. Even today it has never regained its former prominence in Classics.

It is therefore all the more surprising that, approximately a hundred years after the appearance of Nietzsche's scandalous study, the question of the origin of (European) theatre was taken up again; this time, however, the question was asked not by

Classics nor by Anthropology nor by Theatre Studies but by the theatre itself. From the Seventies onwards the German stage, which had long been acquainted with ancient Greek plays,[2] experienced a true 'boom' in productions of them. Staging ancient Greek plays—tragedies as well as comedies—came to serve diverse purposes in terms of different political, social, and cultural developments occurring at the time in Germany. These included, for instance, the so-called 68-movement, the first social-democratic/ liberal government, the RAF (Red Army Faction) terrorist movement, and society's response to it. Amongst a multitude of productions of ancient Greek plays, which were often of high artistic standard, the Berlin Schaubühne's *Antiquity Project* (*Antikenprojekt*) of 1974 stands out as unique. This is because it posed a question which was far from being topical: *What were the origins of theatre?* Why did the Schaubühne take up this quest? How did it deal with it? And what did it achieve by doing so?

THE BERLIN SCHAUBÜHNE'S *ANTIQUITY PROJECT* (1974)

The *Antiquity Project* was one of the most thoroughly prepared productions by the always thoroughly prepared Berlin Schaubühne. The preparations started in 1973 when members set out on a journey to Greece. Extensive literature on ancient Greek theatre was also carefully studied and discussed. On this occasion it was decided not to perform in the small theatre building of the Schaubühne at the Hallesches Ufer, but to create a particular environment for the performance in a huge exhibition hall on the Berlin Fairground. The project consisted of two performances, presented on two successive nights. On the first night there was a performance of *Exercises for Actors*, directed by Peter Stein. On the second night, Euripides' *Bacchae* was performed in a production by Klaus Michael Grüber.

The stage for *Exercises for Actors* was designed by Karl-Ernst Herrmann.[3] On the first night, the floor of the hall, slightly gradu-

---

[2] See Flashar (1991).

[3] For my analyses of the *Antiquity Project*, Peter Stein's production of the *Oresteia* (1980), and Einar Schleef's production of *The Mothers* (1986), I have referred both to my own memory and also to video recordings of the performances, reviews, and programme notes.

ated on three sides, was covered with soil. Seats for the spectators were hollowed out in the soil. This created a single space which barely separated the acting space from that of the spectators. A huge clock hung from the ceiling, reminiscent of a train station. Every five minutes the voice of Bruno Ganz (who would perform Pentheus on the second night) announced the time over a loud-speaker. The actors entered the hall one after the other; they spread out in the space, adopting a relaxed attitude with their heads slightly bowed. At eight o'clock the signal for the beginning was struck.

The *Exercises* consisted of six parts: 'Beginnings', 'The Hunt', 'The Sacrifice', followed by the intermission featuring a satyr play. After the intermission, a kind of initiation rite was performed, and the evening concluded with Prometheus' response to the second *stasimon* of the chorus from the Aeschylean *Prometheus Bound* (436–506). The titles of the first three parts before the intermission, as well as the initiation rite after it, recall a book on ancient Greek sacrificial practices which had appeared a year before the Schaubühne began their preparations for the *Antiquity Project*: Walter Burkert's study *Homo Necans* (1972). Here the Swiss philologist and anthropologist had developed a new theory of sacrifice by pointing to ancient Greek sacrificial practices. He had connected the sacrifice with the hunt and the meal on which the hunters feast after a successful hunting expedition. Burkert had identified three parts of the sacrifice: the beginnings (which consist of cleansing rites, dressing up in new clothes, self-decoration, often sexual abstinence, forming a procession, and all the procedures right up to the killing of the sacrificial animal); the killing of the animal and its dismemberment (*sparagmos*); the burning of the bones on the altar and the shared meal of meat (*ōmophageia*). The titles used by the Schaubühne—'Beginnings', 'The Hunt', and 'The Sacrifice'—drew heavily on this theory. Later, Burkert had also dealt with Greek initiation rites; this part of *Exercises* also alluded to his book. In adopting these very specific headings, *Exercises for Actors* therefore directly referred to the most up-to-date theory about Greek sacrificial rituals.

At eight o'clock, when the signal to begin was given, the actors started to move. They walked, breathing slowly, moving their different limbs and reaching out with their hands. Repeatedly they began the same movements anew: from breathing they developed sounds, and from the sounds there developed screaming.[4] Whatever exercises they performed, the particular differences between the actors were emphasized. 'Walking' was performed by one actor in a refined, elegant way, by the next rather clumsily, and so on.

'Beginnings' is an ambiguous piece. Of course, on one level, it simply means the beginning of the performance. However, since it is the beginning of an 'antiquity project', it also implies much more. It can be taken as the beginnings of theatre in that the human body is the first and foremost material of theatre. Wherever theatre exists human bodies are involved. A performance is created out of the particular possibilities offered by the physical body. It is therefore not completely out of place to understand the beginnings of the *Antiquity Project* as a meditation on the beginnings of theatre.

The second part, 'The Hunt', began with the separation of three protagonists from the community of actors, which was, of course, reminiscent of the separation of the actor from the chorus in Greek theatre and of the further development of theatre: Aeschylus is said to have introduced the second actor and Sophocles the third (Aristotle, *Poetics* 4. 1449ª). In the ancient Greek theatre there were no more than three actors. In Berlin the three actors took over the parts of hunters and victim. The hunters (Otto Sander and Peter Fitz) were dressed in long, light-coloured coats and wore large dark hats and sunglasses. They looked as if they had stepped out of a spaghetti Western. The victim (Heinrich Giskes) looked like something between a human and an animal, a mythical figure. The action of the hunt could thus be located in archaic as well as in modern culture. The tracking down of the victim not only entailed allusions to Burkert's theory of sacrifice and the function of the hunt he had expounded, but it also revealed itself as one of the main subjects of theatre (and later film) from the age of the Greeks until the present day. In the third part, 'The Sacrifice', the actors brought in an object made of animal skulls and bones. They wound woollen threads around it, recalling Burkert's description of how the horns of the sacrificial animal were wrapped up with bandages. The actors danced around the object; they explored different ways of creating a kind of collective body by using their

---

[4] For this description see also Jäger (1974).

individual bodies in particular ways, and experimented with complicated rhythms.

The second and the third parts were as ambiguous as 'Beginnings'. They may have referred to Burkert's ideas about how hunt and sacrifice are related to each other. They may also be taken as a tentative statement concerning the origin of Greek theatre. It was not only Nietzsche and the Cambridge Ritualists who had derived its origin from dismemberment rites. In 1972, that is in the same year as the appearance of Burkert's study, René Girard published his theory of sacrifice, *La Violence et le sacré*. In this book he explained theatre as originating in a crisis within the sacrificial cult. So he, too, connected the origin of Greek theatre with sacrifice. 'The Hunt' and 'The Sacrifice' may well have pointed to this relationship.

On the other hand, these two parts can be seen as anticipating the action of the second night, the performance of *Bacchae*, in particular the tracking down of Pentheus and his dismemberment. Apart from anything else, the actions were complicated exercises for actors, as in the fifth part after the intermission. Both actors and spectators were separated according to sex: a kind of initiation rite was performed. Three actors in each group were undressed, beaten, buried, unburied, smeared with slime, and their faces painted like masks. They had to relearn how to perceive and how to move. Actions were performed (to be picked up again in *Bacchae*), such as the unearthing of bodies, covered with slime. Yet this part could also be associated with yet another theory about the origin of Greek theatre. In *Aeschylus and Athens* (1941), George Thomson had argued that Greek theatre's origins lay in particular initiation rites.

We can conclude, therefore, that *Exercises for Actors* did indeed reflect upon the beginnings of theatre: on different kinds of rituals as possible origins—sacrificial or initiation rituals—and on the human body, which is the basis, main material and foremost condition of theatre. *Exercises* did not, however, attempt to provide evidence to support particular statements. Instead it opened up different possibilities which all stressed the performative. Each piece placed emphasis on the human body, which moves in space and utters sounds, as well as on bodily enactment of ritual patterns such as those in 'The Hunt', 'The Sacrifice', and the initiation rites.

The last part introduced language. Until then, the actors had only used their voices for creating different kinds of sounds and screams. Now the spectators of different sexes were reunited. They were pushed through a narrow opening into another part of the hall. Prometheus was here bound to one of the walls. Two actors were covering him in plaster. As Prometheus moved from stammering the first words of the evening, speaking the monologue cited above, his body steadily disappeared underneath the plaster. When he pronounced his last sentence (*Prometheus Bound*, 505), 'All arts that mortals have come from Prometheus', only his mouth was visible and the words were reduced to stammering again. This part was no less ambiguous than the previous ones. Yet it did introduce a material which, in European theatre, proved to be as fundamental as the human body (language), and the exercises turned out to be exercises in language: the actor tried out different kinds of vocal delivery (melodrama, ridicule, exaggeration, and so on). Nonetheless, language was shown to be not a supplement to the body, but its opponent: the more language developed, the more the body vanished. However, once the body was 'gone', language also ceased to exist and deteriorated into the stammering from which it sprang. This part therefore reflected on the rather complicated relationship between body and language in theatre. Language was developed from a 'bound' body which was incapable of moving; it dissolved itself from the body and became independent of it (just as the texts of Greek plays handed down to us are detached, as disembodied language, from the original performance from which they derive). But, without a body, language in theatre seems to degenerate: in the theatre, language is only feasible as embodied language. Disconnected from the body, language is not able to constitute theatre. So by reflecting on the origins of theatre, on its possible roots in different kinds of rituals as well as on its main materials, primarily bodies and language, the piece actually ended up reflecting on the particular relationship between body and language in the theatre (and perhaps even between performance and text).

In *Exercises for Actors* the statements Peter Stein made on the origins of theatre, or on the relationship between body and language, were not explicit. Rather, he opened up different perspectives on these issues without favouring any particular solution. Moreover, by instructing the actors to perform strange actions such as those in the second, third, and fifth parts, and by exposing the alien nature of such actions, it was intimated that whatever the origins of Greek theatre may be, they are alien and, in the end, incomprehensible.

On the second night there was a production of Grüber's *Bacchae*. A huge planked area marked the field of play in the exhibition hall, and it was embraced by the spectators on two sides arranged at right angles to each other (stage design by Gilles Aillaud and Eduardo Arroyo). The back wall had four openings: on the left, a road-sweeping machine was parked and manned by figures in yellow plastic suits; in the middle were two doors, one closed, the other open to reveal a man dressed in a tuxedo, drinking a glass of champagne and watching the arena; on the right, two horses stood behind a glass pane. On the ceiling there were a number of ventilators and neon lights which lit the hall brightly. Stravinsky's *Apollon Musagète* was played. Dionysus (Michael König), holding a woman's shoe in his hand, was pushed onto the stage on a hospital trolley (see Figure 28). He was naked, except for a G-string—as were all the male figures in the performance. He began the prologue stammering, searching for the word 'I'.

Then the Bacchae made their entrance. They were all dressed differently, each highly individually. They inspected the room, fingered the ventilators and the walls which closed the playing area at the back, turned off the lights, and began to tear up the planks from the floor. Clumps of soil, fruit, lettuce, and wool were thrown up. Finally, they unearthed the elderly Cadmus (Peter Fitz) and Tiresias (Otto Sander), thoroughly covered in slime. Then the naked Pentheus (Bruno Ganz) appeared. His first words were passages from Wittgenstein's diaries, more precisely, the entries from 31 May 1915 and 8 July 1916 on the problems of describing the world by naming: 'There are only two godheads: the world and my independent I.'[5] As Pentheus spoke, the road-sweeping machine drove onto the stage and swept away the 'filth' created by the Bacchae. The yellow figures replaced the boards and Pentheus ordered the neon lights to be turned on again. The Bacchae, who had become immobile, slowly started moving again. They tried to combine the words 'Pentheus' and 'hybris',

---

[5] Wittgenstein (1979), 53 and 74–6: 'Es gibt zwei Gottheiten: die Welt und mein unabhängiges Ich.'

FIGURE 28.   Michael König as Dionysus in *Bakchen*, directed by Klaus Michael Grüber, from *Antiquity Project* in Berlin (1974).

and they delivered exercises on Greek terms such as *orgiazein*, 'to perform a sacred act'.

As the performance continued, there were many other similarly striking and enigmatic images which, superimposed on each other, intersected and cut through the linear succession of the dialogue and the choral passages. When Dionysus and Pentheus met for the first time, they came very close to each other, greeted each other with an intimate kiss, touched each other, and almost melted into one person. When Dionysus persuaded Pentheus to put on women's clothes, so that he could observe the women on Cithaeron safely, Pentheus put on the female shoe which Dionysus had been holding on his entrance. The messenger reporting Pentheus' death remained on the same spot to give his report, as yellow slime dripped down his naked body. He spoke torturously slowly, in a singing vocal tone, listening to each of the sounds he produced.

After Agave (Edith Clever) killed her son, there was no dismembered body lying on the stage. Instead of putting the body of his grandson back together, Cadmus helped Agave to sew together pieces of the suit that the man in the tuxedo had worn: stand-up collar, tails, white shirt, and grey patent leather shoes. They sewed and sewed and sewed—and never came to an end.

In this production, Grüber also focused on the subject determined by the agenda of the last part of the *Exercises for Actors*—the question of the relationship between language and body, text and performance in theatre. He established a totally new kind of relationship between the text and the bodies, actions, objects, and images on stage. On the one hand, there was obviously an interpretative relationship between some stage objects, bodily actions and images, and parts of the text. For example, Pentheus appeared at the same moment that the road-sweeping machine drove onto the stage. This device, as well as Pentheus' order to switch on the lights, could be taken as an interpretation of Pentheus as a man of law and order. On the other hand, there were objects, actions, and images which could scarcely be related to the dramatic text and which triggered associations going far beyond it (the naked, slime-covered bodies, the horses, the sewing together of parts of clothes, the attempts to give various explanations of a Greek term, the inclusion of the Wittgenstein text). The associations they triggered were certainly very different for each different spectator. Ambiguity was the predominant thing generated by the performance.

Moreover, it also revealed a particular attitude towards the past, developing an idea Stein initiated in *Exercises for Actors*—a meditation on the fundamental strangeness of archaic as well as classical Greek culture. Grüber's production demonstrated impressively that the elements used on the stage to stand in for elements of a past world are primarily related to our own world; any meaning we attribute to them, concerning the past world we want to represent or revive, tells more about us and our present than about the past world it is meant to represent, interpret, and explain. On the contemporary stage, a revival of the ancient Greek world—or of any other past world—is impossible. No resurrection of the dead will take place here. The past is lost and gone forever. What remains are only fragments—play texts torn out of their original contexts—which cannot convey their original meaning. They are mute, distant, alien, and because of this it is not possible to stage them as if they were contemporary plays.

Yet the performance did not aim to create the same image of the past for each and every spectator, nor to unite the individual spectators into a community, but rather to highlight the possible differences between the spectators—their individuality. In the same way it also highlighted differences between the members of the chorus. While on the one hand, the means of individualization were bodies dressed differently and which moved differently, on the other, individualization was achieved by using elements which might trigger widely different associations in each spectator, and in this way, arouse various emotions and initiate highly different processes of meaning generation. The performance, therefore, did not aim to create a de-individualizing community either out of the chorus members or out of the spectators. In this regard, it took a pronounced anti-Nietzschean stance.

In another sense, however, there were resonances of Nietzsche throughout the performance. Clearly, the performance did not serve the purpose of conveying the text of *Bacchae* or a particular reading of it. If we want to characterize the relationship between text and performance in Grüber's production, Nietzsche's notion of dismemberment comes into mind. It makes good sense to think about the term *sparagmos*.[6] For, in this case, staging the play meant 'tearing apart' its text. The textual 'body' of *Bacchae*, so to speak, had to be sacrificed in order to give birth to the performance of *Bacchae*. This performance of a Greek tragedy constituted a sacrificial ritual. The sacrifice, however, did not result in the deification of the victim, as Girard describes it, nor in the restoration of the dismembered body. That is to say, the performance did not come into being by putting together the fragments and pieces of the dismembered textual 'body' of the play. Rather, something totally new emerged, permanently reflecting its relationship to the text which, since it remained closed, strange, remote, and, in the end, indecipherable, had to be sacrificed in order to allow the performance to take shape.

In the final image of the performance, Cadmus and Agave appeared to be sewing parts of a contemporary spectator's clothes to the scenes unfolding on stage. Instead of having Cadmus put

---

[6] The Greek word denotes the process of tearing the sacrificial animal apart.

the fragments and pieces of Pentheus' dismembered body back together again, Grüber created images of a never-ending process of stitching and re-stitching which was open to several different readings. It could be read as a commentary on the process of staging Greek—and perhaps other classical—texts. In this process the textual 'body' has to be dismembered. It is accessible not as a whole but only in its single parts and pieces. The performance will thus never be able to convey the text. It may pretend to put together the bits and pieces of the text and to come into being as a restoration, a resurrection on stage. But this is a delusion. The performance can be no more than a sewing together of parts of a contemporary spectator's clothes—sewing and sewing and sewing and never coming to an end. Not even the sacrifice of the text-body will redeem us or admit us into the paradise of an unmediated understanding of ancient Greek tragedy. By performing a sacrificial ritual, the production of a Greek tragedy allows us, at best, to reflect on our fundamental distance from it and perhaps to include some fragments of it into our present theatre, into our contemporary culture. Our distance from the past of Greek tragedy and Greek culture, cannot, in principle, be bridged—at least not by theatre and its performances of ancient Greek plays. Thus the purpose of staging Greek—and other classical—texts is to remind us of this distance and to enable us to find ways of coping with it individually and perhaps to insert fragments of such texts into the context of our contemporary reflections, life, and culture. It cannot accomplish a return to the origins—whatever they might have been. They are gone and lost forever.

Nonetheless, the idea that theatre sprang from a sacrificial ritual is relevant to this performance, even if in a completely different sense. For Grüber's production also reflected on the typical process of staging a text in general in the western tradition. To stage a text means to perform a *sparagmos* and an *ōmophageia*.[7] The participants, the actors, musicians, stage director, and designer dismember the text and incorporate it into a performance piece by piece. They proceed somewhat in the manner of a Greek sacrificial meal as described by Walter Burkert, for they incorporate that which they, a 'priest', or some ruling 'Zeitgeist', have declared to

---

[7] This is the Greek term for the sacrificial meal, during which parts of the animal are torn off and consumed.

be edible. That which appears to them as 'bones', inedible 'innards' or even 'fatty vapour' is left to the 'gods'; that is, they will not be considered in the instance of this particular production. In this sense, each and every production, which comes into being by the process of staging a text, performs a ritual of sacrifice. Grüber's production suggested the outline of an idea of theatre directly connected with ritual sacrifice. Because it proceeds from the text, European theatre is founded on sacrifice and is performed each night as a sacrifice. For the text, disconnected from the bodies of the actors, turns into stammering. It is only by way of its dismemberment that it gains new life, that it can be resurrected. In this respect, the origin of our theatre is indeed sacrificial ritual.

We are now in a position to return to our initial question: Why did the Schaubühne's *Antiquity Project* take up the seemingly outdated quest for the origins of theatre? The performative turn which German culture experienced from the Sixties onwards led to a radical change in staging practices. After the end of the Second World War, until the beginning of the 1960s, the dominant view of the function of theatre was that it had to stage the great texts—the classics—in order to convey the timeless ideas, ethical norms, and values incorporated in them by the poets, to audiences who were hungry for such nourishment after the shattering of all values during the Third Reich. This implied a certain hierarchy: since it is the text which implies such values, it is primary to the performance; without a text there would be no performance. It is the task of the performance to convey the meanings of the text, to be as 'true' to the text as possible. Thus, in the end, it is the text which constitutes theatre.

In the Sixties, this idea was challenged by a new generation of stage directors such as Peter Zadek, Hansgünther Heyme, Claus Peymann, Peter Stein, and Klaus Michael Grüber. They proclaimed not only new forms of political theatre—in a broad sense of the word—but also a new retheatricalization, a deliberate return to the 'proper' means of theatre, such as the human body and its performative as well as expressive potential. Theatre, they believed, needed to develop from a 'hermeneutic', interpretative institution, which conveys timeless values formulated in the texts of the classics, into an unmistakably performative art and an interventionist 'political' institution. The primacy of the text was thus refuted. The classical texts were now read in terms of their potential topicality and performed accordingly. It was no longer the task of the director to interpret the texts and to convey their meanings by way of 'adequate' theatrical means, but to create performances which would work on the senses of the spectators and challenge them to reflect. This would bring out new relationships between actors and spectators and open up new possibilities for aesthetic experience. Some critics furiously denounced this new theatre as 'Regietheater' (director's theatre), which, they argued, so abuses the texts that they have to be protected from the 'tyranny' of the young stage directors.

This was—broadly speaking—the situation to which the *Antiquity Project* of the Schaubühne responded. By taking up the quest for the origin of theatre and by using a classical Greek text, it took a stance within this debate. It did uncompromisingly challenge the criticism that 'Regietheater' is not 'true' to the text by showing that there cannot be anything like truthfulness to the text, that in being staged a text can never keep its so-called 'integrity' unless it is dismembered. The text has to be sacrificed in order to let the performance come into being. Without the dismemberment of the text, there cannot be a performance of the text. In another respect, the *Antiquity Project* strongly supported the shift of the focus from text to performance by featuring the body of the actor as the main material of the theatre—as in *Exercises for Actors*—as well as by the particular use which *Bacchae* made of the actors' bodies. In this sense, 'Regietheater' was proven to be not the theatre of a tyrannical stage director but a theatre which liberates the actor and his body—that is, in the end, an actors' theatre.

Yet the *Antiquity Project* can even be understood as a critique of certain forms of 'Regietheater' which appropriate classical texts as mouthpieces for current political and social concerns. By emphasizing and exposing how strange, distant, alien, and, ultimately, indecipherable, ancient Greek texts are for members of contemporary German culture, *Bacchae* showed that they were unsuitable for simple topical purposes. By dealing with the issue of the origin of theatre, the *Antiquity Project* therefore also dealt with the controversy over the new German theatre, or 'Regietheater'. It justified the reversal of the hierarchy between text and performance, word and body, and, at the same time, problematized attempts to relate classical texts directly to current political and social claims and concerns. It thus marked the distance separating the present and the past from which the text stems, and posed the problem of the inaccessibility of the past. It made it clear that theatre does not allow for an unmediated encounter with the past, that it cannot 'revive' it. The *Antiquity Project* proposed an encounter with the past based on deep intellectual reflection in addition to an encounter with the texts stemming from it. Sacrificing the text, according to this proposal, could not be synonymous with ruthlessly appropriating a text or with radically topicalizing it. Certainly, it meant that the text must be dismembered. But one had to reflect on the purposes of such a dismemberment. The question was therefore raised as to who 'the gods' are, to whom a text is sacrificed—that is, what kind of performance comes into being.

PETER STEIN'S *ORESTEIA* AT THE SCHAUBÜHNE (1980)

Six years after the *Antiquity Project*, the Schaubühne launched another antiquity project which, in many respects, referred to the first. It also addressed the question of theatre's origin, but took quite another stance. While in the first *Antiquity Project* the Schaubühne had used one of the last of the surviving Greek tragedies (*Bacchae* was first produced in 405 BCE), this time they turned to one of the earliest texts and the only surviving trilogy: Aeschylus' *Oresteia* (first performed in 458 BCE). The director was Peter Stein.

The choice of theatrical space was in pronounced antithesis to the first *Antiquity Project* at the Schaubühne. The *Oresteia* was performed in the small theatre of the Schaubühne at the Hallesches Ufer. This production, the final one at this venue, marked the end of an era. A few weeks after the *Oresteia* premiered there, the new Schaubühne theatre, a cinema built by Mendelsohn at the Lehniner Platz (1927/8) and redesigned by Jürgen Sawade, was inaugurated with a repeat performance of the *Oresteia*.

Karl-Ernst Herrmann's spatial design maintained a clear separation between stage and auditorium. Both areas were arranged, however, in a unique way. In an allusion to the Theatre of Dionysus in Athens, the auditorium gradually sloped to the back wall in low, felt-covered steps where approximately four hundred spectators squatted uncomfortably, leaving free a broad passage leading from the door back left to the stage. The stage was raised to a level considerably higher than that of the auditorium, in almost direct provocation of theatre avant-gardists such as Vsevolod Meyerhold and Emil Piscator in the 1920s, or Richard Schechner and Ariane Mnouchkine in the 1960s and 1970s, who despised such raised stages. In the centre of the platform, five steps led from the auditorium to the stage. During the first two parts of the trilogy, *Agamemnon* (subtitled *The Butcher is Butchered*) and *Libation Bearers* (subtitled *The Liberator Turns Mad*), the stage was barely used. Instead it was enclosed by a huge wall made of black panels. A large door in the middle of this 'iron curtain' was open a crack to allow the guardian, the nurse, and particularly Clytemnestra to come out in order to talk to the citizens of Argos from the platform. At the end of both parts, however, it opened wide to allow the *ekkuklēma* to be rolled out. A 'tableau' was created on it summarizing the subtitles: Clytemnestra (Edith Clever), wearing a white, blood-stained blouse, holding up a huge sword dripping with blood, stood with legs astride and head and shoulders raised over the bloody corpses of Agamemnon (Gunter Berger) and Cassandra (Elke Petri). Orestes (Udo Samuel), wearing a white, blood-stained shirt, stretched over the bloody bodies of Clytemnestra and Aegisthus (Peter Fitz), one hand holding a sword, dripping with blood, the other, the branch of an olive tree.

It was not until the intermission before the third part, *Eumenides* (subtitled *The Vampires Bless the City*), that the black wall was first sprayed white (the temple of Apollo) and then, in the course of the performance, completely removed. The stage, linked by several flights of five stairs to the auditorium, was now used by the protagonists: Athene (Jutta Lampe), who sailed in on a kind of swing over the heads of the spectators to reach the stage; Apollo (Peter Simonischek), who rode down to it in an elevator; Orestes; the citizens of Athens, who served as judges sitting at a long, narrow table; and the Erinyes (see Figure 29). During the first two parts it had been quite dark in the auditorium. Light only entered from time to time through the open doors upper left and at both sides in front, paving lanes of light through the darkness. Sometimes the only light came from the dim glow of torches which the chorus of old men used as they shuffled through the auditorium. In the third part, however, the stage was brightly lit.

The closed stage of the first and second parts meant that the auditorium was turned into a stage. In the middle of the steps,

FIGURE 29. Athena and the Erinyes in the 1980 production of *Die Orestie*, directed by Peter Stein in Berlin.

where the spectators squatted, was a table reserved for the twelve old men, the citizens of Argos, dressed in grey, worn-out coats and grey hats. They assembled here again and again, having spread out through the auditorium, amongst the spectators. In the second part, Agamemnon's tomb was erected here, and here Electra (Tina Engel) and her servants, dressed in black garments and headscarves, poured their libations like mourners at a funeral. The auditorium was even used in the third part, on occasion, by various actors, but this was rather the exception. The Erinyes, for example, advanced in formation through the auditorium to the stage, and, after Orestes was acquitted, he departed through the auditorium, shaking hands with various spectators as if thanking them personally for his acquittal.

This use of space related to shifts within the relationship between the auditory space (*auditorium*) and visual space (*theatron*). The almost totally dark space of the first two parts was designed primarily as an auditory space. Human voices were heard in the darkness articulating strange sounds—in a similar way to the figures in the *Exercises for Actors* in the 'hunt' section years before. The old men, for example, produced an insistent murmuring with their lips closed, which gradually became a whimpering, whistling sound. Or the *ololugmos* (ritual cry) could be heard—a sound of screaming, singing, humming with fluttering voice and falsetto, like crickets chirping or like the call of a bird. Most of all, however, the voices articulated verbal sounds. Words emerged from the darkness. A kind of language developed, although the bodies of those uttering it were hardly visible. Such an arrangement might recall the last part of *Exercises*, where the body was disappearing while language emerged, and language deteriorated into stammering when the body was no longer visible. Here, clearly, the relationship between language and body was defined differently, although not in such an extreme or pronounced way.

The way in which the words emerged from the almost invisible bodies was quite remarkable. One of the old men murmured a sentence while others, scattered in space, repeated it, varying its volume, pitch, and tempo. The differently 'orchestrated' sentences of the chorus reached the ears of the spectators from various directions. Somewhere a Greek word was heard, complementing and contrasting the sound of German words with that of a foreign language. The German words and sentences which followed it appeared to be vain attempts to find adequate translations for a Greek term—a device which in some respects recalls the chorus in Grüber's *Bacchae*. Through these strange sounds other meanings emerged. In the auditory space, sound and meaning were directly related to one another. The particular materiality of the voices articulating verbal sounds, the particular sound quality of voice and language, created a specifically new meaning in the confrontation of different sounds. Audiences were thereby made aware of the difficulty of finding an adequate German translation of the Greek terms.

This manner of dealing with language in the performance was not only practised by the chorus. It was typical of the whole production. In discovering ever new vocal-verbal variations, the fragile interdependency of sound and meaning was permanently tested anew, realized, and made obvious to the listener. The procedure was principally made possible by the particular translation used. This was done by Stein himself, taking into account current research as well as previous translations. In comparison with these, Stein's version is immediately striking for its great length, for he refused to make a final decision in favour of any one of all possible variant terms with which to translate something. Instead, he maintained the full spectrum of possible terms.

A translation was thus created which, although it tells the old story with impressive clarity, nonetheless continually points to the difficulties in attributing meaning to it today. Stein's philological precision, his decision not to cast aside a variant which current research had declared possible, did not lead to a 'faithful' translation, but rather questioned the whole notion of such a thing in principle. Each variant sounded different, each sound evoked another meaning. The production decisively refused to convey any 'original' meaning of the ancient and distant story, or even one particular possible present-day meaning. Rather, it opened up the possibility of reflecting on the deeply problematic relationship between historicity and topicality which underlies and is the condition of a theatrical working process drawing on an ancient foreign text as material. In this respect Stein continued in his *Oresteia* what Grüber had achieved in his *Bacchae*. This point was also made by the archaeological reconstruction of objects and actions. The offering of flour presented by the servants on the platform (*Libation Bearers*), or the libations of wine and milk which Electra poured over Agamemnon's tomb, were all performed with the greatest possible precision. Each action was clearly recognizable and describable, though the meaning of each remained obscure and sealed.

The auditory space of the first two parts of the trilogy can be described as a verbal space ('Sprachraum'). When, in the third part, the wall was removed and the stage became visible, the visual space gained at least equal rights with the auditory space. At this point the play was transferred from the auditorium to the stage which, brightly lit, offered a clear focal point for the spectator's gaze. The predominance of language, however, gained in value. Now the actions and images on stage frequently served the purpose of commenting on the spoken words, or emphasizing particular components of their meaning. For instance, after Athene had persuaded the Erinyes to settle down in Athens as Eumenides, the citizens of Athens accompanied them down the steps from the stage to chairs placed between the flights of stairs. Here they tied the same purple garments around them on which Clytemnestra had persuaded Agamemnon to tread when he entered the palace. They were bound so tightly that they could not move. The action on stage was a comment on the act of persuasion, as well as on its content. For the German word 'einwickeln' is ambiguous. It means 'to tie around' as well as 'to talk someone into something', 'to trick someone'. Athene's persuasion of the Erinyes thus entailed the different meanings of 'einwickeln', the consequences of which were acted out on-stage. This entailed a pun on another German term, 'einbinden', which means 'to bind', 'to bandage' and 'to integrate'. Athene promised the Erinyes she would integrate them into the community of Athens, into the *polis*. The citizens of Athens who 'bound' and 'bandaged' them, however, activated another semantic potential of the term. The 'Einbindung' of the Eumenides entailed robbing them of any possible action, immobilizing them. While the tableaux at the end of the first and second parts could be read as illustrations of the subtitles, here the tableau formed by the Eumenides, wrapped in red cloth and thus integrated ('eingebunden') into Athens' social foundation, revealed that the subtitle *The Vampires Bless the City* was no more than a myth—it did not correspond with any reality on stage. So at the end of the performance the visual space superimposed itself over the auditory space—a change to which the image of the never-ending voting process also contributed. Meaning came into existence in and through the visual space.

The relationship between text and performance which Stein established in the *Oresteia* may be understood as the antithesis of the procedure used by Grüber in *Bacchae*. In the Schaubühne *Oresteia*, the birth of theatre emerged from the spirit of language. What was performed there was another meditation on the origins of theatre or, to be more precise, on the origins of *European* theatre—a meditation which openly contradicted the reflections performed by Stein in *Exercises for Actors* and those of Grüber in *Bacchae*. Although Stein retained all the achievements of *Exercises*—such as the physical and vocal training—he took a different stance towards the issue of origin as well as towards the relationship between word and body, text and performance. Whereas in *Exercises* it was ritual—sacrificial and initiatory—which was suggested as the origin of theatre, in the *Oresteia* it was insinuated that theatre originates in language. It is the word ringing out in space which constitutes theatre. Whether this word is preceded or accompanied by bodily actions belonging to a ritual was no longer a question worthy of being pursued. For it was no longer related to the problems which face contemporary theatre.

The implied criticism of 'Regietheater' which Grüber's *Bacchae* had suggested was taken much further here—to the extent that it undermined even Grüber's position, which justified the emergence of 'Regietheater'. Stein's *Oresteia*, in this respect, took a clear stance. The performance comes into being out of language which is laid down in the text. An auditory space is thus created. Within this and beyond this a visual space then takes shape which, finally, may expand on its own. Since, in the auditory space, actors and spectators are united within one space, while the visual space confronts both groups, the transition from the prevalently auditory space to the dominance of the visual space may be understood as bringing about detachment from the ritual community as the differentiation between two groups of people—those who act and those who look on. Although, at first sight, this seems to entail a clear-cut definition of the relationship between ritual and theatre, namely, that theatre begins where the ritual community ends, a closer look obliterates such a distinction. For, if theatre comes into being when a word rings out in space, that is, by creating an auditory space, such a space is always shared by all within it. It is only the visual space which demands a confrontation between actors and spectators.

In the *Oresteia*, Peter Stein insisted on the primacy of the text in European theatre. The handing down of dramatic texts serves two important functions, among others. First, it allows us to deal with the past in a particular way on stage; secondly, it opens up the possibility of a very specific kind of creative process. Peter Stein comments:

It is the absurd miracle of European theatre that it creates dramatic texts which can be handed down and thus, even today, enable an actor to say: 'I am Prometheus'. This is not possible in any other art. When today someone paints in the style of Piero della Francesca and states, I used paint made from eggshells, then it is, at best, a copy. The actor does not copy anything. He embodies the part, as it was embodied 2,500 years ago. Through the text that is handed down and in a rather adventurous way, he is able to make contact directly with something which happened 2,500 years ago.[8]

Such contact is not to be equated with unconditional appropriation. It exposes that which cannot be clarified as something which is obscure and unintelligible, because it has a corrupt tradition. For the tradition is often fragmentary and defective, and the words and actions on today's stage related to it may remain strange and incomprehensible to both the actor and the spectator. The work done by memory ('die Erinnerungsarbeit'), as it was performed in and by the performance is, in this sense, always painful. (Could it be that the pain and torture, to which the poor spectators were exposed as they were forced to squat in a rather uncomfortable position on the steps for nearly eight hours, also alluded to this?) In this respect, Stein's *Oresteia* is not so far removed from Grüber's *Bacchae*. Both productions were fundamentally sceptical about the possibility of any kind of historical knowledge. While *Bacchae* conceded that there might exist the possibility at least of an individual finding ways to cope with the distance from the past and, perhaps, even to find ways of inserting fragments of the past into his or her present thoughts and life, Stein's *Oresteia* highlighted the difference between the *possibility* of some actual knowledge

---

[8] Peter Stein in von Becker (1997). For an edition of Stein's translation of the *Oresteia* see Seidensticker (1997).

about what an object looked like, or how an action was performed, and our *uncertainty* about the potential meanings of such objects and actions. The performances thus suggested that whatever we think we know about the past is a kind of reinvention—a construction, a fantasy.

On the other hand, the existence of the text allows for a particular kind of creative process. The transition from the dominantly auditory space to the predominance of the visual space, a transition which Stein's *Oresteia* performed, depicted a creative process which proceeds from the word and leads to the image on stage. In the beginning was the word laid down in the text and conveyed by it. Stein's *Oresteia* showed emphatically that western theatre is a theatre based on text, and this entails the conditions of its particular possibility of being. In this regard, it openly contradicted Grüber's *Bacchae*. Grüber's and Stein's productions both tried to determine the importance and meaning of text and performance in terms of their own contemporary culture, which increasingly seemed to change from a predominantly textual to a prevalently performative culture, a change indicated by the performative turn of the Sixties. Yet in doing so they took a very different stance from each other. When Grüber defined the process of staging a text as a *sparagmos* and *ōmophageia* of the text, he insisted that the text has to be sacrificed when a new order—that of the performance—is to be created. Sacrificing the text, thus, could mean performing a rite of passage which will perhaps lead us into a new performative culture. Such a performative culture, however, is not conceivable if it does not incorporate parts and pieces of the former textual culture.

Stein's *Oresteia* suggested another view. When the performance comes into being out of the language which is laid down in the text, a new performative culture is only conceivable on the basis of the old textual culture. Only if one proceeds from a text can there come into existence a performative culture able to serve the needs of the contemporary world. In Grüber's *Bacchae*, the quest for the origin of theatre served to justify, in principle, the fundamentally new approach of 'Regietheater'. In Stein's *Oresteia*, on the contrary, it aimed at rejecting it. With this production Stein broke away from 'Regietheater'. He announced a return to the text and to the Apollonian principle. The *Oresteia* marked the beginning of a new era of the Schaubühne.

POSTSCRIPT TO THE *ANTIQUITY PROJECTS*: GRÜBER'S *PROMETHEUS BOUND* IN SALZBURG (1986)

In 1986, Klaus Michael Grüber returned to Greek tragedy. He staged the Aeschylean *Prometheus Bound* at the Salzburg Festival, in the unique environment of the Felsenreitschule. This time his stage designer was Antonio Recalcati. On the broad stage of the Felsenreitschule, set in front of its natural rocks, he built a dark, bleak, eerie landscape, in which only the rock where Prometheus (Bruno Ganz) was bound was recognizable. The rest remained vague and shadowy, more to be guessed or even hallucinated than to be perceived; the only perceptible thing—except the rock—was a kind of a mythic 'world-tree'.

Grüber referred in this production to both of the Berlin Schaubühne's *Antiquity Projects*, especially the work of Stein. In some respects Grüber's *Prometheus Bound* can be understood as a commentary on the different hypotheses about the specific theatrical relationship between body and language proposed by Stein's two productions. In *Exercises for Actors* it had been insinuated that theatre is constituted by bodily actions, that language develops out of such actions and deteriorates into stammering when it dissolves completely from the body. In the *Oresteia*, on the contrary, it was proposed that theatre is born out of language—that an auditory space is created within which theatre begins. Within and beyond such an auditory space a visual space then takes shape. Grüber's *Prometheus Bound*, in a way, played off the first *Antiquity Project* against the second. Even if Prometheus was bound to the rocks, which meant that Bruno Ganz could not execute many bodily actions, it was the seemingly paradoxical relationship between his aching, suffering, almost motionless body and his mighty words, challenging the gods, which created a particular theatrical situation. And even if Angela Winkler, playing Io, used a microphone, which 'distanced' her voice and words from her body, both language and body remained related to each other because of the particular use which the actress made of her body. Grüber's production thus affirmed and modified the idea of the relationship between body and language suggested by *Exercises for Actors*.

It contradicted, however, the concept of the relationship between auditory and visual space proposed by Stein's *Oresteia*. It made clear that, in theatre, a visual space does not develop out of the auditory space which language creates. Rather, both expand simultaneously. This does not mean that they have to correspond to each other; they might exist alongside one another without being clearly related to each other, as was the case here. The somewhat mythical, shadowy, eerie landscape, and the language of the new translation by the poet Peter Handke, which brought into focus a 'modern' view of Prometheus from the perspective of the 'dialectics of Enlightenment', bore no obvious correspondence to each other. However, both demanded that the spectator/listener perceive them; both were able to set his or her imagination in motion. Thus, with this production, Grüber took a decisive stand against the so-called return to the text proclaimed by Peter Stein with and through the *Oresteia*. Even if the text used in a performance is not severely cut or radically changed, this does not mean that it is accorded primacy over the performance. The auditory space, as created by language, may expand, it is true. But it does not constitute theatre. Without a visual space, there is no theatre. It is the visual space, with its moving—or even fixed—bodies, which constitutes theatre.

In this sense, Grüber's production of *Prometheus Bound* appears to be an experiment designed to test Stein's claim. It reduced the mobility of the actors' bodies as far as possible; it expanded the spoken language to a remarkable extent—there were only rare moments without any declamation—and yet, it produced a result that does not support Stein's claim. As the Greek word *theatron* suggests, theatre is visual space, i.e. space to be seen. Language can be added, may even expand to such an extent that it never ceases throughout the course of the performance. Nonetheless, it is not language—let alone the text of a play—which constitutes theatre, but the visual space.

In constructing his experiment, and referring to the two Schaubühne *Antiquity Projects*, Grüber did not deal with the question of the origin of theatre in a historical sense, asking whence it sprang or how it developed (from ritual, for instance), but, as in his *Bacchae* and Stein's *Oresteia*, in a theoretical sense, with the question of what constitutes theatre. The answer he found in his production of *Prometheus Bound* sided with *Exercises of Actors* and contradicted the *Oresteia*. Klaus Michael Grüber has never staged another Greek tragedy subsequently.

EINAR SCHLEEF'S *THE MOTHERS* AT THE FRANKFURT SCHAUSPIELHAUS (1986)

In 1986, Einar Schleef staged Euripides' *Suppliant Women* and Aeschylus' *Seven against Thebes* at the Frankfurt Schauspielhaus. The production, which lasted almost four hours, was entitled *The Mothers*. Schleef started his career in the early 1970s, as a stage director and designer in the GDR at the Berliner Ensemble, but left for West Germany in 1976. He pursued projects in Düsseldorf and Vienna without ever finishing them. *The Mothers* was his first production in the west and until his untimely death in July 2001 remained his only production of Greek drama. In it he created a new form of theatre, a form he developed further in all his following productions.

Schleef created a unique space for *The Mothers*. Except for the back three rows (for elderly or disabled people), all the seats in the auditorium were removed. The floor of the auditorium gradually rose to the back rows in shallow steps where the spectators took their places. From the stage, a kind of catwalk, also sloping in steps, cut through the middle of the auditorium to the back wall, where behind and above the remaining seats it met with a second, narrow stage. Thus, the acting space was spread out in front, behind and in the middle of the spectators so that they were often almost surrounded by the actors.

In *The Mothers* Schleef experimented with what, from now on, would become the trademark of his theatre: the chorus. There were different choruses, all consisting of women: the chorus of widows dressed in black, meeting Theseus (Martin Wuttke) with axes in their hands; the chorus of virgins dressed in white tulle in the first part, red in the second; the chorus of women dressed in black overalls, like workers in a munitions factory. They occupied and ruled the space: the stage in front of the spectators, the catwalk where, particularly in the second part, they ran, hurried, dashed up and down, wearing black metal-toed boots, and the stage behind the spectators. While the choruses in Grüber's *Bacchae* and Stein's *Oresteia* had been intentionally individualized, in *The Mothers* all the members of each chorus not only wore identical clothes but also moved their bodies in the same rhythm, performing the same movements and speaking, whispering, shouting, roaring, howling, screaming, whimpering, and whining the words in unison.

However, this does not mean that the chorus acted as a collective body in which the individuality of the different chorus members dissolved and merged with the others. Rather, the chorus appeared as a permanent battleground between the individual who wants to join the community while having her uniqueness upheld, and the community which strives for total incorporation of all its members and threatens alienation to those who insist on their individuality. Thus, within the chorus, a permanent tension existed between the individual members and the community which they formed, a tension which caused an incessant flow within the chorus, a dynamic of transformation regarding the individual's position in, and relationship to, the community. This tension never vanished; the chorus never transformed itself into a harmonious collective; rather, the tension intensified. Over and over again, it made itself felt as an act of violence done to the individual by the community as well as to the community by the individual.

This latter violence became even more obvious whenever the chorus was confronted with another individual—Theseus or Eteocles. The conflict between Eteocles and the women of Thebes, for instance, was settled by a constant shift of the positions on the catwalk: the women lying on the steps while Eteocles stood upright above them, or Eteocles crouching while the women bent down towards him. The power struggle between the individual and the chorus was fought through a constant change of positions in the space and the force of the voices. When the women suddenly straightened themselves and, literally, shouted Eteocles down solely by the strength of their voices, he fell to his knees and cowered.

A similar permanent tension between individual and community also defined the relationship between actors and spectators. The spatial arrangement which allowed the actors to surround the spectators or to act right in the middle of them suggested the idea of a fundamental unity between actors and spectators, of a single— perhaps even harmonious—community formed out of the two groups. But this unity was permanently challenged. Whenever it came into being, the community was immediately broken up again. Instead of unity, conflicting forms were experienced. This was partly due to the ambiguous spatial arrangement. The catwalk cut through the auditorium. This allowed the actors to perform in the middle of the auditorium, but it could also be experienced as posing a permanent threat of dismemberment in terms of the collective body of the audience which it dissected. Moreover, it exposed the spectators to the violence done to them by the chorus when they trampled up and down the steps right overhead and shouted down to them, or shouted them down so that the audience felt physically attacked. Here, too, a power struggle was fought between the chorus and the audience. The ecstatic chorus aimed to overwhelm the audience, to bring about a state of ecstasy in it as well, which individual members of the audience opposed, either verbally or by leaving the auditorium. There were only rare moments when chorus and auditorium formed a harmonious community—moments of transition before the next outbreak of conflicting forces between the two groups.

In terms of his treatment of the chorus, Schleef can be seen as a disciple of Nietzsche in the sense that Nietzsche claimed that the chorus is the origin of theatre and that tragedy is constituted by the incessant battle between two conflicting principles: that of individualization and that of its destruction, or dismemberment. In his book *Droge Faust Parsifal* (*Drug Faust Parsifal*), Schleef explains:

The classical chorus presents a terrifying image: figures herd together tightly, seek protection amongst each other although they vehemently reject each other as if the proximity of another person might contaminate the air. This endangers the group itself, it will yield to any attack, precipitously and fearfully accept the idea of a necessary sacrifice, ostracize one member to buy its own freedom. Although the chorus is aware of its betrayal, it does not readjust its position, but rather places the victim in the position of someone who is clearly guilty. This is not just one aspect of the classical chorus but also a process which repeats itself every day. The enemy-chorus is not just made up of the millions of ignorant, wretched, looters and asylum seekers, but also alternative thinkers, especially those who speak their native language; they must be destroyed first, no matter how. And yet up to this decisive moment, the classical constellation is alive, if the chorus and the individual are still at war, the relationship of the chorus to the individual continues to rumble, the individuals who were isolated from each other before and as a whole against the chorus which they hope to defeat successfully.[9]

The choruses in *The Mothers*—as in all of Schleef's following productions—were not only characterized by the tensions between

---

[9] Schleef (1997), 14.

individual and community but, moreover, by another equally fundamental tension: that between body and language. It seems inevitable that Schleef—like Grüber and Stein before him—should have linked his contemplation of the origin of theatre to a contemplation of the relationship between body and language in theatre. Both intersected in the chorus.

One might assume that since there was mostly a shared rhythm synchronizing the bodily movements and the vocal recital of the choral odes, there was, if not harmony, at least a correspondence between body and language. The shared rhythm, however, functioned as the site and means of the battle. On the one hand, language tried to force its rhythm on the bodies, to inscribe it onto the bodies and thus to subordinate the bodies to its own symbolic order. On the other hand, the bodies rebelled against such an attempt. They tried to force their rhythm on the language, a rhythm which often distorted the syntactical order, so that the sentences did not make sense any more and the symbolic order of language was destroyed. Neither came off as the winner in this battle; rather, there was a permanent shift between the symbolic order of language and the ecstatic order of the body. While language tried to subordinate the ecstatic body to its symbolic order, the body strove to undermine and to subvert the symbolic order of language by dissolving it in the maelstrom of its ecstasy.

This is what made the choruses of *The Mothers*—and Schleef's choruses in general—a gripping and fascinating experience reminiscent again of Nietzsche's ideas about the birth of tragedy. What was performed by the choruses might be seen as the battle between the Dionysian principle (embodied by ecstatic dancing, running, falling bodies) and the Apollonian principle (embodied by the symbolic order of language). However, in the case of Schleef's choruses, the outcome of the battle was never predictable. As long as the performance continued, the battle moved back and forth between body and language without generating a winner. In theatre, body and language have to join forces, although they have to act simultaneously as opposing forces fighting each other inexorably. A truly tragic theatre can only come into being on this condition.

With *The Mothers* Einar Schleef laid the foundations of a new theatre, a theatre based on the chorus. He continued to develop this concept further until his very last production, *Betrayed People* (performed at the Deutsches Theater, Berlin, in 2001), in which he himself appeared on stage as Nietzsche, reciting from *Ecce Homo* for forty-five minutes. Through *The Mothers* German theatre history from Nietzsche's *Birth of Tragedy* onwards had come full circle. In his once scandalous book, Nietzsche had developed a theory about the origin of ancient Greek theatre in order to lay the foundations for a new theatre, the theatre of the future, which he saw already partly realized in Richard Wagner's musical theatre. Einar Schleef turned to ancient Greek theatre and its origin in the chorus in order to establish a contemporary form of tragic theatre, a theatre which features the complicated and ever-changing relationship between individual and community, a relationship which can never be transferred into a state of harmony or even into balance. Schleef's thinking about the origin of theatre as carried out by the chorus was undertaken in terms of the rebirth of tragic theatre, a theatre of violence which also does violence to its spectators, a theatre which physically and spiritually hurts. Schleef did not resort to ancient Greek theatre in order to emphasize its fundamental strangeness and inaccessibility, nor in an attempt to topicalize it by making references to current social and political themes. He resorted to it because he saw the chorus as the indispensable condition of tragic theatre. And this was what he was striving for—unfortunately in times which had completely lost any sense of the tragic.

CONCLUSIONS

In the early 1970s it became the trend to stage classical plays in the manner of 'Regietheater', so that there was an actual boom in productions of ancient Greek plays in German theatres. Many directors staged several such productions. Some even turned repeatedly to ancient Greek plays—both tragedies and comedies: Robert Ciulli, for example, at the Theater an der Ruhr Mühlheim. Hansgünther Heyme created more than twenty performances of ancient Greek plays (including Hartmut Lange's *Herakles* in 1968—see above, Riley, Chapter 4), or of his adaptation of the Homeric epics, at different theatres. It therefore seems all the more striking that the three stage directors who used productions of Greek plays in order to contemplate the origin of theatre from a historical as well as theoretical perspective created only one production (in the case of Grüber, two), and did not ever create new realizations of Greek drama subsequently (although Stein's *Oresteia* was later revived). In all three cases it made good sense to choose a Greek play in order to think about the origin of theatre. In *Bacchae*, the meditation consisted of making reference to Greek sacrificial practices. The *Oresteia* explored the very idea of a 'transmitted text' by using one of the oldest texts in our tradition. *The Mothers* made the case for a *choric* theatre, the model of which was located in ancient Greek theatre.

In all three cases, thinking about the origin of theatre was intended to lay the foundations for, and/or justify, a new kind of theatre. For Grüber it was his particular realization of 'Regietheater'; for Stein it was a theatre which claims to return to the text and be 'faithful' to it; for Schleef it was a new tragic theatre as a choric theatre. That is to say, thinking about the origin of theatre was designed to establish a *new* origin from which the new tradition would spring. After the 'founding event' of each of these performances, it no longer seemed necessary to resort to ancient Greek drama. The model created by reference to Greek theatre as the origin of European theatre could now be applied to all kinds of plays.

14

The Voices We Hear

Timberlake Wertenbaker

The question I hear again and again is—Why has there been such a resurgence in Greek drama, or drama inspired by the Greek plays, in the last twenty-five years or so? There have been various answers proposed, but I want to put forward a suggestion that I have not heard before. I am going to start not with the Greeks but with Shakespeare. Not even with *Troilus and Cressida* but with *Hamlet*. What is Hamlet to the Greeks, or the Greeks to Hamlet? What links him to them and to us? It is an odd link, an illogical one if you will: it is the ghost of Hamlet's father, and his famous words, 'remember me'.[1] It is the voice of the unappeased ghost, who is condemned to wander the earth because he was 'cut off even in the blossoms of my sin |...| No reckoning made, but sent to my account | With all my imperfections on my head'.[2] In other words, Hamlet's father has died unconfessed. But 'unconfessed' actually means 'without self-knowledge', because what is a confession but a telling of the truth of one's self? The person who dies without having known himself, herself—that person becomes a ghost wandering the earth, unappeased. This is also why Hamlet can not kill Claudius when he sees him praying: Claudius is 'in the purging of his soul',[3] in prayer, in a state of self-knowledge.

I do not know if it was the Greeks who invented the phrase 'know thyself', but they certainly popularized it and made it the sound-bite of Greek philosophy.[4] Know thyself. And with self-knowledge come goodness, proper action, improvement. It was held that only ignorance made us behave badly. I think it is something western civilizations have carried with them down the centuries: the belief that the human being could know himself or herself and that with that knowledge would come, so to speak, a

---

[1] The ghost's final words in *Hamlet*, I. v. 91: 'Adieu, adieu! Hamlet, remember me!'

[2] *Hamlet*, I. v. 76–9.   [3] *Hamlet*, III. iii. 85.

[4] 'Know thyself' (*gnōthi seauton*), the famous inscription on the temple of Apollo at Delphi, much cited by Plato. See especially Socrates' words at *Phaedrus* 229e.

solution, a way to a better life, to rational behaviour, and of course to better societies. Know thyself. When we say 'be rational', or 'don't be so irrational', we mean the same thing: behave with logic, make sense; that is, if you are rational, you will behave better.

Many of the Greek tragedies are tragedies of self-knowledge: Oedipus knows how to solve riddles, but he does not know who he is until the end of *Oedipus Tyrannus*. Creon thinks he knows what it is to be a good statesman, but fails and admits at the end of *Antigone* that he lacked judgement, he was blinded, he had no knowledge.[5] Sophocles' Ajax goes mad—the ultimate failure in self-knowledge. Lack of self-knowledge is tragic and brings on self-destruction: Oedipus blinds himself, Creon loses all, Aeschylus' Agamemnon dies caught in a net. His Orestes finds a sort of Greek 'happy ending' by going to Athens in *Eumenides* and seeking judgement—he comes to know himself as a citizen, and frees himself from the mad pursuit of the Erinyes. So, we could say very simply that lack of self-knowledge brings about a fall. Fine. Clear. Simple.

But look at the tragedies more closely. Who are the blazing characters? Clytemnestra, Electra, Hecuba, Medea, Phaedra, Antigone—women. And what is the relation of these women to self-knowledge? To the rational? None. None at all.

I will not go into the Greek view of women in general because it is rather hard to pinpoint, and I think it is irrelevant: irrelevant because the tragic poets were not interested in portraying women as such—as women, that is. Rather, I think they were portraying the terrifying possibility that maybe the human being was not someone to whom you could say 'know thyself', but someone to whom you would have to say: 'you are unknowable'. In other words, those characters did not have an Aristotelian plot line—first pride, then a fall, then a realization and acceptance—but remained incomprehensible, blinded to themselves, irrational and forever unresolved, haunting the rational mind. And like Hamlet's father's ghost, they remain unappeased, condemned to wander the earth. Look in particular at Orestes and Electra. Orestes' story is clear: he is told he must avenge his father, he does so by killing his mother, he is pursued by the Erinyes, he is judged in Athens. He has a plot, a beginning, middle, and end, pity, terror,

---

[5] Sophocles, *Antigone* 1261–9, 1317–20.

recognition—the whole Aristotelian tragic journey to self-knowledge. But what about Electra? She too is involved in the killing of her mother, but the Erinyes do not pursue her. Where does she go? Does she suffer? Her whole story is one of waiting for Orestes and for vengeance, and then nothing: nothing because no self-knowledge, in the form of either torment or justification, can come to her. She just goes. Unresolved. No one asks her if she is a matricide or a citizen. This is particularly acute in Aeschylus' version of the story in the *Oresteia*, but it is not that different in Sophocles' *Electra* or in Euripides'. Electra does not reach self-knowledge any more than her mother did.

Hecuba, in Euripides' play by that name (see Figure 30), starts as a rational human being. On hearing that her daughter Polyxena is to be a human sacrifice on Achilles' tomb, she argues with great

FIGURE 30.   Agamemnon (L. Peter Callender) is supplicated by Hecuba (Olympia Dukakis) and the chorus (led by Michele Shay) in *Hecuba*, translated by Timberlake Wertenbaker and directed by Carey Perloff (1998).

sense and explains the barbarity of such behaviour to Odysseus. As a Trojan she also appeals to international, mutual laws of behaviour; she even appeals to Greek law. Odysseus argues equally rationally and appeals to *raison d'état*. Soldiers should be rewarded, even with the blood of innocent girls. Hecuba grieves but accepts defeat and her daughter is wrenched from her.[6] However, when she discovers her son has been murdered by Priam's ally Polymestor, then she chooses to become irrational, she calls on the spirits of madness, she pushes herself down into that darkness in order to act and proceed to a bloody revenge on Polymestor, whom she blinds after killing his sons. It is an interesting transformation: a rational person asks for justice, but an irrational one goes and gets revenge. Polymestor, who loses his eyes, his sons, and his reputation, sees her at the end of the play as a rabid bitch with burning eyes.[7] What better image of the unappeased? Of the irrational?

I will not go through every female character. But again, Medea, having killed her children, simply goes off in a chariot, saying surprisingly little—the most unsatisfactory plot ending to one of the most haunting characters of tragedy. She is incomprehensible but believable. Jason spends the whole play justifying his acts. She never does.

Now there is always an exception, or an apparent exception, and I am coming to her: Antigone—the best plotted, most rational character of Greek tragedy, the rebel, the one who follows her own conscience (Figure 31). Antigone disobeys Creon's decree and buries her brother Polyneices. The plot of *Antigone* in fact belongs to Creon. He is the one who starts out blinded and arrogant, and ends self-consciously sorry. Antigone never wavers, nor is her decision reasoned. Again and again she simply appeals to more ancient laws than Creon's decrees, laws she says the state cannot overrule: you honour the dead of your family whether they are enemies or not. She does not justify the law. That is why the passage in which she explains, rationally, why her brother means so much to her (because she is never going to get another one) is of highly dubious authenticity and I have always left it out in

---

[6] This confrontation occurs at Euripides, *Hecuba* 218–440. See Wertenbaker (1996a), 15–26.

[7] Euripides, *Hecuba* 1265. See Wertenbaker (1996a), 56.

FIGURE 31. Joanne Pearce as Antigone with members of the chorus in *The Thebans*, translated by Timberlake Wertenbaker and directed by Adrian Noble, at the Swan Theatre, Stratford-upon-Avon (1991).

translation.[8] Antigone is actually possessed by ancient custom; she herself is haunted by her family ghosts, she invokes them, she is obsessed by them (as we would say), and in the end she joins them. She may indeed be heroic in the classic sense, but she is still unselfconscious. So she is and is not an exception.

There is another curious exception in the other direction—Oedipus. In *Oedipus Tyrannus* he is the most self-conscious of heroes, the one who struggles most with this question of self-knowledge. Fine. But now look at *Oedipus at Colonus* and you find someone going back on everything he has said: you find an angry old man, an irrational one, denying he ever wanted to go into exile. Listen to him:

You might say I myself wanted this and the city reasonably granted my wish. It is true that on the day it all happened [*the day*—i.e. the whole of *Oedipus Tyrannus* when Oedipus discovered his identity], my spirit was boiling, and it would have pleased me to die . . . Only later, when my

---

[8] Sophocles, *Antigone* 900–28.

distress was eased and I understood that my spirit had been excessively harsh on my past failings . . . [9]

Listen to the last words: 'my spirit had been excessively harsh on my past failings'. *Oedipus at Colonus*, written so late in Sophocles' life, lasting hours, is one of the most intriguing plays I have worked on, because Oedipus simply does not make sense. He curses his sons with breathtaking cruelty; he celebrates the future destruction of his house. And, in the end, he does not die: it is a kind of peaceful apotheosis—very beautiful. But it is as if Sophocles, having resolved him in the first *Oedipus*, unresolved him and literally turned him into a ghost.

What then does this have to do with us now? Why do we go back to the plays? I would suggest that after two thousand and some years of philosophy, more than a hundred years of psychology and psychotherapy, after centuries of science, after even, most recently, the Genome Project telling us what is in our genes, after watching the great rational political experiments crumble in our faces, we are beginning to feel what the Greek playwrights suspected but feared to say all along: the human being may perhaps be unknowable—unknowable and ultimately irrational. And it is a terrible thought. Because if unknowable, if irrational, then no amount of science, philosophy, or politics will make us better, will make us behave better, will give us the self-understanding to behave better. It was one of the frightening conclusions of the twentieth century, after the horrors of the Second World War, Chile, and the hot sores of the Balkan wars and Afghanistan, that we do not seem to progress morally as human beings: we know more, but we seem to understand less and less about ourselves. And so the human being is truly an object of fear and pity. And we were warned of this thousands of years ago by the characters, the unappeased characters of tragedy—the women, mostly, who could not know themselves but have called out to us again and again: 'Remember me. Remember me.'

Is this a bleak end? I am not sure. Because if you look at, write, see in performance the unknowable human being, you will not

[9] Sophocles, *Oedipus at Colonus* 431–9. Oedipus completes the sentence by saying, 'then, then, the city drove me out by force—so long afterwards'. The translation is that of Timberlake Wertenbaker, from *The Thebans*, a translation of Sophocles' three tragedies about Oedipus and his family, first performed at the Swan Theatre, Stratford-upon-Avon, in 1991. See Wertenbaker (1997), 58.

close off with the conclusions that have brought so much destruction on our world: you will not insist—even to the death—that this is the right way to love, this is the political system that works, and you are the one who knows best. You will wonder at the human being as Sophocles asked us to in the second chorus of *Antigone*:

> Wonder
> at many things
> But wonder most
> at this thing:
> Man...[10]

In the chorus you are asked to wonder at what humanity can do, but let us now start wondering at what humanity *cannot* do. We cannot conclude ourselves. We cannot bring our plot to an end. We are forever unresolved. It is painful and frustrating. So much of our drama is about the conclusion of revelation, self-knowledge. What happens without it? I think it is why much modern theatre retreats into little stories about small lies, or into a portrayal of mindless violence. Either/or: you know that when you lie you can conclude the plot, while mindless violence ignores the rational and you avoid the question altogether.

I think there is something more interesting at stake. The need for truth, for self-knowledge, is profoundly human. That it may be out of reach, forever out of reach, is profoundly painful and equally human. In *Dianeira*, in which I used Sophocles' *Women of Trachis* as a basis and inspiration, both Dianeira and Heracles face with bitterness the incomprehensibility of it all. 'It was all a waste of breath,' says Dianeira wearily as she kills herself.[11] And to Heracles, the great male hero if ever there was one, comes the bitter thought that everything he has done in obedience to his father Zeus has been for nothing—no reward, no reason, nothing from the gods, deception. Interestingly, it is only after screaming that his agonizing pain, his itching pain has turned him 'into a girl' that he can admit this. *Dianeira* is a play about anger. We are angry when something does not make sense, when the rational, our rational expectations and conclusions, fail us. And yet, beyond anger, there is wonder.

---

[10] Sophocles, *Antigone* 332–3, in the translation of Wertenbaker (1997), 102

[11] The first performance of *Dianeira*, the text of which is published in Wertenbaker, *Plays Two* (2002), was a radio broadcast on Radio 3 on Sunday 28 November 1999.

Wonder
at many things
But wonder most
at this thing:
Man
who
crosses the speckled sea

. . . .
criss-crosses the land

. . . .
traps the wild species of the plains[12]

but who cannot trap himself in his knowledge, who cannot know himself. Who wanders over the earth forever unconcluded and uncertain.

As always, in moments of crisis, we return to the Greek playwrights and we find they have already sketched the terrain. If we are indeed unknowable, endlessly unknowable, it was those ghostly voices of long ago who first whispered the warning: Electra, Hecuba, Medea. And when we tune in once again to the Greek plays it is to hear those voices calling out to us—across centuries, across history—those voices which first sang of the endless, haunting, unappeased, stalking mystery of the human being.

---

[12] Sophocles, *Antigone* 332–44, in the translation of Wertenbaker (1997), 102–3.

15

Details of Productions Discussed

Amanda Wrigley

This chapter comprises a reference list of production details of all the works of modern performance (from theatre, opera, dance, television, and film) informed by one or more Greek tragedies which have been discussed in the text of this volume (hence there are some that pre-date the watershed years of the late 1960s). Since Greek tragedy is the focus of the discussion, all works of ancient comedy and Roman drama have been omitted, with the exception of Seneca, whose tragic works have themselves been considered to be adaptations of Greek tragedies, and modern productions of which are often informed to some extent by their Greek counterparts. Thus, a production entitled *Medea* will relate to the Greek tragedy of that name, unless stated otherwise (for example, Seneca's *Medea*). When the title of the modern work of performance does not make clear to which Greek tragedy the work is related, a brief indication is offered.

The list is arranged chronologically by date of première. When the exact première date of a theatrical, operatic, dance, or television performance has not been uncovered at the time of going to press, it is listed under month and/or year alone. After these productions are film works, listed alphabetically, by year of production. Only the following basic production details are included: author of the script (writer, translator, adaptor, librettist), composer (for opera), director, venue at which the première took place, and the company involved in the production of the work. For films, the country of origin is listed. The names of actors, composers for non-operatic productions, conductors, and individuals responsible for design and choreography are not usually cited.

A 'production' is considered to be a work of modern performance regardless of the length of the run, hence details of important tours and revivals of a work are included in the entry for the original production and not separately. However, when the text discusses a revival of a production which differs significantly from the original production in some way, for example with notable changes in cast, direction, or theatre company, it is recorded separately in the list. For examples of this, see the 1954 and 1955 entries for *Oedipus Rex*, Berkoff's *Greek* of 1980 and 1988, and *Die Orestie*, directed by Stein in 1980 and 1994.

Although the productions gathered together in this chapter are a somewhat random sample of works of modern performance which have been informed by Greek tragedy, in terms of the proportion of works influenced by the three tragedians they are not inconsistent with the larger picture being drawn by the database at the Archive of Performances of Greek and Roman Drama.[1] The database currently holds records for approximately six and a half thousand productions of Greek tragedy which have been staged, sung, danced, televised, or filmed since the Renaissance and up to the present day. Half of these occur before the watershed years of 1968–9, and half after, with the proportional popularity of the three tragedians remaining consistent for the period from the Renaissance to 1968–9, and from then to the present day: half of all productions are informed by Euripides, and roughly one-third and one-fifth are informed by Sophocles and Aeschylus respectively. Interestingly, this general trend is identifiable in the following collation of the works which were selected for discussion by the contributors to this volume.

The database is and will continue to be a work in progress, being constantly revised and added to as a result of the work of the APGRD's Researchers and Graduate Associates, and the information supplied by an international network of friends and colleagues in the worlds of academe and the theatre. Any omissions or errors in the following information remain the responsibility of the author of this chapter alone.[2]

Reference works used include Flashar (1991); Hall, Macintosh, and Taplin (2000); Reid (1993); and Sadie (1992).[3]

---

[1] It is hoped that this will be accessible on the web at www.apgrd.ox.ac.uk by the end of 2004.

[2] Corrections to and additional information for this listing would be gratefully received by the author at apgrd@classics.ox.ac.uk. Information on other amateur and professional productions of Greek and Roman drama, on stage and film, and in opera and dance, performed since the Renaissance to the present day would also be most welcome.

[3] I am indebted to both Edith Hall and Fiona Macintosh for their valuable help in the preparation of this listing. I am also very grateful to Isobel Hurst for her timely and efficient assistance. My thanks also go to a small army of academics, theatre companies, and archivists, too numerous to mention individually here, who have been most generous with their time and resources.

25 January 1659	*Oedipe*; adaptation by Pierre Corneille; performed at the Hôtel de Bourgogne, Paris
Late 1667/ early 1678	*Oedipus*; adaptation by John Dryden and Nathaniel Lee; performed at the Dorset Garden Theatre, London
4 December 1693	*Médée*; opera composed by Marc-Antoine Charpentier; libretto by Thomas Corneille; performed at the Opéra, Paris
10 April 1718	*Oedipe*; adaptation by François-Marie Arouet de Voltaire; performed at the Comédie Française, Paris
Early 1720s	*Philoctetes*; directed by Thomas Sheridan; performed by students at Sheridan's school in Dublin, Ireland
11 November 1772	*Antigona*; opera composed by Tommaso Traetta; libretto by Marco Coltellini; performed at the Imperial Theatre, St Petersburg
16 June 1783	*Philoctète*; adaptation by Jean-François de La Harpe; performed at the Comédie Française, Paris
13 March 1797	*Médée*; opera composed by Luigi Cherubini; libretto by François-Benoît Hoffman; performed at the Théâtre Feydeau, Paris
2 March 1808	*Der Zerbrochene Krug* [*The Broken Jug*]; parodic version of *Oedipus Tyrannus* written by Heinrich von Kleist; directed by Johann Wolfgang Goethe; performed at the Court Theatre, Weimar
28 February 1818	*Philoctetes*; adaptation by Nikolaos Pikkolos; performed in Odessa
1881	*Oedipe roi*; translated by Jules Lacroix; with Jean Mounet-Sully as Oedipus; performed at the Comédie Française, Paris
January 1907	*Playboy of the Western World*; parodic version of *Oedipus Tyrannus* written by J. M. Synge; performed at the Abbey Theatre, Dublin

25 January 1909	*Elektra*; opera composed by Richard Strauss; libretto by Hugo van Hofmannsthal after Sophocles; performed at the Hofoper, Dresden
1909	*Medea*; performed by students at Bryn Mawr College, Bryn Mawr, Pennsylvania
January 1912	*Oedipus Rex*; translated by Gilbert Murray; directed by Max Reinhardt; with John Martin-Harvey as Oedipus and Lillah McCarthy as Jocasta; performed at Covent Garden, London
20 December 1922	*Antigone*; adaptation by Jean Cocteau; directed by Charles Dullin; music composed by Artur Honegger; designed by Pablo Picasso; costumes by Gabrielle (Coco) Chanel; performed at the Théâtre d'Atelier, Paris
7 December 1926	*Oedipus the King*; translated by W. B. Yeats; with Frank McCormick as Oedipus; performed at the Abbey Theatre, Dublin
30 May 1927	*Oedipus Rex*; opera-oratorio composed by Igor Stravinsky; libretto by Jean Cocteau, translated into Latin by Jean Daniélou; performed at the Théâtre Sarah Bernhardt, Paris
12 September 1927	*Oedipus at Colonus*; translated by W. B. Yeats; with Frank McCormick as Oedipus; performed at the Abbey Theatre, Dublin
1927	*Prometheus*; directed and choreographed by Eva Palmer-Sikelianos; performed at the ancient theatre at Delphi (1st Delphic Festival)
20 June 1931	*Die Bakchantinnen*; opera composed by Egon Wellesz using his own libretto; directed by Clemens Krauss and Lothar Wallerstein; performed at the Staatsoper, Vienna
26 October 1931	*Mourning Becomes Electra*; adaptation of the *Oresteia* by Eugene O'Neill; directed by Philip Moeller; with Alla Nazimova as

	Christine (the Clytemnestra figure) and Alice Brady as Lavinia (the Electra figure); performed in New York; Theatre Guild, USA
15 March 1933	*Philoctetes*; in ancient Greek; directed by Milman Parry; music composed by Elliott Carter; with Robert Fitzgerald as Philoctetes, and Harry Levin as Odysseus; performed at Lowell House Hall, Cambridge, Massachusetts; Harvard Classical Club
16 June 1934	*Bacchae*; directed by Eva Palmer-Sikelianos; performed on the athletics field by students at Smith College, Northampton, Massachusetts
June 1935	*Bacchae*; directed by Eva Palmer-Sikelianos; performed by students at Bryn Mawr College, Bryn Mawr, Pennsylvania
13 March 1936	*Oedipe*; opera composed by Georges Enescu; libretto by Edmond Fleg after Sophocles' two Oedipus plays; performed at the Opéra, Paris
3 May 1936	*Les Perses*; with Roland Barthes as Darius; performed in the courtyard of the Sorbonne, Paris, followed by a tour; Le Groupe de Théâtre Antique de la Sorbonne
1937	*Philoctète*; adaptation by André Gide; directed by Jacques Copeau; performed at the Théâtre du Vieux-Colombier, Paris
3 June 1943	*Les Mouches*; informed by the *Choephori* and *Eumenides* of Aeschylus and Sophocles' *Electra*; written by Jean-Paul Sartre; directed by Charles Dullin; performed at the Théâtre de la Cité, Paris
30 November 1943	Sophocles' *Electra*; directed by Alan Schneider; performed at the Catholic University of America, Washington, DC; Speech and Theater Department of the Catholic University of America

4 February 1944

Antigone; adaptation by Jean Anouilh; directed by André Barsacq; performed at the Théâtre d'Atelier, Paris

18 October 1945

Oedipus Rex; translated by W. B. Yeats; directed by Michel Saint-Denis; with Laurence Olivier as Oedipus and Sybil Thorndike as Jocasta; performed at the Old Vic, London; Old Vic Company, England

3 May 1947

Night Journey; ballet based on *Oedipus Tyrannus*; music composed by William Schuman; choreographed by Martha Graham (who took the role of Jocasta); designed by Isamu Noguchi; performed at Cambridge High School, Cambridge, Massachusetts

15 February 1948

Antigone; adaptation (based on Friedrich Hölderlin's translation) written and directed by Bertolt Brecht; performed at the Stadt-theater, Chur, Switzerland

22 February 1948

Le Baccanti; opera composed by Giorgio Federico Ghedini; libretto by Tullio Pinelli; performed at the Teatro alla Scala, Milan

17 March 1950

Oedipus the King; translated by Dudley Fitts and Robert Fitzgerald; directed by Alan Schneider; performed at the Catholic University of America, Washington, DC; Speech and Theater Department of the Catholic University of America

31 March 1951

Ecuba; opera composed by Bruno Rigacci; concert performance in Rome (see entry under 4 May 2002 for the first staged performance)

7 May 1953

Medea; opera composed by Luigi Cherubini; directed by André Barsacq; with Maria Callas as Medea; performed in Florence (16th Maggio Musicale Fiorentino); Teatro Communale di Firenze (see entry under

	13 March 1797 for the first performance of this work)
15 July 1954	*Oedipus Rex*; translated by W. B. Yeats; directed by Tyrone Guthrie; designed by Tanya Moiseiwitsch; with James Mason as Oedipus; performed in the Festival tent at the Stratford Shakespearean Festival, Stratford, Ontario
1954	*Herkules und der Stall des Augias*; an adaptation by Friedrich Dürrenmatt; broadcast on Radio Bern, Switzerland
May 1955	*L'Orestie*; translated by André Obey; directed by Jean-Louis Barrault; music composed by Pierre Boulez; with Barrault as Corypheus and Orestes; performed at the Bordeaux Festival, transferring to the Théâtre Marigny, Paris, later that year; Renaud-Barrault, France
28 June 1955	*Oedipus Rex*; translated by W. B. Yeats; directed by Tyrone Guthrie; designed by Tanya Moiseiwitsch; with Douglas Campbell as Oedipus; performed at the Stratford Shakespearean Festival, Stratford, Ontario
1956	*Oedipus Rex*; film; translated by W. B. Yeats; directed by Tyrone Guthrie; with Douglas Campbell as Oedipus; Canada
20 February 1959	*Heracles*; a reading of William Arrowsmith's translation; directed by Geraldine Lust; performed in the Great Hall of the Cooper Union for the Advancement of Science and Art, New York; Qwirk Productions, USA
Summer 1960	*Die Perser*; translated by Mattias Braun; directed by Hans Lietzau; performed at the Schillertheater, Berlin, with revivals in several East German locations in the seasons 1961–2, 1965–6, 1967–8, and 1968–9

1960	*The Prodigal*; a version of *Orestes* written by Jack Richardson; directed by Rhodelle Heller; performed at the Downtown Theatre, New York
1960	*Never on Sunday*; film in which the plots of *Oedipus Tyrannus* and *Medea* are parodied, with clips of a performance of *Medea* at the Herodes Atticus, Athens; written and directed by Jules Dassin; with Dassin as Homer and Melina Mercouri as Ilya; Greece
11 April 1961	*Revelation in the Courthouse Park*; opera, with scenes from *Bacchae*; composed by Harry Partch using his own libretto; directed by Barnard Hewitt; performed at the University of Illinois at Urbana-Champaign; School of Music, University of Illinois at Urbana-Champaign, USA
1 March 1962	*Die Alcestiade*; opera composed by Louise Talma; libretto by Thornton Wilder, translated into German by H. Herlitschka; performed at the Opera House, Frankfurt
29 May 1962	*King Priam*; opera composed by Michael Tippett using his own libretto, influenced partly by *Hecuba* and *Trojan Women*; performed at the Belgrade Theatre, Coventry (Coventry Festival)
1962	*Edufa*; a version of *Alcestis* written and directed by Efua Sutherland; performed at the Drama Studio, University of Ghana
1962	*Odale's Choice*; adaptation of *Antigone* by Kamau Brathwaite; performed at the Mfantisman Secondary School, Saltpond, Ghana
1962	*Philoctetes*; directed by Masaaki Kubo; performed at the Hibiya Amphitheatre, Tokyo; Greek Tragedy Study Club of the University of Tokyo

1962	*Song of a Goat*; a version of *Agamemnon* by J. P. Clark; directed by Wole Soyinka; performed at the Mbari Centre, Ibadan, Nigeria
1962	*Herakles*; film; directed by Werner Herzog; Germany
13 March 1963	*Alceste*; opera composed by Ton de Leeuw; televised in the Netherlands
20 March 1963	*Herkules und der Stall des Augias*; an adaptation by Friedrich Dürrenmatt; performed at the Schauspielhaus, Zürich
23 December 1963	*Antigona '43*; opera composed by Lyubomir Pipkov; libretto by V. Bashev and P. Panchev; performed in Ruse, Bulgaria
7 April 1964	*Philoctetes*; adaptation by Keith Johnstone; directed by William Gaskill; with Colin Blakeley as Philoctetes; performed at the Old Vic, London, in a double bill with the British premiere of Samuel Beckett's *Play*; National Theatre, England
1 March 1965	*Clitennestra*; opera composed by Ildebrando Pizzetti using his own libretto; performed at the Teatro alla Scala, Milan
10 March 1965	*Les Troyennes*; adaptation by Jean-Paul Sartre; directed by Michael Cacoyannis; performed at the Théâtre National Populaire, Paris
30 April 1965	*Pocodeň Prométheova* [*Prometheus' Torch*]; opera composed by Jan Hanuš; libretto by J. Pokorný; performed at the Národní Divadlo, Prague
27 October 1965	*Herakles*; adaptation by Archibald MacLeish; directed by Alan Schneider; with Rosemary Harris as Megara and Sydney Walker as Herakles; performed at the Lydia Mendelssohn Theater, University of Michigan, Ann Arbor; University of Michigan's Professional Theater Program

with the APA (Association of Producing Artists) Repertory Company, USA

1965   *Persae*; directed by Karolos Koun; premiered at the World Theatre Season in London, and frequently revived; Theatro Technis, Greece

1965   *Song of a Goat*; a version of *Agamemnon* by J. P. Clark; performed at the Commonwealth Festival of the Arts, London

1965   *Les Visions Prophétiques de Cassandre*; cantata composed by Monic Cecconi-Botella; libretto by Aeschylus

2 February 1966   Sophocles' *Électre*; translated and directed by Antoine Vitez; performed at the Théâtre-Maison de la Culture de Caen, followed by a tour

14 June 1966   *Oresteia*; translated by Richmond Lattimore; directed by Alexis Solomos; music composed by Iannis Xenakis; performed at the Greek Theatre, Ypsilanti, Michigan, USA

6 August 1966   *The Bassarids*; opera influenced by *Bacchae*; composed by Hans Werner Henze; libretto by W. H. Auden and Chester Kallman; directed by Gustav Rudolf Sellner; performed at the Salzburger Festspiele

1966   *Medea*; musical composition by Dimitri Terzakis; performed by students at the Musikhochschule, Köln

17 March 1967   *Mourning Becomes Electra*; opera composed by Marvin David Levy, libretto by Henry Butler based on Eugene O'Neill's stage play of the same title (see entry under 26 October 1931); performed at the Metropolitan Opera, New York

19 March 1967   Seneca's *Medea*; part of the text set for male chorus and ensemble by Iannis Xenakis;

directed by Jorge Lavelli; performed at the Théâtre de l'Odéon, Paris

22 October 1967   *The Trojan Women*; opera composed by Margaret Garwood; libretto by H. A. Wiley; performed at P. M. C. Colleges Auditorium, Chester, Pennsylvania; Pennsylvania Opera Company

1967   *The Agamemnon of Aeschylus*; opera composed by Felix Werder; libretto by Gilbert Murray; broadcast on ABC Radio, Australia (see entry under 1 June 1977 for the performance of a revised version of this opera)

1967   *Antigone*; adaptation of Bertolt Brecht's text (for the première of which see entry under 15 February 1948) written by Judith Malina whilst in prison for political protest; performed at the Avignon Festival; Living Theatre Company, USA

1967   *Antigone*; opera composed by William Russo; libretto by A. A. Hoge; performed in Chicago

1967   *Clytemnestra*; musical composition for soprano and ensemble by Dimitri Terzakis; libretto after Aeschylus' *Eumenides*

1967   *Médée*; opera composed by Andor Kovách using his own libretto based on the play by Jean Anouilh; performed in Saarbrücken

1967   *Oedipus*; directed by Karolos Koun

1967   *Edipo Re*; film; directed by Pier Paolo Pasolini; Italy

5 February 1968   *Syllabaire pour Phèdre* [*Spelling-book for Phaedra*]; chamber opera composed by Maurice Ohana; libretto by Raphaël Cluzel and Maurice Ohana; performed at L'Académie de Musique, Paris

1 March 1968   *Orestes*; opera composed by Daniel Jones using his own libretto; broadcast on BBC Radio 4

19 March 1968	Seneca's *Oedipus*; translated by Ted Hughes; directed by Peter Brook; performed at the Old Vic, London; National Theatre, London
24 March 1968	*Prometheus*; opera composed by Carl Orff; libretto in ancient Greek; performed at the Württembergisches Staatstheater, Stuttgart
6 June 1968	*Dionysus in 69*; adaptation of *Bacchae* written and directed by Richard Schechner; performed at the Performing Garage, New York; Performance Group, USA
20 September 1968	*Jertfirea Iphigeniei* [*Iphigenia's Sacrifice*]; opera composed by Pascal Bentoiu; libretto by A. Pop and Pascal Bentoiu; radio broadcast in Bucharest
8 November 1968	*The Passion of Oedipus*; opera based on *Oedipus at Colonus* composed by Roy Travis; performed at the Opera Workshop, University of California, Los Angeles
2 December 1968	*Neutral Ground*; adaptation of *Philoctetes* by Tom Stoppard; directed by Piers Haggard; with Patrick Magee as Philo (the Philoctetes character); broadcast by Thames Television; produced by Granada Television
1968	*The Gods are Not to Blame*; adaptation of *Oedipus Tyrannus* by Ola Rotimi; performed in Nigeria; Olokun Acting Company, Nigeria
1968	*Herakles*: adaptation by Harmut Lange; directed by Hansgünther Heyme; performed in West Berlin
1968	*Orestes*; directed by Jan Kott; performed by students in the open-air Greek theatre at the University of California at Berkeley, USA
1968	*Philoktet*; adaptation by Heiner Müller; directed by Hans Lietzau; performed at the Residenztheater, Munich

10 January 1969	Seneca's *Phaedra*; translated by Edoardo Sanguineti; directed by Luca Ronconi; performed in Rome
8 February 1969	*Rites*; adaptation of *Bacchae* written by Maureen Duffy; directed by Joan Plowright; performed at the National Theatre, London
April 1969	*Oresteia*; performed in Moscow; Slovak National Theatre Company, Czechoslovakia
1969	*Elektra*; opera composed by Leonidas Zoras
1969	*Iphigenia/Titus*; a work using speeches from Goethe's *Iphigenie auf Tauris* conceived, directed, and performed by Joseph Beuys at Experimenta 2, German Academy of the Performing Arts, Frankfurt
1969	*Prometheus Bound*; adaptation by Heiner Müller; directed by Peter Stein; performed in Zurich
1969	*Seven against Thebes*; directed by Manfred Karge and Matthias Langhoff; performed in Berlin; Berliner Ensemble, Germany
Early 1970	'An evening of free Greek music and drama', including readings from *Antigone*, *Trojan Women*, *Philoctetes*, and plays by Aristophanes; directed by Minos Volonakis; held in London; Greek Committee against Dictatorship
*c.*1970s	*Iphigenia in Brooklyn*; satirical cantata composed by Peter Schickele (P. D. Q. Bach)
13 November 1970	*Helen in Egypt*; opera composed by Jonathan Elkus; libretto by J. Knight after H. D.; performed at the University of Wisconsin Opera Theatre, Milwaukee, alongside his *Medea* (see next entry)
13 November 1970	*Medea*; opera composed by Jonathan Elkus using his own libretto; performed at the

University of Wisconsin Opera Theatre,
Milwaukee, alongside his *Helen in Egypt*
(see previous entry)

15 December 1970   *Deafman Glance*; adaptation of *Medea* written and directed by Robert Wilson; per-
formed at the University Theater, Iowa
City, touring to New York and across
Europe the following year

1970   *Appunti per un' Orestiade Africana* [*Notes for
an African Oresteia*]; film; directed by Pier
Paolo Pasolini; Italy

1970   *Comedy of Oedipus: You Killed the Beast!*;
satirical Arabic adaptation of *Oedipus
Tyrannus* by Ali Salem; directed by Galal
El-Sharqawi; performed at the El-Hakim
Theatre, Cairo

1970   *Dionysus in 69*; film; directed by Brian De
Palma, Robert Fiore, and Bruce Rubin;
Performance Group, USA

28 January 1971   *Agamemnon*; music drama by Havergal
Brian using his own libretto, based on
J. S. Blackie's translation; performed at
St John's, Smith Square, London

1971   *Blood: From the Heart of America*; musical
version of the *Oresteia*; libretto by Doug
Dyer; performed at the New York Shakespeare Festival

1971   *Death of Antigone*; chamber opera composed
by Reginald Smith Brindle; performed in
Oxford

1971   *The Eumenides*; musical composition by
Margaret Anne Wheat; libretto after
Aeschylus and Sartre's *Les Mouches*

February 1972   *Ajax*; musical composition by John Eaton;
libretto by John Moore; University of
Washington Contemporary Chamber Ensemble

15 April 1972	*Heracles*; opera composed by John Eaton; libretto by M. Fried based on Sophocles' *Trachiniae* and Seneca's *Hercules on Oeta*; performed at the Opera Theater, Indiana University, Bloomington
1972	*Le Baccanti*; opera composed by Giorgio Federico Ghedini; libretto by Tullio Pinelli; performed in Milan (see entry under 22 February 1948 for première)
1972	*The Death of Iphigenia*; soprano cantata composed by Francis Routh; libretto by Gilbert Murray
1972	*Orestes*; musical composition by Michael Adamis
29 March 1973	*Les Troyennes*; music drama composed by Joanna Bruzdowicz; libretto by J. Luccioni; performed at the Théâtre Gérard Philippe, Paris
2 July 1973	*The Island*; a play, drawing on *Antigone*, written by Athol Fugard, John Kani, and Winston Ntshona; directed by Athol Fugard; The Space Theatre, Cape Town (where the title was given as *Die Hodoshe Span*), followed by international tours, with what will probably be its final revival with the original actors in Europe in 2002
2 August 1973	*The Bacchae of Euripides: A Communion Rite*; adaptation by Wole Soyinka; directed by Roland Joffe; with Martin Shaw as Dionysos; performed at the Old Vic, London; National Theatre, England
1973	*Antigonae*; opera composed by Meyer Kupferman; libretto by Friedrich Hölderlin; performed at the Lenox Arts Center, Stockbridge, Massachusetts
1973	*Clytemnestra's Argument*; choral composition by Elizabeth Gomm

1973	*Odale's Choice*; adaptation of *Antigone* by Kamau Brathwaite; directed by Derek Walcott; performed in Trinidad; Trinidad Theatre Workshop
1973	*The Orphan*; a version of *Orestes* by David Rabe; directed by Jeff Bleckner; performed at the New York Shakespeare Festival (produced in its final form in 1974 by the Manning Street Actors' Theater, Philadelphia, in association with the New York Shakespeare Festival, directed by Barnet Kellman)
7 February 1974	*Bakchen*; directed by Klaus Michael Grüber; with Michael König as Dionysus; performed in an exhibition hall in a Berlin fairground; Schaubühne am Halleschen Ufer, Germany
13 February 1974	*Clytemnestra*; opera composed by Peter Wishart; with Maureen Lehane as Clytemnestra; performed at the Collegiate Theatre, London
24 March 1974	*Prikovaniyat Prometey* [*Prometheus Bound*]; opera-oratorio composed by Lazar Nikolov; performed in Ruse, Bulgaria
21 April 1974	*Iphigenie auf Tauris*; dance drama directed and choreographed by Pina Bausch; music composed by Christoph Willibald Gluck; performed at the Pina Bausch Tanztheater, Wuppertal
21 June 1974	*Trojan Women (Fragments of a Greek Trilogy)*; adapted and directed by Andrei Şerban; performed at Café La MaMa, New York; La MaMa Experimental Theatre Club, USA
30 October 1974	*Edipo y Yocasta*; opera composed by Josep Soler Sardà; libretto based on Sophocles and Seneca; directed by Antoni Ros Marbà; performed in Barcelona (XII Festival Internacional de Música de Barcelona); Quartet

	Polifònic de Barcelona and Orquestra Ciutat de Barcelona (OCB)
1974	*Herakles 5*; adaptation by Heiner Müller; performed in Munich
1974	*Orestes' Argument*; choral composition by Elizabeth Gomm
1974	*Toroia no Onna* [*Trojan Women*]; adapted and directed by Tadashi Suzuki; with Shiraishi Kayoko as Old Woman/Hecuba/Cassandra; performed at the Iwanami Hall, Tokyo, and revived with international tour from 1977–90; Wasedo Sho-Gekijo, Japan
1974	*The Travelling Players*; film drawing on *Choephori* and *Eumenides*; written and directed by Theo Angelopoulos; Greece
17 January 1975	*Medea*; adaptation by Gloria Albee; performed in New York; Westbeth Playwrights' Feminist Collective, USA
Late 1975/ early 1976	*Antigone Prism*; Women's Ensemble of the Berkeley Stage Company, USA
9 January 1976	*Phaedra*; music drama composed by George Rochberg using his own libretto after Racine; performed in Syracuse, New York
Summer 1976	*Medea*; translated and directed by Minos Volonakis; with Melina Mercouri as Medea; performed at Didimoticho, Evros; National Theatre of Northern Greece
1976	*Médée*; cantata composed by Jean Delysse
1976	*Phaedra*; solo cantata composed by Benjamin Britten; libretto by Robert Lowell after Racine; performed at the Aldeburgh Festival, Suffolk
1 June 1977	*Agamemnon*; opera composed by Felix Werder; libretto by Gilbert Murray; performed at the Grant Street Theatre,

Melbourne (see entry under 1967 for the original performance, of which this was a revised version)

19 November 1977   *À Colone*; musical composition by Iannis Xenakis; setting of lines from *Oedipus at Colonus*; performed in Metz, France (Rencontres Internationales de Musique Contemporaine)

1977   Seneca's *Oedipus*; translated by Ted Hughes; directed by Richard Schechner; performed in New York

1977   A collage of Racine's *Phèdre* and *Oedipus Tyrannus*, and French cabaret; performed by Ethyl Eichelberger at Café La MaMa, New York

1977   *Philoktet*; adaptation by Heiner Müller; performed in the German Democratic Republic

1977   *The Return of the Absent*; adaptation of *Oedipus Tyrannus* by Fawzi Fahmi; with Mahmoud Yassin as Oedipus and Aida Abdel-Aziz as Jocasta; performed at the National Theatre, Cairo

1977–80   *Electra Speaks*; third and culminating part of *The Daughter's Cycle*, a play, influenced by the myth of Electra, written by Clare Coss, Roberta Sklar, and Sondra Segal; performed at the Women's Interart Center, New York; Women's Experimental Theatre, USA

4 February 1978   *Medea*; adaptation by Mutsuo Takahashi; directed by Yukio Ninagawa; performed at the Nissei Theatre, Tokyo; Toho Company, Japan

26 July 1978   *Le Nom d'Oedipe: Chant du corps interdit*; version by Hélène Cixous; music composed by André Boucourechliev; directed by Claude Régy; performed in the Main Court-

	yard of the Palais des Papes, Avignon (Avignon Festival)
13 November 1978	*Les Choéphores (Orestia II)*; music drama for radio; composed by Aurel Stroe; radio broadcast in Bucharest (see entries under 1 March 1983 and 1986 for the broadcast of the rest of the trilogy)
1978	*Prometheus*; opera composed by Meyer Kupferman; libretto by Johann Wolfgang Goethe and Meyer Kupferman; Act I Scene II performed at the Manhattan School of Music, New York
1978	*A Dream of Passion*; film drawing on Volonakis's 1976 stage production of *Medea;* written and directed by Jules Dassin; with Melina Mercouri as Maya, the actress playing Medea; Greece
7, 14, and 21 March 1979	*The Serpent Son*; television adaptation of the *Oresteia* written by Kenneth McLeish and Frederic Raphael; directed by Bill Hays; with Claire Bloom as Athene, Helen Mirren as Kassandra, Siân Phillips as Leader of the Furies, Denis Quilley as Agamemnon, Diana Rigg as Klytemnestra, and Billie Whitelaw as leader of the chorus women; televised in three parts on BBC2
3 May 1979	*Medea*; opera composed by Ray Edward Luke; libretto by Carveth Osterhaus; performed at the New England Conservatory, Boston, Massachusetts
1979	*Against Silence*; an adaptation of *Iphigenia in Aulis*; performed in USA; Emmatroupe, USA
1979/80	*Medeas Barn* [*Medea's Children*]; a version created for children by Per Lysander and Suzanne Osten; directed by Suzanne Osten; performed at the Unga Klara Theatre, Stockholm (The Children's Festival)

Late 1970s   *The Rex Family*; planned performance in
                      Kansas City, Missouri; Actors' Sorority

11 February 1980   *Greek*; adaptation of *Oedipus Tyrannus*
                      written and directed by Steven Berkoff;
                      performed at the Half Moon Theatre,
                      London

1 March 1980   *The Cry of Clytaemnestra*; chamber opera
                      composed by John Eaton; performed at
                      the Opera Theater, Indiana University,
                      Bloomington

18 October 1980   *Die Orestie*; adapted and directed by Peter
                      Stein; performed at the Schaubühne am
                      Halleschen Ufer, Berlin (revived in 1994);
                      Schaubühne am Halleschen Ufer, Germany

December 1980   *Medea*; dramatic cantata composed by
                      Ronald Caltabiano using his own libretto;
                      performed at the Juilliard Festival of Con-
                      temporary Music, New York

1980   *Bacchae*; directed by Michael Cacoyannis;
                      with Irene Pappas as Agave; performed at
                      the Circle in the Square, New York

1980   *Medea*; written and performed by Ethyl
                      Eichelberger at Club 57, New York

1980   *Oresteia*; translated by Thanasis Valtinos;
                      directed by Karolos Koun; with Melina
                      Mercouri as Clytemnestra; performed at
                      the ancient theatre at Epidaurus; Theatro
                      Technis, Greece

28 November 1981   *The Oresteia*; translated by Tony Harrison;
                      directed by Peter Hall; music composed by
                      Harrison Birtwistle; designed by Jocelyn
                      Herbert; performed at the National Theatre,
                      London; National Theatre, England

1981   *Bacchae*; directed by Tadashi Suzuki; with
                      Dionysus played by Shiraishi Kayoko, who
                      also played Agave; performed at the Univer-
                      sity of Wisconsin, Milwaukee, later touring

	to Togamura and Tokyo (the premiere was in Tokyo in 1978)
1981	*Jocaste*; written by Michèle Fabien; directed by Marc Liebens; performed in Belgium; Ensemble Théâtral Mobile, Belgium
1981	*Oresteia*; performed in South Africa; Cape Performing Arts Board, South Africa
21 June 1982	*Kommos*; composed by John Buller; setting of lines from Aeschylus' *Persians*; performed at the St Bartholomew's Festival, London
5 December 1982	*Troerinnen*; directed by Christoph Schroth; performed at the Mecklenburg Staatstheater, Schwerin, German Democratic Republic, subsequently touring in 1983 in both East and West Germany, and to Delphi and Athens
1982	*The Black Bacchants*; opera composed by Roy Travis using his own libretto
1982	*Jocasta, or Boy Crazy*; written and performed by Ethyl Eichelberger at S.n.a.f.u., New York
1 March 1983	*Agamemnon (Orestia I)*; music drama for radio; composed by Aurel Stroe; radio broadcast in Bucharest (see entries under 13 November 1978 and 1986 for the broadcast of the rest of the trilogy)
Summer 1983	*Phaedra's Dream*; ballet choreographed by Martha Graham; music composed by George Crumb; with Rudolf Nureyev as Hippolytus in some charity performances; performed at the Athens Festival, touring in 1984 to Paris and New York; Martha Graham Dance Company, USA
8 November 1983	*Gospel at Colonus*; musical adaptation written and directed by Lee Breuer; music composed by Bob Telson; designed by Alison Yerxa; with Morgan Freeman as Preacher

Oedipus, and Clarence Fountain as Singer Oedipus; choral work featured the Blind Boys of Alabama; performed at the Carey Playhouse, Brooklyn, New York (Next Wave Festival); Brooklyn Academy of Music, USA

20 January 1984   *Antygona*; translated by Stanisław Hebanowski; directed by Andrzej Wajda; performed at the Stary Teatr, Kraków

2 July 1984   *Prometheus*; cantata by Theodoros Antoniou; performed in Athens

25 September 1984   *Prometeo*; music drama composed by Luigi Nono; libretto by Massimo Cacciari; performed at San Lorenzo, Venice (revised version performed at La Scala, Milan, the following year)

23 October 1984   *Medea*; opera composed by Gavin Bryars; libretto by Minos Volonakis and the composer; directed by Robert Wilson; performed at the Opéra de Lyon, France (see entry under 3 November 1995 for the performance of the revised version)

1984   *Prometheus Bound*; directed by William Reichblum; performed at Café La MaMa, New York

1984   *The Riot Act*; adaptation of *Antigone* by Tom Paulin; directed by Stephen Rea (who also played Creon); performed in Northern Ireland; Field Day Theatre Company, Northern Ireland

17 September 1985   *Medea*; opera composed by Felix Werder; performed at the College of Advanced Education, Melbourne

December 1985   *The Prometheus Project: Four Movements and a Coda*; directed by Richard Schechner; performed at the Performing Garage, New York

23 February 1986	*Die Mütter* [*The Mothers*]; adaptation of Euripides' *Suppliants* and Aeschylus' *Seven against Thebes* by Hans-Ulrich Müller-Schwefe; directed by Einar Schleef; performed at the Schauspielhaus, Frankfurt
12 March 1986	*Alcestis*; adapted and directed by Robert Wilson; Loeb Drama Center, Cambridge, Massachusetts; American Repertory Theatre
2 June 1986	*Ajax*; adaptation by Robert Auletta; directed by Peter Sellars; with Howie Seago as Ajax; performed at the John F. Kennedy Center for the Performing Arts, Washington, DC, transferring to La Jolla Playhouse, California, before a European tour; American National Theater (see Figure 32)
7 July 1986	*Troades*; opera composed by Aribert Reimann; libretto by Franz Werfel; directed by Jean-Pierre Ponelle; performed at the Nationaltheater, Munich
16, 17, and 19 September 1986	*The Theban Plays*; translated and directed by Don Taylor; with Anthony Quayle as Oedipus and Juliet Stevenson as Antigone; televised in three parts on BBC2
September 1986	*A Mouthful of Birds*; a version of *Bacchae* written by Caryl Churchill and David Lan; directed by Ian Spink and Les Waters; performed at the Birmingham Repertory Theatre, before transferring to the Royal Court, London, in November; Joint Stock Theatre Group, England
1986	Sophocles' *Électre*; translated and directed by Antoine Vitez; performed at the Théâtre National de Chaillot, Paris (see entry under 1990 for the film based on this production)
1986	*Eumenides (Orestia III)*; music drama for radio; composed by Aurel Stroe; radio broadcast in Timişoara, Romania (see

FIGURE 32.   Ajax (played by Howie Seago, who is deaf) admonishes his young son Acere in *Ajax*, directed by Peter Sellars (1986).

entries under 13 November 1978 and 1 March 1983 for the broadcast of the rest of the trilogy)

1986   *Prometheus Bound*; translated by Peter Handke; directed by Klaus Michael Grüber; performed at the Salzburg Festival

21 August 1987   *Kassandra*; musical composition by Iannis Xenakis, setting of lines from *Agamemnon*; performed in Gibellina, Sicily, together with a reduced version of his *Oresteia* (see entry under 14 June 1966)

4 October 1987   *Oedipus*; music drama composed by Wolfgang Rihm; libretto by the composer, using extracts from Friedrich Hölderlin's translation of *Oedipus Tyrannus* and works by Heiner Müller and Friedrich Nietzsche; performed at the Deutsche Oper, Berlin

November 1987   *Medea*; adaptation by Charles Ludlam; directed by Lawrence Kornfeld; performed at the Charles Ludlam Theater, New York; Ridiculous Theatrical Company, USA

1987   *Antigone*; opera composed by József Soproni; libretto based on Jean Anouilh's *Antigone*

1987   *Klytemnestra: The Nightingale of Argos*; written and performed by Ethyl Eichelberger at P.S. 122, New York

1987   *Summer of Medea*; film; directed by Babis Plaitakis; Greece

1987   *Héraklès*; opera-pantomime composed by Ján Zimmer using his own libretto; broadcast on Czechoslovakian television

15 March 1988   *Oedipus Tex*; dramatic oratorio composed by Peter Schickele (P. D. Q. Bach); performed in Minneapolis

19 April 1988   *Phèdre*; opera composed by Sylvano Bussotti using his own libretto; performed at the Teatro dell'Opera, Rome

17 June 1988   *Greek*; opera composed by Mark-Anthony Turnage; libretto adapted by Turnage and Jonathan Moore from Steven Berkoff's stage play of the same title (see entry under 11 February 1980); directed by Jonathan

Moore; performed at the Carl Orff-Saal, Munich (1st Müncher Biennale festival); Ensemble Modern, Germany

29 June 1988   *Greek*; adaptation of *Oedipus Tyrannus* written and directed by Steven Berkoff (who also played DAD); performed at the Wyndham's Theatre, London

1 July 1988   *Medeamaterial*; adaptation by Heiner Müller; directed by Theodoros Terzopoulos; performed at Theater Manufaktur, Berlin, followed by a tour to Italy, Spain, and San Diego, California; ATTIS Theatrical Group, Greece

9 November 1988   *The Love of the Nightingale*; a play, influenced by *Philoctetes*, fragments of Sophocles' *Tereus*, and Ovid, written by Timberlake Wertenbaker; directed by Garry Hynes; performed at The Other Place, Stratford-upon-Avon, England; Royal Shakespeare Company, England

19 November 1988   *The Aspern Papers*; opera composed by Dominick Argento using his own libretto which incorporates elements of *Medea*; performed at the Music Hall, Fair Park, Dallas; Dallas Opera Company, USA

29 November 1988   *Philoctetes*; translated by Kenneth McLeish; directed by Declan Donnellan; performed at the Donmar Warehouse, London (followed by a European tour); Cheek by Jowl, England

15 December 1988   Sophocles' *Electra*; translated by Kenneth McLeish; directed by Deborah Warner; with Fiona Shaw as Electra; performed at The Pit, Barbican Arts Centre, London (revived at the Riverside Studios, London, in December 1991, and at the Templemore Sports Stadium, Derry, Northern Ireland,

	in February 1992); Royal Shakespeare Company, England
1988	*Medea*; film adaptation by Carl T. Dreyer and Preben Thomsen; directed by Lars von Trier; first broadcast on Danish television
31 October 1989	*The Gods are Not to Blame*; adaptation of *Oedipus Tyrannus* by Ola Rotimi; directed by Yvonne Brewster; performed at the Everyman Theatre, Liverpool; Talawa Theatre Company, England
1989	*Honey, I'm Home*; a version of *Alcestis*; performed at Hampshire College, Amherst, Massachusetts; Split Britches Theater Company, USA
1989	*Oedipus Wrecks*; film; written and directed by Woody Allen as part of a series of films entitled *New York Stories*; USA
1989	*Seize the Fire*; film adaptation of *Prometheus Bound* by Tom Paulin; directed by Tony Coe; The Open University
22 August 1990	*Kassandra*; opera, drawing on Aeschylus' *Agamemnon* and Euripides' *Trojan Women*, composed by Nicholas Zumbro; performed at the Theatre of Rhemetia, Khalandri, Athens
8 September 1990	*Oresteia*; version by George Taylor; directed by Michael Chase; performed in a tent in Stroud, England (Stroud Festival); The Mask Studio, England
23 September 1990	*Greek*; film version of opera composed by Mark-Anthony Turnage (see entry under 17 June 1988 for premiere of this work); directed by Jonathan Moore and Peter Maniura; televised on BBC2
27 September 1990	*Greek*; opera composed by Mark-Anthony Turnage; libretto adapted by Turnage and Jonathan Moore from Steven Berkoff's

stage play of the same title (see entry under 11 February 1980); directed by Jonathan Moore; performed at the English National Opera (see entry under 17 June 1988 for première of this work)

1 October 1990   *The Cure at Troy: A Version of Sophocles' Philoctetes*; adaptation by Seamus Heaney; directed by Stephen Rea and Bob Crowley; performed at the Guildhall, Derry (toured Northern Ireland and the Republic before transferring to the Tricycle Theatre, London, in April 1991); Field Day Theatre Company, Northern Ireland

16 November 1990   *Les Atrides* (*Iphigénie à Aulis*, translated by Jean Bollack, opened on 16 November 1990; *Agamemnon* and *Les Choéphores*, translated by Ariane Mnouchkine, opened on 24 November 1990 and 23 February 1991 respectively; and *Les Euménides*, translated by Hélène Cixous, opened on 26 May 1991); directed by Ariane Mnouchkine; performed at the Cartoucherie de Vincennes, Paris, followed by an international tour; Théâtre du Soleil, France

1990   *Antigone/Rites for the Dead*; film adaptation written and directed by Amy Greenfield; Eclipse Productions, USA

1990   Sophocles' *Électre*; film, based on the 1986 stage production directed by Vitez; directed by Hugo Santiago; France

2 March 1991   *In the Border Country*; a television film drawing on the *Oresteia*; written by Daniel Mornin; directed by Thaddeus O'Sullivan; with Sean Bean, Juliet Stevenson, and Saskia Reeves; a Little Bird production broadcast by Channel 4

12 March 1991   *Oedipus the King*; adapted and directed by Jatinder Verma; performed at Tara Arts

	Studio, London, followed by a tour of the UK and Italy; Tara Arts, England
3 May 1991	*Die Antigone des Sophokles nach der hölderlinschen Übertragung für die Bühne bearbaitet von Brecht*; translation (of Bertolt Brecht's adaptation of Friedrich Hölderlin's translation) by Danièle Huillet; directed by Jean-Marie Straub and Danièle Huillet; performed at the Schaubühne, Berlin, and touring to Segesta, Sicily, in August
May 1991	*Medea: SexWar*; operatic adaptation written by Tony Harrison, with passages from the SCUM (Society for Cutting Up Men) Manifesto by Valerie Solanis; directed by Janek Alexander; performed at the Institute of Contemporary Arts, London, followed by a tour; Volcano Theatre Company, Wales
25 June 1991	*Antigone*; music drama composed by Ton de Leeuw using his own libretto; performed in Westergasfabriek, Amsterdam
1 July 1991	*Oresteia*; translated by Kirsti Simonsuuri; directed by Ritva Siikala; performed at the Katajanokan Konehalli, Helsinki; Theatre Raivoisat Ruusut, Finland
5 September 1991	*Three Birds Alighting on a Field*; influenced by *Philoctetes*; written by Timberlake Wertenbaker; directed by Max Stafford-Clark; performed at the Royal Court Theatre, London (revived with changes in 1992)
8 October 1991	*Ajax*; translated by Leconte de Lisle; directed by Stephane Braunschweig; performed at the Théâtre de Gennevilliers (Festival d'automne) in France before transferring to the Riverside Studios, London, in May 1992; Théâtre Machine, France
25 October 1991	*The Thebans*, comprising *Oedipus Tyrannos* (opening on 25 October), *Oedipus at Kolonos*

and *Antigone* (both opening on 26 October); versions by Timberlake Wertenbaker; directed by Adrian Noble; Swan Theatre, Stratford-upon-Avon, England (transferring to the Barbican Arts Centre, London, in 1992); Royal Shakespeare Company, England

2 November 1991 *Backanterna*; opera composed by Daniel Börtz; libretto by Göran O. Eriksson and Jan Stolpe; directed by Ingmar Bergman; performed at the Royal Opera, Stockholm (televised in Sweden on 9 April 1993)

1991 *The Case for Decision Ö* [*Der Fall Ö*]; film, drawing on Franz Fühmann's novel *König Ödipus*, written by Ulrich Plenzdorf; directed by Rainer Simon; Deutsche Film-Aktiengesellschaft (DEFA), Germany

1991 *Medea*; opera composed by Mikis Theodorakis using his own libretto; performed in Bilbao (revised versions performed in Athens on 6 July 1993, and in Meiningen on 5 May 1995)

13 March 1992 *Medeamaterial*; opera composed by Pascal Dusapin; libretto by Heiner Müller; performed at the Théâtre Royal de la Monnaie, Brussels (Ars Musica Festival)

3 May 1992 *La Déesse Athéna*; musical composition by Iannis Xenakis; setting of Aeschylus' *Eumenides* lines 681–708; performed in the Megaron Mousikis, Athens

5 May 1992 *Bakxai*; opera composed by John Buller using the ancient Greek text and some passages from William Arrowsmith's English translation; directed by Julia Hollander; performed at the Coliseum, London; English National Opera

31 May 1992 *Pylades*; chamber opera, drawing on the *Electra*s of Sophocles and Euripides, com-

	posed by George Couroupos; directed by Dionysos Fotopoulos; performed at the Megaron Mousikis, Athens
4 September 1992	*Hecuba*; translated into English by Kenneth McLeish; directed by Laurence Boswell; with Ann Mitchell as Hecuba, and Don Warrington as Polymestor; performed at the Gate Theatre, London; Gate Theatre, England
1992	*Jocaste*; opera composed by Charles Chaynes; libretto by Jacques Lacarrière influenced by *Phoenician Women*; performed in Rouen
1992	*Les Bacchantes inspirées par Euripide*; directed by Lukas Hemleb; performed at the Goethe-Institut, Yaoundé, Cameroon; La Troupe d'Ébène, Cameroon
1992	*Die Antigone des Sophokles nach der hölderlinschen Übertragung für die Bühne bearbaitet von Brecht*; film, using Danièle Huillet's translation of Bertolt Brecht's adaptation of Friedrich Hölderlin's translation, directed by Jean-Marie Straub and Danièle Huillet; Germany and France
17 March 1993	*Antigone*; opera composed by Dinos Constantinides; libretto by Dudley Fitts and Robert Fitzgerald; performed at the Louisiana State University Union Theater, Baton Rouge; Louisiana State University Opera Theater and Baton Rouge Opera
April 1993	Seneca's *Medea*; chamber opera composed by Gordon Kerry; libretto by Justin Macdonnell; performed at the Athenaeum Theatre, Melbourne, followed by a tour; Chamber Made Opera, Australia
16 May 1993	*The Oresteia*; opera composed by Liza Lim; libretto by Barrie Kosky and Liza Lim from Tony Harrison's translation; directed by

	Barrie Kosky; performed at TheatreWorks, Melbourne; Elision Ensemble, Australia
July 1993	*The Persians*; adaptation by Robert Auletta; directed by Peter Sellars; music composed by Hamza El Din; with Howie Seago as Darius; performed at the Salzburg Festival, Austria, followed by an international tour
1 September 1993	*Bacchae*; translation by C. K. Williams, with the choruses given in ancient Greek, set to music by Iannis Xenakis; directed by David Freeman; performed at the Queen Elizabeth Hall, London; Opera Factory, England
28 January 1994	*Antigone: A Cry for Peace*; directed by Nikos Koundouros; performed in the no-man's land at the border between northern Greece and the former Republic of Yugoslavia
29 January 1994	*Die Orestie*; adaptation by Peter Stein, translated into Russian by Boris Shekassiouk; directed by Peter Stein; new production retaining significant elements of the 1980 production; performed at the Academic Theatre of the Russian Army, Moscow, followed by a European tour; Melpomene Society for German–Russian Cultural Exchange, Academic Theatre of the Russian Army, and the Goethe Institutes of Munich and Moscow
3 March 1994	*Philoktetes-Variations*; three plays by John Jesurun, Heiner Müller, and André Gide; directed by Jan Ritsema; Ron Vawter played Philoktetes in each of the three plays; performed at the Kaaitheater, Brussels; co-produced by Kaaitheater, Brussels, and Hebbel-Theater, Berlin
18 May 1994	*La Ville parjure ou le réveil des Erinyes* [*The Perjured City, or the Awakening of*

	the Furies]; adaptation of *Eumenides* by Hélène Cixous; directed by Ariane Mnouchkine; performed at the Cartoucherie de Vincennes, Paris, followed by a European tour; Théâtre du Soleil, France (see entry under 1999 for a film version of this production)
1 June 1994	Seneca's *Thyestes*; translated by Caryl Churchill; directed by James Macdonald; performed at the Green Room, Manchester, transferring to the Royal Court, London, on 7 June; co-produced by Manchester City of Drama and London's Royal Court
2 July 1994	*Iketides* [*Suppliants*]; translated by K. Ch. Myris; directed by Stavros Dufexis; performed at the ancient theatre at Epidaurus; Desmoi Cultural and Artistic Association, Greece
August 1994	*Sarajevo*; three-part opera, the first part of which is influenced by *Trojan Women*, composed by Nigel Osborne; performed at the Royal Festival Hall, London
Summer 1994	*Medea, the Musical*; musical adaptation written and directed by John Fisher; first performed by the Department of Dramatic Arts at the University of California at Berkeley, then touring widely, including a nine-month run at the Stage Door Theatre, San Francisco, from 3 April 1996
28 September 1994	*Ion*; adapted by David Lan; directed by Nicholas Wright; with Jude Law in the role of Ion; performed at The Pit, Barbican Arts Centre, London; Royal Shakespeare Company, England
21 October 1994	*Tegonni, an African Antigone*; adapted and directed by Fémi Òsófisan; performed at the Mary Gray Munroe Theater, Emory University, Atlanta; Theater Emory, USA

October 1994   *Medea*; dance drama written from improvisation by Mark Fleishman; music composed by René Avenant; choreographed by Alfred Hinkel; directed by Mark Fleishman and Jennie Reznek; performed in Capetown, touring to Grahamstown in July 1995 and Johannesburg in 1996; Jazzart Dance Theatre Company, South Africa

12 November 1994   *Clytemnestra*; musical composition for soprano and orchestra composed by Rhian Samuel; performed at St David's Hall, Cardiff (and broadcast on BBC Radio 3 on 5 February 1995); BBC National Orchestra of Wales

29 November 1994   *Ion*; translated by Kenneth McLeish (from 6 to 8 December some performances were given in modern Greek); directed by Nick Philippou; performed at the Lyric Theatre, Hammersmith, London; Actors Touring Company, England

1994   *Agamemnon*; adapted by Charles Mee; directed by Brian Kulick; performed in Los Angeles; The Actors' Gang, USA

2 May 1995   Sophocles' *Electra*; opera composed by Mikis Theodorakis; libretto by Spyros Evangelatos based on Kostas Georgousopoulos; performed at the City Theatre, Luxembourg

17 August 1995   *Bacchae*; opera composed by Theodoros Antoniou; libretto by Keith Botsford; excerpts had been performed in Boston, Massachusetts, on 9 December 1992, but the complete work was first performed at the Herodes Atticus, Athens (Athens Festival)

26 August 1995   *Ode to Phaedra*; opera composed by George Roumanis; libretto by Frank Zajackowski; directed by Daniel Helfgot; televised in the

	USA; KTEH Public Television and Opera San Jose
24 September 1995	*Freispruch für Medea*; opera in two acts composed by Rolf Liebermann; libretto by Ursula Haas; directed by Ruth Berghaus; performed at the Staatsoper, Hamburg; Philharmonisches Staatsorchester Hamburg Switzerland (see the entry under 1 June 2001 for the première of the three-act version of this work)
10 October 1995	*Phoenician Women*; translated by David Thompson; directed by Katie Mitchell; performed at The Other Place, Stratford-upon-Avon, England, transferring to The Pit, Barbican Arts Centre, London, in 1996; Royal Shakespeare Company, England
3 November 1995	*Medea*; opera composed by Gavin Bryars (a revised version of the work performed on 23 October 1984); libretto by Minos Volonakis and the composer; performed at the Tramway, Glasgow; BBC Scottish Symphony Orchestra
1995	*The Labourers of Herakles*; a play, inspired by fragments of the lost tragedian Phrynichus, written by Tony Harrison (who also played Phrynichus); performed at Delphi
1995	*Mighty Aphrodite*; film informed by *Oedipus Tyrannus* and *Hippolytus*; written and directed by Woody Allen; USA
1995	*Soldier Boy*; film, with links to several Euripidean plays, written and directed by Peter Demas; Canada
15 March 1996	*Jason ~~und~~ Medea/Schwarz überwölbt Rot* [*Jason ~~and~~ Medea/Black Enshrouds Red*]; chamber opera composed by Volker Blumenthaler; using the Medea plays of Euripides and Grillparzer, Homer's *Odyssey*,

Ovid's *Metamorphoses*, and texts by Georg
Trakl and Ono no Komachi; performed at
the Nürnberg Tafelhalle, Germany; Neues
Musiktheater Erlangen, Germany

23 March 1996   *The Cure at Troy*; adaptation of *Philoctetes*
by Seamus Heaney; directed by Leland
Patton; with Seamus Heaney's pre-recorded
voice as Heracles; performed at the Loeb
Drama Center, Cambridge, Massachusetts;
American Repertory Theatre Institute for
Advanced Theatre Training, Harvard Uni-
versity

Spring 1996   *The Trojan Women: A Love Story*; adaptation of Euripides and Hector Berlioz's 1859
opera *Les Troyens* by Charles Mee; directed
by Tina Landau; performed at the University of Washington, Seattle

15 May 1996   *Phaedra's Love*; adaptation of Euripides'
Hippolytus and Seneca's *Phaedra* written
and directed by Sarah Kane; performed at
the Gate Theatre, London; Gate Theatre,
England

20 May 1996   *Bacchae*; opera composed by Arghyris
Kounadis; libretto by Kopidakis; performed
in Athens

27 July 1996   *The Darker Face of the Earth*; adaptation
of *Oedipus Tyrannus* by Rita Dove; directed
by Ricardo Kahn; performed at the Angus
Bowmer Theatre, Ashland, Oregon (Oregon
Shakespeare Festival); co-produced by the
Crossroads Theatre, New Brunswick, NJ,
and the John F. Kennedy Center for the
Performing Arts, Washington, DC

17 September 1996   *The Oedipus Plays*; translation of Sophocles'
two Oedipus plays by Ranjit Bolt; directed
by Peter Hall; with Greg Hicks as Tiresias/
Polynices; performed at the Royal National

Theatre, London; Royal National Theatre, England

22 November 1996   *Dionysus 96: The Bacchae of Euripides*; directed by Ramon Arjona IV; performed at the Kennedy Theatre, University of Hawaii at Manoa, Honolulu, Hawaii

19 December 1996   *I Sette Contro Tebe*; translated by Eduardo Sanguineti; directed by Mario Martone and Andrea Renzi; performed at the Teatro Nuovo, Naples; Teatri Uniti, Italy (rehearsal footage from this production was used in Martone's 1998 film)

1996   *Bacchae*; operatic adaptation; libretto by Peter Steadman; directed by Chen Shizheng; performed at the Beijing Children's Theatre, Peking; China National Beijing-Opera Theatre

1996   *Edipo Alcalde* [*The Mayor Oedipus*]; film adaptation by Gabriel García Márquez; directed by Jorge Alí Triana; Colombia, Mexico, and Spain

4 August 1997   *The Red Act Arias*; musical composition by Roger Reynolds influenced by *Agamemnon* (part of a work entitled *The Red Act Project*; see entry under 21 May 1999); libretto by Richmond Lattimore; with Harriet Walker as Narrator; performed at the Royal Albert Hall, London (Proms Festival), and broadcast by BBC Radio 3; BBC Symphony Orchestra and Singers

5 September 1997   *The Iphigenia Cycle*; adaptation of Euripides' two Iphigenia plays by Nicholas Rudall; directed by JoAnne Akalaitis; performed at the Court Theatre, Chicago, Illinois

21 November 1997   *The Bacchae*; translated by Paul Schmidt; directed by François Rochaix; performed at the Loeb Drama Center, Cambridge, Massachusetts; American Repertory Theatre

3 January 1998	*Herkules*; adaptation by Oscar van Woensel; directed by Hein van der Heijden; Transformatorhuis Toneelgroep, Amsterdam; Toneelgroep Amsterdam, Netherlands
20 January 1998	*Phaedra in Delirium*; adaptation, influenced by Euripides' *Hippolytus*, Seneca's *Phaedra*, and Ovid, by Susan Yankowitz; directed by Alison Summers; performed at the Classic Stage Company, New York
22 January 1998	*Herakles*; translated by Gerrit Komrij; directed by Titus Muizelaar; performed at the Stadsschouwberg, Amsterdam; Toneelgroep Amsterdam, Netherlands
15 and 22 February 1998	*The Trojan Women*; directed by Martin Jenkins and Damiano Pietropaolo; music composed by Colin Linden; broadcast in two parts on CBC (Canadian Broadcasting Corporation) Radio 1; CBC
9 May 1998	*Oedipus at Colonus*; opera composed by Theodoros Antoniou; libretto by Giorgos Michaelidis; performed at the Megaron Mousikis, Athens
13 May 1998	*Medea*; adaptation by Alistair Elliot; directed by Kenny Leon; with Phylicia Rashad in the role of Medea; performed at the Woodruff Arts Center, Atlanta; Alliance Theatre Company, USA
June 1998	*Agamemnon*; opera composed by Garrett Fisher; performed at the Nippon Kan Theater, Seattle
June 1998	*Jocasta*; dance drama; music composed by Ruth Schonthal; choreographed by Christine Sang; the libretto was an English reworking of Hélène Cixous's *Le Nom d'Oedipe*; directed by Marya Mazor; performed at the Cornelia Connelly Center for

	Education, New York; Voice and Vision, USA
9 July 1998	*Herakles*; translated by Kenneth McLeish; directed by Nick Philippou; performed at the Gate Theatre, London; Gate Theatre, England
22 July 1998	*Hippolytos: A Dance Drama*; music composed by Jamie Masters; choreographed by Untung Hidayat; adaptation by Jamie Masters; directed by Yana Zarifi; performed at the Faculty of Music, Cambridge (revived in London in November); Thiasos, England
4 September 1998	*Eracle*; translated by Dario del Corno; directed by Andrée Ruth Shammah; performed at the Teatro Olimpico, Vicenza
14 October 1998	*Phèdre*; cantata composed by Naji Hakim; libretto after Racine; directed by John Abulafia; performed at the Royal Festival Hall, London
17 October 1998	*Oedipus*; adapted and directed by Dare Clubb; with Billy Crudup as Oedipus, and Frances McDormand as Merope, his adoptive mother; performed at the Classic Stage Company, New York; Blue Light Theater Company, USA
21 October 1998	*Hecuba*; version by Timberlake Wertenbaker; directed by Carey Perloff; with Olympia Dukakis as Hecuba; performed at the Geary Theater, San Francisco (a revival of the 1995 production at the Center for the Arts, San Francisco); American Conservatory Theater (ACT), USA
1998	*Medea*; opera in traditional Hebei Clapper style; directed by Jinlin Luo; performed across Europe; Hebei Clapper Opera Troupe, China

1998	*Muslim Babae*; adaptation of *Trojan Women* by Sedfrey Ordonez; performed in Manila
1998	*Tegonni, an African Antigone*; adapted and directed by Fémi Òsófisan; performed at the University Arts Theatre, University of Ibadan, Nigeria
1998	*The Photographers*; film adaptation of *Antigone*; directed by Nikos Koundouros; Greece
1998	*Prometheus*; film; written and directed by Tony Harrison; music composed by Richard Blackford; designed by Jocelyn Herbert; Holmes Associates/Michael Kustow production presented by Film Four in association with the Arts Council of England; England
1998	*Rehearsals for War* [*Teatro di Guerra*]; film, using rehearsal footage from Martone's 1996 stage production *I Sette Contro Tebe*; directed by Mario Martone; Italy
February 1999	*Edufa*; a version of *Alcestis* by Efua Sutherland; performed in Nairobi, Kenya
2 March 1999	*Iph ...*; adaptation of *Iphigenia in Aulis* by Colin Teevan; directed by David Grant; performed at the Lyric Theatre, Belfast
23 March 1999	*Trojan Women*; translated by Nicholas Rudall; directed by JoAnne Akalaitis; performed at the Shakespeare Theatre, Washington, DC; Shakespeare Theatre, USA
21 May 1999	*Justice*; musical composition by Roger Reynolds drawing on *Trojan Women, Iphigenia in Aulis*, and *Agamemnon* (part of a work entitled *The Red Act Project*; see entry under 4 August 1997); directed by Tadashi Suzuki; libretto by Roger Reynolds; performed at Shizuoko, Japan (2nd Theatre Olympics)
25 May 1999	*Heracles Trilogy*; directed by Theodoros Terzopoulos; Muhsin Ertugrul Stage, Istan-

bul (11th International Istanbul Theatre Festival), followed by a tour to Japan and Barcelona; co-produced by the International Istanbul Theatre Festival and Attis Theatre, Athens

2 June 1999   *Trojan Women*; directed by Antunes Filho; Muhsin Ertugrul Stage, Istanbul (11th International Istanbul Theatre Festival), followed by a tour to Japan and Barcelona; Macunaima, Brazil

5 August 1999   *The Darker Face of the Earth*; adaptation of *Oedipus Tyrannus* by Rita Dove; directed by James Kerr; performed at the Royal National Theatre, London; Royal National Theatre, England

7 October 1999   *Antigone*; opera composed by Mikis Theodorakis using his own libretto based on Aeschylus' *Seven against Thebes*, Euripides' *Phoenician Women*, and Sophocles' *Antigone*; performed at the Megaron Mousikis, Athens

28 November 1999   *Dianeira*; version of Sophocles' *Trachiniae* by Timberlake Wertenbaker; directed by Catherine Bailey and Timberlake Wertenbaker; with Simon Callow as Nessos, Olympia Dukakis as Nurse, Joseph Fiennes as Helos, Alan Howard as Heracles, and Harriet Walter as Dianeira; broadcast on BBC Radio 3

1 December 1999   *The Oresteia*; an adaptation by Ted Hughes; directed by Katie Mitchell; performed at the Royal National Theatre, London; Royal National Theatre, England

2 December 1999   *Marie Christine*; musical composed by Michael John LaChiusa using his own libretto, a version of *Medea*; performed at the Vivian Beaumont Theatre, Lincoln Center, New York

9 December 1999	*Antigone*; opera composed and directed by John Eaton; performed in the Harold Washington Library Center, Chicago; Pocket Opera Company, USA
1999	*Holy Smoke*; film, drawing on elements of *Bacchae*; directed by Jane Campion; with Kate Winslet and Harvey Keitel
1999	*La Ville parjure ou le réveil des Erinyes*; film, drawing on Mnouchkine's stage production of the same name (see entry under 18 May 1994); directed by Catherine Vilpoux; France
15 March 2000	*Oedipus*; adaptation by David Greig; directed by Graham McLaren; performed as part of a series of plays entitled *The Greeks* at the Old Fruitmarket, Glasgow; theatre babel, Scotland
16 March 2000	*Edipo Re*; translated by Guido Paduano; directed by Mario Martone; performed at the Teatro Argentina, Rome; Teatro di Roma, Italy (see entry under 2000 for a film created from this production)
16 March 2000	Sophocles' *Electra*; adaptation by Tom McGrath; directed by Graham McLaren; performed as part of a series of plays entitled *The Greeks* at the Old Fruitmarket, Glasgow; theatre babel, Scotland
17 March 2000	*Medea*; adapted by Liz Lochhead; directed by Graham McLaren; with Maureen Beattie as Medea; performed as part of a series of plays entitled *The Greeks* at the Old Fruitmarket, Glasgow, before transferring to the Assembly Rooms, Edinburgh (Edinburgh Fringe Festival), prior to an international tour; theatre babel, Scotland
23 March 2000	*Big Love*; version of Aeschylus' *Suppliants* written by Charles Mee; directed by Les

Waters; performed at the Actors' Theatre of Louisville, Kentucky (24th Humana Festival of New American Plays)

9 June 2000 · *Ion*; opera composed by Param Vir; libretto by David Lan; a 'partial staging' directed by Steven Pimlott; performed at Snape Maltings Concert Hall, Suffolk (Aldeburgh Festival)

June 2000 · *Medea in Exile*; opera composed by Douglas Anderson; performed in New York; American Chamber Opera Company

6 July 2000 · *Oedipus*; directed by Tadashi Suzuki; performed at Delphi, and later in New York

14 September 2000 · *Alcestis*; adaptation by Ted Hughes; directed by Barrie Rutter; performed at the Viaduct Theatre, Halifax, Yorkshire, followed by a tour of the UK; Northern Broadsides, England

21 October 2000 · *Tantalus*; adaptation of John Barton's ten-play cycle, which includes material from several Greek epics and tragedies, with additional text by Colin Teevan; directed by Peter Hall and Edward Hall; performed at the Denver Center for the Performing Arts, Denver, Colorado, before a tour of the UK; Denver Center Theatre Company, USA, in association with the Royal Shakespeare Company, England

30 November 2000 · *Herakles*; directed by Jay Scheib; performed at Chashama Theatre, New York; Chashama, USA

2000 · *A Place on Earth* [*Un Posto al Mondo*]; film, drawing on Martone's stage production of *Edipo Re* (see entry under 16 March 2000); directed by Mario Martone; Radio Televisione Italiana, Italy

16 February 2001 · *Mister Heracles*; adaptation by Simon Armitage; directed by Natasha Betteridge

and Simon Godwin; performed at the West Yorkshire Playhouse, Leeds

March 2001   *Herakles*; translated by Wolfgang Heyder; directed by Georg Rootering; performed at the Theater am Kirchplatz, Schaan; Theater am Kirchplatz, Liechtenstein.

April 2001   *Agamemnon*; opera composed by Andrew Simpson; libretto by Sarah Ferrario; workshop production performed at the Catholic University of America, Washington, DC (see entry under 25 April 2003 for first full staging)

1 June 2001   *Medea*; opera in three acts composed by Rolf Liebermann; libretto by Ursula Haas; performed at the Stadttheater Bern, Switzerland (see entry under 24 September 1995 for the two-act version of this work)

3 June 2001   *Zerbrochene Bilder* [*Shattered Pictures*]; 'scenic music' composed by Paul-Heinz Dittrich; libretto includes texts by Heiner Müller (*Verkommenes Ufer*, *Medeamaterial*, and *Landschaft mit Argonauten*), Paul Celan, and Edgar Allan Poe; directed by Iris Sputh and Jonathan Stickhammer; performed at the Schlosstheater, Rheinsberg

6 September 2001   *Oedipus*; version by Blake Morrison; directed by Barrie Rutter; performed at the Viaduct Theatre, Halifax, Yorkshire, followed by a tour of the UK; Northern Broadsides, England

7 September 2001   *Song of a Goat*; version of *Agamemnon* by J. P. Clark; directed by Ahmed Yerima; Muson Centre, Lagos, followed by a tour; National Troupe of Nigeria

20 September 2001   Scenes from *The Oresteia*; translated by Tony Harrison; directed by Felicity Hilton; performed by Diana Quick in the Holywell Music Room, Oxford

17 October 2001	*Antygona*; opera composed by Zbigniew Rudzínski; libretto by Joanna Kulmowa; performed at the Warsaw Chamber Opera
Autumn 2001	*My Deah*; a reading of John Epperson's version of *Medea*; performed at the New York Theatre Workshop
9 November 2001	*The Seven against Thebes*; English translation of Antón Arrufat's Spanish adaptation by Mike Gonzalez; directed by Susan Triesman and Steve King; performed at the Ramshorn Theatre, University of Strathclyde, Glasgow; Actual Theatre Company, Scotland
1 December 2001	*Klytaemnestra's Unmentionables*; written by Rob Grace; directed by Jennifer Wineman; with Bradford Louryk in a one-man performance; performed at the Here Arts Center, New York; Studio 42, USA
30 January 2002	*Medea*; in ancient Greek; directed by Nat Coleman; performed at the Oxford Playhouse; Oxford University Classical Drama Society
12 February 2002	*Medea*; opera in three acts composed by Rolf Liebermann; libretto by Ursula Haas; directed by Jorge Lavelli; performed at the Opéra Bastille, Paris (see entry under 1 June 2001 for the premiere of this work)
22 February 2002	*Die Perser*; adaptation by Durs Grünbein; directed by Niels-Peter Rudolph; performed at the Staatsschauspiel, Dresden
15 March 2002	*Troijan Naiset* [*Trojan Women*]; opera composed by Jani Sivén; libretto by Tapani Mikkola; directed by Ville Saukkonen; performed in Helsinki, touring to Berlin; Helsinki Conservatory
March 2002	*Helen*; adaptation by Ellen McLaughlin; directed by Tony Kushner; performed at

the Public Theater, New York; Public Theater, USA

March 2002   *The Greeks*, comprising sections of *Trojan Women* performed in ancient Greek; directed by Sergey Prokhanov; workshop performance by students of the Russian Academy of Theatre Arts at the Luna Theatre, Moscow

4 May 2002   *Ecuba*; opera composed by Bruno Rigacci; directed by Mignon Dunn; performed at the Conservatory of Music, Brooklyn College, New York; Brooklyn College Conservatory Orchestra, USA (see entry under 31 March 1951 for the first concert performance)

17 May 2002   *Bacchai*; translated by Colin Teevan; directed by Peter Hall; music composed by Harrison Birtwistle; with Greg Hicks as Dionysus/Teiresias/Servant; performed at the Royal National Theatre, London, before touring to Newcastle upon Tyne and Epidaurus; Royal National Theatre, England (see Figure 33)

5 June 2002   *Die Heimkehr des Dionysos* [*The Return of Dionysus*]; 'music drama' composed by Edwin Geist using his own libretto; directed by Vladimir Tarasov; first performed (over seventy years after its composition) at the Russisches Theater, Vilnius, Lithuania

20 June 2002   *Bad Women*; inspired by several Greek tragedies; written and directed by Tina Shepherd and Sidney Goldfarb; performed at the Here Arts Center, New York; Talking Band, USA

4 July 2002   Seneca's *Oedipus*; translated by Ted Hughes; directed by Michael Chase; performed in the Glasshouse Theatre, Stourbridge, England; Glasshouse Productions, England

12 July 2002	*Jocasta*; music drama composed by George Couroupos; libretto by Ioulita Iliopoulou; conducted by Miltos Logiadis; directed by Apostolia Papadamaki; performed in Delphi (XI International Meeting on Ancient Greek Drama)
18 August 2002	*Oedipe*; opera composed by Georges Enescu; libretto by Edmond Fleg after Sophocles' two Oedipus plays; performed at the Usher Hall, Edinburgh (Edinburgh Festival); BBC Scottish Symphony Orchestra (see entry under 13 March 1936 for the première of this work)
29 August 2002	*Oedipus Rex*; opera composed by Igor Stravinsky; directed by François Girard; performed at the Edinburgh Playhouse (Edinburgh Festival); Canadian Opera Company (see entry under 30 May 1927 for the première of this work)
August 2002	*Herakles*; translated by Mairi Yossi; directed by Thymios Karakatsanis; performed extensively across Greece (première as yet unidentified); National Theatre of Northern Greece
19 September 2002	*The Children of Herakles*; translated by Ralph Gladstone; directed by Peter Sellars; performed at the Bottroper Lichthof, Bottrop (Ruhr Triennial Arts Festival), Germany, followed by a tour to Italy and France before transferring to the Loeb Drama Center, Cambridge, Massachusetts, in January 2003; American Repertory Theatre, in association with the Ruhr Triennial Arts Festival
2 October 2002	*Ariel*; adaptation of *Iphigenia in Aulis* and *Oresteia* by Marina Carr; directed by Conall Morrison; performed at the Abbey Theatre, Dublin

FIGURE 33. Agave (William Houston), holding the head of Pentheus, in *Bacchai*, directed by Peter Hall (2002). The masks were made by Vicki Hallam.

19 October 2002	*Medea*; opera composed by Adriano Guarnieri; conducted by Pietro Borgonovo; directed by Giorgio Barberio Corsetti; first performance of the complete work at the PalaFenice, Venice
2002	*The Bacchae*; film adaptation written and directed by Bradford Mays; with William Shephard (who played Pentheus in *Dionysus in 69*; see entry under 6 June 1968) as Cadmus; USA
23 January 2003	*Médée*; opera composed by Michèle Reverdy; libretto adapted by Kai Stefan Fritsch and Bernard Banoun from Christa Wolf's *Medea-Stimmen*; performed at the Opéra National, Lyon
29 January 2003	*Women of Troy*; directed by Jenny Green and Robert Kennedy; performed at the Belvoir Street Downstairs Theatre, Sydney; Hoi Barbaroi Productions, Australia
January 2003	*Mythos*; Hebrew drama drawing on the *Oresteia* written and directed by Rina Yerushalmi; with Yousef Sweid as Orestes; performed in Tel Aviv; Itim Ensemble, Israel
5 February 2003	*Iphigenia*; adaptation of *Iphigenia in Aulis* by Edna O'Brien; directed by Anna Mackmin; performed at the Crucible Theatre, Sheffield; Sheffield Theatres, England
13 February 2003	*Antigone*; translated and directed by Conall Morrison; performed at the Town Hall Theatre, Galway, and subsequently touring to other Irish venues; Storytellers Theatre Company, Republic of Ireland
7 March 2003	*Oedipe sur la Route*; opera composed by Pierre Bartholomée; libretto by Henri Bauchau, based on his novel; directed by Philippe Sireuil; performed at the Théâtre Royal de la Monnaie, Brussels

20 March 2003	*YokastaS*; a play, drawing on *Oedipus Tyrannus*, by Richard Schechner and Saviana Stanescu; performed at La MaMa Experimental Theatre Club, New York
25 April 2003	*Agamemnon*; opera composed by Andrew Simpson; libretto by Sarah Ferrario; performed at the Catholic University of America, Washington, DC (see entry under April 2001 for an earlier workshop production)
13 May 2003	*Ödipus in Kolonos*; translated by Peter Handke; directed by Klaus Michael Grüber; performed at the Burgtheater, Vienna (Wiener Festwochen)
Autumn 2003	*Antigone*; adaptation by Blake Morrison; directed by Barrie Rutter; performed at the Cattle Market, Skipton, Yorkshire, followed by a tour of the UK; Northern Broadsides, England

References

ADORNO, THEODOR (1966), *Negative Dialektik*, Frankfurt. Translated into English by E. B. Ashton (1973), *Negative Dialectics*, New York.

ALFORD, C. F. (1992), *The Psychoanalytic Theory of Greek Tragedy*, New Haven, CT, and London.

ALI, TARIQ (1978), *1968 and After: Inside the Revolution*, London.

ALLAIN, PAUL (2002), *The Art of Stillness: The Theatre Practice of Tadashi Suzuki*, London.

ANG, IEN (1985), *Watching Dallas: Soap Opera and the Melodramatic Imagination*, English translation by Della Couling, London.

ANGELOPOULOS, T. (1997), *10 3/4: Screenplays*, vol. i, Athens.

ANSORGE, PETER (1975), *Disrupting the Spectacle: Five Years of Experimental and Fringe Theatre in Britain*, London.

ARMEL, ALIETTE (1999), 'Les visages d'Antigone', in Armel (ed.), *Antigone: figures mythiques*, Paris, 7–92.

ARMITAGE, SIMON (2000), *Mister Heracles*, London.

ARONSON, ARNOLD (2000), *American Avant-Garde Theatre*, London and New York.

ARROWSMITH, WILLIAM (1956), *Heracles*, in William Arrowsmith, Walter Brynner, and Richmond Lattimore, *Euripides*, vol. ii, Chicago, IL, and London.

——(1959), *The Bacchae*, in William Arrowsmith, Emily Townsend Vermeule, and Elizabeth Wyckoff, *Euripides*, vol. v, Chicago, IL, and London.

ARRUFAT, ANTÓN (1968), *Los Siete contra Tebas*, Havana.

ARTAUD, ANTONIN (1938), *Le Théâtre et son double*, Paris.

AULETTA, ROBERT (1986), '*Ajax*, adapted from Sophocles', *Theater* 18.1, 18–35.

——(1987), *Ajax, adapted from Sophocles by Robert Auletta*, Amsterdam.

——(1993), *The Persians by Aeschylus: A Modern Version*, Los Angeles, CA.

AUSTIN, NORMAN (1999), 'Homer and the sunrise in Derek Walcott's *Omeros*', *Classical World* 93, 29–42.

AVISAR, ILAN (1988), *Screening the Holocaust: Cinema's Images of the Unimaginable*, Bloomington, IN.

BALL, HUGO (1974), *Flight Out Of Time: A Dada Diary*, New York.

BALME, CHRISTOPHER (1999), *Decolonizing the Stage: Theatrical Syncretism and Post-Colonial Drama*, Oxford.

BANNING, YVONNE (1999), 'Speaking silences: images of cultural difference and gender in Fleishmann and Reznek's *Medea*', in Marcia Blumberg and Dennis Walder (eds.), *South African Theatre As/And Intervention*, Amsterdam and Atlanta, GA, 41–7.

BARDEL, RUTH (2001), 'Casting shadows on the Greek stage', D.Phil. thesis, University of Oxford.

BARKER, CLIVE, and SIMON TRUSSLER (1994, eds.), *Jan Kott: An Eightieth Birthday Celebration*, published as *New Theatre Quarterly* 10.40.

BARLOW, SHIRLEY (1996, ed.), *Euripides: Heracles*, Warminster.

BARNES, CLIVE (1968), 'Development of the environmental experience and audience involvement of *Dionysus in 69*', *New York Times*, 19 November, 52.

BARNOUW, ERIK (1962), *The Television Writer*, New York.

BARRAULT, JEAN-LOUIS (1961), *The Theatre of Jean-Louis Barrault*, translated from the French by Joseph Chiari, London.

BARTHES, ROLAND (1970*a*), *S/Z*, Paris.

—— (1970*b*), *L'empire des signes*, Geneva.

—— (1972), 'Putting on the Greeks', in *Critical Essays* (= *Essais critiques* (Paris 1964)), translated from the French by Richard Howard, Chicago, IL, 59–66.

—— (1975), *Roland Barthes par Roland Barthes*, Paris.

BAUDRILLARD, JEAN (1991), 'The reality gulf', *The Guardian*, 11 January, 25.

—— (2002), *Screened Out*, translated from the French by Chris Turner, London.

BECKETT, SAMUEL (1958), *Endgame*, New York.

—— (1986), *The Complete Dramatic Works*, London.

—— (1995*a*), *Eleuthéria*, Paris.

—— (1995*b*), *Eleuthéria*, translated from the French by Michael Brodsky, New York.

BENJAMIN, JESSICA (1988), *The Bonds of Love: Psychoanalysis, Feminism, and the Problem of Domination*, New York.

BERKOFF, STEVEN (1994), *The Collected Plays*, vol. i, London and Boston, MA.

—— (1996), *Free Association: An Autobiography*, London and Boston, MA.

BERNAL, MARTIN (1987), *Black Athena: The Afroasiatic Roots of Classical Civilization*, vol. i, London.

BIERL, ANTON (1996), *Die Orestie des Aischylos auf der modernen Bühne*, Stuttgart.

BILLINGTON, MICHAEL (1993), 'A tragedy of our time', *The Guardian*, 16 August, 4–5.

BIRRINGER, JOHANNES (1991), *Theatre, Theory, Postmodernism*, Bloomington, IN.

BLISS, MICHAEL (1983), *Brian De Palma*, London.

BOUZEREAU, LAURENT (1988), *The De Palma Cut: the Films of America's Most Controversial Director*, New York.

BRADBY, DAVID (2002), 'Cultural politics and theatrical practice in the history of the Théâtre du Soleil', in David Bradby and Maria Delgado (eds.), *The Paris Jigsaw: Internationalism and the City's Stages*, Manchester and New York, 113–31.

BRADBY, DAVID, and MARIA DELGADO (2002, eds.), *The Paris Jigsaw: Internationalism and the City's Stages*, Manchester and New York.

BRADBY, DAVID, and ANNIE SPARKS (1997), *Mise en Scène: French Theatre Now*, London.

BRATHWAITE, KAMAU (1967), *Odale's Choice*, London.

BRECHT, BERTOLT (1990), *Sophocles' Antigone adapted by Bertolt Brecht, based on the German translation by Friedrich Hölderlin and translated into English by Judith Malina*, New York.

BRECHT, STEFAN (1969), Review of *Dionysus in 69*, *The Drama Review* 43, 156–68.

——(1978), *The Theatre of Visions: Robert Wilson*, Frankfurt am Main.

BREITINGER, ECKHARD (1996), 'Theater in Afrika heute: politisches Umfeld und "angepasse Ästhetik"', in Peter Meyns (ed.), *Staat und Gesellschaft in Afrika: Erosions-und Reformprozesse*, Hamburg, 243–58.

BREUER, L. (1989), *Gospel at Colonus*, New York.

BREWSTER, BEN, and LEA JACOBS (1997), *Theatre to Cinema: Stage Pictorialism and the Early Feature Film*, Oxford.

BROCKETT, OSCAR G. (1999), *History of the Theatre*, 8th edn. with revisions by Franklin J. Hildy, Boston, MA, and London.

BROICH, ULRICH (1997), 'Postkoloniales Drama und griechische Tragödie', in Hellmut Flashar (ed.), *Tragödie: Idee und Transformation*, Stuttgart and Leipzig, 332–47.

BROOK, PETER (1987), *The Shifting Point, 1946–1987*, New York.

BROWN, CALLUM G. (2001), *The Death of Christian Britain*, London and New York.

BRUSTEIN, ROBERT (1968), 'The democratization of art', *The New Republic*, 10 August, 18–19.

BRYANT-BERTEIL, SARAH (2000), '*The Trojan Women: a Love Story*: A postmodern semiotics of the tragic', *Theatre Research International* 25.1, 40–52.

BUDELMANN, FELIX (forthcoming), 'Greek tragedies in West African adaptations', in Barbara Goff (ed.), *Classics and Colonialism*.

BURIAN, PETER (1997), 'Tragedy adapted for stages and screens: the Renaissance to the present', in Pat Easterling (ed.), *The Cambridge Companion to Greek Tragedy*, Cambridge, 228–83.

BURKERT, WALTER (1966), 'Greek tragedy and sacrificial ritual', *Greek, Roman and Byzantine Studies* 7, 87–121.

—— (1972), *Homo Necans: Interpretationen altgriechischer Opferriten und Mythen*, Berlin. Translated into English by Peter Bing (1983), *Homo Necans: The Anthropology of Ancient Greek Sacrificial Ritual and Myth*, Berkeley, CA.

BYG, BARTON (1995), *Landscapes of Resistance: The German Films of Danièle Huillet and Jean-Marie Straub*, Berkeley, CA.

CAMUS, ALBERT (1970), *Selected Essays and Notebooks*, translated from the French by Philip Thody, Harmondsworth.

CANNING, CHARLOTTE (1996), *Feminist Theaters in the USA: Staging Women's Experience*, New York and London.

CARTLEDGE, PAUL (2000), 'Greek political thought: the historical context', in Christopher Rowe and Malcolm Schofield (eds.), *The Cambridge History of Greek and Roman Political Thought*, Cambridge, 11–59.

CARTMELL, DEBORAH, and IMELDA WHELEHAN (1999, eds.), *Adaptations: From Text to Screen, Screen to Text*, London.

CASE, SUE ELLEN (1988), *Feminism and Theatre*, Basingstoke.

CAUGHIE, JOHN (2000), *Television Drama: Realism, Modernism, and British Culture*, Oxford.

CAVE, RICHARD (1980), *Terence Gray and the Cambridge Festival Theatre*, Cambridge.

CHALVRON-DEMERSAY, SABINE (1999), *A Thousand Screenplays: The French Imagination in a Time of Crisis*, English translation by Teresa Lavender Fagan, Chicago, IL, and London.

CHAMPAGNE, LENORA (1984), *French Theatre Experiment since 1968*, Ann Arbor, MI.

CHESTER, LEWIS, GODFREY HODGSON, and BRUCE PAGE (1969), *An American Melodrama: The Presidential Campaign of 1968*, London.

CHIOLES, JOHN (1993), 'The *Oresteia* and the avante-garde: three decades of discourse', *Performing Arts Journal* 45, 1–28.

CHODOROW, NANCY (1978), *The Reproduction of Mothering: Psychoanalysis and the Sociology of Gender*, Berkeley, CA.

CHRISTIE, IAN (2000), 'Between magic and realism: Medea on film', in Edith Hall, Fiona Macintosh, and Oliver Taplin (eds.), *Medea in performance 1500–2000*, Oxford, 144–65.

CHURCHILL, CARYL, and DAVID LAN (1986), *A Mouthful of Birds*, London.

CIXOUS, HÉLÈNE (1978), *Le Nom d'Oedipe: chant du corps interdit*, Paris. Translated as *The Name of Oedipus: Song of the Forbidden*

Body, in Christiane P. Makward and Judith G. Miller (1994, eds.), *Plays by French and Francophone Women*, Ann Arbor, MI, 247–326.

—— (1994), *La Ville parjure*, Paris.

CLARK, J. P. (1961), *Song of a Goat*, Ibadan.

CLASZ, CARY (1991), 'An introduction to theatre history in relation to society', Part IV, unpublished manuscript accessible at http://members.aol.com/clasz/PartFour.html (last accessed November 2002).

CLEMENTS, A. (2000), *Mark-Anthony Turnage*, London.

CLENDINNEN, INGA (1999), *Reading the Holocaust*, New York and Cambridge.

CLINTON, WILLIAM J. (1996), *Between Hope and History: Meeting America's Challenges for the 21ˢᵗ Century*, New York

COLAKIS, MARIANTHE (1993), *The Classics in the American Theater of the 1960s and Early 1970s*, Lanham, MD.

—— (1996), 'What Jocasta knew: alternative versions of the Oedipus myth', *Classical and Modern Literature* 16.3, 217–29.

CORCORAN, NEIL (1998), *The Poetry of Seamus Heaney: A Critical Study*, London.

COSS, CLARE, SONDRA SEGAL, and ROBERTA SKLAR (1980), 'Separation and survival: mothers, daughters, sisters—The Women's Experimental Theater', in Hester Eisenstein and Alice Jardine (eds.), *The Future of Difference*, Boston, MA, 193–235.

—— (1983), 'Notes on the Women's Experimental Theatre', in Karen Malpede (ed.), *Women in Theatre: Compassion and Hope*, New York, 235–44.

CRAIG, EDWARD GORDON (1983), *Craig on Theatre*, ed. J. Michael Walton, London.

CROW, BRIAN, and CHRIS BANFIELD (1996), *An Introduction to Post-Colonial Theatre*, Cambridge.

CURB, ROSEMARY, PHYLLIS MAEL, and BEVERLEY BYERS PITTS (1979), 'Catalog of Feminist Theaters—Parts 1 and 2', *Chrysalis* 10, 51–75.

DASGUPTA, GAUTAM (1979), 'Theatre and the ridiculous: a conversation with Charles Ludlam', in Bonnie Marranca and Gautam Dasgupta (eds.), *Theater of the Ridiculous*, Baltimore, MD, and London, 77–91.

DAVIES, ROBERTSON, TYRONE GUTHRIE, BOYD NEEL, and TANYA MOISEIWITSCH (1955), *Thrice the Brinded Cat Hath Mew'd: A Record of the Stratford Shakespearean Festival in Canada*, Toronto.

DAVIS, GREGSON (1997a, ed.), *The Poetics of Derek Walcott: Intertextual Perspectives = South Atlantic Quarterly* 96.2.

—— (1997b), ' "With no Homeric shadow": the disavowal of epic in Derek Walcott's *Omeros*', in Gregson Davis (ed.), *The Poetics of Derek Walcott: Intertextual Perspectives = South Atlantic Quarterly* 96.2, 321–33.

DAVIS, JACK, with KEITH CHESSON (1988), *Jack Davis: A Life-Story*, Melbourne.

DEANE, SEAMUS (1991, ed.), *The Field Day Anthology of Irish Writing*, Derry.

—— (2002), 'Field Day's Greeks (and Russians)', in Marianne McDonald and J. Michael Walton (eds.), *Amid Our Troubles: Irish Versions of Greek Tragedy*, London, 148–64.

DECREUS, FREDDY (2000), 'The *Oresteia*, or the myth of the western metropolis between Habermas and Foucault', *Grazer Beiträge* 23, 1–21.

—— (forthcoming), 'Postmodernism and the staging of classical tragedy'. Lecture delivered in November 2002 at the APGRD.

DE LAURETIS, TERESA (1987), *Technologies of Gender: Essays on Theory, Film, and Fiction*, Bloomington, IN.

DELGADO, MARIA, and PAUL HERITAGE (1996), *In Contact with the Gods? Directors Talk Theatre*, Manchester and New York.

DENARD, HUGH (2000), 'Seamus Heaney, Colonialism, and the Cure', *Performing Arts Journal* 66, 1–18.

DERRIDA, JACQUES (1967*a*), *De la grammatologie*, Paris.

—— (1967*b*), *L'Écriture et la différence*, Paris.

—— (1981), *Dissemination*, translated from the French by Barbara Johnson, Chicago, IL.

DOVE, RITA (1996), *The Darker Face of the Earth*, Brownsville, OR.

DRABECK, BERNARD A., and HELEN E. ELLIS (1986, eds.), *Archibald MacLeish: Reflections*, Amherst.

DUFFY, MAUREEN (1973), *Rites*, in Victoria Sullivan and James Hatch (eds.), *Plays by and about Women*, New York, 345–77.

—— (1983), *Rites*, in Michelene Wandor (ed.), *Plays by Women*, vol. ii, London.

DUPONT, FLORENCE (1991), *Homère et Dallas: Introduction à une critique anthropologique*, Paris.

DÜRRENMATT, FRIEDRICH (1954), *Herkules und der Stall des Augias*, Zurich. Reprinted in Friedrich Dürrenmatt (1988), *Werkausgabe in siebenunddreissig Bänden*, Zurich.

EAGLETON, TERRY (1998), *The Eagleton Reader*, Oxford.

—— (2002), *Sweet Violence: The Idea of the Tragic*, Oxford.

EASTERLING, PAT (1997, ed.), *The Cambridge Companion to Greek Tragedy*, Cambridge.

EL DIN, HAMZA (1996), *Available Sound—Darius*, Lotus Records, Salzburg.

ELLEY, DEREK (1976), 'The fall of the Roman Empire', *Films and Filming* 22.5, 18–24.

—— (1984), *The Epic Film: Myth and History*. London.

ELLMANN, MAUD (1994, ed.), *Psychoanalytic Literary Criticism*, London and New York.

EPPERSON, JOHN (2001), '*My Deah*', the unpublished typescript can be requested from the author at info@lypsinka.com.

ESSLIN, MARTIN (1974), 'Aristotle and the advertisers: the television commercial as drama', *Kenyon Review*, Fall. Reprinted in Martin Esslin (1980), *Mediations: Essays on Brecht, Beckett and the Media*, New York, 228–42.

EYRE, RICHARD, and NICHOLAS WRIGHT (2000), *Changing Stages: A View of British Theatre in the Twentieth Century*, London.

FABIEN, MICHÈLE (1981), *Jocaste*, in *Didascalies* 1, Brussels. Translated into English by R. Miller, in Françoise Kourilsky and Catherine Temerson (1988, eds.), *Plays by Women: An International Anthology*, New York, 77–101.

FANON, FRANTZ (1967a), *Black Skin, White Masks*, translated from the French by Charles Lam Markmann, New York.

——(1967b), *Wretched of the Earth*, translated from the French by Constance Farrington, Harmondsworth.

FERRIS, DAVID F. (2000), *Silent Urns: Romanticism, Hellenism, Modernity*, Stanford.

FINN, HOLLY (2001), 'Goddesses versus guerillas', *Financial Times Weekend Section*, 3 February, 11.

FISCHER, ERNST (1959), *Von der Notwendigkeit der Kunst*, Dresden. Translated into English by Anna Bostock (1963), *The Necessity of Art*, Harmondsworth.

FISCHER-LICHTE, ERIKA, MICHAEL GISSENWEHRER, and JOSEPHINE RILEY (1990, eds.), *The Dramatic Touch of Difference*, Tübingen.

FLASHAR, HELLMUT (1991), *Inszenierung der Antike: Das griechische Drama auf der Bühne der Neuzeit, 1585–1990*, Munich.

——(1997, ed.), *Tragödie: Idee und Transformation*, Stuttgart and Leipzig.

FLETCHER, BERYL S., and JOHN FLETCHER (1985), *A Student's Guide to the Plays of Samuel Beckett*, revised 2nd edn., London.

FOLEY, HELENE (1975), 'Sex and state in ancient Greece', *Diacritics* 5.4, 31–6.

——(1978), 'Reverse similes and sex roles in the *Odyssey*', *Arethusa* 11, 7–26.

——(1981), 'The conception of women in Athenian drama', in Helene Foley (ed.), *Reflections of Women in Antiquity*, London and New York, 127–67.

——(1985), *Ritual Irony: Poetry and Sacrifice in Euripides*, Ithaca, NY, and London.

——(1999), 'Modern performance and adaptation of Greek tragedy' (1998 Presidential Address to the American Philological Association), *Transactions of the American Philological Association* 139, 1–12.

FOLEY, HELENE (1999–2000), 'Twentieth-century performance and adapatation of Greek tragedy', in Martin Cropp, Kevin Lee, and David Sansone (eds.), *Euripides and Tragic Theatre in the Late Fifth Century* (*Illinois Classical Studies* Special Issues 24 and 25), Champaign, IL, 1–13.

—— (2001*a*), *Female Acts in Greek Tragedy*, Princeton, NJ, and Oxford.

—— (2001*b*), '*Tantalus*', *American Journal of Philology* 122, 415–28.

—— (forthcoming *a*), 'The Millennium Project: *Agamemnon* in the United States', in Fiona Macintosh, Pantelis Michelakis, Edith Hall, and Oliver Taplin (eds.), *Agamemnon in Performance, 458 BC–2002 AD*, Oxford.

—— (forthcoming *b*), 'Adaptation of Greek tragedy by American women playwrights', *Proceedings of the X International Meeting on Ancient Greek Drama, Delphi, Greece, 30 June–9 July 2000*.

FORT, B. (1997), 'Theater, history, ethics: an interview with Hélène Cixous on *The Perjured City or The Awakening of the Furies*', *New Literary History* 28.3, 425–56.

—— (1999), 'Spectres d'Eschyle: *La Ville parjure* d'Hélène Cixous', in Mireille Calle-Gruber (ed.), *Hélène Cixous: croisées d'une oeuvre*, Paris, 443–6.

FOTOPOULOS, DIONYSSIS (1986), *Stage Design: Costumes*, Athens.

FOUCAULT, MICHEL (1969), *L'archéologie du savoir*, Paris.

—— (1978), *The History of Sexuality*, translated from the French by Robert Hurley, New York.

FRAZER, JAMES G. (1890), *The Golden Bough: A Study in Comparative Religion*, London.

FREEMAN, SANDRA (1998), 'Bisexuality in Cixous's *Le Nom d'Oedipe*', *Theatre Research International* 23.3, 242–8.

FREUND, PHILIP (1970), *Jocasta*, in *Three Poetic Plays*, London, 94–170.

FRIEDLANDER, SAUL (1992, ed.), *Representing the Holocaust*, Cambridge, MA, and London.

FÜHMANN, F. (1968), *König Ödipus: Gesammelte Erzählungen*, Berlin.

GALINSKY, G. KARL (1972), *The Herakles Theme*, Oxford.

GAMEL, MARY-KAY (1999), 'Staging ancient drama: the difference women make', *Syllecta Classica* 10, 22–42.

GAUTHIER, R.-G., and E. ERTEL (1992), *La Tragédie grecque: les Atrides au Théâtre du Soleil*, Paris.

GERVAIS, DAVID (2002), 'Ted Hughes' *Oresteia*', *The Cambridge Quarterly* 31, 139–54.

GIAVARINI, L. (1992), 'Antigone, sauvage', *Cahiers du cinéma* 459, 38–41.

GIBBS, JAMES (1986), *Wole Soyinka*, Basingstoke.

GILL, A. A. (1999), *Starcrossed*, London.

GILROY, PAUL (1993), *The Black Atlantic*, London and New York.

GIRARD, RENÉ (1972), *La Violence et le sacre'*, Paris. Translated into English by Patrick Gregory (1977), *Violence and the Sacred*, Baltimore, MD.

GLADSTONE, RALPH (1955), *Heracleidae*, in Ralph Gladstone, David Grene, Richmond Lattimore, and Rex Warner, *Euripides*, vol. i, Chicago, IL, and London.

GOFF, BARBARA (forthcoming, ed.), *Classics and Colonialism*.

GOFFMAN, ERVING (1956), *The Presentation of Self in Everyday Life*, Edinburgh.

——(1976), *Gender Advertisements*, Washington, DC.

GOLDHILL, SIMON (1984), *Language, Sexuality, Narrative, the Oresteia*, Cambridge.

——(1986), *Reading Greek Tragedy*, Cambridge.

GOLDING, WILLIAM (1995), *The Double Tongue*, London.

GORDIMER, NADINE (1999), *Living in Hope and History: Notes From Our Century*, New York.

GRAHAM, MARTHA (1961), *Night Journey*, in *Martha Graham: An American Original in Performance*, Kultur Video, West Long Branch, NJ.

——(1973), *The Notebooks of Martha Graham*, New York.

GREEN, ANDRÉ (1979), *The Tragic Effect: The Oedipus Complex in Tragedy*, translated from the French by Alan Sheridan, Cambridge.

GREER, GERMAINE (1970), *The Female Eunuch*, London.

GRIFFITH, MARK (1977), *The Authenticity of Prometheus Bound*, Cambridge.

GROTOWSKI, JERZY (1968), *Towards a Poor Theatre*, Holstebro.

GUGELBERGER, GEORG M. (1991), 'Decolonising the canon: considerations of third world literature', *New Literary History* 2, 505–24.

HALL, EDITH (1989), *Inventing the Barbarian: Greek Self-Definition through Tragedy*, Oxford.

——(1992a), 'A decent funeral', *Times Literary Supplement* 4653 (5 June), 18.

——(1992b), 'Sexualised violence', *Times Literary Supplement* 4668 (18 September), 20.

——(1993), 'Asia unmanned: images of victory in classical Athens', in John Rich and Graham Shipley (eds.), *War and Society in the Greek World*, London, 108–33.

——(1996, ed.), *Aeschylus' Persians*, with translation, introduction and commentary, Warminster.

——(1997a), 'The sociology of Athenian tragedy', in Pat Easterling (ed.), *The Cambridge Companion to Greek Tragedy*, Cambridge, 93–126.

HALL, EDITH (1997*b*), 'Greek plays in Georgian Reading', *Greece and Rome* 44, 59–81.

—— (1997*c*), 'Talfourd's ancient Greeks in the theatre of reform', *International Journal of the Classical Tradition* 3, 283–307.

—— (1998), 'Ithyphallic males behaving badly: satyr drama as gendered tragic ending', in Maria Wyke (ed.), *Parchments of Gender: Deciphering the Bodies of Antiquity*, Oxford, 13–37.

—— (1999*a*), 'Medea and British legislation before the First World War', *Greece and Rome* 46, 42–77.

—— (1999*b*), 'Sophocles' *Electra* in Britain', in Jasper Griffin (ed.), *Sophocles Revisited: Essays Presented to Sir Hugh Lloyd-Jones*, Oxford, 261–306.

—— (2000), 'Medea on the 18th-century London stage', in Edith Hall, Fiona Macintosh, and Oliver Taplin (eds.), *Medea in Performance 1500–2000*, Oxford, 49–74.

—— (2002), 'Tony Harrison's *Prometheus*: a view from the Left', *Arion* 10, 129–40.

—— (forthcoming), 'Childbirth and family crisis in ancient drama'.

HALL, EDITH, and FIONA MACINTOSH (forthcoming 2004), *Greek Tragedy and the British Stage 1660–1914*, Oxford.

HALL, EDITH, FIONA MACINTOSH, and OLIVER TAPLIN (2000, eds.), *Medea in Performance 1500–2000*, Oxford.

HALL, PETER (2000), *Exposed by the Mask: Form and Language in Drama*, London.

HALL, STUART (1990), 'Cultural identity and Diaspora', in Jonathan Rutherford (ed.), *Identity, Community, Culture, Difference*, London, 222–37.

HAMILTON, SABRINA (1993), 'Split Britches and the *Alcestis* lesson: "What is this albatross?"', in Ellen Donkin and Susan Clement (eds.), *Upstaging Big Daddy: Directing Theater as if Gender and Race Matter*, Ann Arbor, MI, 133–49.

HANISCH, CAROL (1969), 'The personal is political', in *Feminist Revolution* (published by Redstockings Women's Group), New York, 204–5.

HARDWICK, LORNA (2000), *Translating Words, Translating Cultures*, London.

—— (2003*a*), 'Classical drama in modern Scotland: the democratic stage', in Lorna Hardwick and Carol Gillespie (eds.), *Crossing Boundaries through Greek Tragedy*, Selected Proceedings of the Open Colloquium, Milton Keynes.

—— (2003*b*), 'Ancient Greek drama on the modern European stage: identities and performance', in Cristina Chimisso (ed.), *Exploring European Identities*, Milton Keynes, 263–70.

HARDWICK, LORNA (2003c), *Reception Studies, Greece & Rome New Surveys in the Classics* 33, Oxford.

—— (forthcoming), 'Refiguring classical texts: aspects of the post-colonial condition', in Barbara Goff (ed.), *Classics and Colonialism.*

HARDWICK, LORNA, PAT EASTERLING, STANLEY IRELAND, NICK LOWE, and FIONA MACINTOSH (2000, eds.), *Theatre: Ancient and Modern*, Milton Keynes.

HARDWICK, LORNA, and CAROL GILLESPIE (2003, eds.), *Crossing Boundaries through Greek Tragedy*, Selected Proceedings of the Open Colloquium, Milton Keynes.

HARRISON, GEORGE W. M. (2000, ed.), *Seneca in Performance*, Swansea and London.

HARRISON, JANE ELLEN (1912), *Themis: A Study of the Social Origin of Greek Religion*, Cambridge.

HARRISON, TONY (1986), *Theatre Works, 1973–1985*, Harmondsworth.

—— (1990), *The Trackers of Oxyrhynchus*, London.

—— (1991), *A Cold Coming: Gulf War Poems*, Newcastle upon Tyne.

—— (1992), *The Gaze of the Gorgon*, Newcastle upon Tyne.

—— (1998), *Prometheus*, London.

HARTIGAN, KARELISA V. (1995), *Greek Tragedy on the American Stage: Ancient Drama in the Commercial Theater, 1882–1994*, Westport, CT, and London.

—— (2002), *Muse on Madison Avenue: Classical Mythology in Contemporary Advertising*, Frankfurt am Main.

HAYMAN, RONALD (1979), *Theatre and anti-Theatre: New Movements since Beckett*, New York.

HEANEY, SEAMUS (1983), *Sweeney Astray*, Derry.

—— (1990), *The Cure at Troy: A Version of Sophocles' Philoctetes*, London.

—— (1996), *The Spirit Level*, London.

—— (2002), '*The Cure at Troy*: production notes in no particular order', in Marianne McDonald and J. Michael Walton (eds.), *Amid Our Troubles: Irish Versions of Greek Tragedy*, London, 171–80.

HERBERT, JOCELYN (1993), *A Theatre Workbook*, London.

HERSH, ALLISON (1992), ' "How sweet the kill": orgiastic female violence in contemporary re-visions of Euripides' *Bacchae*', *Modern Drama* 35, 409–23.

HEXTER, RALPH, and DANIEL SELDEN (1992, eds.), *Innovations of Antiquity*, New York.

HOLDEN, AMANDA (2001, ed.), *The New Penguin Opera Guide*, London.

HÖLDERLIN, FRIEDRICH (1970), *Sämtliche Werke und Briefe*, ed. Günther Mieth, Munich.

430 *References*

HORTON, ANDREW (1997), '"What do our souls seek?"': an interview with Theo Angelopoulos by Andrew Horton', in Andrew Horton (ed.), *The Last Modernist: The Films of Theo Angelopoulos*, Westport, CT.

HUGHES, JUDITH (1990), *Reshaping the Psychoanalytical Domain: The Work of Melanie Klein, W. R. D. Fairbairn, and D. W. Winnicott*, Berkeley, CA, and London.

HUGHES, TED (1969), *Seneca's Oedipus*, London.

INNES, CHRISTOPHER D. (1981), *Holy Theatre: Ritual and the Avant Garde*, Cambridge.

——(1993), *Avant Garde Theatre, 1892–1992*, London and New York.

INSDORF, ANNETTE (1983), *Indelible Shadows: Film and the Holocaust*, New York.

IRIGARAY, LUCE (1974), *Speculum de l'autre femme*, Paris.

JACKSON, RUSSELL (2000, ed.), *The Cambridge Companion to Shakespeare on Film*, Cambridge.

JAFFE, D. (1976), 'Archibald MacLeish: mapping the tradition', in W. French (ed.), *The Thirties: Fiction, Poetry, Drama*, 2nd edn., Florida, 141–8.

JÄGER, GERD (1974), '. . . wie alles sich für mich verändert hat', *Theater heute* 3, 12–20.

JAMESON, FREDERIC (1971), *Marxism and Form: Twentieth-Century Dialectical Theories of Literature*, Princeton, NJ.

——(1972), *The Prison-House of Language: A Critical Account of Structuralism and Russian Formalism*, Princeton, NJ.

JEFFORDS, SUSAN (1993), 'Can masculinity be terminated?', in Steven Cohan and Ina Rae Hark (eds.), *Screening the Male: Exploring Masculinities in Hollywood Cinema*, London and New York, 245–62.

JEFFREYS, JOE E. (1996), 'An outre entrée into the para-ridiculous histrionics of drag diva Ethyl Eichelberger: a true story', dissertation, New York University.

JOHNSON, ELEANOR (1983), 'Notes on the process of art and feminism', in Karen Malpede (ed.), *Women in Theatre: Compassion and Hope*, New York, 245–51.

JONES, CLAUDIA (1995 (1949)), 'An end to the neglect of the problems of the Negro woman', in *Words of Fire: An Anthology of African American Feminist Thought*, New York. (Originally published in the periodical newspaper *Political Affairs*.)

JONES, E. (1953), *Sigmund Freud: Life and Work*, vol. i, *The Young Freud, 1856–1900*, London.

JUNEJA, RENU (1992), 'Derek Walcott', in Bruce King (ed.), *Post-Colonial English Drama: Commonwealth Drama since 1960*, London, 236–66.

KABBANI, RANA (1986), *Europe's Myths of Orient: Devise and Rule*, London.

KALB, JONATHAN (1998), *The Theatre of Heiner Müller*, Cambridge.

KANE, SARAH (1996), *Phaedra's Love*, in *Blasted and Phaedra's Love*, London, 63–103.

KARPINSKI, MACIEJ (1989), *The Theatre of Andrzej Wajda*, translated from the Polish by Christina Paul, Cambridge.

KAUFMANN, WALTER (1968), *Tragedy and Philosophy*, New York.

KEELEY, EDMUND, and PHILIP SHERRARD (1982, eds.), *George Seferis: Collected Poems*, London.

KENNELLY, BRENDAN (1991), *Euripides' Medea, A New Version*, Newcastle upon Tyne.

KERR, WALTER (1968*a*), 'Come dance with me, Who me?', *New York Times*, 16 June, D1.

——(1968*b*), 'The delusion about illusion', *New York Times*, 21 July, D1.

KERSTEN, HEINZ (1991), Review of *Der Fall Ö*, *Der Tagesspiegel*, 4 April.

KIERNANDER, ADRIAN (1993), *Ariane Mnouchkine and the Théâtre du Soleil*, Cambridge.

KING, BRUCE (2000), *Derek Walcott: A Caribbean Life*, Oxford.

KLEIN, MELANIE (1957), *Envy and Gratitude: A Study of Unconscious Sources*, London.

——(1961), *Narrative of a Child Analysis: The Conduct of the Psychoanalysis of Children as seen in the Treatment of a Ten Year Old Boy*, London.

KNOX, BERNARD (1979), *Word and Action: Essays on the Ancient Theater*, Baltimore, MD, and London.

KOTT, JAN (1970), *The Eating of the Gods: An Interpretation of Greek Tragedy*, London.

KOURILSKY, F. and TEMERSON, CATHERINE (1988), *Plays by Women: An International Anthology*, New York.

KRAUS, M. (1985), 'Heiner Müller und die griechische Tragödie', *Poetica* 17, 299–339.

KUCKHOFF, ARMIN-GERD (1987), 'Der Friedensgedanke im antiken Drama', in Maria Erxleben (ed.), *Der Friedensgedanke im antiken Drama*, Stendal, 9–29.

KYRIAKOS, K. (2002), *From Stage to Screen: A Spherical Approach to the Relation Between Greek Cinema and Theatre*, Athens. (In Greek: *Apo ti skini stin othoni: sfairiki proseggisi tis schesis tou ellinikou kinimatografou me to theatro*.)

LAERMANS, RUDI (1994), 'Halfway to the grave', *Theater* 25, 71–91.

LAHR, JOHN (1993), 'Inventing the enemy', *The New Yorker*, 18 October, 103–6.

LANGE, HARTMUT (1988), *Vom Werden der Vernunft und andere Stücke fürs Theater*, Zurich.

LANGER, LAWRENCE (1995), *Admitting the Holocaust*, Oxford.

LEATHERMAN, LEROY (1966), *Martha Graham, Portrait of the Lady as an Artist*, New York.

LEFÈVRE, ECKARD (2000), 'Sophokles und Heiner Müllers *Philoktet*', in Susanne Gödde and Theodor Heinze (eds.), *Skenika: Beiträge zum antiken Theater und seiner Rezeption. Festschrift zum 65. Geburtstag von Horst-Dieter Blume*, Darmstadt, 419–38.

LEFKOWITZ, MARY, and GUY ROGERS (1996, eds.), *Black Athena Revisited*, Chapel Hill, NC, and London.

LESTER, ELENORE (1969), 'Professor of the Dionysiac theater', *New York Times*, 27 April.

LEYSHON, ROBERT (1999), 'Laughing in the beginning and listening at the end: directing Fugard in Barbados', in Marcia Blumberg and Dennis Walder (eds.), *South African Theatre As/And Intervention*, Amsterdam and Atlanta, GA, 75–81.

LONG, JOSEPH (2002), 'The Sophoclean killing fields: an interview with Frank McGuinness', in Marianne McDonald and J. Michael Walton (eds.), *Amid Our Troubles: Irish Versions of Greek Tragedy*, London, 263–82.

LUDLAM, CHARLES (1989), *Medea*, in *The Complete Plays of Charles Ludlam*, New York, 802–13.

LYOTARD, JEAN-FRANÇOIS (1970), 'Oedipe juif', *Critique* 26, 530–45.

—— (1971), *Discours, figure*, Paris.

LYSANDER, PER, and SUZANNE OSTEN (1975), *Medea's Children*, translated from the Swedish by Ann-Charlotte Harvey, Charlottesville, VA.

MCCORKLE, J. (1986), 'Remapping the new world: the recent poetry of Derek Walcott', *Ariel* 17, 3–14.

MCDONALD, MARIANNE (1983), *Euripides in Cinema: The Heart Made Visible*, Philadelphia.

—— (1992), *Ancient Sun, Modern Light: Greek Drama on the Modern Stage*, New York.

—— (1997), 'When despair and history rhyme: colonialism and Greek tragedy', *New Hibernia Review* 1.2, 57–70.

—— (2000), 'Black Dionysus: Greek tragedy from Africa', in Lorna Hardwick, Pat Easterling, *et al.* (eds.), *Theatre: Ancient and Modern*, Milton Keynes, 95–108.

—— (2001), *Sing Sorrow: Classics, History, and Heroines in Opera*, Westport, CT, and London.

—— (2002), 'The Irish and Greek tragedy', in Marianne McDonald and J. Michael Walton (eds.), *Amid our Troubles: Irish Versions of Greek Tragedy*, London, 37–86.

McDonald, Marianne, and J. Michael Walton (2002, eds.), *Amid Our Troubles: Irish Versions of Greek Tragedy*, London.

McDowell, Colin (2002), 'Fashion moment: Greek goddess', *The Sunday Times Style Section*, 27 October, 8.

Macintosh, Fiona (1994), *Dying Acts: Death in Ancient Greek and Modern Irish Tragic Drama*, Cork.

—— (1995), 'Under the blue pencil: Greek tragedy and the British censor', *Dialogos* 2, 54–70.

—— (1997), 'Tragedy in performance: nineteenth- and twentieth-century productions', in Pat Easterling (ed.), *The Cambridge Companion to Greek Tragedy*, Cambridge, 284–323.

—— (2000*a*), 'Introduction: the performer in performance', in Edith Hall, Fiona Macintosh, and Oliver Taplin (eds.), *Medea in Performance 1500–2000*, Oxford, 1–31.

—— (2000*b*), 'Medea transposed: burlesque and gender on the mid-Victorian stage', in Edith Hall, Fiona Macintosh, and Oliver Taplin (eds.), *Medea in Performance 1500–2000*, Oxford, 75–99.

—— (2001), 'Alcestis on the British stage', *Cahiers du GITA* 14, 281–308.

—— (2002), 'Oedipus in Africa', *Omnibus* 42, 8–9.

—— (forthcoming *a*), 'Medea between the wars', in J. Dillon and S. Wilmer (eds.), *Rebel Women: Festschrift for Marianne McDonald*.

—— (forthcoming *b*), *Oedipus Tyrannus: A Production History*, Cambridge.

Macintosh, Fiona, Pantelis Michelakis, Edith Hall, and Oliver Taplin (forthcoming, eds.), *Agamemnon in Performance, 458 BC–2002 AD*, Oxford.

MacKinnon, Kenneth (1986), *Greek Tragedy into Film*, London and Sydney.

MacLeish, Archibald (1967), *Herakles*, Boston, MA.

McNamara, Brooks, Jerry Rojo, and Richard Schechner (1975), *Theatres, Spaces, Environments: Eighteen Projects*, New York.

MacNeice, Louis (1979), *Collected Poems*, 2nd edn., London.

McRobbie, A. (1978), *'Jackie': An Ideology of Adolescent Femininity*, University of Birmingham Centre for Contemporary Cultural Studies Occasional Paper 53 (April).

Mallie, Eamonn, and David McKittrick (2002, eds.), *Endgame in Ireland*, London.

Malnig, Julie, and Judy C. Rosenthal (1993), 'The Women's Experimental Theatre: transforming family stories into feminist issues', in Peggy Phelan and Lynda Hart (eds.), *Acting Out: Feminist Performances*, Ann Arbor, MI, 201–14.

Mandel, Oscar (1981), *Philoctetes and the Fall of Troy: Plays, Documents, Iconography, Interpretations*, Lincoln, NE.

Mandela, Nelson (1995), *Long Walk to Freedom*, reprint of 1994 edn., London.

MARCUSE, HERBERT (1955), *Eros and Civilization: A Philosophical Inquiry into Freud*, Boston, MA.

MARTONE, MARIO (1998), *Teatro di guerra: un diario*, Milan.

MEE, CHARLES L. (1998), *The Trojan Women: A Love Story*, in *History Plays*, Baltimore, MD, and London, 159–251. Also accessible at www.panix.com/~meejr (last accessed November 2002).

MEYER-THOSS, GOTTFRIED (2002), *Peter Sellars*, Berlin.

MICHELAKIS, PANTELIS (2001), 'The past as a foreign country? Greek tragedy, cinema and the politics of space', in Felix Budelmann and Pantelis Michelakis (eds.), *Homer, Tragedy, and Beyond: Studies in Greek Literature in Honour of P. E. Easterling*, London, 241–57.

MILLETT, KATE (1970), *Sexual Politics*, New York.

MILNER, LARRY S. (2000), *Hardness of Heart, Hardness of Life: The Stain of Human Infanticide*, Lanham, MD.

MORRIS, SARAH P. (1992), *Daidalos and the Origins of Greek Art*, Princeton, NJ.

MÜLLER, HEINER (1966), *Philoktet; Herakles 5*, Frankfurt am Main.

——(1998), *Werke*, ed. Frank Hörnigk, vol. i, Frankfurt am Main.

NAREMORE, JAMES (2000), 'Introduction: film and the reign of adaptation', in James Naremore (ed.), *Film Adaptation*, New Brunswick, NJ, 1–16.

NGŨGĨ WA THIONG'O, (1972), 'Wole Soyinka, Aluko and the satirical voice', in *Homecoming: Essays on African and Caribbean Literature, Culture and Politics*, London.

——(1983), *Barrel of a Pen: Resistance to Repression in Neo-Colonial Kenya*, Oxford.

——(1986), *Decolonising the Mind*, Oxford, Nairobi, Portsmouth, NH.

——(1993), *Moving the Centre: The Struggle for Cultural Freedom*, Oxford, Nairobi, Portsmouth, NH.

——(1997), *Writers in Politics*, 2nd edn., Oxford.

NICHOLS, GRACE (1983), *I Is a Long-Memoried Woman*, London.

NIETZSCHE, FRIEDRICH (1993), *The Birth of Tragedy out of the Spirit of Music*, translated from the first German edition of 1872 by Shaun Whiteside, ed. Michael Tanner, London.

NOONAN, M. (1999), 'Performing the voice of writing in the in-between: Hélène Cixous's *La Ville Parjure*', *Nottingham French Studies* 38, 67–79.

O'CONNOR, JOHN (1968), 'Against the incoherent', *Wall Street Journal*, 22 October, 20.

O'HEALY, A. (1999), 'Revisiting the belly of Naples: the body and the city in the films of Mario Martone', *Screen* 40.3, 239–54.

OKPEWHO, ISIDORE (1991), 'Soyinka, Euripides and the anxiety of empire', *Research in African Literatures* 30.4, 32–55.

OLANIYAN, TEJUMOLA (1995), *Scars of Conquest: Masks of Resistance*, Oxford.

O'MAHONY, JOHN (2000), 'The mighty munchkin' (profile of Peter Sellars), *The Guardian Saturday Review*, 20 May, 6–7.

O'NEILL, EUGENE (1961), 'Memoranda on masks', in Toby Cole (ed.), *Playwrights on Playwriting*, New York, 65–9.

O'RAWE, DES (2000), '(Mis)translating tragedy: Irish poets and Greek plays', in Lorna Hardwick, Pat Easterling, *et al.* (eds.), *Theatre: Ancient and Modern*, Milton Keynes, 109–24.

ÒSÓFISAN, FÉMI (1999*a*), 'Theater and the rites of post-Négritude remembering', *Research in African Literatures* 30.1, 1–11.

——(1999*b*), *Recent Outings*, Ibadan.

OTTE, WERNER (2001), 'Die Wunde der Revolution. Heiner Müllers *Philoktet* im Spannungsfeld von Rationalitaet und mythischem Zwang', dissertation, University of Salzburg.

PADEL, RUTH (1996), '*Ion*: lost and found', *Arion* 4, 216–24.

——(2000), *I'm a Man: Sex, Gods and Rock 'n' Roll*, London.

PALMER-SIKELIANOS, EVA (1993), *Upward Panic: The Autobiography of Eva Palmer-Sikelianos*, edited by John P. Anton, Chur and Philadelphia.

PAPPENHEIM, MARK (1993), 'The Greeks had a word for it', *The Independent*, 16 August.

PARKER, JAN (2000), 'Profound ambiguities in Sophocles' and Anouilh's *Antigone*', in Lorna Hardwick, Pat Easterling, *et al.* (eds.), *Theatre: Ancient and Modern*, Milton Keynes, 125–35.

PARKER, R. B. (1986), 'The National Theatre's *Oresteia*, 1981–82', in Martin Cropp, Elaine Fanthan, and S. E. Scully (eds.), *Greek Tragedy and its Legacy*, Calgary, 337–57.

PARNES, UZI (1988), 'Pop performance, four seminal influences; the work of Jack Smith, Tom Murrin—the Alien Comic, Ethyl Eichelberger, and the Split Britches Company', dissertation, New York University.

PARTCH, H. (1991). *Bitter Music: Collected Journals, Essays, Introductions, and Librettos*, ed. with an Introduction by T. McGeary, Urbana, IL.

PASOLINI, PIER PAOLO (1967), *Edipo Re: Un Film di Paolo Pasolini*, Arco Films, Milan: Garzanti (1990). With English subtitles, Water Bearer Films Inc., New York.

PATSALIDIS, SAVAS, and ELIZABETH SAKELLARIDOU (1999, eds.), *(Dis)Placing Classical Greek Theatre*, Thessaloniki.

PAVIS, P. (1986), 'The classical heritage of modern drama: the case of postmodern theatre', *Modern Drama* 29, 1–22.

PAVLIDES, MEROPE (1986), 'Restructuring the traditional: an examination of Hélène Cixous' *Le Nom d'Oedipe*', in Karelisa V. Hartigan (ed.),

Within the Dramatic Spectrum, University of Florida Department of Classics Comparative Drama Conference Papers 6, New York and London, 151–9.

PERCY, NORMA (2002), 'Putting history on television', in Eamonn Mallie and David McKittrick (eds.), *Endgame in Ireland*, London, 1–11.

PETKOVIC, NIKOLA (1997), 'Re-writing the myth: rereading the life: the universalizing fame in Pier Paolo Pasolini's *Edipo Re*', *American Imago* 54, 39–68.

PICON-VALLIN, B. (2001), *Le Film de théâtre*, Paris.

PLENZDORF, U. (1988), *Filme*, vol. ii, Rostock.

PLUGGÉ, DOMIS EDWARD (1938), *History of Greek Play Production in American Colleges and Universities from 1881 to 1936*, New York.

PODUSKA, DONALD M. (1999), 'Classical myths in music: a selective list', *Classical World* 92.3, 195–276.

POLLARD, R. (1995), 'From ancient epic to twentieth-century opera: the re-invention of Greek tragedy in Tippett's *King Priam*', M. Litt. thesis, Newcastle University.

POLYCHRONAKI, VENIA (2001), 'Frieze frame', *The Guardian Weekend*, 3 February, 42–3.

RABE, DAVID (1993), *The Orphan*, in *The Vietnam Plays 2*, New York.

RAMAZANI, J. (1997), 'The wound of history: Walcott's *Omeros* and the post-colonial poetics of affliction', *Proceedings of the Modern Literature Association* 112.3, 405–15.

RAPHAEL, FREDERIC, and MCLEISH, KENNETH (1979), *The Serpent Son*, Cambridge.

RASCAROLI, LAURA (2003), 'A present and a true city? Naples in Mario Martone's cinema', in Ewa Mazierska and Laura Rascaroli, *From Moscow to Madrid: Postmodern Cities, European Cinema*, London and New York.

RASS, M. (2000), 'Dem Text einen Körper geben—Jean-Marie Straub/ Danièle Huillet und das Theater', in Volker Roloff and Scarlett Winter (eds.), *Theater und Kino in der Zeit der Nouvelle Vague*, Tübingen, 151–63.

REBELLATO, DAN (1999), *1956 and All That: The Making of Modern British Drama*, London.

REHM, RUSH (1992), *Greek Tragic Theatre*, London.

——— (2002), 'Supplices, the satyr play: Charles Mee's *Big Love*', *American Journal of Philology* 123, 111–18.

REID, JANE DAVIDSON (1993), *The Oxford Guide to Classical Mythology in the Arts, 1300–1990s*, Oxford.

RICH, ADRIENNE (1979), 'When we dead awaken: writing as revision', in Adrienne Rich, *On Lies, Secrets, and Silence*, New York, 33–50.

RICHARDS, SHAUN (2000), 'Into that rinsing glare? Field Day's Irish tragedies', *Modern Drama* 43.1, 109 ff.

RICHARDSON, JACK (1960), *The Prodigal*, New York.

RIEDEL, VOLKER (2000), *Antikerezeption in der deutschen Literatur vom Renaissance-Humanismus zur Gegenwart*, Stuttgart.

RIEU, E. V. (1946), *Homer, The Odyssey*, Harmondsworth.

ROLOFF, VOLKER, and SCARLETT WINTER (2000, eds.), *Theater und Kino in der Zeit der Nouvelle Vague*, Tübingen.

RORTY, RICHARD (1979), *Philosophy and the Mirror of Nature*, Princeton, NJ.

ROSSLYN, F. (1998), 'The hero of our time: classic heroes and post-classical drama', in Lin Foxhall and John Salmon (eds.), *Thinking Men: Masculinity and its Self-Presentation in the Classical Tradition*, London and New York, 183–96.

ROTIMI, OLA (1971), *The Gods are Not to Blame*, Oxford.

ROUHANI, FUAD (1998), *The Persians*, translated into modern Persian, Bethesda, MD.

ROWLAND, ANTONY (2001), *Tony Harrison and the Holocaust*, Liverpool.

RUCK, K. (1976), 'Duality and the madness of Heracles', *Arethusa* 9, 53–75.

RUTHERFORD, JONATHAN (1990), 'A place called home: identity and the cultural politics of difference', in Jonathan Rutherford (ed.), *Identity, Community, Culture, Difference*, London, 9–27.

SADIE, STANLEY (1992, ed.), *The New Grove Dictionary of Opera*, London and New York.

SAÏD, EDWARD (1978), *Orientalism*, London.

—— (1993), *Culture and Imperialism*, London.

SAVARESE, N. (1992), *Teatro e spettacolo fra Oriente e Occidente*, Bari.

SCHANZE, HELMUT (1979), 'Das Theater nützt dem Fernsehen. Nützt das Fernsehen dem Theater? Zur bisherigen Adaption der Dramen- und Theatertradition im Fernsehen der Bundesrepublik', in Helmut Kreuzer and Karl Prümm (eds.), *Fernsehsendungen und ihre Formen*, Stuttgart, 115–30.

SCHECHNER, RICHARD (1965–6, 1968), 'Approaches: work in progress', in Richard Schechner (1969), *Public Domain: Essays on the Theater*, Indianapolis, IN, 43–91.

—— (1967), 'In warm blood: the *Bacchae*', in Richard Schechner (1969), *Public Domain: Essays on the Theater*, Indianapolis, IN, 93–107.

—— (1968a), 'The politics of ecstasy', in Richard Schechner (1969), *Public Domain: Essays on the Theater*, Indianapolis, IN, 209–28.

—— (1968b), 'Speculations on radicalism, sexuality, and performance', *The Drama Review* 13, 89–110.

SCHECHNER, RICHARD (1968c), 'Theatre and revolution', *Salama-gundi* 2.2, 11–27.

—— (1968d), 'Beyond nude dancing', *New York Times*, 16 June, 68.

—— (1969), *Public Domain: Essays on the Theater*, Indianapolis, IN.

—— (1970, ed.), *The Performance Group: Dionysus in 69*, New York.

—— (1971), 'Actuals: primitive ritual and performance theory', *Theatre Quarterly* 1.2, 49–66.

—— (1973), 'Nakedness', in Richard Schechner (1994), *Environmental Theater*, New York, 87–124.

—— (1982), 'Intercultural performance', *Drama Review* 26.2.

—— (1985), *Between Theater and Anthropology: Intercultural Studies of Theatre and Ritual*, Philadelphia.

—— (1988), *Performance Theory*, London.

—— (1993), *The Future of Ritual: Writings on Culture and Performance*, London and New York.

—— (1994), *Environmental Theater*, New York.

—— and WILLA APPEL (1990, eds.), *By Means of Performance: Inter-cultural Studies of Theatre and Ritual*, Cambridge.

—— and MADY SCHUMAN (1976, eds.), *Ritual, Play, and Performance: Readings in the Social Sciences/Theatre*, New York.

SCHENK, R. (1991), Review of *Der Fall Ö* by Rainer Simon, *Filmspiegel* 7.

SCHLEEF, EINAR (1997), *Droge Faust Parsifal*, Frankfurt am Main.

SCHWARZ, DANIEL R. (1999), *Imagining the Holocaust*, New York.

SEGAL, CHARLES (1982), *Dionysiac Poetics and Euripides' Bacchae*, Princeton, NJ. Reprinted with additional afterword in 1997, Princeton, NJ.

—— (1986), *Interpreting Greek Tragedy: Myth, Poetry, Text*, Ithaca, NY, and London.

—— (1997), *Dionysiac Poetics and Euripides' Bacchae*, 2nd edn., Princeton.

SEGEL, HAROLD B. (1987), *Turn-of-the-century Cabaret*, New York.

SEIDENSTICKER, B. (1997, ed.), *Die Orestie des Aischylos, übersetzt von Peter Stein*, Munich.

SELLARS, PETER (1989), 'Peter Sellars' talk at Carnuntum' (a transcript of a lecture delivered in August 1989), in Marianne McDonald (1992), *Ancient Sun, Modern Light: Greek Drama on the Modern Stage*, New York, 89–95.

SHAY, JONATHAN (1995), *Achilles in Vietnam: Combat Trauma and the Undoing of Character*, New York.

SHELLARD, DOMINIC (1999), *British Theatre since the War*, New Haven, CT, and London.

SHEPARD, RICHARD (1969), 'Not on marquee, but in spotlight: the audience', *New York Times*, 7 February, 30.

SHEPHARD, WILLIAM HUNTER (1991), *The Dionysus Group, American University Studies*, Series 26, Theatre Arts, vol. v, New York.

SIEGRIST, CHRISTOPH (1997), 'Mythologie und antike Tragödie in der DDR', in Hellmut Flashar (ed.), *Tragödie: Idee und Transformation*, Stuttgart and Leipzig, 348–67.

SIERZ, ALEKS (2001), *In-yer-Face Theatre: British Drama Today*, London.

SILVERBERG, ROBERT (1969), *The Man in the Maze: Science Fiction*, London.

SIMON, BENNETT (1988), *Tragic Drama and the Family: Psychoanalytic Studies from Aeschylus to Beckett*, New Haven, CT, and London.

SIMON, JOHN (1968), 'The stage', *Commonweal* 88 (28 July), 504.

SMELIANSKY, ANATOLY (1999), 'Russian theatre in the post-communist era', in Robert Leach, Victor Borovsky, and Andy Davies (eds.), *A History of Russian Theatre*, Cambridge, 382–406.

SMETHURST, MAE (2000), 'The Japanese presence in Ninagawa's *Medea*', in Edith Hall, Fiona Macintosh, and Oliver Taplin (eds.), *Medea in Performance 1500–2000*, Oxford, 191–216.

—— (2002), 'Ninagawa's production of Euripides' *Medea*', *American Journal of Philology* 123.1, 1–34.

SMITH, MICHAEL (1968), Review of *Dionysus in 69*, *Village Voice*, 13 June, 41.

SOLOMON, ALISA (1997), *Re-Dressing the Canon: Essays on Theatre and Gender*, London.

SOLOMON, JON (2001), *The Ancient World in the Cinema*, revised edn., New Haven, CT.

SOMER, R. F. (1988), 'The public man of letters', in B. A. Drabeck, H. E. Ellis, and S. Rudin (eds.), *The Proceedings of the Archibald MacLeish Symposium, May 7–8, 1982*, Lanham, MD, 115–21.

SONCINI, SARA (1999), 'Rewriting the Greeks in contemporary British drama: the metatheatre of Timberlake Wertenbaker and Tony Harrison', in Savas Patsalidis and Elizabeth Sakellaridou (eds.), *(Dis)Placing Classical Greek Theatre*, Thessaloniki, 73–83.

SOYINKA, WOLE (1967), *A Dance of the Forests*, Oxford.

—— (1973), *The Bacchae of Euripides*, London.

—— (1976), *Myth, Literature, and the African World*, Cambridge.

SPATHES, DIMITRIS (1986), 'Sophocles' *Philoctetes* in N. Pikkolo's adaptation: the first performance of an ancient Greek tragedy in modern Greek theatre history' (in Greek), reprinted in *O Diaphotismos kai to Neollenniko Theatro* [*The Enlightenment and the Modern Greek Theatre*], Thessaloniki, 145–98.

SPILLIUS, E. B. (1983), 'Some developments from the work of Melanie Klein', *International Journal of Psychology* 64, 321–32.

SPOCK, BENJAMIN (1946), *The Common Sense Book of Baby and Child Care*, New York.

STANFORD, W. B. (1976), *Ireland and the Classical Tradition*, Dublin.

——(1984), *Ireland and the Classical Tradition*, 2nd edn., Dublin.

STEHLÍKOVÁ, EVA (2001), 'Productions of Greek and Roman drama on the Czech stage', *Eirene* 37, 71–160.

STEINER, GEORGE (1961), *The Death of Tragedy*, London.

——(1984), *Antigones*, Oxford.

STEINER, RUDOLF (1960), *Speech and Drama*, translated from the German by Mary Adams, London.

STEPHENS, F. (1964), *Theatre World Annual 1965*, London.

STOPPARD, TOM (1998), *Neutral Ground*, in *Plays Three*, London, 73–128.

STRAUB, JEAN-MARIE, and DANIÈLE HUILLET, (1992), *Antigone de Sophocle, Version allemande de Friedrich Hölderlin retravaillée pour la scène par Bertolt Brecht: Texte découpé par Jean-Marie Straub en 147 plans cinématographiques et traduit en français par Danièle Huillet*, Toulouse.

——(2001), 'Antigone, cinéma, théâtre', in B. Picon-Vallin, *Le Film de théâtre*, Paris, 106–22.

SULLIVAN, DAN (1968), 'Theatre: *Bacchae* updated in garage', *New York Times*, 7 June, 35.

SULLIVAN, J. P. (2001), 'The social ambience of Petronius' *Satyricon* and *Fellini Satyricon*', in Martin M. Winkler (ed.), *Classical Myth and Culture in the Cinema*, rev. edn., Oxford, 258–71.

SUTHERLAND, EFUA (1967), *Edufa*, London.

SWEENEY, JOHN (1997), 'Prometheus unbounded', *The Observer*, 13 July, 3.

TAPLIN, OLIVER (1971), 'Significant actions in Sophocles' *Philoctetes*', *Greek, Roman and Byzantine Studies* 12, 25–44.

——(1977), *The Stagecraft of Aeschylus*, Oxford.

——(1978), *Greek Tragedy in Action*, London.

——(1987), 'The mapping of Sophocles' *Philoctetes*', *BICS* 34, 69–77.

——(1989), *Greek Fire*, London.

——(1997), 'The chorus of mams', in Sandie Byrne (ed.), *Tony Harrison: Loiner*, Oxford, 171–84.

——(2002), 'Contemporary poetry and classics', in T. P. Wiseman (ed.), *Classics in Progress*, Oxford, 1–19.

——(forthcoming), 'The Harrison version', in Fiona Macintosh, Pantelis Michelakis, Edith Hall, and Oliver Taplin (eds.), *Agamemnon in Performance, 458 BC–2002 AD*, Oxford.

TARTT, DONNA (1992), *The Secret History*, New York and London.

TAYLOR, ELLA (1989), *Prime-Time Families: Television Culture in Post-war America*, Berkeley, CA, Los Angeles, CA, London.

TAYLOR, LIB (1995), 'Deaf sign language as a language for the stage', *Studies in Theatre Production* 12, 65–81.

TERADA, REI (1992), *Derek Walcott's Poetry: American Mimicry*, Boston, MA.

THIEME, JOHN (1999), *Derek Walcott*, Manchester.

THOMSON, GEORGE (1941), *Aeschylus and Athens*, London.

TIPPETT, M. (1980), 'The resonance of Troy: essays and commentaries on *King Priam*', in *Music of the Angels: Essays and Sketchbooks*, ed. M. Bowen, London.

——(1995), *Tippett on Music*, ed. M. Bowen, Oxford.

TOPOUZES, KOSTAS (1992, ed.), *Sophocles' Philoctetes*, Athens.

TRILSE, CHRISTOPH (1975), *Antike und Theater Heute*, Berlin.

TURNER, E. G. (1957), 'Subjects for declamations', *The Oxyrhynchus Papyri* 2400, 107–9.

TURNER, VICTOR (1986), *The Anthropology of Performance*, New York.

TYTELL, JOHN (1995), *The Living Theater: Art, Exile, and Outrage*, New York.

UNSWORTH, BARRY (2002), *The Songs of the Kings*, London.

VAN DYCK, KAREN (1998), *Kassandra and the Censors: Greek Poetry since 1967*, Ithaca, NY.

VAN STEEN, GONDA A. H. (2000), *Venom in Verse: Aristophanes in Modern Greece*, Princeton, NJ.

——(2001), 'Playing by the censors' rules? Classical drama revived under the Greek junta (1967–1974)', *Journal of the Hellenic Diaspora* 27.1–2, 133–94.

VAN ZYL SMIT, BETINE (1992), 'Medea and apartheid', *Akroterion* 37, 73–81.

——(2001), 'Medea becomes politically correct', in Bernhard Zimmermann (ed.), *Rezeption des antiken Dramas auf der Bühne und in der Literatur*, Stuttgart, 262–83.

VASUNIA, PHIROZE (2001), *The Gift of the Nile: Hellenizing Egypt from Aeschylus to Alexander*, Berkeley, CA, Los Angeles, CA, London.

VERMA, JATINDER (1998), '"Binglishing" the stage: a generation of Asian theatre in England', in Richard Boon and Jane Pastow (eds.), *Theatre Matters: Performance and Culture on the World Stage*, Cambridge.

VERNANT, JEAN-PIERRE (1979), *Myth and Society in Ancient Greece*, translated from the French by Janet Lloyd, Brighton.

——(1983), *Myth and Thought among the Greeks*, translated from the French, London.

VERNANT, JEAN-PIERRE (1991), *Mortals and Immortals: Collected Essays*, ed. Froma Zeitlin, Princeton, NJ.

VERNANT, JEAN-PIERRE, and PIERRE VIDAL-NAQUET (1988), *Myth and Tragedy in Ancient Greece*, translated from the French by Janet Lloyd, New York.

VIDAL-NAQUET, PIERRE (1986), *The Black Hunter: Forms of Thought and Forms of Society in the Greek World*, translated from the French by Andrew Szegedy-Maszak, Baltimore, MD.

VINCENDEAU, GINETTE (2002), 'Introduction', in Ginette Vincendeau (ed.), *Film/Literature/Heritage: A Sight and Sound Reader*, London, xi–xxxi.

VITEZ, ANTOINE (1995), *Écrits sur le théâtre*, vol. ii, Paris.

—— (1997), *Écrits sur le théâtre*, vol. iv, Paris.

VON BECKER, PETER (1997), 'Die Sehnsucht nach dem Vollkommen', *Der Tagesspiegel*, 1 October, 16.

VON GUNDEN, KENNETH (1991), *Postmodern Auteurs: Coppola, Lucas, De Palma, Spielberg and Scorsese*, Jefferson, NC.

WALCOTT, DEREK (1981), *The Fortunate Traveller*, NewYork.

—— (1986), *Collected Poems 1948–1984*, New York.

—— (1990), *Omeros*, London.

—— (1993), *The Odyssey: A Stage Version*, London.

—— (1998), *What the Twilight Says*, London.

WALSH, JOHN (1990), 'Bard of hope and harp', *The Sunday Times*, 7 October.

WALTON, J. MICHAEL (1987), *Living Greek Theatre: A Handbook of Classical Performance and Modern Production*, New York.

—— (2002), 'Hit or myth: the Greeks and Irish drama', in Marianne McDonald and J. Michael Walton (eds.), *Amid Our Troubles: Irish Versions of Greek Tragedy*, London, 3–36.

WARDLE, IRVING (1993), 'Centre stage for activist's elegy', *The Independent on Sunday*, 18 August, 16.

WARRACK, JOHN, and EWAN WEST (1992), *The Oxford Dictionary of Opera*, Oxford.

WERTENBAKER, TIMBERLAKE (1985), *The Grace of Mary Traverse*, London.

—— (1988), *Our Country's Good: Based on the Playmaker, a Novel by Thomas Keneally*, London.

—— (1992), *Three Birds Alighting on a Field*, London.

—— (1995), *The Break of Day*, London.

—— (1996a), *Hecuba by Euripides, Translated and Adapted by Timberlake Wertenbaker*, Woodstock, London, Melbourne.

—— (1996b), *Timberlake Wertenbaker: Plays One*, London.

——(1997), *Sophocles: Oedipus Tyrannos, Oedipus at Kolonos, Antigone, Translated by Timberlake Wertenbaker*, London.

——(1998*a*), *After Darwin*, London.

——(1998*b*), *Filumena by Eduardo de Filippo, Translated by Timberlake Wertenbaker*, London.

——(2000), *The Ash Girl*, London.

——(2001), *Credible Witness*, London.

——(2002), *Plays Two*, London.

WETMORE, KEVIN J. (2002), *The Athenian Sun in an African Sky*, Jefferson, NC, and London.

WHITAKER, RICHARD (2002), 'Translating Homer in an African context', in F. Montanari *et al.* (eds.), *Omero tremila anni dopo*, Rome, 523–33.

——(2003), 'Issues in multi-cultural translation: translating *The Iliad* into Southern African English', in Lorna Hardwick and Carol Gillespie (eds.), *Crossing Boundaries through Greek Tragedy*, Selected Proceedings of the Open Colloquium, Milton Keynes.

WHITE, C. L. (1977), *The Women's Periodical Press in Britain, 1946–76*, London.

WHITELAW, BILLIE (1995), *Billie Whitelaw. Who He?*, London.

WILES, DAVID (2000), *Greek Theatre Performance: An Introduction*, Cambridge.

——(2003), *A Short History of Western Performance Space*, Cambridge.

WILLIAMS, DAVID (2000, ed.), *Collaborative Theatre: The Théâtre du Soleil Sourcebook*, London.

——(2002), ' "Towards an art of memory": Peter Brook in Paris', in David Bradby and Maria Delgado (eds.), *The Paris Jigsaw: Internationalism and the City's Stages*, Manchester and New York, 37–52.

WILMER, STEVE E. (1999), 'Seamus Heaney and the Tragedy of Stasis', in Savas Patsalidis and Elizabeth Sakellaridou (eds.), *(Dis)Placing Classical Greek Theatre*, Thessaloniki, 221–31.

WILSON, BRYAN R. (1969), *Religion in a Secular Society*, London.

WILSON, EDMUND (1941), *The Wound and the Bow: Seven Studies in Literature*, New York.

WILSON, PETER (2002), 'The musicians among the actors', in Pat Easterling and Edith Hall (eds.), *Greek and Roman Actors: Aspects of an Ancient Profession*, Cambridge, 39–68.

WINKLER, JOHN J., and FROMA ZEITLIN (1990, eds.), *Nothing to do with Dionysos? Athenian Drama in its Social Context*, Princeton, NJ.

WINKLER, MARTIN M. (2001, ed.), *Classical Myth and Culture in the Cinema*, rev. edn., Oxford.

WITTGENSTEIN, LUDWIG (1979), *Notebooks 1914–1916*, Second edition, edited by G. H. von Wright and G. E. M. Anscombe, Oxford.

WOLF, CHRISTA (1996), *Medea-Stimmen*, Munich.

World Theatre (1957) 6.4 (a special issue on Greek tragedy).

WORTH, KATHARINE (1990), 'Enigmatic influences: Yeats, Beckett, and Noh', in Masaru Sekine and Christopher Murray (eds.), *Yeats and the Noh: A Comparative Study*, Gerrards Cross, 145–58.

——(1998), 'Words for music perhaps', in Mary Bryden (ed.), *Samuel Beckett and Music*, Oxford, 9–20.

WREN, CELIA (2002), 'In Medea Res', *American Theatre* 19.4, 22–5.

WRIGLEY, AMANDA (2002), 'Review of Royal National Theatre's *Bacchai*, 2002', *JACT Review* 32, 12–14.

——(forthcoming), '*Agamemnon*s on the Archive Database', in Fiona Macintosh, Pantelis Michelakis, Edith Hall, and Oliver Taplin (eds.), *Agamemnon in Performance, 458 BC–2002 AD*, Oxford.

WYKE, MARIA (1997), *Projecting the Past: Ancient Rome, Cinema, and History*, New York and London.

YEATS, W. B. (1982), *Collected Plays*, London and Basingstoke.

ZEITLIN, FROMA (1978), 'The dynamics of misogyny: myth and myth-making in the *Oresteia* of Aeschylus', *Arethusa* 11, 149–84. Reprinted in John Peradotto and J. P. Sullivan (1984, eds.), *Women in the Ancient World: The Arethusa Papers*, Albany, NY, and in Froma Zeitlin (1996), *Playing the Other: Gender and Society in Classical Greek Literature*, Chicago, IL, and London, 87–119.

——(1982), *Under the Sign of the Shield: Semiotics and Aeschylus' Seven Against Thebes*, Rome.

——(1985), 'Playing the other: theater, theatricality, and the feminine in Greek drama', *Representations* 11, 63–94. Revised in Froma Zeitlin (1996), *Playing the Other: Gender and Society in Classical Greek Literature*, Chicago, IL, and London, 341–74.

——(1993), 'Staging Dionysus between Thebes and Athens', in Thomas H. Carpenter and Christopher A. Faraone (eds.), *Masks of Dionysus*, Ithaca, NY, and London, 147–82.

——(1996), *Playing the Other: Gender and Society in Classical Greek Literature*, Chicago, IL, and London.

Index

military and militarism:
  cinema comments on role of 6
  Heracles and 16, 117–18, 121,
    122–5, 127, 128
  Müller on power of 151–2
  violence 127, 138–40;
    domestic 114, 133–4
Miller, Arthur 118, 317
Millett, Kate 13, 38, 39, 110
mime 28, 279–81, 318
mind 36–46, 257, 313–68
  see also origins of theatre;
    psychoanalysis; self-
    knowledge
miners, Harrison's *Prometheus*
  and 22, 176, 185–93, 194,
  214
Miroto, Martinus *178*, 197
misunderstanding,
  collective 182–3
Mitchell, Katie; *Phoenician
  Women* 20
Mnouchkine, Ariane 28–9, 35, 36,
  261, 345
  Les Atrides 28–9, 173, 257, *258*,
  259
mobility, reduction of
  actors' 270–1, 354
modernism 30, 246–7, 262
Moiseiwitsch, Tanya *252*, 318
moon missions, Apollo 8
moral awareness, theatre and 77,
  184
morality plays, medieval 58
Morris, Sarah; *Daidalos and the
  Origins of Greek Art* 229
Morrison, Blake; *Oedipus* 32 n. 60,
  43
Morrison, Jim 9
Moscow 4, 43–4
mother-figure, Kleinian 37, 314,
  325
Mounet-Sully, Jean 315–16

Mülheim, Theater an der
  Ruhr 359
Müller, Heiner:
  Beckett's influence 35
  Description of a Picture 22
  Herakles 5 114, 151
  influence on Louryk 96
  Medeamaterial 151, 292–3
  and Oedipus 151, 299, 313
  Philoktet 11, 18, 150–3
  plays premiered in Munich 18,
    151
  and *Prometheus Bound* 151, 175
multilingual performances:
  Orghast 40, 176
  South African 239, 241
multi-media works 22–3
  Guarnieri's *Medea* 286, 294, 304
Munich 18, 151
music 31
  ancient Greek 286, 289, 292
  in Beckett 272, 273, 278–81, 282
  see also opera; rock music
Musker, John 217
myth:
  Aeschylean primacy over
    character 261
  misogynistic, of origin 99, 110
  universality 189

Nairobi, Kenya 234 n. 36
Napoleon I, Emperor of
  France 213
'nation' language 234
National Theatre Company,
  British:
  Beckett's *Play* 274–6, *275*
  Duffy's Rites 106
  O'Brien's *Birds* 4
  Philoctetes 274 n. 15
  Soyinka's *The Bacchae of
    Euripides: A Communion
    Rite* 236–7